TENNESSEE:
The Dangerous Example

TENNESSEE:

The Dangerous Example

Watauga to 1849

by

MARY FRENCH CALDWELL

AURORA PUBLISHERS, INC.
NASHVILLE/LONDON

CONTENTS

v

List of Illustrations

Honorable Winfield Dunn, governor of Tennessee, signs the Bicentennial Proclamation commemorating the two-hundredth anniversary of the Watauga Association.

STATE OF TENNESSEE

PROCLAMATION

BY THE GOVERNOR

WHEREAS, TWO HUNDRED YEARS AGO THIS YEAR THE FIRST INDEPENDENT GOVERNMENT ON THE NORTH AMERICAN CONTINENT WAS SET UP BY A GROUP OF PIONEERS IN THE WATAUGA RIVER AREA OF EAST TENNESSEE; AND

WHEREAS, THESE HARDY MEMBERS OF THE WATAUGA ASSOCIATION DECLARED THEMSELVES FREE OF BRITISH RULE FOUR YEARS BEFORE THE DECLARATION OF INDEPENDENCE; AND

WHEREAS, THE BRITISH GOVERNMENT TOOK NOTICE OF THIS ACTION OF THE TENNESSEE SETTLERS, TERMING IT A "DANGEROUS EXAMPLE TO THE REST OF THE COLONIES;" AND

WHEREAS, TOO FEW PEOPLE IN AMERICA TODAY ARE AWARE OF THE IMPORTANT PART TENNESSEANS OF THE WATAUGA ASSOCIATION TOOK IN LAYING THE GROUNDWORK FOR THE AMERICAN REVOLUTION AND THE FREE GOVERNMENT WE NOW ENJOY; AND

WHEREAS, WE ARE NOW IN THE MIDST OF PLANS TO CELEBRATE OUR NATION'S 200TH BIRTHDAY IN 1976:

NOW, THEREFORE, I, WINFIELD DUNN, AS GOVERNOR OF THE STATE OF TENNESSEE, DO HEREBY PROCLAIM THIS YEAR 1972 AS THE

WATAUGA ASSOCIATION 200TH ANNIVERSARY YEAR

AND URGE ALL OUR CITIZENS TO RECOGNIZE THE PRECEDENCE SET BY THIS GROUP OF PIONEERING TENNESSEANS.

IN WITNESS WHEREOF, I HAVE HEREUNTO SET MY HAND AND CAUSED THE GREAT SEAL OF THE STATE OF TENNESSEE TO BE AFFIXED AT NASHVILLE ON THIS THE 12TH DAY OF JUNE, 1972.

GOVERNOR

ATTEST:

SECRETARY OF STATE

In this book Mary French Caldwell writes the inspiring history of the first independent government of English-speaking people in America, and how these early settlers of Tennessee and their descendants helped spread their example of freedom across the continent.

Their Watauga Association, founded in 1772, was described as "a dangerous example" by the colonial governor of Virginia, Lord Dunmore, in a letter meant to warn King George III. Not long thereafter the Revolution began. In warfare on the western frontier, where the British used Indian allies in ferocious attacks on the settlements, the settlers prevailed. And more besides: they helped George Rogers Clark capture the Illinois country, and in the Carolinas they turned the British back toward final defeat at Yorktown.

Jackson at New Orleans, Houston in Texas, Polk in the White House when the United States raised our flag on the Pacific shore—these too were Tennesseans, and Mrs. Caldwell relates their deeds.

Thus *Tennessee: The Dangerous Example* is a book that needed to be written and published, and with special appropriateness for the time of America's Bicentennial.

It is Mrs. Caldwell's fifth book and follows forty years after her first, *Andrew Jackson's Hermitage,* and only five years after her fourth, *Tennessee: The Volunteer State.* Her books are products of lifelong devotion to her Tennessee homeland, to the task of compiling the facts, and to the art of telling the story.

Robert A. McGaw
Chairman, Tennessee Historical Commission

Tennessee: The Dangerous Example fills a long existing void in Tennessee history by consolidating in one volume the diverse aspects of the Watauga settlement and the many exciting developments that followed therefrom. Written with skill and obvious dedication, this book will long stand as an eloquent narrative of the birth and early growth of Tennessee and of her contribution to the nation. Mrs. Caldwell has thoroughly and profoundly researched the often difficult background to the stirring events she recounts and *Tennessee: The Dangerous Example* may well be the definitive work on this fundamental period in our history.

It is particularly appropriate that publication of *Tennessee: The Dangerous Example* should take place as we are planning the commemoration of the bicentennial of the American Revolution. The part played by the overmountain men in the founding of our country is often overshadowed by the more graphic campaigns that occurred in the East, but they fought the unknown and the savage, while the armies of Washington faced an organized but predictable enemy. The deeds and the sacrifices of the Watauga settlers and those who followed will long live in the annals of human courage and spirit, and it is fortunate that Mrs. Caldwell has devoted her talent to the telling of their story.

William L. Barry
Chairman, Tennessee American Revolution Bicentennial Commission
Assistant Attorney-General, State of Tennessee

Preface

As is true of many important experiments, the first free government set up on the continent of North America had a simple, almost obscure beginning. That it missed passing almost unnoticed in the early days of its infancy is due to the discerning and apprehensive eyes of the last colonial governor of Virginia, the Earl of Dunmore, who warned the British Secretary of State in 1774, that unless His Majesty, George III, granted people along the western frontiers titles to land beyond the Appalachian Mountains ". . . nothing can stop the concourse of people that actually draw toward them."

Furthermore, he informed him, "In effect we have an example of the very case, there being actually a set of people in the back part of this colony, bordering on the Cherokee country, who finding that they could not obtain the land they fancied . . . have settled upon it without, and contented themselves with becoming in a manner tributary to the Indians, and having appointed magistrates, and framed laws for their present occasions, and to all intents and purposes, erected themselves into, though an inconsiderable, yet a separate State; the consequence of which may prove hereafter detrimental to the peace and security of the other colonies; it at least sets a dangerous example to the people of America, of forming governments distinct and independent of his majesty's authority. . . ."

This "dangerous example" was, of course, the Watauga Association, founded in 1772—four years before the American Declaration of Independence—by the little band of pioneers who had followed William Bean to his settlement at Boone's Creek on the Watauga River. No written documents describing this historic event have yet been brought to light, but its existence was verified in the petition addressed to "The Hon. Provincial Council of North Carolina." This document bore the receipt date of August 22, 1776, and was, naturally, written prior to that time.

After stating their case and describing their government in detail, the Wataugans petitioned:

"We now submit the whole to your candid and impartial judgment. We pray your mature and deliberate consideration in our behalf, that you may annex us to your Province . . . in such manner as may enable us to share in the glorious cause of Liberty; enforce our laws under authority, and in every respect become the best members of society."

Even before their petition was received by North Carolina, they raised "a company of fine riflemen" and sent a platoon under the command of young Felix Walker, clerk of the Watauga Association, to the South Carolina coast, where, at Sullivan's Island in June 1776, it helped repulse the British fleet which threatened Charleston. After remaining near Charleston for a short time, word came from beyond the mountains that the Indians were planning an attack on the Watauga and neighboring settlements, and Walker led the volunteers back to defend their own homes and to shield the eastern colonies from invasion. They, and others, throughout the Revolutionary War, not only fought the Indians at home, but also sent volunteers to fight the British east of the mountains. So began Tennessee's long and honorable record of volunteer service, which won for it the nickname: "Tennessee, the Volunteer State."

Yet, even as they fought the British and the Indians, they were engaged in an amazing series of experiments in state-making. From 1769, when William Bean built his cabin on Boone's Creek, until 1796, when Tennessee took its place as the sixteenth state of the Federal union, a period of only twenty-seven years, they lived under and were thoroughly familiar with at least nine forms of government:

(1) British colonial governments. (2) 1769-1772, as "tributary to the Indians"; (3) 1772-1775, the Watauga Association; (4) 1775-1777, Washington District, North Carolina; (5) 1777-1784, Washington County, North Carolina; (6) 1784-1788, the Free State of Franklin; (7) 1788-1790, Washington County, a second time. (8) 1790-1796, The Territory of the United States South

of the River Ohio; (9) June 1, 1796, the sovereign State of Tennessee.

Certainly, by 1796, these over-the-mountain men were thoroughly capable of making their own laws and drafting their own constitution. Thomas Jefferson called theirs "the least imperfect and most republican" system of government yet adopted by an American state. In less than fifty years after they had achieved statehood, Tennesseans, marching shoulder to shoulder with thousands of other Americans, had carried the "dangerous example" of independent government by free men to the distant shores of the Pacific.

As the American people prepare to celebrate the bicentennial of their independence, it is fitting that not only Tennessee, but the entire nation, pay tribute to these pioneer empire builders who, four years before the American Declaration Independence, had established their own government and have enjoyed it, without interruption, for two hundred years.

The following pages are devoted to telling something of their story.

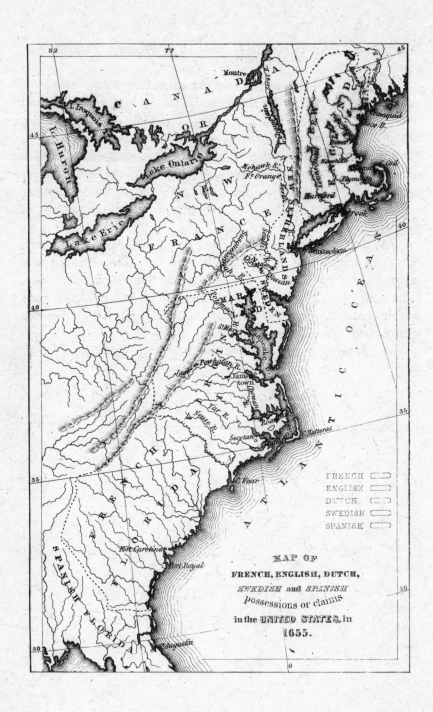

MAP OF
FRENCH, ENGLISH, DUTCH,
SWEDISH and *SPANISH*
Possessions or claims
in the UNITED STATES, in
1655.

FRENCH
ENGLISH
DUTCH
SWEDISH
SPANISH

CHAPTER I

The Enchanted Valley

Encirclement by major European powers of land which now lies within the borders of the present state of Tennessee and some of her neighboring states was accomplished by the middle of the eighteenth century. France, England and Spain each asserted, in vague, overlapping terms, their claims to it and the extensive territory surrounding it, but none of them actually accomplished the founding of permanent settlements, which, after all, is the only means of establishing ownership of the land. It was as if fate had decreed that this beautiful, fertile country, nestled in the heart of the continent, be reserved for a new breed of men, a new way of life. For many years before the state of Tennessee came into being, this land, watered by the Tennessee River and its tributaries, was known simply as the "Tennessee Country." It was a part of the great watershed of the Mississippi River and, because of France's claims to the entire Mississippi valley, was often spoken of as the "French waters."

The claim of France to this territory was based upon her extensive explorations, from her strong bases in Canada, to her settlements at the mouth of the Mississippi and along the coast of the Gulf of Mexico. Her priests, noted for their religious zeal in converting the heathen, and her traders accompanied her explorers, thereby strengthening her claims to the lands through which they traveled. Their presence had a tremendous impact upon not only the explorations, but on the settlements which followed them. By the late 1600s several traders—notably one Jean Couture—had traveled from the Mississippi River, crossed the mountains and had appeared in South Carolina.

Spain, as early as 1539, had sent out a lavishly equipped expedition, commanded by De Soto, to establish her claims to the interior of the continent. Members of this expedition were the first white men to approach, and, perhaps, to enter, the land now included in

1

the territory of Tennessee. De Soto himself died of a fever and was buried not far from the present city of Memphis, in the waters of the mighty river he had discovered. Members of the party, seeking to keep his body from falling into the hands of hostile Indians, conducted his funeral ceremonies at night and committed it to his river's keeping.

Spain's chief claims to land in the New World, however, had to do with the vast territory which stretched along the southern border of the United States—from Florida, on the Atlantic Ocean, to California, on the Pacific. It was not until the middle of the nineteenth century that this territory finally became a part of the United States.

England, which had already established strong colonies along the eastern seaboard, had pushed her frontiers westward to the Appalachian Mountains. She, too, had a strong claim to the land beyond the mountains and, like the others, professed ownership to all lands between these mountains and the Pacific Ocean.

Much of this beautiful land lies today within the territories of the states of Tennessee, Kentucky, the Carolinas, Alabama and Mississippi; but, in reality, it belongs to none of them, for this great watershed of the Tennessee River and its tributaries cannot be confined by man-made boundaries. Its loveliness is a thing of the spirit—no more capable of being held to earth than the sky, the sunlight, or the winds that blow little clouds and great storms alike across its peaks, its coves and wide, green valleys. It is not strange that the first white men who explored its waters and followed their meanders to the distant Mississippi and the Gulf of Mexico had to battle for years before they actually possessed it. The red men who inhabited it loved it with such fervor that, with all the strength they possessed, they repelled each advance. In the end, of course, the insatiable curiosity, the courage, the ingenuity, the determination—even the greed—of the white man prevailed; but not without a gigantic struggle which forms one of the most dramatic chapters in American history. England, like France and Spain, by the middle of the eighteenth century, was looking with covetous eyes toward the rich lands beyond the mountains. All of these European nations were torn by war, court intrigues and secret

DeSoto's Discovery of the Mississippi. Published by Johnson, Fry & Company, New York, from the original picture by Powell.

Burial of DeSoto in the Mississippi. From *Sartain's Magazine.* Engraved by John Sartain from an original drawing by James Hamilton.

treaties as they struggled for supremacy, not only in Europe, but also in the New World. Yet, in spite of their far-reaching strength and powers, it remained for plain, unassuming men from Britain's American colonies to make the final conquest. This was done gradually, without ceremony and without the permission of either England or her colonial governments. But it was done effectively and irrevocably.

Long before its settlement the beauty and fertility of this transmontane country were well known in both the eastern colonies and in the most powerful courts of Europe. It was not, however, until the British colonists were well established east of the mountains that conditions which led to its occupation developed. Among the most important of these was the rapidly increasing population of the eastern colonies, which had resulted in the taking up of the most desirable lands along the seaboard and the pushing of many settlers toward the less fertile lands along the western frontiers. This population was composed largely of less successful men who had little opportunity to establish themselves in the lower country; of young people seeking new lands and better opportunities for advancing their fortunes; of travelers and explorers; and of ambitious men who saw in this rich transmontane land tempting opportunities for acquiring vast estates and great wealth—even for the founding of a new and independent state, which, by the waterways emptying into the great Mississippi River, could market its products on the Gulf Coast and, thence, to the countries of Europe.

In addition to these material inducements to cross the mountains, there were other, even more vital reasons. Relations between Great Britain and her American colonies were becoming more and more strained. Among the most serious of these reasons were the passage, by the British Parliament, of laws restricting American trade and American liberties; the levying of unjust and excessive taxes; the enforcement of these and other unpopular acts at the hands of petty colonial officials, whose unscrupulous and cruel oppression was becoming intolerable; and the widespread corruption of local courts and governments. Furthermore, provision had been made for carrying serious offenders to England for trial. Inhabitants of the western frontiers suffered intensely under these abuses, for courts were held among them seldom, or, in many cases, not at all. Even when courts were held, it was difficult to get a fair trial, or to escape the heavy penalties often inflicted by them.

As these abuses increased and exciting tales continued to trickle in about the beauty and fertility of the country beyond the mountains, men began to think seriously of its occupation. They knew that great dangers and hardships would have to be faced in its settlement, but they were beginning to feel that this vast land of promise would be well worth the price of taking it. Hunters, Indians and traders continued to tell great tales of the abundance of game, the richness of the soil, the pleasant climate, the excellent waterways, and its surpassing beauty. But they did not neglect to recount also stories of attacks from hostile Indians and the hardships of their lives in the wilderness. Many of their listeners decided to see this land for themselves, joined parties of "long hunters" and remained for months at a time exploring it. Thus they became fully acquainted with its desirability, as well as its disadvantages. The disadvantages, however, were beginning to seem small in light of the increasingly intolerable oppressions of the mother country and her colonial officials. One major difficulty faced them: Great Britain was strongly opposed to the extension of her colonial frontiers beyond the Appalachian Mountains. Her purpose at that time was to hold this land as Indian hunting-grounds and as a buffer state between her eastern colonies and the French and hostile Indians to the west.

Yet, in spite of this attempted restraint, the number of white men who ventured into this alluring, forbidden country increased, and so did the number of their fascinating tales. A few of their stories still survive in old manuscripts carefully preserved in various state and national archives. Some of them have been printed and are available to the modern reader. One of the most delightful is the story of Herbert's Spring, located at the beginning of the western watershed, told by James Adair.

"From the head of the southern branch of Savannah-river," Adair wrote, "it does not exceed half a mile to a head spring of the Mississippi water, that runs through the middle and upper parts of the Cheerake nation, about a north-west course,—and joining other rivers, that empty themselves into the great Mississippi. The above fountain is called 'Herbert's spring' and it was natural for strangers to drink thereof, to quench thirst, gratify their curiosity, and to have it to say they had drank of the French waters. Some of our people who went only with the view of staying a short time, by some allurement or other, exceeded the time appointed, at their return, reported either through merriment or superstition, that the spring had such a natural bewitching quality that whoever drank of it, could not possibly quit the nation, during the tedious space of seven years." [1]

It was not a fairly-tale enchantment, however, which first led men to build their homes in this inviting country and to take advantage of occupying the rich land which lay before them. Nor, in spite of the fact that Adair's story of Herbert's Spring and other tall tales make delightful reading, is it possible to escape the grim reality which French claims to this rich territory presented to Britain's American colonies. Ownership of the Mississippi valley, with its vast watershed and wealth of navigable streams, was being held in the balance. That the British colonies were taking the French threat to their trade and for the ownership of the disputed Mississippi valley very seriously is fully evident in various writings and legislative records of the half century which immediately preceded the founding of the white man's first settlement in the transmontane country in 1769. On this subject the South Carolina records are particularly interesting. This colony, because of her proximity to the French and Spanish settlements of the lower South, was particularly concerned, not only about the protection of her important fur trade, but also about the actual danger of French-incited Indian attacks upon settlements along her borders. To understand more fully the significance of the situation, it is helpful to review briefly some of the legislative records of this period.

As early as October 4, 1698, the South Carolina Journals of the Commons House of Assembly recorded the passage of resolutions which provided:

". . . That ye Virginians be Prohibited from Trading in this Province. . . .

"That the french Kings Subjects be Discouraged from making any further Progress in ye Indians trade in This Province. . . ."

That both the French and the Indian trade continued to be matters of grave concern is shown in many other entries, in these and other colonial records.

"November 16, 1700—Sat. morning . . . Ordered that Mr Speaker Ralph Izard, Esqr; and Mr Robt Stevens, be a committee to Joyne with a Committee of the upper House to address the Lords Proprs: that their Lordships would take such Methods as are most Necessary for the removal of ye french That are Settled on Masseshippe River, which we have great reason to believe will much Prejudice This settlement, and that the said Address, be Laid before the House at the next sitting."

"Feb. 25, 1701. . . . Upon the message brought from the upper house by Landgrave Edmund Bellinger relating to 4 french men belonging to Cannada that came from the Mississhippe River, & that the Governr: desired this house to give our advise how these men should be disposed of: & whether 15 more of the sd french in the sd River should be admitted to Come into this Settlement. . . ."

Thursday, February 26, 1701. ". . . According to yesterdayes order the house Entered ino ye debate relating to those french men that Came from Canada upon the debate on ye above order.

"Resolved that ye french men belonging to Cannada that came from Mississhippe be treated as friends in Amity with us & yt the Governor be desired to order them to return back as soon as possible & yt no encouragement be given them to return here with any furrs. . . ."

Other entries concerning the French, Spanish, and Indian questions also make interesting reading:

August 14, 1701—(Governor's message) "I have One Thing more Gentlemen to recommend to your Serious Consideration which is ye French Settlement which is on ye Sea Coast on ye Mississhippi River . . . and St Augustine I am informed that they have made two Settlements . . . about 120 Miles to ye Southward of St Augus-

tine. They already begin to incite our Indians to trade with them—
our Indians are in Love with their liberality and Conversation. It is
possible there may (be) a Warr in Europe or that if there be we
may not be Invaded But Warr or peace we are sure to be always
in danger & under ye trouble to Charge of keeping out Guards:
even in time of Peace so long as those french live so near to us to
put you in mind of the french of Canada's Neighbourhood to the
Inhabitants of New England is to Say enough on this Subject:

Thursday, August 21, 1701—"This House being Informed
That the french and Spanyard have Designs to Ataque This Colony
if Warr Breaks out. . . ."

Tuesday, August 26, 1701. "Order'd That the Governr be addressed To Take Such Care for Securing Our friendly Injans to
our Interest and from being Drawn from us by ye french Settled
to ye Southward of St Augustine as he Shall Think most Expedi-
ent. . . . "

On August 28, 1701, still further plans to protect the South
Carolina frontier against the French, Spanish and Indians were
taken up, and the subject was one which continued to command
the attention, not only of South Carolina, but of the other British
colonies for many years.

Governors and legislative bodies of Virginia were also faced with
similar problems, as is shown by Governor Dinfiddie's letter to
Governor Glen of South Carolina, in 1754. This communication,
which tells of George Washington's mission into the western country to ascertain the state of affairs among the Indians and French
settlements, reads in part as follows:

". . . That I might be truly inform'd w't steps the French had
taken on the Ohio prejudicial to His m'y's (Majesty's) Int't I
thought proper to send a Gent'm to the French Com'd't on whose
return I have the Hon'r to give y'r Excellenc'y part in the following
Intelligence. On his arrival at the Ohio, Major Washington, (the
Gent. whom I sent out) found that the French had taken post on
that River and built a Fort wherein they had mounted 8 P's Cannon six Pound'rs and that they had in readiness materials for other
Forts, w'ch they declar'd their intentions to Erect on that River
particularly at Logstown, the place destin'd for their chief resi-

dence as soon as the Season w'd permit them to embark and for w'ch Purpose he saw 220 Canoes ready finish'd besides a great number block'd out. Having delivered his Credentials and my Letter he complain'd to the Com'd'r of the violence that had been offered His M'y's Subjects in seizing their Effects and making Prisoners of their Persons to w'ch he answer'd' That the Co'ty had belonged to them, that no English Man had a right to trade upon those waters and that he, (the Com'd'r) had Orders to make every Person Prisoner that attempted it on the Ohio or the waters of it. Maj'r Washington learned that the French had four forts on the Mississippi, besides their strong settlem't at New Orleans, where they have above 1400 men in garrison, that by means of the River Oubasch (Wabash) they have communication between Canada and the Mississippi and some Forts on the Oubash to cover and protect this Comunicat'n. . . ." [2]

From this time forward George Washington was to play an important part in defeating the French plan to control and occupy the Mississippi valley. The intervention of foreign powers and their cruel practice of inciting the Indians to warfare against the white settlements was not ended, however, even with the defeat of the British in the Revolutionary War.

Under both British and American rule the western country passed through several stages of this colonial and foreign intervention in its relations with the Indian tribes. And to this malicious and deliberate use of the Indians to fight their battles against the white settlers may be traced much of the blame for the cruel wars which drenched the frontier with blood for many years. First, as is briefly shown in previously quoted documents of South Carolina and Virginia, it was the French who were instigating Indian warfare against the western frontiers of the British colonies. Then, it was Britain who, during the Revolutionary War, used the same tactics to incite the Indians against the struggling young American settlements in the present East and Middle Tennessee and Kentucky. Later, during the second war with England in 1812, it was again the British, who, with the collaboration of the Spanish settlements in Florida, armed and incited the Indians to attacks against American settlements. It was the fiendish massacre at Fort Mims, August

8

30, 1813, which brought Andrew Jackson into the field against the Indians, the Spanish at Pensacola and, later, the British at New Orleans.

Efforts were made by the early settlers of both Kentucky and Tennessee to establish friendly relations with the Indians, but long years of foreign influence had already created an atmosphere of hostility which could not be overcome. It was deadly war—on both sides—a war cruel beyond the wildest flights of imagination and fought, necessarily, to the bitter end. Having had, for something over a half-century, some taste of what Indian warfare could be, it is still difficult to understand how a little handful of white men dared to cross the mountains with their families and establish homes in the west.

Yet, in spite of all these difficulties, there was a strong sentiment favoring development of the transmontane lands in both England and the American colonies. By the middle of the eighteenth century serious exploration of this country was undertaken and great tracts of land were granted to men who were obligated to settle it. As early as 1747 the Ohio Company was organized by several leading men of Virginia, and Christopher Gist, who lived on the Yadkin River in North Carolina, was selected to locate and examine the lands for them.[3] The Virginia Provincial Council, in 1749, authorized the Loyal Land Company to enter and survey an 800,-000 acre tract of land. Obligated to locate these lands and settle occupants within a period of four years, the Loyal Company obtained the service of Dr. Thomas Walker, "a man of good education, discernment and well established in Virginia" to explore the grant.

Dr. Walker, who had already begun his explorations of the western country, found that the gap in the mountains discovered by Governor Spotswood and his Knights of the Golden Horseshoe, in 1716, was the lowest and best passage through the Appalachian range. He named it Cumberland Gap in honor of the Duke of Cumberland, son of the reigning monarch, George II. He gave the same name to the Cumberland River, whose headwaters he had discovered in his earlier travels.

The stage was rapidly being set for the opening of this new coun-

try. Two important events contributed greatly to the movement—
the treaty of Fort Stanwix in November, 1768, and the increasing
persecution of citizens along the western borders of Virginia and
the Carolinas by agents of the British Government. The Stanwix
Treaty, by which the powerful Six Nations relinquished their title
to a vast expanse of western lands, removed, at least partially, the
danger of Indian attacks on the proposed settlements and resulted
in the first rush of emigrants toward the west. Only a hardy few
formed the advance guard, but after they had led the way, others
quickly followed.

France's effort to maintain her claims to the Mississippi valley
and the stubborn resistance of England, instead of being quieted,
were intensified by the outbreak of the Seven Years' War in Europe
and its American counterpart, the French and Indian War (1754-
1763). When this bloody war was finally concluded, great changes
took place in the titles to American territory. France lost the whole
St. Lawrence valley to England; Spain lost Florida to the same
power and also ceded her lands west of the Mississippi River to
France. Yet, in spite of her victories on the battlefields and on the
high seas, England was actually losing more than she had gained
in America. A large part of her great colonial empire was rapidly
slipping from her grasp and her entire colonial system was endangered.

As early as December, 1768, French statesmen were convinced
that separation of Britain's American colonies from their mother
country was imminent.

"Without exaggerating the projects or union of the Colonies,"
wrote Du Chatelet to Choiseul, "the time for their independence is
very near. Their prudent men believe the moment not yet come; but
if the English government undertakes vigorous measures, who can
tell how far fanaticism for liberty may carry an immense people,
dwelling for the most part in the interior of the continent, remote
from imminent danger? . . . Three years ago the separation of the
English Colonies was looked upon as an object for the next generation; the germs were observed, but no one could forsee that they
would be so speedily developed. This new order of things, this
event which will necessarily have the greatest influence on the whole

political system of Europe, will probably be brought about within a very few years."

Choiseul,[4] in his reply, agreed with Du Chatelet's [5] opinion and assured his fellow statesman that the Spanish court at Madrid would be promptly informed on the subject.

Du Chatelet's prediction was well founded, for all of America was astir. Such men as George Washington and his friend, George Mason, were already pondering measures to be presented at the forthcoming sessions of the Virginia House of Burgesses.

"Our lordly masters in Great Britain," Washington wrote to Mason on April 5, 1769, "will be satisfied with nothing less than the deprivation of American freedom. Something should be done to maintain the liberty which we have derived from our ancestors. No man should hesitate for a moment, to use arms in defense of so valuable a blessing. We have already proved the inefficiency of addresses to the throne and remonstrances to Parliament. How far their attention to our rights and privileges is to be awakened by starving their trade and manufacturers, remains to be tried. . . ."

While the American policy of refusing to buy English goods was already proving effective, it was not enough to halt the progress of British oppression. The majority of the members of Parliament and advisers to the throne were deaf to the American pleas, but the ears of London merchants and manufacturers became increasingly alert as they saw their colonial trade disappearing. Fleets and a standing army might invade Boston, but armed men could not force the Americans to drink British tea, nor to use other items on the mother country's trade lists. Neither was there a law which could force a man to buy a new coat for himself, nor a gown for his wife. A few far-seeing Britons saw in this oppression of Americans a direct threat to their own hard-won liberties and, on this ground, some of the great statesmen of the period rose in passionate defense of the colonists.

"It is not a question of one refractory Colony," warned Isaac Barre, "the whole country is ripe for revolt. Let us come to the point. Are the Americans proper subjects for taxation? I think they are not. I solemnly declare I think they will not submit to any law imposed upon them for the purpose of revenue.

11

"On a former occasion the noble Lord North told us that he would listen to no proposition for repeal until he saw America prostrate at his feet. To offset this is not as easy as some imagine; the Americans are a numerous, a respectable, a hardy, a free people. But were it ever so easy, does any friend to his country really wish to see America thus humbled? In such a situation, she would serve only as a monument to your vengeance and your folly. For my part, the America I wish to see is America increasing and prosperous, raising her head in graceful dignity, with freedom and firmness asserting her rights at your bar, vindicating her liberties, pleading her services and conscious of her merit. This is the America that will have the spirit to fight your battles, to sustain you when hard pushed by some prevailing foe and by her industry will be able to consume your manufactures, support your trade, and pour wealth into your towns and cities. If we do not change our conduct toward her, America will be torn from our side. I repeat it; unless you repeal this law, you run the risk of losing America." [6]

In January, 1769, Edmund Burke, one of the greatest of all champions of the American colonists, speaking against the pernicious provision of carrying Americans to England for trial, made this prophecy:

"Suppose you do call over two or three of these unfortunate men; What will become of the rest? 'Let me have the heads of the principal leaders,' exclaimed the Duke of Alva; these heads are Hydra's heads. Suppose a man is brought over for High Treason; if his witnesses do not appear, he cannot have a fair trial. God and nature oppose you." [7]

These warnings were of no avail. Britain pursued her ruthless course, and French statesmen, watching cautiously from the sidelines, pointed to a golden opportunity for their court and for Spain. The far-sighted Du Chatelet, writing to Choiseul, said:

"An attempt to seize the defenders of American liberties would precipitate the revolution. How great will be the indignation of the Americans, when they learn that Britain, without receiving their representations, without hearing their agents, treats them as slaves and condemns them as rebels. They will never recognize the right

12

claimed by Parliament; even if they bear with it, their hearts will breathe nothing but independence, and will own no other country than the wilderness their industry has fertilized. Henceforward, the Colonies are divided from the Metropolis in interests and principles; and the bonds of their dependence will be severed on the first opportunity. Spain and France should adopt towards them general principles, entirely different from those which have been practised till now; and, even at the risk of transient inconveniences, should depart from the ancient prohibitory laws of commerce. The two courts must consider whether it is for their interest to second the revolution which menaces England, at the risk of consequences which may a little later result from it for the totality of the New World; and whether the weakening of a common enemy can compensate the risk of such an example to their own colonies. . . ."

Bancroft continues on the subject, stating that the letter from Du Chatelet to Choiseul "excited the most attentive curiosity of Louis XV and every one of his Council. An extract of it was sent to ascertain the sentiments of the Catholic King. . . ."

While this letter was studied in the greatest courts of Europe, the Americans continued to oppose England's abusive policies, and Parliament considered further measures to force American submission. All of the parties were well aware of the value of the territory west of the Allegheny Mountains and considered it in their discussions. But the land itself was already in the hands of the victors—the home builders. They would love it, cherish it and hold it for their own against all comers.

"Spain," Bancroft pointed out, "valued Louisiana as a screen for Mexico; and England, in turn, held the valley of the Mississippi from jealousy of France; not to colonize it . . . John Finley, a backwoodsman of North Carolina, who in this year (1768) passed through the Kentucky country, found not one white man's cabin in all the enchanting wilderness. . . . It was Hillsborough's purpose to prevent colonization, and to hold the territory through friendship of the savages. . . . But this design was shattered by actual settlements in the Illinois and Wabash; the roving disposition of the Americans; and the avarice of the British officers who coveted profit from the concession of lands. . . ." [8]

13

THE DANGEROUS EXAMPLE

In the meantime, the fur trade and commerce with the Indian tribes had grown to such proportions that all three of the great powers, at one time or another, established posts in the Mississippi valley. The ownership and history of these posts is as complicated as the European history of that day, for, like all possessions in the New World, they were subject to the constantly shifting whims, the court intrigues, the secret treaties and constant maneuvering of English, French and Spanish officials. Saint Louis, west of the Mississippi, increased in population and acquired importance as a trading post, but the population of Illinois had shown some decrease, and in 1768, "totaled scarcely more than 1,358, of whom rather more than three hundred were Africans. Kaskaskias had six hundred white persons and three hundred Negroes. . . ."

While these posts were established primarily for trade, it was inevitable that traders and soldiers, seeing the rich lands about them, should bring in slaves and establish themselves and their families on plantations. All the major European powers still clung to their dreams of building rich colonies in the New World.

Through treaties with the Cherokees at Hard Labour in South Carolina in October, 1768, and with the Six Nations at Fort Stanwix the following month, vast tracts of land were ceded to the British Crown. These negotiations were followed by a great rush toward the western boundaries of the Carolinas and Virginia where hundreds of restless, adventurous men and women stood poised, waiting for the slightest pretext upon which they might dash forward to claim princely estates in the transmontane country. Many had already chosen sites for their future homes.

Virginia had received, but was not too much impressed, during this critical period, by its new governor, Lord Botetourt, who arrived, amidst great pomp and formal ceremonies, to assume office in 1768. By display of courtly trappings, England was seeking to impress the Virginians with the power and dignity of the British Crown.

He was instructed also to call a new legislature, to closet its members, as well as those of the Council, and to humor them in almost anything except explicit denial of the authority of Parliament.

Following his instructions, the new governor appeared in full splendor and, in May, 1769, was carried to the opening session of the House of Burgesses in his state coach, drawn by six white horses. He appeared before the assembly in person and, among other things, suggested a new treaty by which the western boundaries of Virginia would reach deeper into the Cherokee country. He entertained members lavishly at his own table and, by his natural charm, made himself exceedingly agreeable. But neither his popular stand on western expansion nor his delightful personality changed the irrevocable determination of his guests. George Washington, Patrick Henry, the Lees, Carters and young Thomas Jefferson, then serving his first term in the House of Burgesses, were frequently at his table. Still neither legislators nor citizens deviated from their stern resolves. Botetourt was received on all sides with the greatest of courtesy, but members of the House of Burgesses declared for their body the sole right of imposing taxes and, furthermore, they advocated ". . . a concert of the Colonies in care for the violated rights of America. . . ."

Furthermore, it "laid bare the flagrant tyranny of applying to America the obsolete statute of Henry the Eighth; and it warned the King of the dangers that would ensue if any person in any part of America should be seized and carried beyond the sea for trial. It consumated its work by communicating its Resolutions and asking the concurrence of every legislature in America."

While Virginia was thus engaged in asserting American rights, groups in South Carolina were driven to more drastic action. Here people suffered under a judicial system which provided that court processes might be served and fees collected in the province, but that courts were held only in the capital city of Charleston. This left the remote districts at the mercy of dishonest officers and denied their citizens recourse to the courts. They met this situation by taking affairs into their own hands and "regulating" their own disputes or business. From this attempt to provide necessary local self-government, they became known as "regulators."

Similar groups of Regulators were also active in North Carolina, where the unscrupulous Governor Tryon, aided and abetted by Edmund Fanning, went to even greater extremes. Titles to property were challenged and exhorbitant fees were charged for recording

15

new deeds; juries were packed; men were arrested and imprisoned on the slightest provocation; the cost of any lawsuit became prohibitive; and to already heavy taxes was added the graft of illegal tax collectors. To combat these evils the Regulators of North Carolina arose in great numbers. Revolt flamed high in Orange, Anson, Rowan, and Mecklenburg counties, where countless citizens were outlawed and forced to flee for their lives to that one and only haven open to them—the trackless west. They, their families, and their friends, formed the backbone of the western movement.

Tennessee's first historian, Judge John Haywood, who was personally acquainted with many of the men that were so persecuted and who had their stories from their own lips, wrote:

"The royal force, under command of Gov. Tryon, met the 'Regulators' near the Great Alamance, on the 16th of May, 1771, and defeated them, killing about two hundred of them on the field of battle. Some of them were taken by the victors and hanged; others took the oath of allegiance, and returned home; others fled to Holston. . . ." [9]

Among those who fled to the western wilderness were Daniel Boone, from the Yadkin, who removed in 1769 or 1770; and James Robertson, from Wake County in North Carolina, early in 1770. Robertson, Haywood says:

". . . visited the delightful country on the waters of the Holston, to view the new settlements which then began to be formed on the Watauga. When he came to the Watauga in 1770, he found one Honeycut living in a hut, who furnished him with food for his subsistence. He made a crop this year on the Watauga. . . ."

After remaining with Honeycut for several months, tending his crop of corn and exploring the country, Robertson began his return trip to North Carolina. As he made this lonely journey he became lost and, after riding for several days in his attempt to find his way, he came to a precipice so steep that his horse could not cross it, so he had to abandon him. Meanwhile, the constant rain had wet his powder so that he could not obtain food. After wandering on foot for about two weeks, weak, emaciated and on the verge of starvation, he miraculously met two hunters.

16

Judge John Haywood, author of Tennessee's first history. Photo courtesy of State of Tennessee Tourism Development Division.

"But there is a Providence which rules over the destinies of men," Judge Haywood comments, "and preserves them to run the race appointed for them. Unpromising as were the prospects of James Robertson at that time . . . yet the God of nature had given him an elevated soul, and planted in it the seeds of virtue, which made him in the midst of discouraging circumstances look forward to better times."

The hunters gave him food and, after much persuasion on Robertson's part, permitted him to ride on one of their horses. So it was that one of the greatest of the pioneers of the Tennessee country was saved and left to "run the race appointed for him." He returned promptly to the Yadkin and soon brought his family out to settle in the Watauga.

The Treaty of Fort Stanwix, 1768, had greatly encouraged the formation of settlements west of the mountains, which were soon progressing with increasing vigor, in spite of the known dangers and difficulties. A short time before Robertson's appearance on the Watauga, perhaps early in 1769, the first cabin was built and the first hearth-fire was kindled in the home of a permanent settler. This was a simple, commonplace act, but one which announced quietly to the world that the advance guard of the conquerors of the great Mississippi valley had come! It is quite probable that these first settlers, William Bean and his wife, Lydia, had no thought of the international significance of their act. In fact, they may never have known that, some five years later, their presence, with that of a few relatives and friends who had come out to join them, would be discussed with fear and foreboding in the greatest courts of Europe. They and others were far too busy and too much concerned with the daily problems which confronted them to bother about the far-reaching consequences of their actions.

William Bean had chosen for his home a lovely site on the Watauga River at Boone's Creek, where he and Daniel Boone had camped on one of their early hunting trips. It was only one of the many beautiful spots he might have selected, for all of them were not only beautiful, but were fertile, well-watered and offering rich returns for the labors of cultivating them. As these hunters returned to their eastern homes, it was natural for them to report the

17

presence of women and children in this new country and to persuade their own families to join in the trek to the west.

In May, 1769, Boone, having prevailed upon John Findley to guide him, set out for the Kentucky country, leaving his wife and young children to shift for themselves at their peaceful habitation on the banks of the Yadkin River in North Carolina. As they pushed into the wilderness they found buffalo in great herds, grazing fearlessly; deer, bears, and the smaller beasts were encountered in great numbers; the streams abounded in fish, and the air was filled with huge flocks of birds. The larger animals, finding their way to watering places and salt licks, made trails which could be traveled with comparative ease, and war traces of the Indians crossed and recrossed the wilderness, but much of the travel of Boone and his small exploring party was away from even these crude trails. Daniel Boone sought out the very heart of the wilderness. But, as summer waned, only one man—John Stewart—was left with him. The others had slipped away on their own mysterious missions—perhaps to join other explorers and French traders on the Cumberland River, or to follow the rivers which led to the Mississippi and, finally, down that great stream to Natchez and the Gulf of Mexico.

While hunting on the Kentucky River, Boone and Stewart were captured by a band of Indians, but, fortunately, made their escape. Shortly afterward, they were joined by Squire Boone, Daniel's brother. Stewart did not survive long, however. He was killed by the Indians and the two Boones were left alone in the wilderness. When the spring of 1770 arrived, their supplies were exhausted and Squire returned to the eastern settlements, leaving Daniel to the solitude of his Kentucky forests. He had no salt and possessed neither horse nor dog, but, aside from the disturbing thought of his wife and children left alone for so many months, he existed quite happily until July, 1770, when his brother, faithful to his promise, met him at the camp they had built the previous year. Boone, however, soon returned home to the Yadkin, where he began preparations for removal to his western paradise. This time he would carry with him his patient wife, his family and as many friends and neighbors as could be persuaded to join him.

18

Daniel Boone in hunting attire, from the original painting by Chappel. Reproduced by Johnson, Fry & Company, New York.

To Boone, perhaps, more than to any other has accrued the chief honor for the exploration and settlement of Kentucky, as well as for portions of the Tennessee country. Little is known of John Findley, except that he was apparently the first hunter and explorer of this "dark and bloody ground," and that he served as Boone's guide because of his previous knowledge of the country. John Stewart is remembered especially because he was the first man known to have lost his life in the long, arduous battle to possess the rich domain which he had helped discover. But Boone had scarcely begun his career. His fame and chief accomplishments lay ahead.

One of the most important events of this great period of exploration was George Washington's tour of the Ohio River country in 1770. His chief purpose in this journey was to establish claims and protect the rights of the soldiers and officers, who had served with him in the French war, to the 200,000 acres bounty which had been granted to them by the colony of Virginia. Beyond this, it had even greater benefits in encouraging the opening of these rich lands to a vast population already waiting eagerly to possess it. In order to select suitable tracts for his men, it was necessary for him to descend the Great Kanawha River and to make a careful inspection of the territory through which he passed.

Washington was a great sportsman, but he had not only a love of hunting and living in the primeval forests, but was also an excellent judge of the quality and location of tracts which would be suitable for early settlement. His journey began with the hunting season of the Indians, when game abounds and the woodlands have reached their full growth. For lovers of Nature, it was a delightful time and, for serious explorers, an excellent time to assess the fertility of the land by viewing it at the height of its productivity. Animals were well fed and plentiful and so fearless that even the usually timid deer were often seen as they came down to the water's edge to drink. Great flights of ducks and geese and pigeons filled the air with the whirr of their wings and countless flocks of wild turkeys marched by in full sight and undisturbed. The voyagers, easily killing by day the game they needed for their evening meal, feasted on the best the land had to offer.

The journey was not without its dangers, however, for the Indians were still hostile and resented the encroachment of the white men. Soon, however, news of Washington's appearance on their waters sped through the Indian towns, for many of them had fought with the French against the English and were already aware of the importance of his name.

One old chief, leading several members of his tribe, approached Washington's encampment and, through an interpreter, addressed him with great reverence, saying that he had heard of his being in that part of the country and had come a great distance to see him. Continuing, he told Washington that he was one of the warriors in the service of the French, who had lain in ambush on the banks of the Monongahela and had played great havoc with Braddock's army.

"He and his young men," Washington Irving relates [10] "had singled out Washington, as he made himself conspicuous riding about the field of battle with the general's orders, and had fired at him repeatedly, but without success; then they had concluded that he was under the protection of the Great Spirit, had a charmed life, and could not be slain in battle. . . ."

Often, during the progress of this journey, Washington walked far into the forests, examining the kinds and the growth of trees, which, to a skilled woodsman, reveal much of the fertility and nature of the soils. Here and there he blazed trees, marking the corners of his soldiers' tracts and taking into account even the most minute details of the nature of the land. It was an adventurous journey, not without many real dangers, especially on the return trip through the bitter cold of an unusually severe winter. On the whole, however, it was most enjoyable to a man like George Washington, and of definite benefit to the men who had served loyally in the ranks he commanded.

At this same time Daniel Boone was still exploring his land of promise—the Kentucky country—with forty adventurers, who, from the Clinch River plunged westward under the leadership of James Knox. These men, and others like them, who ventured into the wilderness for long periods—sometimes months, or even years—were called, because of their extended stays, "the long hunters." Most of them eventually found their way back to their eastern homes and returned with their families and friends to form settlements; others found their way down the Cumberland River to the great limestone bluffs where the city of Nashville now stands. Here they found even richer country, indeed a hunter's paradise, covered with luxuriant forest growth, as well as tall, thick cane, in which countless animals roamed and the whirr of the wings of great flocks of fowl was almost deafening. The bellowings of buffaloes could be heard from great distances from the Great Salt Lick, and other animals gathered here to drink the refreshing waters and lick the salt-rich rocks. Some of the bolder hunters and explorers pushed on to the Mississippi and floated down its broad waters to Natchez and other parts of the far South. The wilderness was alive with restless men—the home-makers and the empire-builders.

American colonial leaders, notably Benjamin Franklin, and even some of the more liberal representatives of the British crown, advocated settlement of the transmontane country, but the royal edict, proclaimed in 1763, at the time of the ending of the French and Indian War, forbidding such settlement was still in effect. However, inhabitants along the western borders of the colonies had already proven themselves an unruly lot and had given much evidence that the uneasiness of the British monarch was not without foundation. It was apparent that if they were permitted to cross the mountains, they might easily get entirely out of hand. There was also the disquieting thought that they might join the Spanish and French settlements in the far South, for their markets and, likewise, their chief interest, would necessarily follow the natural course of the western waters to the sea.

This opposition, along with the inability to obtain legal titles to the land, had a slight tendency to discourage settlement of this fabulous country—but only a very slight one. The certain hostility of Indian tribes was also a disadvantage, but neither, in the face of difficulties they knew existed in the eastern colonies, constituted an insurmountable obstacle. Adventurous, ambitious and, some-

21

times, desperate men, do not wait for assurances of safety and security, so a hardy few, in defiance of all restrictions, while possession was still the greater part of the law, kept moving themselves and their families to new homes and a new life beyond the mountains. But these adventurers were not a lawless mob—nor were they in ignorance of the customary processes of law and order. At their earliest opportunity, they worked out their own means of providing a type of government suited to their own needs.

At their earliest convenience, although it was forbidden by the British government, they sought titles to their lands by direct purchase or lease, from the Indians. Their case was too urgent to permit compliance with ancient rules and regulations, but they were careful to respect the rights and freedoms guaranteed by English laws which their forbears had obtained after their long struggle for justice and freedom from oppression by a monarchical government. Now, however, they were their own masters. Many of them dared not go back to the mother colonies, for there was a price on their heads. Others did not wish to go, for they, fleeing poverty and oppression, also sought new opportunities in a new land. All of them looked forward to possessing a place where they, unmolested by the tax collectors and oppressive laws, might enjoy the fruits of their labors and where their children might have a chance to build a life for themselves in this rich, new land.

Bean was soon followed by a stream of emigrants from Virginia and the Carolinas. By 1772, a number of able men who were destined to take leading parts in the settlement and development of this far-reaching wilderness, had established themselves at choice sites on the Holston and Nolichucky, as well as the Watauga Rivers and their tributaries. This steady stream of emigrants, Ramsey says:

". . . embraced within their limits men of very different and opposite traits of character. Most of them were honest, industrious, enterprising men, who had come there to improve their condition, by subduing and cultivating new lands in the West. But others had arrived among them, who had fled from justice in their own country, and hoped to escape the demand of the law, and the punishment of crime, by a retreat to these remote and inaccessible frontiers. There, from the existing condition of affairs, they found

Covered bridge over the Watauga River. Photo courtesy of State of Tennessee Tourism Development Division.

safety from prosecution, and certainly from conviction through the regular channels of the law. . . ."

The emigrants who had settled on the North Holston, in what are now Sullivan and Hawkins counties, were believed to be in Virginia and, therefore, considered themselves to be under the law and protection of that province. The settlements south of Holston River were, admittedly, within the boundaries of North Carolina.

This became fully apparent as the result of running lines in accordance with terms of the treaty held at Lochaber, South Carolina, October 18, 1770. Governor Botetourt of Virginia, increasingly aware that citizens of that province were pressing further and further into the Indian country, arranged this treaty in an effort to placate the restless citizens on his western frontiers. The line run in compliance with the Lochaber treaty began at the intersection of the North Carolina-Cherokee line, about seventy miles east of the Long Island of the Holston River and, in order not to trespass upon this sacred meeting place, or "beloved island," of the Cherokees, carried the line westward until it reached within six miles of the Long Island. Thence, it continued to the mouth of the Great Kanawha River.

Col. John Donelson, who, in 1780, was to command the flotilla which left Fort Patrick Henry, at the Long Island, to make its historic voyage to the site of the present city of Nashville surveyed the line in 1771. Anthony Bledsoe, about the same time, made a private survey which, like Donelson's, revealed that the three settlements which thought they were in Virginia were actually within the boundaries of North Carolina.

Alexander Cameron, British Indian agent among the Cherokees, a deputy of John Stewart, then ordered all persons who had made settlements beyond the Donelson line to move. The inhabitants of the Brown settlement on the Nolichucky River withdrew to the Watauga. The Watauga settlement and the Carter's Valley settlement remained undisturbed, but in what they considered a very serious position.

"The settlers," Haywood wrote, "uneasy at the precarious tenure by which they occupied the lands, desired to obtain a permanent title. For this purpose, in the year of 1772, they deputed James

23

Robertson and John Boone to negotiate with the Indians for a lease; and for a certain amount in merchandise, estimated at five or six thousand dollars, muskets, and other articles of convenience, the Cherokees made a lease to them for eight years of all the country on the waters of the Watauga." [11]

Fortunately, in this crisis, there continued to be peace between the Indians and the settlers. Even more fortunately, many of the leading Cherokees insisted that the Wataugans be permitted to remain on the land, provided that they would not make further encroachments.

This happy ending to immediate difficulties which confronted the Wataugans was marred by a dangerous event which could easily have wiped out all of the white settlements.

After the treaty granting the lease was signed, the settlers staged a great celebration—racing, athletic events and other frontier amusements. Many of the Indians remained to take part in it, but, toward the end of the day, some white men, apparently from Wolf Hills, killed one of the Indians.

"This act," Ramsey says, "alike atrocious, inhuman and impolitic, gave great offence and produced much alarm. The inhabitants felt that it was not only wrong, but that it would expose them to the retaliatory vengeance of the outraged Cherokees. At this crisis the wisdom and intrepidity of Robertson saved the infant settlements from extermination. He undertook a journey to the Indian nation, one hundred and fifty miles distant, in order to pacify them, and allay the irritation produced by this barbarous and imprudent act. The attempt was hazardous in the extreme; but the safety of the whites demanded the mission, and he proceeded at once to the chief town of the Cherokees, met their head men, and declared to them that his people viewed the horrid deed which had been perpetrated with deepest concern for their own character, and with keenest indignation against the offender, whom they intended to punish as he deserved whenever he could be discovered. The Indians were appeased by this incident of condescension in the white people, and of the discountenance which they gave to the miscreant. The settlers were saved from their fury, and Robertson began to be looked upon as an intrepid soldier, a lover of his countrymen, and as a man of uncommon address, in devising means of extrication from difficulties." [12]

Meanwhile, the settlements were gaining in population and in strength.

Judge Haywood describes the three settlements, known usually as the Holston Settlements, as follows:

"In the same year (1772) Jacob Brown, with one or two families from North Carolina, settled on the Nolichucky River, where, keeping a small store of goods, he ingratiated himself with the Indians; and made with them a contract for lands on the waters of that river, similar to the former. (The Watauga lease.) In both instances the property advanced to purchase the goods was reimbursed by selling out the lands in small parcels, to individuals for the time the lease was to last.

"Soon after the arrival of Mr. Robertson on the Watauga, some persons settled in Carter's Valley, fourteen or fifteen miles above where Rogersville now is. All the country was then supposed to be a part of Virginia, and it soon became settled from Wolf Hills (now Abington, Virginia) to Carter's Valley. The river was deemed the boundary line between North Carolina and Virginia. Parker and Carter opened a store in the valley, which the Indians robbed. When Henderson's Treaty was held with the Cherokees in 1774, and again in 1775, these merchants came to the meeting, and demanded Carter's Valley as compensation for the injury they had sustained, to extend from Cloud's Creek to Chimney Top Mountain of Beech Creek. The Indians were willing to give the valley, provided an additional price was thrown into the bargain. Parker and Carter agreed to the proposal, and took Robert Lucas as a partner to enable them to advance the additional price. Parker and Carter leased their lands to job purchasers, but when, sometime afterwards, it began to be suspected that the lands lay in North Carolina and not in Virginia, the purchasers refused to hold under them." [13]

While these negotiations gave a certain security to the lands which the Wataugans occupied, there was a constantly increasing need for the establishment of a formal government. This truth being fully recognized, they, with the fine show of courage which had

25

brought them west in the first place, set themselves to remedying the situation.

Sometime in the spring of 1772 the Wataugans came together and, as Ramsey puts it, "exercised the divine right of governing themselves." [14] They formed a written association and articles for the management of their general affairs. Five commissioners were appointed, by the decision of a majority of whom all matters in controversy were settled; and the same tribunal had entire control in all matters affecting the common good.

"The Government was paternal and patriarchal—simple and moderate," Ramsey continues, "but summary and firm. The Articles by which the Association was governed have not been preserved. They formed, it is believed, the first compact for civil government anywhere west of the Alleghenies, and would make a valuable and exceedingly interesting contribution to the historical literature of the Great West, and a most desirable addition especially to these annals. But after the most diligent inquiry and patient search, this writer has been unable to discover them."

Since no documents have yet been brought to light on the formation of the Watauga Association, it has been impossible for positive statements to be made on the details of this unique and entirely original form of government. A few authentic statements concerning it were brought out four years later in the 1776 petition of "Washington District" for annexation of the province of North Carolina. It appears that there were five "commissioners" who also functioned as a court, the members of which, it is generally agreed were: James Robertson, John Sevier, John Carter, Charles Robertson and Zachariah Isbell. Brief sketches of these men were given by Ramsey and later writers.

James Robertson, whom Andrew Jackson and many others have called "The Father of Tennessee," was born in Brunswick County, Virginia, June 28, 1742, of Scotch-Irish ancestry. He was of a quiet manner, wise and deliberate in his decisions, and possessed of indomitable courage, which saved many desperate situations during the early days in both East Tennessee and Middle Tennessee settlements. His skill in managing the Indians, as well as his fearlessness and excellent strategy when it was necessary to wage war

James Robertson, called "The Father of Tennessee," by Andrew Jackson and others. Photo courtesy of State of Tennessee Tourism Development Division.

John Sevier, a great leader in the development west of the Allegheny Mountains. Photo courtesy of State of Tennessee Tourism Development Division.

George III, from an engraving in R. Campbell & Company's edition of Hume's *History of England*.

against them, made him one of the great heroes of the times. Theodore Roosevelt said that Robertson and Sevier were two of the three greatest leaders in the development west of the Allegheny Mountains, George Rogers Clark being the third.

John Sevier was of an entirely different nature, but he and Robertson complemented each other, the qualities of one blending with those of the other. Sevier was born in Rockingham County, Virginia, September 23, 1745, of French Huguenot ancestry, the original family name in France being Xavier. One of the best estimates of his character and accomplishments is given by the late John Trotwood Moore:

"He was a gentleman by birth and breeding. While not a learned man, he was extremely intelligent and was a friend and correspondent of many of the most prominent and able statesmen of the times, including Madison and Franklin. It was said that he was the handsomest man in Tennessee. He was tall, with blue eyes and brown hair, of slender build and erect military carriage. He was fluent and gallant, generous and convivial, of gay, pleasure-loving temperament; yet his manners were polished and he had a great natural dignity. He was impulsive, yet, in his campaigns with the Indians, prudent and judicious. He was especially fond of two things: popularity and Indian fighting; and he was successful in both roles. He fought thirty-five battles and all victoriously; and he was undoubtedly the most popular man in Tennessee during his lifetime."

John Carter, who also came from Virginia, was one of the great pioneer leaders of Tennessee. He was possessed of great wisdom and dependability and was one of the most popular men in the settlements. Settling originally in Carter's Valley, he soon left to reside in the Watauga Valley. Here he was chosen to head the court of law established by the Watauga Association and later was also chairman of the Committee of Thirteen.

Charles Robertson of South Carolina was chosen as a trustee of the Watauga Association and, when lands were leased, and later purchased from the Indians by the settlers, they were conveyed to him. He was known for his wisdom and good sense, particularly in regard to business dealings and in the management of public affairs.

Zachariah Isbell, like the others, was a favorite of the settlers.

27

He was held in high esteem, particularly because of his long and able service in military operations and in other matters concerning the welfare of the settlements.

Along with the Robertsons, the Seviers and other large and powerful families of the frontier, was that of Gen. Evan Shelby. He was born in Wales in 1720 and, when he was about fifteen, emigrated with his father to Maryland, where he became a prominent figure in Indian border warfare. He came to the Holston in 1771 and settled at King's Meadows, near the present city of Bristol, Tennessee-Virginia. He held the rank of colonel in the Virginia service and, at the time the Walker-Henderson line was run in 1779 and his place was found to be in North Carolina, his office was vacated, and William Campbell was promoted to the full rank of colonel in his stead. Isaac Shelby, his son, who came to the Holston with him, was, at first, a lieutenant, then a captain. In the spring of 1779 he was elected a member of the Virginia legislature. Thomas Jefferson soon promoted him to the rank of major and placed him in command of the guards who were to accompany the commissioners extending the line between Virginia and North Carolina. This line showed that his residence was within the limits of North Carolina, so he was immediately appointed a magistrate and a colonel in the county of Sullivan, North Carolina. Gen. Evan Shelby, with his five sons, worked in unison with the settlers on the Watauga and the Nolichucky and played an important part in defending and developing all of the transmontane settlements.

These, in brief, were among the leaders in the over-the-mountain settlements when the Watauga Association was formed and put into action. There were many others who also played important parts in developing this new country. Apparently, the nearest contemporary authority we have on the subject states that "they appointed magistrates and framed laws for their present occasion, and to all intents and purposes, erected themselves into, though an inconsiderable, yet a separate state."

The above reference is taken from a letter written by the Earl of Dunmore, the last British governor of Virginia, to the Earl of Dartmouth, British secretary of state, Williamsburg, May 16, 1774. It reads:

". . . Whatever may be the law with respect to the title, there are, I think, divers reasons which should induce his majesty (George III) to comply with their petition, so far at least, as to admit the petitioners and their acquisitions, if not into this government, into some other. For if the title should be thought defective, it would still, at such a distance from the seat of authority, be utterly impractical to void it, or prevent the occupying of the lands, which being known to be of an extraordinary degree of fertility, experience shows that nothing (so fond as the Americans are of migration), can stop the concourse of people that actually begin to draw toward them; and should the petition be rejected, your lordship may assure yourself, it is no chimerical conjecture, that, so far from interrupting the progress of their settlement, it would have a direct contrary tendency, by forcing the people to adopt a form of government of their own, which it would be easy to frame in such a manner as to prove an additional encouragement to all the dissatisfied of every other government, to flock to that. In effect, we have an example of the very case, there being actually a set of people in the back part of this colony, bordering on the Cherokee country, who, finding they could not obtain titles to the land they fancied, under any of the neighboring governments, have settled upon it without, and contented themselves with becoming in a manner tributary to the Indians, and have appointed magistrates, and framed laws for their present occasions, and to all intents and purposes, erected themselves into, though an inconsiderable, yet a separate State; the consequence of which may prove hereafter detrimental to the peace and security of the other colonies; it at least sets a *dangerous example* to the people of America, of forming governments distinct from and independent of his majesty's authority." [15]

Lord Dunmore and, indeed, all of Virginia, before many months would be hearing more of this ". . . set of people . . ." who were endangering the other colonies by their ". . . dangerous example. . . ." At about the time the above letter was written, trouble was brewing with the Indians—particularly with the Shawanees.

"The Shawanees," said Bancroft, "the most warlike of all the Indians, prowled from the Allegheny river to what is now Sullivan

29

county in Tennessee. . . . They despised the other warriors, red or white; and made a boast of having killed ten times as many of the English as any other tribe." [16]

One of their warriors returned with the scalps of forty men, women and children and atrocity was piled upon atrocity. The alarm of the emigrants increased from the Watauga to the lower Mononga- hela and frequent expresses sped to Williamsburg pleading for assistance. Dunmore, following the wishes of the assembly, in May, 1774, ordered the militia of the frontier counties to be em- bodied for defense. By September he, himself, with a body of militia, was on the march to the Delawares and the Six Nations, where he renewed peace with portions of these tribes. According to plans, he was then to proceed to the mouth of the little Kanawha and to rendezvous with the four regiments of militia from the fron- tier counties, which Gen. Andrew Lewis had been ordered to raise. Gen. Evan Shelby raised more than fifty men in the transmontane settlements. Among them were his son, Isaac Shelby, James Robert- son, Valentine Sevier and many others who shouldered their rifles and marched out to take their place in history as the first volunteers of the future Tennessee, the Volunteer State, and to play a con- spicuous part in the battle at Point Pleasant. A list of all these first volunteers is not available, but on a roster of Evan Shelby's com- pany which served in this historic campaign, the following names appear:

James Shelby, John Sawyers, John Findlay, Henry Span, Daniel Mungle, Frederick Mungle, John Williams, John Camack, Andrew Torrence, George Brooks, Isaac Newland, Abram Newland, George Ruddle, Emanuel Shoatt, Abram Bogard, Peter Forney, William Tucker, John Fain, Samuel Vance, Samuel Fain, Samuel Handley, Samuel Samples, Arthur Blackburn, Robert Handley, George Arm- strong, William Casey, Mack Williams, John Stewart, Conrad Navè, Richard Park, John Riley, Elijah Robertson, Rees Price, Richard Holliway, Jarrett Williams, Julius Robinson, Charles Fielder, Ben- jamin Graham, Andrew Goff, Hugh O'Gullion, Patk. St. Lawrence, James Hughey, John Bradley, Barileel Maywell, and Barnett O'Gullion. Of the noncommissioned officers, it is only known that

John Sawyers, James Robertson, and Valentine Sevier, were three orderly sergeants.[17]

These over-the-mountain men, with the remainder of General Lewis' command, made their way through the rugged mountains, now brilliant with their autumn foliage, and descended the Kanawha, arriving at Point Pleasant, on the sixth of October. The expected message from Dunmore was not awaiting them, so they made camp, hoping for his early arrival and strengthening their position in preparation for an Indian attack.

Early in the morning of Monday, October 10, Valentine Sevier and James Robertson were out hunting game when they discovered signs of the presence of a large body of Indians. Dashing back to camp to give warning, they found there a young man, who with a companion had been out in search of deer when they were fired upon by the Indians and his companion killed instantly. The Indians had already crossed the river and were preparing for battle.

Colonel Lewis went into action immediately, ordering out two divisions—the Augusta troops, under his brother Charles Lewis and the Botetourt troops under Fleming. At sunrise the Indians opened with a heavy fire upon both divisions. Fleming was shot three times and Charles Lewis was fatally wounded. Had it not been for reinforcements, the troops would have given away under the merciless onslaught of the enemy. But the Indians, too, were paying a heavy price in the hard-fought battle which lasted until about noon. Only the fanatical shouting of their chief, the noted Cornstalk, of "Be strong! Be strong!" kept them in the desperate contest. Both sides fought furiously, sometimes close enough to attack each other with tomahawks and hunting knives. Finally, the Indians retreated and made their escape through the thick underbrush. The Americans won a brilliant victory, but they paid a heavy price for it in killed and wounded.

"This battle," Bancroft says, "was the most bloody and best contested in the annals of forest warfare. . . . The heroes of that day proved themselves worthy to found states. Among them were Isaac Shelby, the first governor of Kentucky; William Campbell, the brave George Matthews; Fleming; Andrew Moore, afterwards a senator of the United States; Evan Shelby, James Robertson, and

31

Valentine Sevier. Their praise resounded not in the backwoods only, but through all Virginia."

After the hard-fought and costly victory at Point Pleasant, the delayed junction with Dunmore and his troops was effected, but Colonel Lewis and his command found, to their great displeasure, that Dunmore was unwilling to push deeper into the Shawanee country to punish these Indians for their depredations and murders on the frontiers. The crisis created by his arbitrary action came near to creating a mutiny among Lewis' troops.[18]

As Dunmore approached he had been met by a flag of truce from the Indians, borne by a white man named Elliott. His readiness to treat with them instead of striking a blow of annihilation against these warriors who had been drenching the frontiers with the blood of their friends and families, infuriated Lewis' men to such an extent that he had the greatest difficulty in keeping them under control. Colonel Lewis himself was enraged that Dunmore would not permit him to crush the enemy now within his grasp and his men, eager for revenge, were ready to follow him regardless of Dunmore's orders. All of them were suspicious of Dunmore's motives in making a "soft peace," for rumors of his treachery were already rife in their camp. Dunmore, however, in a violent rage, drew his sword upon Lewis, threatening him with instant death if he continued his disobedience.

Having made an uneasy peace with Lewis and his men, Dunmore then proceeded to negotiate a treaty with Cornstalk and other Shawanee head men. In this treaty the Shawanees relinquished their claims to the lands south of the Ohio River, but this was of no particular value, because the Cherokees and other southern tribes, who had driven the Shawanees out of it long since, also had vague claims to the land. Actually, Dunmore, by the terms of this treaty, had done less to quiet the frontiers than the backwoodsmen had accomplished through the beating they had given them—without his aid—at the battle at Point Pleasant. However, the governor returned to Virginia as a conquering hero and was highly praised by certain loyalist elements in that province.

The salutary effects of this hard-fought battle, however, gave at least a temporary respite to the frontiers. Daniel Boone, in particular, benefited from it, for now he could carry out his cherished plan to lead a band of settlers into his beautiful Kentucky country. His attempt to accomplish this in the fall of 1773 had been thwarted by a bloody attack by hostile Indians. At that time he had organized a large and well-equipped body of emigrants, including his own family and four or five other families whom he had persuaded to go out with him. With them he advanced towards Cumberland Gap and now, since the little party was joined in Powell's valley by forty well-armed hunters, the caravan numbered about eighty persons. Passing through a narrow defile on the fifth of October, they were startled by the terrific war-cry of Indians in ambuscade and were furiously attacked. Some of the men rushed to assail the Indians in ambush, while others dashed to the protection of the women and children. A terrific conflict followed immediately and, for a short time, there was such a scene of consternation and confusion that it appeared as if the whole party would be massacred by their assailants. Soon, however, it was clear that the fierce and resolute resistance by the men of Boone's party had so surprised and frightened the Indians that they fled in all directions. It was a baptism of blood for the heroic women of the party, for before this time no white woman or no family had crossed the Cumberland mountain range.

The first fire of the Indians had, however, taken its toll. Six men of Boone's party—including his own son, aged about twenty—were killed and a seventh was wounded. Yet, early in 1775, following Dunmore's peace, all of them—men, women and children—began making plans to resume their journey for what Ramsey calls Boone's "darling project of planting a colony upon the Kentucky River, which he had seen, and, desirous of obtaining the consent of the Cherokees, had stimulated Col. Richard Henderson and others of North Carolina, to effect a treaty with them for that purpose. . . ."

After the tragic attack of 1773, however, the Boone party fell back to settlements on the Clinch River, in Virginia, where they remained until after the consumation of Henderson's Transylvania treaty and purchase.

Henderson, impressed by Boone's account of the desirability of the Kentucky country, soon had associated with him an influential body of men, who had sufficient capital to undertake the project. Among them were Thomas Hart, John Williams, James Hogg, Nathaniel Hart, Leonard H. Bulloch, John Luttrell and William Johnston. The next step was a visit to the Cherokee country by Colonel Henderson, Col. Nathaniel Hart and Daniel Boone. Acting as their guide was Thomas Price, a trader, who knew the Cherokee country well, understood the language and was acquainted with their head men and their customs. During their tour, the party visited most of their villages and talked at length with their principal chiefs. At length, the red men agreed to a council for the purpose of negotiating a treaty for the purchase of the great tract of land which lay between the Kentucky and the Cumberland Rivers and promised to attend such a council at the Sycamore Shoals of the Watauga the following March.

Accordingly, at the appointed date, March, 1775, they arrived at the meeting place in a formidable body of about twelve hundred chieftains, warriors, women and children. Negotiations began and continued for several days with great formality and not a little pathos and drama.

One of the most touching pleas against the proposed treaty was made by Oconostota, an aged chief, whose eloquent oration recited a tragic story of the white man's progress in the acquisition of Indian lands.[19] He began with an account of the flourishing state in which his nation once was, and told in detail of the encroachments of the white people upon the retiring and constantly diminishing nations of Indians, who gave up their homes and departed from the lands of their ancestors, to gratify the insatiable greed of the white man for more land. Whole nations, he pointed out, had melted away in their presence, like balls of snow before the sun, and had hardly left their names behind, except as imperfectly recorded by their enemies and destroyers.

It was once hoped, he declared, that the white men would not be willing to travel beyond the mountains, so far from the ocean to which their commerce was carried on, and their connections maintained with the nations of Europe. But now that hope had vanished; they had passed the mountains and had settled upon the Cherokee

34

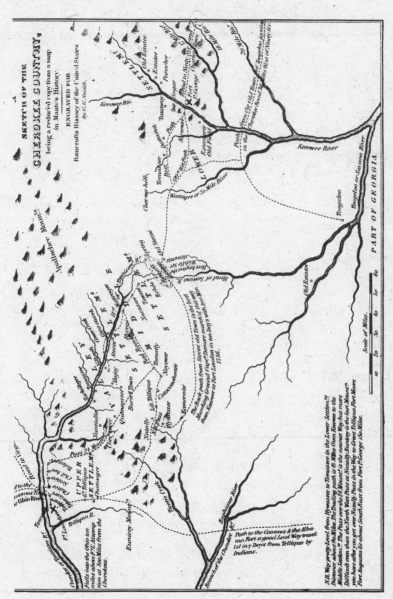

Sketch of the Cherokee country, engraved for Bancroft's *History of the United States* by. G. G. Smith.

lands, and wished to have their usurpations sanctioned by the confirmation of a treaty. When that should be obtained, he prophesied, the same encroaching spirit would lead them upon other lands of the Cherokees. New cessions would be applied for, and, finally, the country which the Cherokees and their forefathers had so long occupied, would be called for, and the small remnant which then may exist of this nation, once so great and formidable, would be compelled to seek a retreat in some far-distant wilderness, there to dwell but a short time, before they would again behold the advancing banners of the same greedy host, who, not being able to point out any further retreat for the miserable Cherokees, would then proclaim the extinction of the whole race. He ended with a strong exhortation to run all risks, and to incur all consequences, rather than to submit to any further dilaceration of their territory.

Another great speech—and the Cherokees were noted for their eloquence—was delivered by the fiery young chieftain, Dragging Canoe, who later led a dissenting group of young warriors down the Tennessee River to establish the Chickamauga Towns in the vicinity of the present city of Chattanooga. At a critical point in the negotiations, Dragging Canoe jumped dramatically into the center of the circle surrounded by the treaty-makers and delivered a powerful argument against yielding any more territory to the white men, and a long-remembered warning. Pointing to the west, he shouted:

"There is a dark cloud hanging over that country—it is a dark and bloody ground. You will pay a heavy price if you take it from us. . . ."

As future events proved, Dragging Canoe's prophecy and threat not only came true, but he himself, by his long, relentless war against the Cumberland and the Kentucky settlements, was the chief instrument in their fulfillment.

However, after a full and frank debate, the treaty was finally agreed upon and signed on March 17, 1775, in spite of the objections of the dissenting chiefs. An idea of the vast size of the purchase and the conditions under which it was agreed upon by the Cherokees may be gained from the writings of Archibald Henderson, a descendant of Col. Richard Henderson.

". . . the area purchased, some twenty millions of acres, included almost all of the present State of Kentucky, and an immense tract in Tennessee, comprising all of the territory watered by the Cumberland River and its tributaries. . . . This historic treaty, which heralds the opening of the West, was conducted with absolute justness and fairness by Judge Henderson and his associates. No liquor was permitted on the treaty ground; and Thomas Price, the ablest of the Cherokee traders, deposed that he at that time understood the Cherokee language, so as to comprehend everything which was said and to know that what was observed on either side was fairly and truly translated; that the Cherokees perfectly understood what lands were the subject of the treaty. . . . The amount paid by the Transylvania Company for the imperial domain was ten thousand pounds sterling, in money and goods. . . ." [20]

That Daniel Boone, who had undoubtedly participated in preparations for the treaty, was present during the negotiations very little, if at all, is shown by the fact that his name has not been found among the records of its proceedings. It is also true that a fortnight before it was concluded Boone had been commissioned by Colonel Henderson to form a party of competent woodsmen to blaze a passage through the wilderness. On March 10, this party of thirty-six axe-men under Boone's leadership, started out from their rendezvous at the Long Island of the Holston, to engage in the arduous labor of cutting out the Transylvania Trail.

Henderson was not successful, however, in founding a new settlement in Kentucky. The treaty of Sycamore Shoals was repudiated by Virginia and North Carolina. He was rewarded at a later date by Virginia, which granted him 200,000 acres of his own choice in Kentucky, and by North Carolina, which granted to him and his associates 190,000 acres in Powell's Valley, where some emigrants were already making their homes. The important thing, and the chief thing which made the settlement of these wild lands possible, was the success of negotiations with a large portion of the Cherokee nation at the Sycamore Shoals treaty. It undoubtedly diminished, though it could not entirely remove immediate Indian attacks upon the infant settlements.

But great and disturbing events were taking place in America with lightening rapidity. The eastern colonies, from their sea-coasts to their most remote inland settlements, were seething with unrest. There were many leading men in all of them who felt that separation from the mother country was close at hand, but, knowing the grave consequences which an irreparable break would involve, they hesitated before taking the final step.

Suddenly, the question was decided for the hesitating, doubting ones. On April 19, 1775, the first battle for America's independence was fought at Lexington, Massachusetts. News of it spread like wildfire through the colonies and to the distant settlements beyond the mountains. Soon the line was sharply drawn between those who had decided that American independence was worth fighting for, if they must, and the Tories, who chose to continue their loyalty to the British Crown. But the Americans, who outnumbered the Tories in most places, were soon preparing to take over the local governments and were making preparations to join in a great, concerted effort to win their independence. North Carolina was among the first to take positive, aggressive action. In Mecklenburg County, a meeting of citizens convened on the nineteenth of May—exactly one month after the Battle of Lexington—and, continuing until two o'clock the next morning, declared:

". . . we, the citizens of Mecklenburg County, do hereby dissolve the political bonds which have connected us to the mother country, and hereby absolve ourselves from all allegiance to the British Crown and abjure all political connection, contact or association, with that nation, who have wantonly trampled on our rights and liberties and inhumanly shed the blood of American patriots at Lexington. . . ."

Furthermore, they declared themselves a free and independent people, ". . . under the control of no power, other than that of our God, and the general government of the Congress. . . ." [21]

The declaration, in full, contained some twenty "resolves." Its author was Dr. Ephraim Brevard, one of the seven sons of a widowed mother, who was a well-trained medical doctor and a graduate of Princeton University. The twenty forceful, well-written "resolves" bear eloquent testimony to the sometimes forgotten fact that many of the constitution makers in the colonies, and, even the supposedly unlettered backwoodsmen beyond the mountains, were actually well-educated for their times.

Abraham Alexander was chairman of the convention and John McKnitt Alexander, its secretary. Delegates were: Hezekiah Alexander, Adam Alexander, Ezra Alexander, Waightstill Avery, Ephraim Brevard, Hezekiah Jones Balch, Richard Barry, Henry Downs, John Davidson, William Davidson, John Flenniken, John Ford, William Graham, James Harris, Senr., Robert Irwin, William Kennon, Neill Morrison, Matthew McClure, Samuel Martin, Thomas Polk, John Phifer, Ezekiel Polk (grandfather of President James K. Polk), Benjamin Patton, Duncan Ocheltree, John Queary, David Reese, William Willson, and Zacheus Willson, Senr."

The Rev. Hezekiah Balch naturally conducted devotions on this historic occasion.

As the day and the night of deliberations wore on, a crowd of excited, deeply concerned citizens surrounded the courthouse, where their delegates, through the long hours, debated and finally agreed upon some twenty history-making resolves. At last, with the dawn, the delegates appeared and the resolves were read to the eager crowd—not once, but many times during the day as fresh crowds gathered.

It appears, however, that the Mecklenburgers were a little ahead of their times. After they had completed their resolves, they sent copies, by the fastest express, to the North Carolina members of the Continental Congress, then meeting in Philadelphia, and to the North Carolina Provincial Congress. Neither of these bodies, however, took any action on the subject, for many American leaders still had hopes of an honorable reconciliation with the mother country.

Even Thomas Jefferson, in a letter to Dr. William Small, written on May 7, 1775, said: "When I saw Lord Chatham's bill, I entertained high hope that a reconciliation could have been brought about. The difference between his terms and those offered by our Congress might have been accommodated. . . ."

This, along with the rapid succession of history-making events, overshadowed the Mecklenburg resolves and, in time, they were almost forgotten. So much so, in fact, that some fifty years later, the very fact of their existence was questioned by eminent authorities. The ensuing debates and sometimes bitter arguments which resulted from this questioning, however, established not only the authenticity, but the importance of Mecklenburg's courageous action.[22]

But the time had come when there could no longer be any hope for reconciliation, nor any doubting that the hour of decision was upon the Americans. They could not continue to exist under present abuses, and, in spite of the generosity and genuine desire on the part of many great British leaders in Parliament and elsewhere, the stubborn determination of His Majesty, George III, and the majority of his government, to subdue his American subjects and conquer their rebellious spirit not only continued, but increased in intensity. Preparation for the full outbreak of hostilities, which most leading Americans were now convinced was inevitable, went forward rapidly, efficiently and with outstanding displays of courage.

In no part of this young, determined America was the crisis met with more sincere, wholehearted support and devotion than among the backwoodsmen west of the mountains.

War in the east, however, was not their major concern. A closer and more dangerous threat was fast developing, as Great Britain's plans for subjugation of the three most southern colonies unfolded. The British fleet would attack the coasts of the Carolinas and Georgia, while strong Indian attacks would be launched against their western borders. The latter necessitated, of course, as their first move, the complete destruction of the infant transmontane settlements. In addition to this, the British planned to land troops in West Florida and march a strong force through the Creek and Chickasaw nations, intending to enlist large numbers of Indian warriors for a major attack on the western settlements.

John Stuart, British superintendent of Indian affairs with the southern tribes, was placed in charge of negotiations for carrying out this plan.

"Early in the year of 1776," Ramsey states, ". . . Stuart received his instructions from the British War Department, and immediately dispatched to his deputies, resident among the different tribes, orders to carry into effect the wishes of his government. Alexander Cameron, a Highland officer who had fought for

39

America in the French war, was at this time Agent for the Cherokee nation. Receiving his orders from Stuart, he lost no time in convoking the chiefs and warriors and making known to them the designs of his government. He informed them of the difficulties between the King and his American subjects, and endeavoured to enlist them in favour of the monarch.

"The Indians could scarcely believe that the war was real—a war among savages that speak the same language being unknown . . ." But by presents in clothing, and promises of the plunder from the conquered settlements, as well as reclaiming their use of the hunting grounds which they had sold to the whites, Cameron succeeded, eventually, in gaining to the British interests a majority of the head men and warriors." [23]

The first steps toward executing this plan had been taken late in 1775, for in January, 1776, sixty chiefs of the Overhill Cherokees, who were completely under the influence of John Stuart, visited him in Pensacola, seeking powder, lead and supplies necessary to prosecute such a war. Responding at once to their requests, Stuart had sixty horses loaded with the supplies and sent to the Cherokee country, placing his younger brother, Henry Stuart, in charge of the caravan.

Both the leaders of the western settlements and the Continental Congress were well informed on every detail of this move on Stuart's part. In order to attempt to win the Indians to the American cause, continental commissioners called them to a conference at Fort Charlotte, but the Indians refused to attend and Willie (pronounced Wylie) Jones, one of the commissioners, reported that, in his opinion, hostilities against the white settlements would soon begin.

In June, 1776, Jones wrote:

"I conjecture that, whenever any one of the Southern Colonies shall be attacked on the seacoast, they will attack the same Province on the frontiers." [24]

Jones also reported the arrival of Henry Stuart in the Overhill country with thirty or forty loads of ammunition. It should be noted that Jones was one of the staunchest friends of the western settlements and that he rendered services of inestimable value to them during these critical years. In gratitude, the settlers named the first town established in the Tennessee country for him— Jonesboro—which stands today as Tennessee's oldest city and a lasting memorial to him.

Judge Williams called him ". . . a sagacious leader in North Carolina, who in 1776 advocated the recognition of the western people and had been their consistent friend. . . ."

As the British succeeded in their plan of inciting the Indians to a cruel and barbaric warfare, the over-the-mountain-men became thoroughly aware of their precarious situation. Knowing that in their remote and isolated position they had very little chance of surviving alone, they sought some degree of protection by seeking annexation, first, unsuccessfully, to the province of Virginia, and, secondly, to North Carolina.[25] Their second petition, with its historic account of the organization and operation of the Watauga Association, and its plea for the privilege of serving in ". . . the glorious cause of Liberty . . ." was, fortunately successful and they began at once to gird themselves for wholehearted participation in the war for American independence.

Their petition to North Carolina is one of the most important documents bearing upon the early history of Tennessee. For many years, it rested untouched in the Archives of North Carolina, but finally, that dean of Tennessee history, J.G.M. Ramsey, unearthed it and published it in full. He tells the story of his ". . . diligent inquiry and patient search . . ." for this and other records of the Watauga and other pioneer settlements of Tennessee, of some of his failures and of this outstanding success. Speaking of the Watauga Association court and other pertinent details, he wrote:

". . . The laws of Virginia were taken as the standard of decision. Of this court, of its decisions and proceedings, little or nothing is certainly known. The records are, probably, all lost. No research of the writer has been successful in discovering them; he has examined in vain the several offices in Tennessee, and also the state archives at Richmond and Raleigh. At the latter place, by the courtesy of Governor Reed, the present executive of North Carolina, he was allowed free access to all public papers of that state. No trace of the records of the Watauga Court was to be found; but his painstaking search was richly compensated by the discovery, in an old bundle of papers, lying in an upper shelf, almost out of reach, and probably not seen before for seventy-five years, of a petition and remonstrance from Watauga settlement, praying, among other things, to be *annexed,* whether as a county, district or other division, to North Carolina. The document appears to be in the handwriting of John Sevier, and is probably his own production. The name of the chairman, John Carter, is written by a palsied hand. It is remarkable that about sixty years afterwards, his grandson, the late Hon. W. H. Carter, from exactly the same Watauga locality, was president of the convention that formed the present constitution of Tennessee. The others are all names since, and at the present time, familiar to Tennesseans.

"This document is, throughout, replete with interest; is full of our earliest history; breathes in the warmest patriotism, and is inspired with the spirit of justice and liberty. . . ." [26]

(This, one of the most important documents relating to early Tennessee history, is printed in full—page 365 Appendix.)

CHAPTER II

The Dangerous Example and the Revolutionary War

With the petition for annexation to North Carolina, a new step was taken in the development of the infant Wataugan Republic. It is apparent that the petitioners, even before their prayer for annexation was completed, signed and delivered to the Province of North Carolina, had chosen a new name, for they designated themselves as ". . . inhabitants of Washington District. . . ." They, as free, independent citizens, went forward with confidence, anticipating full participation in the new government of North Carolina and pledging not only themselves and their trusty rifles to the common cause of Liberty, but offering cheerfully to contribute their just share of the expenses of government and of supporting the military, by offering their private fortunes, as well as their skilled experience in frontier warfare.

Ramsey offers the opinion that the name, Washington District, may have been suggested by John Sevier, who, undoubtedly, had the opportunity of meeting and knowing the then Colonel Washington in Williamsburg and elsewhere in Virginia:

". . . It is not known to this writer," Ramsey continues, "that the authorities or people of any other province had previously honoured Washington by giving his name to one of its towns or districts—a district, too, of such magnificent dimensions, extending from the Allegheny Mountains to the Mississippi. A most suitable tribute of respect to the exalted character and enlarged patriotism of the Father of his Country! The pioneers of Tennessee, were, probably, the first thus to honor Washington." [1]

That Washington District was soon properly annexed to the Province of North Carolina and thereby authorized to send representatives to the Provincial Congress, which convened at Halifax on November 12, 1776, is an established fact, though records of this period are vague as to the exact date or nature of such action. It is quite possible that they followed up, in person, the delivery of their petition without waiting for a formal invitation. Indeed, considering the disordered condition of the times, and the nature of the frontiersmen, it is entirely probable that such was the case.

It was at this history-making session that North Carolina's Bill of Rights and State Constitution were adopted.

". . . Amongst the members of this Congress," Ramsey says, "were Charles Robertson, John Carter, John Haile and John Sevier, from 'Washington District, Watauga Settlement.' Her remote and patriotic citizens, on the extreme frontier, thus participated in laying the foundation of government for the free, sovereign and independent State of North Carolina."

But now the real drama was beginning—a great earth-shaking drama which would shape the lives of millions of men in the years to come—a drama in which the plain man—he, who heretofore, had had no part in controlling his political destiny—would stride to the center of the stage and take the part of leading man. Henceforth he would establish his independent governments, make his own laws and determine who should, or should not, be his rulers.

The first guns of the American Revolution had already been fired and, though they were far removed from their mountain home when they roared out their challenge, the over-the-mountainmen's ears were attuned to the sound of battle and they responded wholeheartedly, with the greatest strength they could muster—and at once.

In fact, even while the Wataugans were in the process of drafting and signing their petition for annexation to North Carolina, they were setting up their own military organization and taking prompt and efficient action to provide for the protection of their own homes, as well as for defense of the eastern seaboard. In their petition they had reported:

". . . We now proceed to give you some account of our military establishments, which were chosen agreeable to the rules of established convention, and officers appointed by the committee. This being done, we thought it proper to raise a company on the District service, as our proportion, to act in the common cause on the seashore. A company of fine riflemen were accordingly enlisted, and put under Capt. James Robertson, and were actually embodied, when we received sundry letters and depositions (copies of which we now enclose to you,) you will readily judge there was occasion for them in another place, where we daily expected an attack. We therefore thought it proper to station them on our own Frontiers, in defense of the common cause, at the expense and risque of our own private fortunes, till further orders, which we flatter ourselves will give no offence. . . ."

There was no lack, in these critical days, of the numerous letters and depositions, as well as verbal reports on the progress of the British-Indian conspiracy, which was now approaching consummation. Nor were the men of the "western waters" slow to recognize the dangers which were confronting them. With the outbreak of the Revolutionary War in the east, they had set to work, not only to organize their military establishments, but to build new forts and to strengthen the few old, inadequate ones. Couriers were dispatched in every direction, and women and children from vulnerable outlying settlements were brought in to Fort Watauga and to Eaton's Station.

It is a remarkable fact that there had not been an Indian war since the settlement began, some seven years earlier, and that there was not a fort or blockhouse from Wolf Hills westward. Eaton's Station, some five or six miles from the Long Island, had been built in advance of the settlement and was garrisoned by a small body of men who fortified it on the alarm of the approaching Indians.[2] It is difficult to identify a number of the other forts and stations which were built during the Revolutionary period and later, so there is considerable confusion in attempting to give an accurate history of them. Fortunately, there had been a lull in Indian hostilities following Lord Dunmore's war of 1774 and the Transylvania Purchase by Richard Henderson and others in the spring of 1775. During this brief respite, the Holston settlements were strengthened in population and Daniel Boone's party was permitted to begin permanent settlement of the Kentucky country. Only a short time had passed, however, before Indian raids de-

scended in full fury. These were to last, in varying intensity, for
nearly two decades.

Speaking of those years in the Tennessee and Kentucky country,
the veteran Indian fighter and, later, United States senator from
Missouri, Thomas Hart Benton, wrote in later years:

". . . Then was witnessed the scenes of woe and death, of
carnage and destruction, which no words of mine can ever paint;
instances of heroism in men, of fortitude and devotedness in
women, of instinctive courage in little children, which the annals
of the most celebrated nations can never surpass. Then was seen
Indian warfare in all its horrors—that warfare which spares de-
crepit age, nor blooming youth, nor manly strength, nor infant
weakness; in which the sleeping family awake from their beds in
the midst of flames and slaughter; when virgins were led off captive by savage monsters; when mothers were loaded with their
children and compelled to march; and when, unable to keep up,
were relieved of their burden by seeing the brains of infants beat
out on a tree; when slow consuming fire of the stake devoured its
victims in the presence of pitying friends, and in the midst of
exulting demons; when corn was planted, the fields were ploughed,
the crops were gathered, the cows were milked, water was brought
from the spring, and God was worshipped, under the guard and
protection of armed men; when night was the season for traveling,
the impervious forest the highway, and the place of safety most
remote from the habitation of man; when every home was a fort,
and every fort subject to siege and attack. Such was the warfare
in the infant settlements of Kentucky and Tennessee, and which
the aged men, actors in the dreadful scenes, have related to me
so many times. . . ." [3]

It should be remembered that England, fully aware of the
cruelties practiced by her Indian allies, used them pitilessly against
men, women and children, who had, but lately, been her loyal,
devoted subjects. The British-Indian war, along the entire western
frontier—from Detroit to Florida—was as much a part of the
Revolutionary War as the more formal and much less barbaric
attacks by British military forces east of the mountains. This war,
along the western borders of the Southern colonies and against the

feeble Holston, Watauga and Nolichucky settlements, was waged with relentless intensity and the men on these "western waters" found themselves under the painful necessity, from 1776 until 1782, of fighting on both fronts. It is a matter of record that they fought brilliantly and successfully on both.

Their first task, however, was to handle the large number of Tories in their midst who were organizing to join the Indians and British in the impending attack. Somewhat prior to this time these people, who were still loyal to the mother country, had been scattered throughout the settlements, but as actual hostilities approached, most of them had moved into the Nolichucky settlement, which was the one nearest the Indian country. The Wataugans were fully aware of the British-Indian conspiracy, for, on May 19, Nathan Read took an oath before John Carter,[4] one of the Justices of Watauga, that he was present on May 18 at the house of Charles Robertson, when a stranger—unknown to anyone present—came up to Robertson's gate and delivered a letter, dated May 9, signed by Henry Stuart, brother of John Stuart, the British superintendent of Indian affairs.

The unusual conditions under which this letter was delivered confirmed both the suspicions and the fears of the settlers. A number of other reports, giving approximately the same information regarding the British-Indian-Tory conspiracy, had also reached the settlements adding considerable proof of its authenticity. Some of them revealed that the Tories, on the approach of the British-Indian troops, had been instructed to display white flags to identify them as friends and allies.

"Gentlemen," the Stuart letter read, in part, "some time ago Mr. Cameron and myself wrote you a letter by Mr. Thomas, and enclosed a talk we had with the Indians respecting the purchase you lately made of them on the Rivers Watauga, Nollichuckey, etc. We are since informed that you are under grave apprehensions of the Indians doing mischief immediately. But it is not the desire of his Majesty to set his friends and allies, the Indians, on his liege subjects: Therefore, whoever you are that are willing to join his Majesty's forces as soon as they arrive at the Cherokee nation, by

47

repairing to the King's standard, shall find protection for themselves and their families, and free from all danger whatever; yet, that his Majesty's officers may be certain which of you are willing to take up arms for his Majesty's just right, I have thought fit to recommend it to you and every one that is desirous of preventing inevitable ruin to themselves and their families, immediately, to subscribe a written paper acknowledging their allegiance to his Majesty King George, and that they are ready and willing, whenever they are called on to appear in arms in defence of the British right in America . . . they are to be free from every kind of insult and danger . . . inform them that his Majesty will immediately land an army in West Florida, march them through the Creek and Chickasaw Nation, where five hundred warriors from each nation are to join them, and then come to Chota, who have promised their assistance, and then to take possession of the frontiers of North Carolina and Virginia, the same time that his Majesty's forces make a diversion on the sea coast of those Provinces. . . ."

No longer in doubt about their danger, from within and from without, two companies took prompt and effective action—one from the Watauga, commanded by Capt. James Robertson, and the other from the Holston, commanded by Capt. John Shelby. They gathered up some seventy suspects and ordered them to take an oath of allegiance to the American cause. Those who refused to do so were driven from the settlements. This very real threat of a Tory-British alliance in the West, as well as the impending Indian attack, made it necessary for the Wataugans to retain the two companies they had raised to protect their own homes and to meet the foe before he reached the western borders of the provinces of North Carolina and Virginia, instead of sending them to the seacoast, as they had planned.

However, it was destined that the Wataugans would be ably represented at Britain's first challenge to the South and to participate in the great American victory which resulted in keeping the would-be invaders out of Charleston for a period of four years. While it is true that it was only a small, token force which had this honor, it was enough to add a few more laurels to the ones which the western marksmen had won at Point Pleasant in 1774 and to assure the easterners that the over-the-mountain-men were ready to fight shoulder-to-shoulder with them.

About the time it was decided to keep on their own frontiers the two companies which had been raised for participation in action east of the mountains, young Felix Walker, who had been serving as clerk of the Watauga Association, returned from a visit to his father. While there he had been authorized to raise volunteers for service on the Carolina seaboard.

"I went to Mecklenburg County," he wrote in later years, "and meeting with some recruiting officers, by recommendation of Gen. Thomas Polk, I was appointed Lieutenant in Capt. Richardson's company, in the Rifle Regiment commanded by James Huger, then a Colonel; and was there furnished with money for the recruiting service. I returned to Watauga and on my way throughout the country, I recruited my full proportion of men, and marched them to Charleston in May, 1776, joined the Regiment and was stationed at James Island.

"Sir Peter Parker with his whole fleet arrived in the Bay while we were stationed on the Island. General Lee arrived in Charleston and took command of the troops, but did not tarry long; he went on to Savannah to assist the Americans against the British and Indians, and to regulate the troops. Sir Peter Parker commanded an attack on Fort Moultrie on Sullivan's Island on the twenty-eighth of June, 1776, was repulsed with the loss of two British men-of-war and a number of men; did not succeed in the reduction of Charleston." [5]

This was Walker's terse account of the repulse of the British fleet, which stopped the proposed reduction of the South in this attack. It was one of the most important battles of the Revolutionary War.

Another young man, Morgan Brown, who later became a prominent citizen of Tennessee, gives a more vivid account of his participation in this battle. It was the duty of Brown's outfit to range in companies to keep order and suppress the Tories. Taking the field early in 1776 it gravitated toward Charleston, reaching that neighborhood in May, 1776, and soon was encamped on Sullivan's

49

Island about two or three weeks before the British fleet appeared in sight.

"Every day," Brown wrote, "seemed to bring us nearer to the critical moment which would put our military skill and bravery to the test, when on the 26th of June, early in the morning, we saw a rocket rise high in the air from the admiral's ship. . . . We stood prepared at the water's edge, looking at the main body apparently preparing for action; when from behind an oyster bank . . . about sixty yards distant, three or four hundred British rose up and deliberately fired at us! This was a complete surprise, for we had not the least suspicion of such a party being there. But what surprised us equally as much, not one of us was touched, not a single shot took effect. . . ." [6]

Continuing, Brown tells how his company returned the fire:

". . . Not such was our fire at the British. Our rifles were in prime order, well proved and well charged; every man took deliberate aim at his object, and it really appeared that every ball took fatal effect. It might have happened that several balls struck the same person, and no doubt it was the case, but the proportion which fell never to rise again was great. This fire taught the enemy to lie close behind their bank of oyster shells, and only show themselves when they rose to fire! But even with this precaution they were cut off very fast, for ours was a certain aim and deadly fire. We had no thought of drawing a trigger without an object . . . their numbers diminished very fast, until, in the space of an hour they had ceased fire altogether. . . ."

Some of these western marksmen quite probably helped man the cannon in the still uncompleted Fort Moultrie. This fort, which ordinarily would have been leveled by the first fire from the British ships, was constructed of soft, palmetto logs, which received the cannonballs without shattering, making the fort practically impregnable. Meanwhile, the steady and accurate fire from Fort Moultrie's cannon was taking a deadly toll aboard the British ships.

Could it have been that one of the western marksmen was responsible for the uncomfortable but, undoubtedly, humorous predicament in which Sir Peter Parker found himself, as the result of

Major General William Moultrie, designer of the first American flag flown in South Carolina. Painted by Col. J. Trumbull, engraved by Edward Scriven.

the expert aim of some unknown American? *Life Magazine* generously permits us to repeat its version of the incident:

". . . Fought out in the North, the British late in 1779 turned to the South. They had tapped at Charleston in 1776 but had been beaten back by the gunners at Sullivan's Island (Fort Moultrie)— one ball carried away the seat of Sir Peter Parker's pants and, according to an old ballad, 'propelled him along on his bumpas.' So they held on to the other major Southern port, Savannah, and concentrated on the North. . . ." [7]

In this battle the over-the-mountain-men served with Francis Marion, later to be known as the celebrated "Swamp Fox." Strangely enough, in 1781, they served again with him in the "mopping up" operations in South Carolina following Cornwallis' surrender. Moultrie and Marion were familiar with Indian-style fighting, both having served in earlier expeditions against the Cherokees.

It was here at Fort Moultrie that over-the-mountain-men fought under the first American flag flown in South Carolina—probably the first one in the South. It was designed by General Moultrie, who tells its story:

". . . About this time (the battle at Sullivan's Island) the Cherokee sloop of war arrived. A little time after we were in possession of Fort Johnson, it was thought necessary to have a flag for the purpose of signals (as there was no national flag at that time). I was desired by the council of safety to have one made, upon which, as the state troops were clothed in blue, and the fort was garrisoned by the first and second regiments, who wore a silver crescent on the front of their caps; I had a large blue flag with a crescent in the dexter corner, to be in uniform with the troops. This is the first American flag which was displayed in South Carolina. . . ." [8]

It was also the flag which, when shot from its staff during a critical point in the battle, was retrieved by Sergeant Jasper, who jumped over the ramparts to rescue it. The day following the battle he was presented with a handsome sword by Governor Rutledge of South Carolina.

The part which future Tennesseans played in this important battle, long overlooked by historians, was brought to light and

51

published by the late Judge Samuel Cole Williams—first, in an article in the Tennessee Historical Magazine and again in his book, *Tennessee During the Revolutionary War.*[9]

The battle at Sullivan's Island was one of the most spectacular and hardest fought of the Revolutionary War. In the brief time it was in progress thousands of shots were fired—over seven thousand balls were picked up on the island a few days after the battle. It was a surprising, almost incredible, victory for the Americans and had a far-reaching effect upon the future progress of the war—not only in stirring rather reluctant leaders into action, but also in lifting the morale of the people.

". . . When the news of this glorious defeat (of the British) reached Congress," wrote one early American historian, "it kindled into a flame that spark of liberty, which prudence and caution had long smothered, in that honorable body; and it burst forth into the declaration of independence. The colonists were now well prepared for such an event, and the declaration of independence was hailed by America, as the salvation of the nation. . . ."[10]

After participating in the repulse of the British fleet, Walker's platoon remained on the South Carolina coast for several weeks, where it assisted in repairing damages and strengthening Fort Moultrie and the defenses on Sullivan Island. General Lee, reporting on this work to Governor Rutledge, stated that there was much to be done for the security of Sullivan's Island. Huger's men volunteered to do this work, and it is quite possible that the volunteers from the western country worked with them.

When they had been in the service at Charleston a few weeks, news was received of the outbreak of Indian hostilities beyond the mountains, and as Walker later recorded in his *Memoir,* it was necessary for the Wataugans to hasten home.

"The war becoming general through the American provinces," he wrote, "the British stimulating the Indians on the frontiers, the Cherokees breaking out and murdering the inhabitants of Watauga and Holstein, where my property and interest lay, I was constrained to resign my commission, contrary to the wishes of my commanding officer, and to return home to engage against the Indians."

It was fortunate indeed that only Walker's platoon had been

allowed to leave the western settlements, for while Clinton and Parker were threatening Charleston, the massive British-Indian invasion got underway in the West. Had either the attack on the South Carolina coast or the Cherokee invasion succeeded, the cause of the American Revolution would have been seriously crippled. Had both been victorious, it might easily have failed almost before it began.

Invasion of the transmontane country was, perhaps, the greater of the dangers, for had the hordes of Indians been able to get a foothold along the sparsely settled frontiers of the southern colonies, they could have been reinforced and maintained in constantly growing strength until British forces from the North and East, with the aid of their fleet, were able to unite with them.

There had been no letup in preparations for resisting the British-inspired Indian invasion of the settlements, since the first knowledge that it was brewing at the outbreak of the Revolutionary War. But, at best, the defenses were far from adequate and the white settlers were greatly outnumbered by their savage foes. However, they were hard at work, building new forts, strengthening the old stations and bringing women and children from the weak outlying settlements into the protection of stronger shelters. Each day brought the time of attack closer and closer.

Fortunately, among the Indians, the white settlers had a compassionate and powerful friend, who was determined to prevent them from being slaughtered in a surprise attack. She was Nancy Ward, "Beloved Woman" of the Cherokees, who, as she watched the final preparations for a march of seven hundred warriors against the white settlements, determined to warn them of the impending danger.

To this end, she called in her friend, Isaac Thomas, a well-known Indian trader and a good American, told him the story, provided him with a fast express and dispatched him posthaste to warn her white friends. With him were William Fallin and two other men who accompanied him as far as the Holston settlements. The fate of all the western settlements and of the colonial frontiers, which would lie ahead of the advancing foe, once they had been conquered, hung by a slender thread.

At the time Thomas and Fallin arrived, John Sevier, with a considerable group of settlers, was at the yet uncompleted Fort Lee, on Nolichucky River, at Limestone Creek. Sevier, then a lieutenant, had been given the responsibility of building and defending this fort, which was at the edge of the settlements nearest the Indians and was, therefore, subject to the first attack. Realizing the seriousness of the situation, Sevier immediately sent warnings to other settlers, dashed off a hurried note to the officers of Fincastle County, and sent Thomas to deliver it. This note, dated at Fort Lee, July 11, 1776, read:

"Dear Gentlemen:—Isaac Thomas, Wm. Fallin, Jarot Williams, and one more, have this moment come in by making their escape from the Indians and say that six hundred Indians and whites were to start for this fort, and intend to drive through the country up to New River before they return.' John Sevier."

Had not Fate, in the comely person of Nancy Ward, stepped in, this small body of men at Fort Lee might well have been wiped out by a surprise attack, and the stronger fort on the Watauga, as well as the rest of the settlements, would, unavoidably, have fallen. Her timely and humane warning, however, put them on the alert in time to concentrate their defenses and, through some miracle, to repel this and other attacks.

In his *Indian Wars and Warriors*, A.V. Goodpasture says:

"This woman held the office of Beloved Woman, which not only gave her the right to speak in council, but conferred such great power that she might, by the wave of a swan's wing, deliver a prisoner condemned by the council, though already tied to the stake. She was of queenly and commanding presence and manners, and her house was furnished in a style suitable to her high dignity. Her father is said to have been a British officer, and her mother a sister of Attakullakulla. She had a son, Little Fellow, and a brother, Long Fellow (Tuskegetchee), who were influential chiefs. The latter boasted that he commanded seven towns, while thirteen others listened to his talks; and though he had once loved war and lived at Chickamauga, at the request of his nephew, General Martin, he had moved to Chestua, midway between Chota and Chickamauga, where he stood like a wall between bad people and

54

his brothers, the Virginians. Like her distinguished uncle, Nancy Ward was a consistent advocate of peace, and constant in her good offices to both races." [11]

Bryan Ward was Nancy Ward's husband, it is generally agreed, not her father. Her daughter, Betsy, was the Indian wife of Gen. Joseph Martin. Many others of her descendents were allied with prominent white families. Like her uncle, Attakullakulla, she was the consistent friend of the white people and, in her own right, she held the love and respect of both races. Her decision to warn the white settlers of the impending invasion was in the interest of both the white people and the Cherokees.

The settlers about Fort Lee became very much alarmed at the news brought in by Thomas, and all except about fifteen volunteers set out at once for Fort Caswell on the Watauga, carrying with them as much as possible of their livestock and belongings. Consequently, it became necessary to abandon Fort Lee, and its little garrison hastened to join the forces on the Watauga before the Indians descended upon them. This precipitous action, while criticized later by William Tatham, served the dual purpose of preventing the slaughter of its inhabitants, had they remained, and of strengthening Watauga for the coming attack. [12]

The invasion was well planned and strongly supported by both the British and the Indians. It was divided into three sections: one, under Old Abram of Chilhowee, was to attack the Watauga and Nolichucky settlements; another, under the Raven of Chota, was to fall upon the Carter's Valley settlements; and the third, headed by Dragging Canoe, was to attack the settlements near the Long Island—still the "beloved island" of the Cherokees. Having accomplished this, they were to pass on into Virginia and continue their slaughter.

As they approached the settlements, they broke up into three separate bodies. The Raven separated from the others near the bend of the Nolichucky River, following the main Great War Trail across the Holston. Both Old Abram and Dragging Canoe went on up the Nolichucky Valley.

The major engagements, however, took place near the Long Island and at Fort Caswell on the Watauga. In the former, the defenders, on being informed that the Indians were approaching, decided to march out and meet them, rather than permit them to attack the fort and the nearby cabins which it protected. The ensuing battle, known as the Battle of Long Island Flats, took place on the level land near the island, on July 20, 1776. An excellent report, prepared by all of the captains who participated in it, was sent to Col. William Preston and was published in the Virginia *Gazette*.

"On the 19th (July, 1776) our scouts returned, and informed us that they had discovered where a great number of Indians were making into the settlements; upon which alarm, the few men stationed at Eaton's completed a breast-work sufficiently strong, with the assistance of what men were there, to have repelled a considerable number; sent expresses to the different stations and collected all the forces in one body, and the morning after about one hundred and seventy turned out in search of the enemy. We marched in two divisions, with flankers on each side and scouts before. Our scouts discovered upwards of twenty meeting us, and fired on them. They returned the fire, but our men rushed on them with such violence that they were obliged to make a precipitate retreat. We took ten bundles and a good deal of plunder, and had great reason to think some of them were wounded. This small skirmish happened on ground very disadvantageous for our men to pursue, though it was with greatest difficulty our officers could restrain their men. A council was held, and it was thought advisable to return, as we imagined there was a large party not far off. We accordingly returned, and had not marched more than a mile when a number, not inferior to ours, attacked us in the rear. Our men sustained the attack with great bravery and intrepitity, immediately forming a line. The Indians endeavoured to surround us, but were prevented by the uncommon fortitude and vigilance of Capt. James Shelby, who took possession of an eminence that prevented their design. Our line of battle extended about a quarter of a mile. We killed about thirteen on the spot, whom we found, and have the greatest reason to believe that we could have found a great many more, had we had time to search for them. There were streams of blood every way; and it was generally thought there was never so much execution done in so short a time on the frontiers. Never did troops fight with greater calmness than ours did. The Indians attacked us with the greatest fury imaginable, and made the most vigorous efforts to surround us. Our spies really deserved the greatest applause. We took a great deal of plunder and many guns, and had only four men greatly wounded. The rest of the troops are in high spirits and eager for another engagement. We have the greatest reason to believe they are pouring in great numbers on us, and beg the assistance of our friends.

James Thompson	John Campbell
James Shelby	William Cocke
William Buchanan	Thomas Madison [13]

The James Shelby, who displayed such "uncommon fortitude and vigilance," was a brother of Isaac Shelby, to whom many of his exploits are sometimes credited. He was one of the great soldiers of the pioneer period, but death cut short his career in the early days of Indian fighting in Kentucky. William Cocke, who was an important figure for a long period of Tennessee history, was one of the men who urged that the Indians be met outside of the fort, instead of waiting for them to attack. He was also one of the officers who wisely suggested a return to the stations at the close of day. For this act, he was accused by some of cowardice, but by others was praised for his wisdom.

The battle formation of the Indians in this encounter was unique, having a cone-shaped center, with wings curving outward, like a bracket reversed at the ends, which came near to proving disastrous for the white men. Only swiftness and cool-headedness on their part kept them from being thrown into confusion by it and prevented them from being outflanked.[14]

Dragging Canoe, until wounds and a broken thigh made it necessary for him to be carried from the field, fought like a mad man. He mingled with his warriors, shouting, encouraging them, and assuring them of victory.

"The Unakas (the whites) are running! The Unakas are running!" he shouted. "Come scalp them!"

But it was his warriors who were running from the field—not the "Unakas."

The most serious threat to the settlements was Old Abram's attack on Fort Caswell on the Watauga. The defense was made under the command of Colonel John Carter. Serving under him were Capt. James Robertson, then thirty-four years old, and Lt. John Sevier, not quite thirty-one—both destined to serve the western country with conspicuous wisdom and gallantry for a period of almost forty years after this historic battle was fought.

The Watauga attack came without warning in the early morning of July 21, 1776, although for some days the settlers, fully aware of the danger, had gathered in the fort and were preparing, as best they could, to defend themselves. The number available for the defense had been increased by the arrival of the little garrison from Fort Lee and others who brought their families in for protection. The defenders now numbered about seventy-five. Women, also present in considerable numbers, not only cared for their children and performed their usual household tasks under siege, but also proved valuable aides during the battle. These women went bravely about their daily tasks—even going outside the fort to milk the cows. On the morning of the attack, a few of the most daring ones lingered outside the fort to complete their work, when the Indians fell upon them and, only by the narrowest margin, did they reach the great gates of the fort before they closed upon them. That is, all but one—a young woman of unusual grace and beauty—who failed to reach the gates before they were shut. She was closely pursued by the yelling, fleet-footed savages, who evidently preferred to capture, rather than to kill her. It appeared inevitable that she could not escape them and, to reopen the gates would mean that the whole company within the fort would be massacred and the fort itself lost. Had she not possessed the strength and speed of a deer, she would, indeed, have fallen into their clutches. She dashed madly toward the stockade and, seeing the closed gates, zigzagged back and forth, eluding her pursuers, until she was near the side of the fort opposite the main entrance. Lieutenant Sevier, seeing her predicament, rushed to her rescue, shot the Indian nearest her, reached over the parapet and drew her quickly into his protecting arms. She was "Bonnie Kate" Sher-

58

rill, who was destined, four years later, to become the second wife of her rescuer.

Virginia had responded promptly to John Sevier's plea for aid which Nancy Ward's messenger had carried to the officers of Fincastle County, but it was not in time to participate in the present great battle. The then Col. Evan Shelby, of the North Holston settlements, set out with one hundred men, as did Virginia rangers. Before any of them arrived, however, the battle had ended and the Indians, unable to reduce the fort, had retired.

Before the siege was lifted a man named James Cooper, with a boy, Samuel Moore, ventured out of the fort to bring boards to cover the roof of their cabin. The Indians fell on them at once and Cooper, seeking to protect himself, tried to dive into the river. The water was too shallow and he was overtaken and scalped. Hearing his screams, John Sevier started to the rescue, but Capt. James Robertson, seeing that the Indians outnumbered the defenders, and that it would require all the men he commanded to protect the women and children from massacre, would not permit him, or those who would have accompanied him, to leave the fort. The firing and screaming, which was so distressing to those within the fort, Robertson believed, was a feint on the part of the Indians to draw his men outside the gates, so he forbade Sevier and his party to attempt a rescue.

Perhaps no single incident illustrates more effectively the difference between these two men, who were destined to play leading parts in the history of Tennessee. Sevier, with his superb, spectacular courage, his dashing manners and his impetuous nature, performed superhuman feats without a moment's hesitation. Robertson, none the less brave, was slower, quieter, and more given to weighing the consequences of his actions. They formed a magnificent pair and each, because of the virtues of the other, was able to render greater service to their people.

The unfortunate youth, Samuel Moore, was taken captive into the Cherokee nation and was later tortured and burned at the stake. This fiendish act was the work of Dragging Canoe. Troops later reported that they found in his house "seven scalps hanging up, nicely painted, and just in front of the town, a stake to which

59

Dragging Canoe, a short time before, had bound a small boy and burned him to death while a war dance was held. Later, when treaty negotiations were in progress, Dragging Canoe, knowing that the whites had been so aroused by his cruelties that they would kill him on sight, did not dare appear in person, but was represented by his agents.

Another captive taken at this time was Lydia, the wife of William Bean. When hostilities broke out, she was captured by the Indians as she attempted to make her way from her home on Boone's Creek to Fort Caswell. She, too, was condemned to death at the stake, but the sentence was postponed while she was questioned concerning the condition of the white settlements. Another prisoner—a white man who understood the Cherokee language— repeated the questions to her and gave her replies to the Indian chiefs.

"How many forts do the white people have? Where are these forts? Can they be starved out? Do they have any powder and lead?" they asked. She answered their questions so as to leave the impression that the settlements were well supplied with ammunition and food and that they were fully capable of defending themselves. After conferring a few minutes, the chief told the white man to say to her that she would not be killed, but that she had to go with them to their towns and teach their women to make butter and cheese.

The Indian men, having had a taste of the white woman's bread and dairy products, were now dissatisfied with their own crude fare and often captured white women, who were ordered to teach their women the mysteries of preparing civilized food. They were especially fond of the white people's bread and called the white captives who taught their women this art "bread women." Mrs. Bean, in addition to being the mother of the first white child born in these pioneer settlements, and a heroine in her own right, might also be called the first home economics teacher of the yet-to-be State of Tennessee. The Cherokees, having developed this taste for civilized foods, had already begun getting some of their meats from herds of beef and dairy cattle, as well as from domestic fowls.

After she was taken into the Indian towns Mrs. Bean's life was

60

still at the mercy of the whims of her captors. At one time she barely escaped the fate of the Moore boy and was actually bound and carried to the top of a mound to be burned, when she was rescued by Nancy Ward.[15] Later, without being seriously harmed, she was returned to her home. Scores of other women and children were taken captive. Some of them escaped without serious injury, others were tortured and abused to such an extent that they died, even though not burned at the stake. Children sometimes grew to maturity among the Indians and were finally returned to their people, unable to speak a word of their mother tongue. Some of them, having lost their families, preferred to remain among the Indians, where they were often greatly respected and loved. Neither age, frailty, nor helpless infancy exempted people from these harrowing experiences.

The portion of the Cherokee invasion directed against the Carter's Valley settlement, led by the Raven of Chota, was carried out by no more than one hundred warriors. This section was sparsely settled and the families who were able to do so fled to the stronger forts, or back into Virginia, for protection.

The Raven broke his force up into small bands, which moved in fan shape. The westernmost flank harassed the settlements on the Clinch River in Virginia, while others bore down on neighborhoods near Wolf Hills (Abington) and carried death and destruction as high up as Seven Mile Ford of Holston. The summer's end left the settlements bleeding and torn by these attacks, but with a hard-won victory to their credit. A new season and a new campaign against the enemy lay ahead.

This invasion had so thoroughly alarmed the eastern settlements that they decided to take steps immediately to convince the Indians of the danger and futility of listening to the "talks" of the British. They began at once to organize four separate expeditions to strike into the heart of the Indian country and to chastise the towns so severely that they would not be able to strike in force again at the white settlements which protected their frontiers.

North Carolina placed about twenty-four hundred men under the command of Gen. Griffith Rutherford, who laid waste to their country on the Oconaluftee and Tuckasegee rivers and on the headwaters of the Hiwassee and Little Tennessee. Eighteen hundred men, or more, sent out by South Carolina, destroyed their towns and settlements on the Savannah and Col. Samuel Jack led about two hundred Georgians to the Chattahoochee and the Tugaloo, where they left a path of destruction. But the fourth, and most important of all, was the Virginia expedition led by Col. William Christian against the hostile Cherokee towns and, particularly, against the Chickamauga settlements, stronghold of Dragging Canoe and his rebellious young warriors.

The Cherokee country was desolated from the Virginia line to the Chattahoochee, and the loss of life was shocking. Over fifty of their towns were burned, their fields laid waste, their orchards cut down, horses and cattle killed or driven off, their property plundered. The few who escaped were hiding in the mountains, subsisting as best they could on wild game and nuts. A few had managed to get to Florida, where they became the charges of John Stuart, who had led them into this unfortunate situation. There was nothing left for them to do but to sue for peace, which was finally achieved through the treaty at De Witt's Corner, in South Carolina, on May 20, 1777, and that at the Long Island of the Holston, on July 20, 1777.

In September, 1776, Col. William Christian of Virginia arrived at the Long Island of the Holston with a considerable body of men, to carry out a punitive expedition against the Cherokee Nation. Here he found Lieut.-Col. William Russell, who had constructed a fort, which he had named Patrick Henry, in honor of the Governor of Virginia, and had it ready for the anticipated troops. While this expedition was not entirely inspired by the late Cherokee invasion, it was greatly accelerated and strengthened by the late hostilities. Early in the summer of 1776, plans were already afoot for the protection of the frontiers. But now the execution of them had become a necessity, for the protection of both the eastern colonies and the western settlers.

"In fact," Judge Williams points out, "the authorities of Virginia, of Georgia and of the Carolinas before July, 1776, had anticipated and feared that the Cherokees, under the influence of John Stuart, his brother Henry, and Alexander Cameron, would co-operate with the British forces in the plan to subdue the Southern Colonies." [16]

All of the Southern colonies had, in fact, discussed means of protecting the frontiers and had taken some steps toward that end; but, so engulfed were they in their own problems that the first dangerous blow had fallen before plans had been put into effect. Fortunately, the frontiersmen, aided by Nancy Ward's warning, had been able to withstand this first onslaught, but they had been greatly weakened by it, and were still subject to almost daily attacks by roving bands of marauding Indians. Only by carrying swift and terrible war into the enemy country could their incursions be prevented.

On October 1, Colonel Christian's forces set out for the Cherokee country, leaving behind at Fort Patrick Henry about one hundred men under the command of Capt. William Witcher of Pittsylvania County, Virginia. Christian was reinforced by men from the Nolichucky and Watauga settlements, commanded by Capt. James Robertson, and a company of light horse under Capt. John Sevier. The rest were infantry. With them were two chaplains, equipped with their rifles, as well as their Holy Bibles and they were fully capable of using either to advantage. They were the Reverend Charles Cummings and the Reverend Joseph Ray—the first of many of that hardy breed of men of God who followed their charges into the wilderness, fought shoulder to shoulder with them when necessary, and, with a rifle resting conveniently across the front of their pulpits, preached hell-fire and damnation to those who dared to forsake the straight and narrow way.

This army, which now had been reinforced by three or four hundred members of the North Carolina militia, commanded by Col. Joseph Williams, Colonel Love, and Major Winston, now numbered some eighteen hundred, or two thousand men, including packhorse men and bullock drivers. They were well armed with rifles, tomahawks and hunting knives. As they moved forward, they sent sixteen spies toward the place where the crossing of the French Broad River was to be made.

The major portion of the body had crossed the Holston at the Great Island, marched eight miles, and encamped at Double Springs, on the headwaters of Lick Creek, where it waited for the reinforcements from Watauga. When these arrived, they set out for the Cherokee towns, some two hundred miles away. Swampy lands near the French Broad River and the threat of Indians, warning the white men not to cross that stream, made the progress slow and cautious, but the army succeeded in making a passage through the heavy cane brakes and the swamps near the mouth of Lick Creek, where they made camp for the night. The beeves and packhorses did not get through until midnight, however.

At this encampment, Alexander Harlin brought in the information that a body of three thousand Indians stood ready to dispute the passage of the French Broad. His statement was verified by Colonel Christian's spies, who had found, at the head of the Nolichucky, recently abandoned camps which indicated the presence of large numbers of Indians. Harlin was sent back to the Indians with the message that Colonel Christian intended not only to cross the French Broad, but to push on to the Tennessee River and the Cherokee towns on that stream.

The next day's march was taken up with great caution and, since the country was entirely unknown to the military commanders, that veteran trader among the Cherokees, Isaac Thomas, was chosen as their guide.

He conducted the army along a narrow, but plain, war path up Long Creek to its source, and down Dumplin Creek to a point a few miles from its mouth, where the war path struck across the ford of French Broad, near what has since been known as Buckingham's Island. As they came down Dumplin, and before they reached the river, the army was met by Fallen, a trader, having a white flag in his rifle. Christian directed that he should not be disturbed and that no action should be taken of his embassy. He departed immediately and gave the Indians the information that the whites, as numerous as trees, were marching into their country.

When news of Christian's expedition reached the Cherokee Nation, a body of one thousand warriors had rushed to the Big Island of the French Broad to offer resistance.

The great war path which led through it was considered as the gate to the best part of their country; and the island being the

Junction of the Tennessee and French Broad Rivers a few miles above Knoxville.

The winding Tennessee River

key to it, the Indians determined to maintain and defend that point to the last extremity.

It was from this place that Fallen was sent to Colonel Christian with the flag of truce, which the latter chose to ignore. While Fallen was on this mission another trader, named Starr, earnestly harangued the assembled warriors, telling them that the Great Spirit had chosen to make two races, one of white clay and the other of red clay and that he intended the white men to conquer and subdue the red men. In persuasive tones, he pled with them to forsake their plan to defend the island and to return to their villages, or hide in the mountains. Finally, the warriors heeded his advice and, without waiting for Fallen's return, they broke up their encampment, destroyed all traces of it, and scattered in all directions.

Whether due to Starr's persuasive powers, or Fallen's warning that the approaching white army was as numerous as trees of the forest, the Cherokees made no attempt to continue their campaign at this advanced outpost.

Meanwhile, unaware that his opponents were fleeing, Christian prepared carefully for his crossing of the French Broad. On reaching that river, he ordered every man to kindle a good fire and strike up tents, as if he intended to encamp there for several days. During the night, he sent a large detachment down the river to another island, with orders to effect a crossing in the darkness and, in the morning, to come up the stream on the southern bank, where it would help the remainder of the army to make a daylight crossing. The orders were carried out, although the waters at the lower ford were so deep and swift that the men had to cross in platoons, four abreast, and braced against each other in order to avoid being swept downstream. The water, at one point, reached almost to the men's shoulders, making it necessary not only for them to struggle against the swift current, but also to keep their guns and powder dry by holding them above their heads.

The army crossed successfully the following morning, but they found that their quarry had fled—not even a trace of their recent encampment was to be seen. Puzzled, but still cautious, Colonel Christian paused for one day to dry the baggage and supplies which had been soaked in crossing the river. They then pushed on toward the Cherokee towns.

Following the valley of Boyd's Creek, down the Ellejay to Little River, and thence to the Tennessee, they saw not a single Indian. The total disappearance of the enemy increased Colonel Christian's suspicions and, expecting strong resistance at the Tennessee River, he ordered his men as they approached the crossing to that stream to follow him at a run until they came to the river. Still no enemy greeted this dashing approach. The army, with its packhorses, the bullock drivers, and the supplies, pushed through the town of Tamotlee, above the mouth of the Tellico River. The following morning the march was continued to the Great Island Town, which, likewise, was entered without resistance.

· The fertile lands of the neighborhood furnished a supply of corn, potatoes and other provisions, and the Indian huts made comfortable bivouacs for the troops. For these reasons, the commander made this place temporary headquarters and a center for future operations. A panic had seized the Cherokee warriors, and not one of them could be found. Small detachments were sent out from time to time to different parts of the nation, but finding no enemy to contend against, they adopted a policy of laying waste and burning their fields and towns. In this manner Neowee, Tellico, Chilhowee and other villages were destroyed.[17]

Certain villages, like the "beloved" town of Chota, the city of refuge, which had not been guilty of making war, and a few others, were exempted. The village in which the Moore boy had been burned at the stake was left in ashes. During the invasion of these towns an occasional warrior was discovered and killed, but no men were taken prisoner. Finally, Colonel Christian, having nothing more for his army to do, succeeded in bringing in enough warriors to effect a temporary peace and to obtain their agreement to bring the leaders of the nation in for a formal treaty of peace at the Long Island of the Holston the following May. The camp at the Great Island Town was then broken up, and the army marched through Chota, recrossed the Tennessee, and returned to the settlements. In a campaign of about three months duration, not one man had been killed and the few who had become ill as the result of hardship and exposure recovered.

Colonel Christian's conduct of this campaign was not without its critics. His leniency toward the Indians, while undoubtedly humane and admirable, was not appreciated by the frontiersmen who often found the scalps of their own loved ones displayed in these Indian villages.

Another incident, which caused great confusion and resentment in camp, was Colonel Christian's cordial reception of Nathaniel Gist (father of the celebrated Sequoyah, who invented the Cherokee alphabet). Gist had already offended many Virginians, as well as the western settlers, by his conduct among the Cherokees, but, probably thinking better of the course he was pursuing, he eventually returned to Virginia where he served, with the rank of colonel, under George Washington. Many members of Christian's command were for putting Gist to death when he appeared in their camp, but Christian did not even put him in irons.[18]

As to his final dealings with the Cherokee chiefs, Colonel Christian reported to Patrick Henry:

"I wrote The Raven that, as he wished to speak to me, I was now here and found that his nation would not fight; that I was willing to hear him and the other chiefs; that I did not come to war with women and children but to fight with men; that his people had better be on their guard, because if they did not comply with my terms after seeing me I should see them safe from camp and then consider them as enemies. . . .

"Tomorrow I expect The Raven, Oconostota, The Carpenter and many others of the Chiefs; and I suppose in three days I can open a treaty or begin to destroy the towns and pursue the Indians toward the Creeks. I know, sir, that I could kill and take hundreds of them and starve hundreds by destroying their corn, but it would be mostly women and children, as the men retreat faster than I can follow, and I am convinced that Virginia State would be better pleased to hear that I showed pity to the distressed and spared the suppliants rather than that I should commit one act of barbarity in destroying a whole nation of enemies. I believe that all the old warriors and all the women of the nation this side of the Hills (the Alleghenies) were averse to the war, and the rest of them were led by Cameron, sometimes by bribing them and at others by threatening them."

Neither the expedition nor the peace talks produced anything of permanent value, for the Indians had no respect for the lofty motives which inspired Colonel Christian's mercy. Even his demand that Cameron and Dragging Canoe be turned over to him failed, for the Raven, then serving as war chief in place of the aging Oconostota, pointed out that they had fled—Cameron to the Alabama country and Dragging Canoe down the Tennessee River to the rapidly growing Chickamauga towns, where, supplied by British goods, he and a renegade band would continue to harass the settlements.

Col. Joseph Williams, voicing criticism of Christian, wrote from Citico Town on November 6, to the North Carolina Provincial Congress that nothing had been done, but burning five of their towns and making an unsatisfactory, patched-up, kind of peace.[19]

While there can be little doubt that, from a military standpoint, Christian's mild campaign left much to be desired and the peace treaty he had arranged was made only after long delay, it did quiet the older Cherokee towns temporarily. The effects of the Cherokee invasion and Christian's expedition into their nation are summed up by Ramsey:

"The unexpected invasions made by the hitherto peaceable Cherokees upon the infant settlements, retarded for a time the rapid growth and enlargement by which they had been for five years, so signally distinguished. But the remarkable success that had followed the unaided efforts of some of the stations, to repulse the assailants and to defend themselves, left little ground of apprehension for the future. Not one emigrant deserted the frontier or crossed the mountains for safety. On the other hand, the campaign that had been carried into the heart of the enemy's country had done more for the new settlements than the mere security it afforded from present assault or future invasion. The volunteers who composed the command of Christian were, many of them, from the interior counties of North Carolina and Virginia. In their marches they had seen and noticed the fertile valleys, the rich uplands, the sparkling fountains, the pellucid streams, the extensive grazing and hunting grounds, and had felt the genial influences of the climate of the best part of East Tennessee. Each soldier, upon his return home, gave a glowing account of the adaptation of the country to all the purposes of agriculture. The story was repeated from one to another, till upon the Roanoke and Yadkin the people spoke familiarly of the Holston, the Nolichucky, the French Broad, Little River and the Tennessee. Particular places were selected, springs designated and points chosen as centres of future settlements. A flood of emigration followed to strengthen, build up and enlarge the little community already planted across the mountain." [20]

But there was much bitter fighting ahead. The Revolutionary War had scarcely begun, and Dragging Canoe's warriors knew no restraining hand. During the winter and early spring of 1776-1777 there were constant incursions by small bodies of warriors from the new towns on Chickamauga Creek.

Spring came and passed, but the Cherokees still failed to come in to make the treaty they had promised Colonel Christian. Nathaniel Gist, who had returned to Virginia and had won George Washington's confidence, now proved his sincerity and his worth. He was sent out to use his influence with the Indians, arriving at Fort Patrick Henry late in March. It was the end of June, however, before the treaty actually got underway. Significantly, it was a treaty with the old men. Attakullakulla and Oconostota, now aging and growing feeble, came in and were seated on two benches which had been covered with three matched coats—the place of honor which their position in the council demanded. Old Tassel was spokesman for the Indians and Waightstill Avery for the white men. But even the old men were uneasy; they resented the encroachment already made by the Watauga and Nolichucky settlements and feared to enter into further negotiations.

William Tatham, who recorded these talks, in translating Old Tassel's oration, succeeded in capturing for posterity some idea of the dignity and pathos of this aging chieftain's remarks—and more than a little of the tragedy which was inevitable as the primitive

69

ways of the red man gave way to the civilization of the whites. He outlined Old Tassel's speech as follows:

"You say: Why do not the Indians till the ground and live as we do? May we not, with equal propriety, ask, why the white people do not hunt and live as we do? You profess to think it no injustice to warn us not to kill our deer and other game from the mere love of waste; but it is very criminal in our young men if they chance to kill a cow or a hog for their sustenance when they happen to be in your lands. We wish, however, to be at peace with you, and to do as we would be done by. We do not quarrel with you for killing an occasional buffalo, bear, or deer on our lands when you need one to eat; but you go much farther; your people hunt to gain a livelihood by it; they kill our game; our young men resent the injury, and it is followed by bloodshed and war.

"This is not a mere affected injury; it is a grievance which we equitably complain of and it demands permanent redress.

"The Great God of Nature has placed us in different situations. It is true that he has endowed you with superior advantages; but he has not created us to be your slaves. *We are a separate people!* He has given each their lands, under distinct considerations and circumstances; he has stocked yours with cows, ours with buffalo; yours with hogs, ours with bear; yours with sheep, ours with deer. He has given you an advantage in this, that your cattle are tame and domestic, while ours are wild and demand not only larger space for range, where we are to hunt and kill them; they are, nevertheless, as much our property as other animals are yours, and ought not to be taken away without our consent, or for some equivalent."

The arguments continued and the treaty was finally concluded on these unsatisfactory notes. While it yielded to the white men certain additional lands, it was apparent that the chiefs attending the talks did not have the power to enforce the terms to which they had agreed. In fact, they admitted openly that Dragging Canoe, now engaged in founding the towns of the seceding element on Chickamauga Creek, would not be bound by it. The chiefs also blamed him for the constant attacks on the settlements and said they were unable to prevent them. In an effort to save the situation, the North Carolina commissioners appointed the sagacious James Robertson temporary Indian agent and directed him to repair to Chota in company with the warriors returning from the treaty, there to reside until otherwise ordered by the governor.

Robertson was further instructed to discover, if possible, the disposition of Dragging Canoe towards this treaty, also that of Judge Friend, Lying Fish, and others who did not attend it, and whether there was any danger of a renewal of hostilities by one or more of these chiefs. He was also to find out about the conversations between the Cherokees and the southern, western and northern tribes of Indians. He was to search in all the Indian towns for persons disaffected to the American cause, and have them brought before a justice of the peace, to take the oath of fidelity, in case of refusal, to deal with them as the law directed. Travelers into the Indian nation without passes, such as the third article of the treaty required, were to be secured. He was immediately to take possession of all the horses, cattle and other property belonging to the people of North Carolina, and to restore them to their owners. He was to inform the government of all occurrences worthy of notice, to conduct himself with prudence and to obtain the favor and confidence of the chiefs; and in all matters with respect to which he was not particularly instructed, he was to exercise his own discretion, always keeping in view the honor and interest of the United States and of North Carolina.

This is undoubtedly the most remarkable assignment in American history! The amazing part about it is that, in the person of James Robertson, the commissioners had the one man on the continent who was capable of serving the American cause in all of the major features of the assignment. Most men, attempting such a mission, would have been killed, either by the Indians or by white men attempting to elude justice.

Before the chiefs departed for the Cherokee country, however, there was a most unusual celebration. Guns were fired, the Indians were plied with food and drink, and the young braves engaged in a dance. But on this occasion there was a dual reason for celebration. It was July 4, 1777—the first anniversary of the American

Declaration of Independence on the soil of the future state of Tennessee.

It became apparent with the passing months, however, that another expedition—this time against the trouble-making Chickamauga towns—would be necessary. There, Indians—flourishing under the leadership of the relentlessly hostile Dragging Canoe—continuously harassed the settlements. Their tomahawks dripped with the blood of men, women, and children, and their dwellings were decorated with the fresh scalps of their innocent victims. Cabins were burned, horses and goods were stolen, and no trail was safe from their attacks. Each day these towns, reinforced by restless young warriors who resented the rule of their aged, peacemaking chiefs, increased in strength and warlike spirit. Stuart and Cameron, acting for the British, kept them well supplied with goods and the tools of war. To share the spoils there soon came a band of renegade whites from some of the eastern colonies, and also from Canada and the French and Spanish settlements to the south. Added to their number were also Indians from other tribes—outlawed by their own people—who joined the Chickamauga towns in order to share the British goods and the plunder from raids on the white settlements. Dragging Canoe's hatred of the white man bore harvest after harvest of bitter fruit.

Meanwhile, similar dangers threatened the Kentucky settlements. The fort which Daniel Boone had built in the spring of 1775 was subject to constant attack. The women of this fort—Boone's wife and daughters and the hardy few who had gone out with them—were the first white women in the Kentucky country and, likewise, the first to pay the price for the foolhardy courage which made settlement of the West possible.

On July 14, 1775, Daniel Boone's daughter, Jemima, and two of her young friends—Betsey and Frances Callaway—happened to be outside the fort, when one of the small bands of Indians which had been constantly lurking in the neighborhood surprised them and took them captive. Their rescue, performed promptly by their sweethearts and fathers, with other men from the fort, was accomplished after a desperate race to overtake the girls and their

72

captors. By remarkably good luck, and by the foresight of one of the girls, who managed to break twigs to mark their passage, the rescuers soon caught up with them and the girls were returned to their families unharmed. It was one of the few happy endings in a long and tragic story.

Minor attacks continued through the years 1775 and 1776, and, in the year of the "three sevens"—1777—called the "bloody year," the very existence of Boonesborough and the younger settlement at Harrodsburg was in peril. The forts at these points were attacked simultaneously by large bodies of Indians on April 15, 1777, and for several weeks were under siege. During May and June, the Indians made every effort to destroy both strongholds; but, regardless of their repeated efforts, they failed to scale the sturdy walls, to set fire to them, or to force the courageous inhabitants to surrender.

On July 4, 1777, a body of two hundred Indians attacked Boone's fort with great fury, but after two days and nights they were finally repulsed. One man of Boone's garrison was killed, while the Indians left seven dead warriors behind them.[21] The Kentuckians exhibited great military skill and determination in defending their position, but in spite of their courage and tenacity, their situation had become desperate. Thus they observed the first anniversary of American independence.

Capt. William Bailey Smith, who, like Boone, had lived in the Watauga settlements, carried news of their critical position to their old friends and neighbors there. A company was promptly organized and, under Smith's command, set out at once to the rescue, exhibiting once more the volunteer spirit of the western frontiersman. They reached Boone on July 25, 1777, and a body of Virginians, commanded by Colonel Bowman, arrived on August 20. Boone later said,

". . . From now on we began to strengthen, and from thence for the space of six weeks we had skirmishes with the Indians in one quarter or another almost every day." [22]

From the time the frontiersmen volunteered to join in Dunmore's war in 1774, and played such a conspicuous part in the victory at Point Pleasant, they had never, regardless of their own needs or weakness, failed to answer a cry for help from their besieged countrymen. Neither the Kentucky nor the Holston settlements could have survived without such brotherly cooperation.

George Rogers Clark, who was in Kentucky during these attacks, had been traveling in the western country since 1775. He had become convinced that some means of quieting the Indians and putting down the British influence in the Ohio country was essential to the future of the Holston and Kentucky settlements and to the success of the American Revolution.

In his travels, says Lossing, ". . . he [Clark] was at once impressed with the importance of that fertile region and the necessity of making it secure for settlements. . . . During the years of 1775 and 1776, he traversed the vast regions of the wilderness south of the Ohio, studied the character of the Indians . . . and sought to discover a plan by which a tide of emigration might flow unchecked into that paradise of the continent. He soon became convinced that the British garrisons at Detroit, Kaskaskia, and Vincennes, were the nests of those vultures who preyed upon the feeble settlements of the west, and deluged the virgin soil with the blood of the pioneers. Virginia, to which province this rich wilderness belonged, was at that time bending all her energies in advancing the cause of independence within her borders east of the Alleghenies, and the settlers west of the mountains were left to their own defense. . . ." [23]

Clark, fully convinced of the necessity of reducing the hostile forts in the Ohio country, submitted a plan for this purpose to Virginia in December 1777. His scheme was approved, and Governor Henry and his council were so warmly interested that all the preliminary arrangements were soon made. Two sets of instructions were given to him—one public, ordering him to proceed to the defense of Kentucky; the other private, directing him to attack the British at Kaskaskia. His force consisted of only four companies; but, as the records of their achievements show, their services were out of all proportion to their small numbers.

Early in the spring of 1778, according to plan, Clark rendez-

George Rogers Clark, engraved by T. B. Welch from a portrait by J. B. Longacre after an original painting by J. W. Jarvis.

Simon Kenton, engraved by R. W. Dodson from a portrait by L. W. Morgan painted for the *National Portrait Gallery*.

voused on Corn Island, at the Falls of the Ohio, 607 miles from Fort Pitt. Here he received an invaluable addition to his forces in the person of Simon Kenton, one of the boldest pioneers of the West, who was then a young man of twenty-two years.[24]

Kenton's romantic story was that when a boy of sixteen, back in Virginia, he had engaged in a fist fight with a young man who had married his fiancee, and, believing he had killed him, fled into the wilderness beyond the mountains. Here he hunted and trapped with the renegade, Simon Girty; lived among the Indians and engaged in one dramatic adventure after another. He served as a spy for Dunmore in 1774 and was of great assistance to Clark in his campaigns. When, in 1782, he learned that he had not killed his rival, he returned to Virginia and brought members of his family to Kentucky.

Leaving the Falls, Clark proceeded to the mouth of the Tennessee River (now the site of Paducah, Kentucky), where he met a group of hunters who were familiar with the country. These men volunteered to serve as guides and also gave him important information concerning the condition of the garrison at Kaskaskia, stating that they believed a surprise attack against it would be successful.

The expedition then dropped down the Ohio to the proper point on the Illinois shore, concealed their boats, and commenced their march through the wilderness to Kaskaskia. They arrived in the neighborhood of the town toward the evening of July 4, 1778, and remained until dark, undiscovered by any of the people. Before midnight the town and garrison were in the possession of the Kentuckians.

Philip Rocheblave, the British commander, was surprised in bed and taken prisoner; but his wife, whom the polite Kentuckians would not disturb, managed to secure or destroy most of his papers. Enough were found to show, however, that the British were inciting the Indians to hostilities and these papers were sent, with the commandant himself, to Virginia. There was no bloodshed in this conquest and, in a few days, Clark's wise policy secured the respect of the French settlers, and they accepted the government of Virginia.

An equally successful move was made against the important British supply post at Cahokia, and soon the key post of Vincennes was captured and the flag of the young American republic floated over its ramparts.

Clark, who by now had been promoted to the rank of colonel, continued his successes in dealing with the Indians and, during the autumn of 1778, busied himself with negotiations with the various tribes of the vicinity. This state of affairs ended abruptly on January 29, 1779, however, when Colonel Clark was informed that the British Governor Hamilton had marched a force from Detroit and now occupied Vincennes. The days of bloodless conquest had ended and Clark was now confronted, not only by the present threat, but also by the certainty of the appearance of a large British force which would attempt to retake Kaskaskia in the spring. Prompt attack was his only hope and, accordingly, in February, 1779, his little band of 175 was on the march, sometimes wading in icy waters which reached their armpits. Soon they appeared again before Vincennes.

An inhabitant whom they had taken captive was sent in with demands for a prompt surrender. The townspeople were greatly alarmed, believing that it was a new expedition of fierce fighters from Kentucky. They could not, some of them reported later, have been more astonished if the armed men had dropped from the skies, for it seemed impossible that they could have come through the icy waters which then flooded the country.

Governor Hamilton refused to yield to the wishes of the people, who favored surrender without resistance, so a siege, which lasted fourteen hours, began. The next day both the town and the fort were surrendered to the Americans and Governor Hamilton and members of his garrison were captured and carried to Virginia as prisoners of war. The British colors were lowered once more and the Stars and Stripes hoisted to take their place. A round of thirteen guns proclaimed the victory, and that night Colonel Clark and his cold, exhausted troops rested in warmth and comfort.

The importance of Clark's expeditions cannot be overestimated, for, had they failed, the British might have succeeded in their plan to unite the Indians from Detroit to Augusta and, in one con-

76

certed movement, to wipe out the Kentucky and Holston settlements and then fall on the western frontiers of Virginia, the
Carolinas and Georgia, where they hoped to meet with victorious
British forces which were to sweep through these provinces to join
them.

The destinies of these western settlements were closely inter-
woven, not only with one another, but with those of the American
forces east of them, who were fighting courageously for complete
independence from Britain.

While Clark was fighting on the Ohio, the Kentuckians had
weakened their own forces to aid him. The Wataugans, in turn, sent
a small force to strengthen the Kentucky stations, although they
themselves were constantly contending against bands of marauding
Indians, as well as against an increasing number of Tories, who
continued to come into the frontiers and, combining with robbers
and other disorderly groups, prowled around the weaker neighborhoods, committing all kinds of depredations and murder. Finally,
the settlers took things into their own hands, apprehended the
leaders in these crimes and shot several of them. In a short time,
these stern measures restored some degree of safety to the frontiers.

The increasing menace of Dragging Canoe's warriors could not
be disposed of so effectively. Three years had now elapsed since
that rebellious warrior had stalked out of the peace talks at Sycamore Shoals and had withdrawn to the wild, picturesque country
of Chickamauga Creek, refusing to be bound by agreements made
by the older chiefs and persisting mercilessly in his war against
the white men. Each day brought more recruits to his ranks and
greater strength to his rapidly growing towns.

As the situation grew more and more serious, Capt. James
Robertson was selected by Governor Caswell of North Carolina as
Superintendent of Indian Affairs and was instructed to take steps
to counteract the depredations of the Indians and the intrigues
of British agents. Accordingly Robertson held conciliatory talks
with the Raven at Chota.

"But these conciliatory talks were misunderstood by the deluded
savage," Ramsey states. "Savunca and some of the more aged chiefs
were disposed to peace, but were unable to repress the warlike at-

titude of Dragging Canoe and his hostile tribe, the Chickamaugas. This tribe of the Cherokees at first occupied the borders of Chickamauga Creek, but afterwards extended their villages fifty miles below, on both sides of the Tennessee."

Few white men were then familiar with the weird country to which Dragging Canoe had fled; but strange stories were told by the Indians. They themselves, it is said, moved some of their earlier villages because of a fear of witches, or some other greatly dreaded spirit, which was not strange, for the country was, indeed, awe-inspiring.

Here, the Tennessee River, in some bygone geological era, had forced a passage through tall ranges of the mountains, and, because of its rapid descent and unnaturally compressed waters, broke into a series of whirlpools and rapids, which roared, boiled and dashed madly against the great boulders forming the river's treacherous, irregular bed. These wild waters began at the base of another of nature's masterpieces—Lookout Mountain—which towers above the winding waters and rich valleys, often clothed in clouds and mists, or standing out grandly in clear weather, as a mighty watch-tower which commands mile after mile of indescribably beautiful countryside. The romantic Tennessee still follows its ancient pattern through these lands—in a perfect outline of an Indian moccasin. The lands stand today as a memorial to the Indians who fought so fiercely to hold them.

On down the river, some thirty-six miles below the present city of Chattanooga, the darkest and most forbidding spot of this strange country was found—Nickajack Cave. This cave, as described by Ramsey, is, at its mouth, ". . . about thirty yards wide, arched over with pure granite, this being in the centre about fifteen feet high. A beautiful little river, clear as crystal, issues from its mouth. The distance which this cave extends into the mountains has not been ascertained. It has been explored only four or five miles. At the mouth the river is wide and shallow, but narrower than the cave. As you proceed further up the stream the cave becomes gradually narrower, until it is contracted into the width of the river. It is beyond this point explored only by water in a small canoe. . . ." [25] (Today the waters of a man-made lake have buried it.)

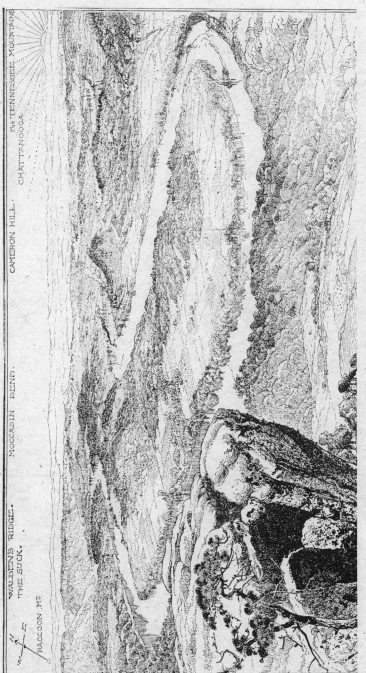

WALDEN'S RIDGE. MOCCASIN BEND. CAMERON HILL. The TENNESSEE MOUNTAINS.
THE SUCK. CHATTANOOGA.
RACCOON MT

A Sketch of Moccasin Bend from Lookout Mountain.

Nickajack Cave

The aboriginal name of the cave was Tecallassee, but that of Nickajack, (said to have been originally "Nigger Jack" for a runaway black man who was among its mixed population) was given to it during pioneer days. Its history is a mixture of bloody and well-authenticated stories and of endless legends and superstitions. So strong were the superstitions that the Indians glided swiftly by in their canoes, and the hunters generally avoided stopping near this gloomy spot. The fact that it eventually became a den of thieves and robbers made it even more dreaded, for the bad men who then sheltered and concealed themselves there were far more dangerous than the evil spirits feared by the Indians.

By the early part of 1779, it had become apparent that the settlers on the Holston and its tributaries, as well as those in Kentucky, would have no relief from hostilities until the Chickamauga towns were subdued. Patrick Henry, then governor of Virginia, who had already put George Rogers Clark in the field, took another step designed to strengthen him and, at the same time, to relieve both the Holston and Kentucky settlements.

Writing to Governor Caswell of North Carolina on January 8, 1779, Governor Henry stated that he had ordered Col. Evan Shelby to raise three hundred men in his district and go at once to Chickamauga and "totally destroy that and every other settlement near it which the offending Indians occupy." [26] His suggestion that North Carolina raise two hundred men to join the expedition met prompt response in the General Assembly, which was then in session. Nine thousand pounds was voted for supplies and a resolution was passed providing that two hundred men ". . . under a lieutenant colonel and four captains be taken from the Washington County (North Carolina) militia by voluntary enlistments if they can be so procured. . . ."

Maj. Charles Robertson, who represented Washington County in the North Carolina senate, was advanced to the rank of lieutenant colonel and placed in command. Major Jesse Walton, then serving in the North Carolina lower house, was placed in charge of supplies and ordered to return home at once with Robertson to prepare for the expedition. There was no difficulty in obtaining volunteers.

Virginia had provided some two hundred pounds for Colonel

Shelby's boats and the larger ones were probably built at the Long Island under his direction. Smaller craft, made in the Indian fashion, by hollowing out trunks of the great poplar trees of the vicinity, were constructed by the backwoods volunteers, who had been instructed to bring their axes and their adzes, as well as clothing and rifles to the rendezvous. Some of the troops probably met at the Long Island, but the main rendezvous of Robertson's and Shelby's troops took place on April 1 at the mouth of Big Creek on the Holston, the home and fort of James Robertson.

The first phase of the campaign—reduction of the Chickamauga towns—was carried out under the joint command of Charles Robertson and Shelby. The second—reinforcement of George Rogers Clark's expedition—was to be commanded by Col. John Montgomery, who had been with Clark at Kaskaskia and had been sent back to Virginia with de Rocheblave, the captured commandant. Montgomery, then a captain, had been instructed to recruit troops for Clark and, as the result of success in both missions, had been promoted to the rank of lieutenant colonel.

In his instructions to Colonel Montgomery, Patrick Henry showed that he was fully aware of the importance of both of these western expeditions:

". . . You will cause the proper vessels for transporting the troops down the Cherokee (Tennessee) River to be built and ready. Let no time be lost in doing this. Captain Isaac Shelby, it is desired, may prepare the boats, but if he can't do it you must get some other person . . . .

"I need not tell you how necessary the greatest possible dispatch is to the good of the service in which you are engaged. Our party at Illinois may be lost, together with the present favorable disposition of the French and Indians there, unless every moment is improved for their reservation; and no future opportunity, if the present is lost, can ever be expected so favorable to the interest of the Commonwealth. . . .

"You receive 10,000 pounds, cash, for Colonel Clark's corps, which you are to deliver to him, except 200 pounds for Captain Shelby to build the boats and whatever incidental expenses happen necessarily on your way. . . ." [27]

80

No funds were furnished Shelby for the subsistence of his troops, so he had to purchase supplies on his own credit. The individual soldiers usually left home well supplied with as much dried meat and other food as they could carry. Once in the field, they were as skilled as the Indians in fending for themselves, but like the Indians, when hunting was poor and provisions were exhausted, they went hungry.

On April 10, the crude, hastily assembled flotilla began its descent of the Holston River and, from its confluence with the French Broad, where the Tennessee (or the Cherokee) River has its beginning, followed the meanders of that mighty stream into the enemy country. A spring flood had raised the waters of the Tennessee, making them as turbulent and as powerful as the warriors who rode their surging crests. Expert seamanship was necessary for the management of the slender canoes, as well as for the larger craft; but these men of the western waters were as skillful and as much at home on their magnificent streams as they were on land. This expedition into the Chickamauga settlements was the first of many amphibious landings in the enemy country—landings which had to be made good, for the swift currents of the western waters made speedy retreat upstream impossible.

At dawn one morning about the middle of April, the fleet reached the mouth of Chickamauga Creek, entirely undetected by the Indians. Turning into this stream, the advance units discovered an Indian asleep at a fish trap and, with him as their guide, the troops waded through a flooded canebrake and entered the town of Chickamauga. This town, which was nearly a mile long, was governed by two important chiefs—Dragging Canoe and Big Fool. The Indians, about five hundred strong, astounded at the invasion of their town by water, fled to the mountains without offering any resistance.

John McCrosky of Sevier County took a party and followed the fleeing Indians across the river and dispersed a camp of them which he found on Laurel Creek. Another party took Little Owl's town, and other towns were in like manner taken and burned. Isaac, and all the other sons of Evan Shelby were out in this campaign. Shelby's command numbered about three hundred and fifty men and Montgomery's about one hundred and fifty.

With the fall of the Chickamauga towns, valuable military supplies including twenty thousand bushels of corn, a large number of fine horses, and other valuable goods, fell into the hands of the victors. These were disposed of in public and carefully recorded private sales, instead of being distributed among the troops. The larger part of these stores had been supplied by the British in preparation for the proposed attacks on the western frontiers and southern colonies which had been planned by Governor Hamilton, before he was taken prisoner by George Rogers Clark at the capture of Vincennes, thus crushing the northern portion of the British-Indian conspiracy.

While Clark had not had the opportunity of ordering or planning the attack on the Chickamauga towns, he had hopes for some such action, as is shown in his letter of April 29, 1779, to Thomas Jefferson:

". . . Many of the Cherokees, Chickasaws, and their confederates are, I fear, ill disposed. It would be well if Colonel Montgomery should give them a dressing, as he comes down the Tennessee. . . ." [28]

Once the Chickamauga towns were destroyed, Colonel Montgomery's men assembled their portions of the captured supplies and floated down the Tennessee to join Clark. The remainder of the force destroyed or sank their boats and such supplies as they could not carry with them and began their homeward march by a new land route north of the Tennessee River. Of this march, Ramsey says:

"They passed by the place since known as Post Oak Springs, crossed the Emory and Clinch a little above their confluence, and the Holston some miles above its junction with the French Broad. They were the first troops that had seen the richest lands of the present Hamilton, Rhea, Roane and Knox, and the north part of Jefferson counties, and seen as they were in all the beauty and verdure of May, it is not strange that a new and increasing current of emigration was at once turned to this beautiful and inviting country. . . ." [29]

Several of the men were still on foot, but horses taken at the Chickamauga towns furnished mounts for many of them on their homeward journey. Col. Evan Shelby bought a black horse, about six years old, for one hundred and twenty pounds, and other officers and men availed themselves of the opportunity to buy horses, cattle and goods captured in the Chickamauga towns.

Evan Shelby and his remarkable family had already made valuable contributions to the development and the defense of the transmontane settlements, but they were, for years to come, to figure brilliantly in the history of Kentucky and Tennessee. He had been an officer at the battle of Kenhawas and, before that, was in the military service of Virginia, serving as a captain of rangers under Braddock, leading the advance under General Forbes when Fort DuQuesne was captured. After the Chickamauga campaign, he became a general in the Virginia militia.

Thomas Jefferson, reporting to George Washington in a letter written at Williamsburg on June 23, 1779, spoke of the sale of these goods and gave an interesting resume of the situation in the West.

"Sir," he wrote, "I have the pleasure to enclose you the particulars of Colonel Clarke's success against St. Vincennes, as stated in his letter but lately received; the messenger, with his first letter, having been killed. I fear it will be impossible for Colonel Clarke to be so strengthened, as to enable him to do what he desires. (i.e. To capture Detroit.) Indeed, the express who brought the letter gives reason to fear St. Vincennes is in danger from a large body of Indians collected to attack it, and said, when he came from Kaskaskias, to be within thirty leagues of the place. I also enclose you a letter from Colonel Shelby, stating the effect of his success against the seceding Cherokees, and Chuccamogga. The damage done them, was killing a half dozen, burning eleven towns, twenty thousand bushels of corn, collected probably to forward to expeditions which were to have been planned at the council which was to meet Governor Hamilton at the mouth of the Tennessee, and taking as many goods as sold for twenty-five thousand pounds. I hope these two blows coming together, and the depriving them of their head, will in some measure, effect the quiet of our frontiers this summer. We have intelligence, also, that Colonel Bowman, from Kentucky, is in the midst of the Shawanee country, with three hundred men, and hope to hear a good account of him. The enclosed order, being in its nature important, and generally interesting, I think proper to transmit to you, with the reasons for supporting it. It will add much to our satisfaction to know it meets your approbation.

"I have the honor to be, with every sentiment of private respect and public gratitude,

"Sir, your most obedient, and most humble servant

"Th. Jefferson." [30]

The well-timed expedition against the Chickamaugas, combined with the removal of Governor Hamilton and his associates to Virginia as prisoners of war, not only prevented the proposed meeting of the British and the Indians at the mouth of the Tennessee River, but completely disorganized the major movements of the enemy in the West. Furthermore, the Montgomery-Shelby campaign against the Chickamauga towns was a successful demonstration of the feasibility of using the water route, in preference to the more dangerous and difficult land route, to the Ohio and Cumberland rivers. Its example undoubtedly influenced the choice of this same route, a few months later, by Col. John Donelson and other leaders, who, like Shelby, built boats on the upper Holston and embarked from Fort Patrick Henry on December 22, 1779, with the pioneer flotilla which carried settlers to the Great Salt Lick on the Cumberland River.

It was also about this time that the death of John Stuart, the British superintendent of Indian Affairs, occurred in Florida. This interrupted the flow of British goods and propaganda which had been constantly inciting the southern tribes to rise against the Americans.

It should be pointed out here that, in the greater number of histories of this period, the part of the western settlements in winning the Revolutionary War is either entirely ignored or greatly minimized. The late Judge Samuel Cole Williams, in his carefully documented and interestingly written volume on Tennessee in the Revolutionary War, records, as only an eminent lawyer is capable

84

of doing, an account of the part which the earliest pioneers of the Tennessee and the Kentucky country played in winning American freedom. He presents carefully annotated document after document to support his case, citing frequently the writings of such men as George Washington, Thomas Jefferson, Patrick Henry and many others, who recognized and were deeply appreciative of the part the westerners played in the struggle. He also delved deeply into British documents related to these stirring times.

Referring to the capture of Governor Hamilton and the death of John Stuart, Judge Williams wrote:

"With these two master-manipulators removed, all the Southern Indian tribes were discouraged: the great plan for a pincer movement from the north and south against the western frontiermen faded out. Cameron, though grown old in age and service, was yet the chief dependence of the British in the upper country. Distraught, but still resolute, the old Scotchman soon made another effort to rally his red adherents. In July, 1779, from the Chickamaugas he dispatched a runner as far as the Middle Towns of the Cherokees, exhorting, cajoling and threatening, in an effort to bring all branches of the Cherokees into concerted action. Again is there demonstration that there was throughout the struggle for American independence a 'War of the Revolution in the West,' and that the campaign of the spring of 1779 was not an insignificant part of it. . . ." [31]

The tide was running in favor of the British in Georgia and the Carolinas and it was important to them to see that the westerners were held in check by the Indians and not allowed to send manpower to assist the hard-pressed colonies east of the mountains.

"This," Williams concludes, "in 1779-80, as in 1776-77, was the strategy of the British. As the eastern patriots were growing groggy under repeated blows, scores of youngsters in the West were coming into or toward lusty manhood, and ready, many of them eager, to march across the mountain ranges and confront the enemy."

Thus the western settlements ended their first decade in 1779, with victory for the American cause in the Northwest and Southwest; but with impending disaster in Georgia and the Carolinas. Both situations stimulated emigration to the country beyond the

mountains: the former, because it advertised the ability of the settlers to take care of themselves; and the latter, because of the increasing numbers, who, driven before the advancing British in the
East, found sanctuary in the western wilderness. These conditions
contributed also to the establishment of the proposed settlement at
the Great Salt Lick on the Cumberland River during the winter
and early spring of 1779-80.

The year 1780 was a critical one in both the East and the West.
The British, at war for five years and still unable to subdue the
rebellious colonies, decided to attempt another attack on the coast
of South Carolina and, to this end, sent Sir Henry Clinton—still
smarting from his defeat on this coast in 1776—with Lord Cornwallis, in a fleet commanded by Admiral Arbuthnot, with orders
to take Charleston. They left Sandy Hook the day after Christmas,
1779, but it was not until March 30 that the actual attack began;
and not until May 16 that they succeeded in taking the city.[32]

With the fall of Charleston, the British were now able to push
towards the interior, to ravage South Carolina and North Carolina,
threaten Virginia, and maintain their hold on Georgia, which had
come into their possession after the fall of Savannah on December
29, 1778, and the occupation of Augusta which followed. These
were dark days indeed for the American cause. After the fall of
Augusta, Gen. Elijah Clarke and other leading Georgians fled to
the Watauga settlements, and from there, continued to fight for
the cause of American independence. Their families, as refugees,
were warmly received by the Wataugans. The fall of Charleston
and the advance of the British through the Carolinas now drove
many citizens of these commonwealths to the haven beyond the
mountains. Even Governor Caswell of North Carolina, who had
many friends in the Watauga, sought temporary shelter for his
family among them. Here, the refugee women and children participated in the rude life of the frontier and the men, united with the
western militia, continued to fight heroically for the American
cause. Soon they were prepared to recross the mountains to add
their strength—and their now famous rifles—to the American
forces in the East.

As early as March 19, 1780, at a meeting of Washington County his pioneer battles. Valentine Sevier, John's brother, and his sons, were also prominent in the Holston and, later, in the Cumberland settlements. The father, Valentine Sevier, Senior, born in London some time before 1740, emigrated to America, settling in Shenandoah county, Virginia, where his son John was born in 1744. From there the senior Sevier, with his family, emigrated to the West, settling on the Holston in what was later Sullivan County. From there he moved to Watauga, where he settled permanently. It was a virile, happily endowed family and one which rendered long and invaluable service to the future state of Tennessee and the American Republic.

One thing is certain:—if a Sevier did not participate in a given campaign, the careful historian will usually find that he was well and honorably employed elsewhere. During the pioneer years, certain men were spared to fight beyond the confines of their own settlements, while others, whose services were equally important, were retained to protect the settlements, often standing between helpless women and children and certain massacre by hostile Indians. The only thing which kept the Indians at bay was their knowledge that the frontiersmen never left the forts and cabins on the Holston, Watauga and Nolichucky, unless they were well manned. Often, during these years, John Sevier, Charles Robertson and others alternated in the command of military campaigns on the eastern side of the mountains, because of the necessity of keeping sufficient men to protect their families at home.

The portion of Sevier's regiment which was commanded by Maj. Charles Robertson reached McDowell a few days ahead of Shelby's men, who arrived at the encampment on July 25. Almost immediately, they were put into action against units of the British who, under the command of that spectacular military genius, Col. Patrick Ferguson, were now threatening that part of North Carolina. From this time until Ferguson's defeat at King's Mountain in the early autumn, the "over-the-mountain men" fought shoulder to shoulder with their eastern comrades in many important engagements, including the American victory at Musgrove's Mill, on August 18, 1780, following which they were hotly pursued by the British.

After this attack at Musgrove's, the mountain men were planning an attack on Ninety-Six, which, they had been informed, the British held with a weak force. Some of the men were actually mounting their horses, while Clarke and Shelby were discussing final plans for the march, when Colonel McDowell's express, Francis Jones, dashed up with a letter from Governor Caswell, announcing the total defeat of General Gates (the Continental commander in the South) near Camden and ordering McDowell and all of his detachments to move out of the enemy's path. News of the disaster was accepted at once, for Colonel Shelby was familiar with Governor Caswell's handwriting, thus removing the possibility that this might be a British ruse to disperse the opposition. Shelby and Clarke realized that they must make a swift retreat, for it was certain that Ferguson, hoping to retrieve the prisoners the mountain men had taken, would soon be on their heels. Instead of abandoning the prisoners, however, they allotted one to each of three horsemen, who were to take turns in carrying him, and continued their headlong race to escape their pursuers. They had also thought of removing the flints and making each prisoner carry his own gun. For forty-eight hours, in the heat of a southern summer, and encumbered with seventy prisoners, they raced westward. Many of them became so exhausted that their faces and eyes were so swollen that they were hardly able to see.

Following these brief victories and the precipitous retreat, Colonel Clarke led an expedition to Augusta, but was unsuccessful in taking it from the British. Refugees from both Georgia and the Carolinas continued, in even greater numbers, to seek shelter in the Watauga and Holston settlements. Clarke eventually rejoined his friends in the fighting beyond the mountains.

Gates' defeat at Camden, attended by the dispersal of Sumpter's corps, caused British hopes for a swift and easy victory to soar again. Lord Cornwallis, now awaiting supplies from the conquered port of Charleston, expected to make a rapid conquest of the Carolinas; to pass on through Virginia, and continue into Maryland and Pennsylvania without meeting serious resistance.

Ferguson, meanwhile, operated nearest the western frontiers of North Carolina and had, in person, supported the advance units

Isaac Shelby, engraved by A. B. Durand from a painting by Jouett.

under DePeyster, which had been sent in pursuit of the fleeing mountain men. Neither his men nor the Loyalists who had gathered to his standards had fared too well, however, at the hands of these lusty fighters. One of the Tories, who had fallen into the hands of Captain Robert Sevier's light-horsemen, had been ". . . subjected to the indignity of a coat of tar and feathers. . . ." [34]

Failing to overtake the racing westerners and effect a rescue of the prisoners, and not daring to push further into the wilderness, Ferguson set up camp at Gilbert Town. Here he soothed his wounded dignity by continuing his raids and dispatching threatening messages to Colonel Shelby and the Wataugans. His emissary was Samuel Phillips, one of Shelby's troopers, who had been taken prisoner and released on parole on condition that he carry the messages across the mountains. Writing in insolent language, he threatened that he would soon cross the mountains, burn the settlements and hang all the leaders. Phillips fulfilled his pledge to Ferguson by delivering the messages, but offset this unpleasant duty by giving to Shelby much valuable information concerning the strength of the British troops.

Shelby immediately mounted his fastest horse and rode some forty (other accounts say sixty) miles to confer with John Sevier. Finding that Sevier was attending a horse race and barbecue, he joined him there, and, while the races and festivities continued, the two of them discussed, for two days, the alarming situation and completed plans for raising every available rifleman and making a surprise attack on Ferguson. They would not wait for him to cross the mountains. They then selected the Sycamore Shoals, on the Watauga, as the place of rendezvous and September 25 as the day.

In the meantime, Lord Cornwallis had advised Ferguson of Clarke's unsuccessful attempt to take Augusta, and had ordered him to intercept the retreating troops and refugees. It was while attempting to carry out this order that Ferguson approached the scene of his last and most important battle.[35] Whether due to accident or to carefully planned strategy, it happened that Ferguson commanded the British units nearest the western mountain men, who, of all Americans, were the most skilled in the use of the rifle.

"When the disputes between the mother country and her colonies were verging toward hostilities," Draper states, "the boasted skill of the Americans in the use of the rifle was regarded as an object of terror to the British troops. These rumors operated on the genius of Ferguson, and he invented a new species of rifle, which could be loaded with greater celerity, and fired with more precision than any then in use. He could load his newly constructed gun at the breech, without using a ramrod, and with such quickness and repetition as to fire seven times in a minute . . . He was regarded as the best rifle shot in the British army, if not the best marksman living. . . ." [36]

His exploits, some of which were performed in the presence of George III, created a great sensation in England.

But, beyond the mountains there were men who had been trained in the grim school of Indian warfare and who, themselves, in their frontier shooting matches and hunts, had learned some spectacular tricks of their own. They cleaned their Deckard rifles, filled their powder horns and their shot pouches, and made ready to march against Ferguson, with the confidence born of long experience. The chief difficulty which confronted Sevier and Shelby now was finding mounts for all of the volunteers and persuading a sufficient number of men to remain behind to protect the settlements.

The means of financing the expedition, however, had raised some questions. Sevier, in attempting to borrow money on his own responsibility, found that the citizens, in purchasing lands, had placed practically all the cash of the community in the hands of the entry-taker, one John Adair, Esq., who soon proved that he was not only a great patriot, but a quick and logical thinker.

"Colonel Sevier," he said, "I have no authority by law to make that disposition of this money. It belongs to the impoverished treasury of North Carolina, and I dare not appropriate a cent of it to any purpose. But, if the country is over-run by the British, Liberty is gone. Let the money go, too. Take it. If the enemy, by its use, is driven from the country, I can trust that country to justify and vindicate my conduct. Take it." [37]

Sevier and Shelby made personal pledges of responsibility for the fund, which was used largely to purchase ammunition, and the matter of financing the campaign was quickly settled. Clothing for the troops was attended to quite simply by the women of the settlements. "Bonnie Kate," John Sevier's bride of a few months, took the lead and worked feverishly to prepare her husband and his sons for the march.

"Had the Colonel's ten children been sons," she said in later years, "and large enough to serve in that expedition, I could have fitted them out." [38]

She was also champion of her sixteen-year old stepson, who begged to go, but had no horse.

"Here," she said, "is another of our boys that wants to go with his father and brothers to the war—but we have no horse for him, and, poor fellow, it is a great distance to walk!"

A horse was found for him and he went along with the rest of them.

Now in readiness to march, the frontiersmen gathered at the Sycamore Shoals of the Watauga on the morning of September 25, the appointed time for the rendezvous. What a scene and what a gorgeous setting for this history-making event!

It is reconstructed vividly by one of the greatest of Tennessee historians, the late Judge Samuel G. Heiskell, of Knoxville, Tennessee—a brilliant lawyer and judge, as painstaking in his historical writings as he was in the preparation of legal documents, or in handing down an important decision, but, in this case, lapsing into sheer poetry!

"It must have been a very animated scene," he wrote, "on that morning of September 25th, 1780. It is impossible to tell just how many persons were there. It would be very entertaining to know all that was done by the assembled soldiers and citizens. It must go without saying that the dress of both women and children and the men was a pioneer dress of make and fabric. There must have been the shoeing of horses, and final consultations between friends and families, and numbers of women and children and horses and dogs, and great bustle and animation over the departure. The Watauga River, which this assemblage was to render historical in the annals of Tennessee, flowed by. Roane Mountain was in the distance; and stretching away is the beautiful Watauga Valley. The fort is there, and John Sevier on a fine horse, such as he always rode, and "Bonnie Kate," and the Reverend Samuel Doak, in his white stockings and, let us hope, minus that intolerable skull cap with which his appearance has been disfigured in the picture that has come down to us. Nowhere on earth is a September morning more divinely perfect than at Sycamore Shoals, in Carter County, Tennessee, and nowhere has nature more lavishly poured out her beauties.

"Isaac Shelby has done his part, and has brought two hundred and forty men, John Sevier has brought two hundred and forty men, and Colonel Campbell has brought two hundred men, and before the grand start was made for the mountains, the glad spectacle was observed of Arthur Campbell coming with two hundred more from Washington County, Virginia. There were about one hundred and sixty of McDowell's men there. These mountain men were not troubled with baggage; each man's entire equipment was a blanket, a tin cup, a wallet of parched corn meal mixed with maple sugar, and now and then a skillet or a bowie knife. The weapon was the Deckard rifle with its thirty-inch barrel. . . ." [39]

Further on in his narrative, Heiskell comments on the dress of the mountain men and quotes the description of the hunting shirt and the official status given to it by George Washington.

" 'The hunting shirt, the emblem of the Revolution,' wrote George Washington Parke Custis, 'is now banished from the national military, but still lingers among the hunters and pioneers of the Far West.' This national costume was adopted in the outset of the Revolution and was recommended by Washington to the Army in the most eventful period of the War of Independence. It was a favorite garb of many of the officers of the line. The British beheld these sons of the mountain and the forest thus attired with wonder and admiration. Their hardy looks, their tall, athletic forms, their marching in Indian file with the light and noiseless step peculiar to their pursuit of woodland game, but, above all, to the European eyes, their singular and picturesque costume, the hunting shirt, with its fringes, wampum belts, leggins and moccasins, the tomahawk and knife; these, with the well known death-dealing aim of these matchless marksmen, created, in the European military, a degree of awe

The gathering at Sycamore Shoals for the Battle of King's Mountain, from the painting by Lloyd Branson. The artist's magnificent painting of the actual battle was destroyed in the Imperial Hotel fire in Knoxville. Sycamore Shoals photo courtesy Tennessee State Museum and State of Tennessee Tourism Development Division.

and respect for the hunting shirt which lasted with the War of the Revolution. And should not Americans feel proud of the garb, and hail it as national, in which their fathers endured such toil and privation in the mighty struggle for independence—the march across the wilderness—the triumphs of Saratoga and King's Mountain? But a little while, and, of a truth, this venerable emblem of the Revolution will have disappeared from among Americans, and will be found only in museums, like ancient armour, exposed to the gaze of the curious." [40]

No account of the historic scene at Sycamore Shoals on that beautiful September morning would be complete without a description of the fine horses for which the settlements had been combed. Not only were they beautifully shaped and strong—they were fleet and sure-footed, in spite of the rough mountain trails. Like the men who rode them, they were of fine stock and had great stamina. The greater number of them, quite probably, were the fine Chickasaw horses, for which that nation of Indians was noted. Even after the turn of the century, these Chickasaw horses were often advertised in the early Tennessee newspapers. They were descended from the magnificent barbs which the early Spanish explorers left on the continent. It is possible, also, that some of them were of the fine breed which was prized in the eastern colonies, and which later was a great favorite with Tennessee racing horse breeders. But, be that as it may, one thing is certain: the western warriors could never have moved so swiftly and fought so brilliantly had they not had fine, dependable mounts. They were made for each other—these men and horses. Both were superb, and both are the proud heritage of the present-day, horse-loving state of Tennessee. It is significant that this crucial expedition was planned by Sevier and Shelby at a horse race!

Everything was well in hand by the end of the first day of the rendezvous, and the following morning, final preparations for getting on the march were soon completed. Significantly, before the frontiersmen began their march, the entire body of soldiers and spectators assembled for a religious service conducted by the Reverend Samuel Doak, in which he, in an eloquent, but necessarily

brief sermon, prayed that these warriors might smite the foe with
". . . the sword of the Lord and of Gideon. . . ."

A quiet solemnity had descended upon the assembly as Doak's
eloquent plea for Divine aid and guidance reverberated in the
autumn air. Then, farewells were said, and, if these heroic women
had tears to shed, they saved them until they had sent their men-
folk on their way with cheerful courage. Then, suddenly, the final
commands rang out. Lithe, strong men leaped into their saddles
and their sensitive mounts, responding to the touch and voices of
their riders, dashed forward at a spirited gallop. Finally, the musical
sound of their hooves on the rocky trails grew fainter and fainter,
fading, at last, into silence.

Slowly, the women with their children, and the men who, most
unwillingly, were left behind to protect them, returned to their
usual tasks and began a long, long period of waiting and hoping
and praying.

Little attention had been paid to the matter of a commanding
officer until the expedition was well on its way. Finally, on October
4, after a conference of the colonels, it was agreed that steps
should be taken to remedy the situation, so Colonel McDowell was
dispatched to General Gates near Hillsborough, asking him to appoint such an officer, saying, among other things:

". . . we think such a body worthy of your attention, and would
request you to send a General Officer to take command . . . Our
troops being all Militia, and but little acquainted with discipline,
we could wish him to be a gentleman of address, and able to keep
proper discipline without disgusting soldiery. . . ."

This request was little more than a gracious gesture to Gates,
however, for pending his reply, Col. William Campbell was chosen
to be the chief in command, with the reservation that he would
serve merely to execute the plans which would be decided upon
daily by all the colonels.

With the apparently loose organization, which was soon to prove
extremely effective, the mountain men neared Gilbert Town, where
Ferguson had but lately been encamped. He, informed of their
approach, engaged in a series of puzzling retrograde movements,
designed, apparently, to secure time for reinforcements from Corn-

96

wallis to reach him and to allow Tory members of his force, whom he had permitted to visit their homes, to return to their commands. The backwoodsmen, seeking to contact him, found that he was retiring toward South Carolina in three separate forces—one attempting, still unsuccessfully, to intercept Colonel Clarke on his retreat from Augusta.

It was now decided to separate the best marksmen and fastest horses from the slower moving portions of the troops in order to speed up the pursuit. At daybreak on October 6, after a night spent in picking the best men and horses, the chase began. In thirty-six hours they halted only once—and that for an hour at the Cowpens, where they were met by four hundred men commanded by Col. James Williams. Here, again, the swiftest horses and the best shots were chosen, and the hard-riding, straight-shooting force dashed off again after Ferguson.

Three of the colonels suggested a halt to rest the exhausted horses, but Shelby, knowing the urgency of a swift stroke before Ferguson could be reinforced, refused and galloped off with a small escort.[41]

"I will not stop until night," he said, "if I follow Ferguson into Cornwallis' camp." At the time, Cornwallis' camp was at Charlotte.

In a short while Shelby's party ran into and captured an advance post of Ferguson's army and it was soon found that he had established himself on King's Mountain. This eminence was, in the opinion of the backwoodsmen, scarcely worthy of being termed a mountain—but Ferguson considered it an inpregnable position and boasted that ". . . if all the rebels of hell should attack him, they could not drive him from it." It was nameless when the British occupied it, but Ferguson quickly christened it "King's Mountain"—a name which it has borne since that day. It was, however, a more powerful position than its size or height indicated, occupied and defended as it was, by Ferguson. If the bayonet, instead of the rifle, had decided the battle, Ferguson might well have made good his boast; but, as Lee points out, his position was ". . . more assailable by the rifle than defensible with the bayonet. . . ."[42] But neither of these deadly tools of warfare actually decided the battle, for it was not to be fought according to the old rules, nor was its

97

outcome to be determined either by the position of the contending armies or by the type of weapon. The decisive element, in this case, was the new spirit which dominated the Americans. They did not move in masses, like automatons governed by an ancient ritual, nor were they dependent upon the commands of a few officers.[43]

"When we encounter the enemy," Shelby instructed his troops on the eve of battle, "don't wait for the word of command. Let each of you be his own officer, availing yourselves of every advantage that chance may throw in your way. If in the woods, shelter yourselves and give them Indian play; advance from tree to tree, pressing the enemy and killing and disabling all you can."

Ferguson's men were no mean adversaries and, in the beginning, it appeared that they had every advantage: a record of successful engagements, an apparently impregnable position, and the hope of early reinforcements. Many of them armed with swords, bayonets and the new rapid firing rifle of their commander's own design, and drilled by that master marksman himself. Small wonder that the British scorned these "back water" men.

While the British barricaded themselves behind their wagons and the great rock ledges of the "bald," or open space on the level summit of the mountain, the westerners approached its heavily wooded base, where they dismounted and hitched their horses, detailing a few men as guards. The drenching rain which had fallen for several hours let up about noon on October 7, giving each man an opportunity ". . . to throw the priming out of his pan, pick his touch-hole, prime anew, examine his bullets, and see that everything was in readiness for battle . . ."[44] Obsolete words now, but once the familiar ritual of a man making a cherished rifle ready for its deadly work!

By early afternoon the American troops were in position and, at three o'clock, Colonel Shelby's and Colonel Campbell's regiments began the attack, keeping the enemy under constant fire while the right and left wings were advancing to surround them. This was accomplished in about five minutes and the fire became general all around.

Cleveland, Shelby, Campbell, in turn advanced and, from

sheltered positions, poured deadly fire into Ferguson's ranks. The answer, in each case, was a heavy bayonet charge which forced them to fall back in great disorder. They recovered quickly, however, found shelter, reloaded their rifles and attacked again. The British held their fire until the end of each bayonet charge; then they fired their rifles, retreated with great precision, reloading as they retraced their steps, as they had been taught to do by Ferguson. While they were going through this carefully rehearsed routine, however, the sharp-sighted riflemen below them, taking deadly aim, picked them off swiftly, one at a time. The British were also at a disadvantage because they fired downhill and often overshot their target. As a result, their bullets rattled harmlessly overhead, instead of reaching their mark.

Ferguson, throughout the battle, dashed in and out among his troops, blowing a shrill silver whistle, fighting with his sword when in close quarters, and in every way living up to his reputation as a brave and gallant officer. Less can be said for his wisdom. DePeyster, never an advocate of the stand at King's Mountain, pled for surrender when it was first evident that the battle was lost. Someone put up a white flag, but Ferguson, dashing up on his white charger, cut it down. Soon another was raised and again Ferguson cut it down—but this time, apparently, he broke his sword at the hilt, for it was later found so on the battlefield.

Now realizing that there was no hope, Ferguson sought to escape capture by the hated "back water" men and, with two escorts, attempted to charge through the enemy lines. They were turned back, and Ferguson received a fatal wound. De Peyster raised the white flag of surrender.

But the fighting did not cease at once, for the mountain men, having been deceived by the two earlier flags, would not stop until they were sure. Then, too, some of them, remembering Tarleton's massacre of Buford's men at Waxhaws, had personal scores to settle. Significantly, they had chosen "Buford" as their battle cry that day.

Young Joseph Sevier was among the last to stop fighting. His uncle, Robert Sevier, had been mortally wounded, but the boy had heard that it was his father, Col. John Sevier. Sobbing hysterically, he screamed:

"The D--d rascals have killed my father, and I'll keep loading and shooting till I kill every --------- one of them!" [45]

Only when his father rode into sight did the boy stop shooting.

The battle had lasted scarcely an hour, [46] but for that one brief hour the little mountain had been a blazing inferno, made more terrible for the British by the Indian-like yells of the backwoodsmen. When they had first attacked, De Peyster had said to Ferguson:

"There are the same yelling devils that were at Musgrove's Mill!"

But what a place that one hour made for itself in history!

The historian Bancroft says in his address commemorating the seventy-fifth anniversary of the battle:

"All honor must be awarded in the South, since she was left alone in her utmost perils. The romance of the American Revolution had its scenes for the most part in the South; and the Battle of King's Mountain . . . was the most romantic of all. . . . The American army for the south was routed and dispersed; Charleston was in the power of the enemy; the government scattered . . . Such was the almost hopeless distress . . . (when) the tidings penetrated the hardy dwellers on the Watauga, the Nolichucky, and the three forks of the Holston. All the difficulties which stood in their way could not make them hesitate . . . meeting from remote districts, they had to organize themselves on the instant for action with unity. The movement commends itself still more to our admiration as a voluntary act of patriotism. It was planned by no Congress— it was ordered by no Executive. . . ." [47]

Ramsey commented in like vein:

"Nor was it the authority or influence of the state, that led to this hazardous service. Many of them knew not whether to any or to what state they belonged. Insulated by mountain barriers, and in consequent seclusion from their Eastern friends, they were living in the enjoyment of a primitive independence, where British taxation and aggression had not reached. It was a gratuitous patriotism that incited the backwoodsmen. . . ." [48]

The frontiersmen's services in the American Revolution were not

100

yet done, but in King's Mountain they had made their most important single contribution to the American cause. In the ten years since the founding of the first settlement, they had fought not only on their own doorsteps, but in the Kentucky settlements, at Charleston, Augusta, Vincennes, Kaskaskia and in the Carolinas. Had not the arrival of the British fleet off the capes of Virginia, while George Rogers Clark was in Richmond seeking support for a long-hoped-for campaign against Detroit, prevented fulfillment of his plans, they would gladly have helped him reduce that British stronghold.

Another year would pass before Cornwallis' surrender at Yorktown—they would see still more important service east of the mountains—but now the die was cast, as far as the American Revolution was concerned—the outcome was assured.

After the British had surrendered, both the yelling and the firing ceased and all was quiet, but for the groans and cries of the wounded and dying. The late afternoon sunlight cast long shadows over the grotesque forms of the dead, which lay among the fallen leaves—some of them reddened by the frost of crisp October nights and some by the blood of brave men—British and American. Ferguson's body, ". . . in all its gore and glory . . ." lay in state on the spot where his soldiers had watched his final, gasping breath, and a strange procession passed before his bier— his own defeated men and the mountaineers, curiously examining the fallen foe and carrying their wounded, that they, too, might see him—impotent in death and defeat. His possessions, with other plunder, were carried away by the victors: Colonel Sevier was given his silken sash; Colonel Campbell, some of his correspondence; Colonel Shelby, the silver whistle which, a few moments earlier, had sounded its shrill battlecry; and Capt. Joseph McDowell, portions of his china table service.

Ferguson was buried on the mountain where he had made his last stand. A local legend has it that a fine looking red-headed girl, called Virginia Sal, camp follower or cook on his personal staff, was killed in the battle and buried with him in a single grave. Another girl, Virginia Paul, the legend continues, rode through the battle and the gory scenes which followed it with apparent unconcern, was taken prisoner and carried with others to the neighborhood of Morgantown, North Carolina.[49]

When the burial rites of both sides had been completed, the mountain men hastened from the scene to escape possible pursuit by Cornwallis. The plunder and most of the prisoners were sent to Virginia; Colonel Campbell, Shelby and Cleveland returned to Hillsboro, North Carolina, where they made an official report to General Gates. Sevier and his men leaped into their saddles and dashed homeward as fast as their horses could carry them, knowing that they had left only a weak force to defend their homes. Furthermore, word had come to them that the Indians, incited by the British, were again preparing to go on the warpath.

They were still faced with the necessity of fighting the war on two fronts, for that portion of the Revolutionary War being fought east of the mountains between the British and the Americans was not ended, and there was the constant danger that Cornwallis, reinforced by the British fleet, might yet be victorious. With Georgia and the Carolinas overrun and Virginia threatened, the prospects for an American victory were by no means promising, so the men on the western waters continued to alternate between defending their own homes and lending a hand to their hard pushed brethren east of the mountains.

However, it was the emergency which confronted them on the western front which necessarily claimed their attention as they returned from their victory at King's Mountain. Being fully aware of this danger, John Sevier, on turning homeward, dispatched a company of swift horsemen under the command of George Russell, in advance of his main body. On reaching the Watauga, Russell found the Indian traders, Ellis Harlin and Isaac Thomas, who had been sent from the Cherokee towns by Nancy Ward to warn the settlers that a large body of warriors was on the march.

Russell's company made hurried preparations to meet the invaders and, when Sevier's command arrived, they were reinforced and ready to ride with him. Without a day's rest and pausing only long enough, tradition has it, to enjoy a hearty meal prepared by "Bonnie Kate" and the other women of the settlement, he and his weary men filled their wallets with food, replenished their powder

insisted on joining the command, totaling some seven or eight hundred men, took up the march against the Indian towns. Christmas day, 1780, found a large number of troops quartered around the sacred village of Chota, where Nancy Ward had come to intercede for the peace-loving portions of her nation. It was here that she generously sent a small herd of beeves to feed the hungry men, and, by so doing, came near to disrupting the army.

Colonel Clarke, of Sevier's command, had been in the Indian country for at least two weeks longer than the others—and, like the rest, had been subsisting on parched corn, haws, grapes, nuts and what scant meat they could find—saw the beeves and ordered his men to slaughter them. Martin drew his sword and ordered his men to take the beef, which had already been quartered and hung up. Clarke resented this and, in a few minutes, the two men were engaged in a fierce fist-fight. Both were literally giants—six feet tall, broad-shouldered and weighing probably two hundred pounds. This incident caused much hard feeling between the Washington County troops on the one hand and those from Sullivan and Virginia on the other. It also added fuel to the fire of criticism which John Sevier was already receiving from certain quarters.

Back in the settlements, there were those who saw in Sevier's dash against the approaching Indians, without waiting for Campbell and Martin to join him, an attempt to add to his personal laurels—still fresh and green from his gallant participation in the battle at King's Mountain. It was an unjust accusation, for Sevier's consistent policy that the best defense is attack and that the most desirable field of battle is the enemy country, was well known and fully approved on the western waters. These criticisms were born of jealousy and were forerunners of greater ones yet to come. The "back water men" were intensely partisan and, when they took sides, either in war or politics, they had a way of fighting wholeheartedly and to the finish. The losers, though at a temporary disadvantage, never knew when they were whipped and kept coming back for more. These traits had a natural outlet during the days of Indian fighting, but when they were carried over into later periods, they sometimes resulted in unbecoming—but highly exciting—

encounters. With such a background, it is easy to understand why politics in Tennessee has never been a tame sport.

Finding that the Cherokee warriors had fled, the only course left to the invaders was to weaken the Indian nation through the destruction of towns, grain and cattle. The torch was applied to several villages, including the sacred village of Chota, and the army, after penetrating the populous sections on the Tellico and Hiwassee rivers, turned homeward on New Year's Day, 1781. They carried few prisoners, and those more for their own protection than as trophies of war. Nancy Ward, with most of her immediate household, was taken to the Long Island of the Holston, (the "Beloved Island" of the Cherokees) where she was left in the care of Maj. Joseph Martin, her son-in-law.

Thomas Jefferson, writing on February 17, 1781, mentioned her presence in the settlements:

"Nancy Ward seems rather to have taken refuge with you. In this case her inclinations ought to be followed as to what is to be done with her." [51]

Martin, on his return, found that marauding bands from the Chickamauga towns were molesting the settlements in Powell's Valley and, for several weeks, was engaged in putting them down.

Sevier, too, on reaching home, found new calls for action. In South Carolina, Gen. Nathaniel Greene, who had succeeded Gates as commander in the South, was threatened by Cornwallis, who had now united the British forces and was attempting to redeem the defeats of King's Mountain and Cowpens. In answer to Greene's call for help, Sevier dispatched Maj. Charles Robertson with three small companies, not daring to send a larger force from the already weakened western settlements. Then he, with a command of approximately the same size, undertook one of the most dangerous expeditions of his career.

Constant depredations on the Nolichucky settlements caused Sevier to think that the raiders were from the Middle Towns of the Cherokees. These towns, located in remote coves so high up in the mountains that they had rarely been visited by the white man, caused the Indians to have a feeling that they were safe from invasion, so they had grown bold. Regardless of their almost inaccessible position and the small force at his command, Sevier, early in March, 1781, set out on an expedition against them. One hundred and thirty men accompanied him. His officers were Maj. Jonathan Tipton and Capts. David McNabb, James Stinson and Valentine Sevier. They took Tuckasegee town, and after that, about fifteen other small towns were destroyed. In the neighborhood of fifty warriors were killed and a number of women and children were taken prisoners. From these prisoners, Sevier carried ten as hostages to his home, where most of them lived on his estate for three years.

It was very likely during the residence of these Indians on the Sevier plantation that his daughter Ruth learned to speak the Cherokee language. She later married Richard Sparks, who had been captured by the Indians when he was four years old and had remained in the Indian nation until he was sixteen. During those years he had been a playmate of the powerful chief, Tecumseh, and his brother, the Prophet. Sparks became a protége of Sevier, who used his knowledge of the Indians to great advantage. He acquired the rank of colonel in the army and, until his death, about 1815, was prominent in Mississippi.

In spite of the difficult terrain encountered on this expedition, only one man, Capt. James Stinson, who suffered a broken arm, was injured. Under Sevier's orders, he was accompanied home by Major Tipton, who was instructed to return to his command. Tipton, perhaps dreading a second trip over trails so rough and steep that even the sure-footed mountain horses had to be led, did not rejoin his command and Sevier, with perhaps unjustified harshness, ordered his commission revoked. This treatment may have stemmed from earlier arguments concerning incidents connected with the battle of Boyd's Creek, or from other unreported incidents which contributed to the growing rift between the two men. Certainly, it did nothing to pour oil on the troubled waters. Both were acknowledged leaders in the western country—but, also, both were often high-tempered, dictatorial men.

Meanwhile, Maj. Charles Robertson's command, which fought with Greene at Guilford Courthouse, North Carolina, March 16, 1781, was defeated. Yet, in the final analysis, they helped Greene win a victory. Their expert use of the rifle exacted such a heavy price from Cornwallis that his army was greatly weakened and his future, final defeat was assured. As Charles James Fox, the British statesman, remarked: "Another such victory would destroy the British army!"

The British were destined to win other victories before they were finally vanquished; but they did not guess the cost of their brutality to the hapless citizens in their line of march. In the furnace of their cruelty was forged a sword which proved to be the chief instrument of their defeat in their second war against the United States in 1812. Andrew Jackson, when only a boy, looked on with blazing eyes while they overran the countryside about the Waxhaws settlement and matched, when occasion permitted, his yet undeveloped strength against their might. Throughout his life he had a clear memory of Cornwallis' invasion of the Carolinas in 1780 and his advance, with such officers as the infamous Lt. Col. Banastre Tarleton and his Tory-British Legion into the Waxhaws settlement. He remembered also the days when Lord Rawdon had encamped his forces on the plantation of his uncle, Major Crawford, for here he had the opportunity to examine the enemy at close range.

It was about this time that he, then thirteen years and four months of age, with his brother Robert, aged sixteen, presented themselves to Maj. (later general) William Richardson Davie, asking enlistment in his dragoons. Robert was received readily enough and Andrew, in spite of his extreme youth, was accepted, presented with a pistol by Major Davie, and assigned to the duties of messenger and orderly. He was an excellent rider, knew the roads and the countryside well, and was alert to everything going on in the neighborhood, so he proved to be a valuable aide to Major Davie.

Even before his enlistment, Andy was thoroughly familiar with military drill and camp life, for he had tagged after his older brother, Hugh, and their friends and relatives as they drilled and marched about the Waxhaws settlement. More than that—he had seen with his own eyes war at its worst, when Tarleton, in a mad chase from Charleston, in an effort to catch Col. Abram Buford and his command, overtook them at the Waxhaws, where the tragic massacre of Buford's men took place. Accepting as truthful,

Nathaniel Greene, hero of the Battle of Guilford Courthouse, 1781. Painting by Col. J. Trumbull, engraved by J. B. Forrest.

William R. Davie, who enlisted Andrew Jackson, then thirteen years of age, for military duty in the Revolutionary War. Engraved by J. B. Longacre from a drawing by M. Vanderlyn in 1800.

the false statements made in Tarleton's demand for unconditional surrender, Buford had ordered the white flags of surrender to be displayed and arms thrown down, but ignoring this symbol of civilized warfare, Tarleton fell upon his disarmed victims with sword and bayonet, mercilessly slaughtering them in what was, undoubtedly, one of the most disgraceful episodes of the Revolutionary War, and one which was not at all in accord with the honorable code observed by most officers—American and British. Young Andy helped his mother and others tend the wounded and dying who were brought from the battleground to the little log church used by the Waxhaws Presbyterian congregation. He heard from dying men the tragic story of death by bayonet and sword, after they had laid down their arms in surrender and now begged for quarter. Forever after, such ruthless slaughter of unarmed men was known as "Tarleton's Quarter." Andy himself was destined to have a taste of similar brutality before his youthful military career was ended.

During this period he was captured by a party of British soldiers and ordered to guide them to the home of an American officer, Major Thompson. He accepted the orders quietly and set out with them for Thompson's house—but, instead of leading them by the usual route to the plantation, which would bring them close to the residence before they could be seen, he took them through an open field, knowing quite well that they would be in full view at least a half mile from the house. His ruse was successful and Major Thompson, seeing their approach, jumped onto his horse, swam it across a swollen stream, and made his escape.

The British, angered when they realized that Andrew had done this intentionally, carried him on as a prisoner. It was during his captivity that he was ordered to clean the muddy boots of a British officer who, when he refused to perform this menial task, struck at him with his sword.

"The sword-point," he recalled in later years, "reached my head and left its mark there as durable as on the soul, as well as on the fingers. . . ." [52]

Had he not raised his hand to ward off the blow, it might easily have fallen with full force upon his head and quickly killed him.

His wounds, like those of his brother and their friends, were un-tended by the British, for they, fearing that Major Thompson, who had made his successful escape, would join with Major Taylor and overtake them, hurried the prisoners to Camden. The prisoners were dismounted and marched on foot, without food or water, and, even while being driven through swollen streams, were pre-vented from drinking.

At Camden he and the others were placed in the jail, a spot from which they were afforded a full view of the American army, when it marched on Camden and took its position at Hobkirk's Hill. In later years, Jackson himself related the story.

"About sunset," he recalled, "a carpenter with some soldiers came into our room with a plank, and nailed up the window look-ing toward Gen. Green's encampment; some tories who were in the company, abused us very much, told us Green was on their lines without artillery, and they intended to make a second Gates of him and hang us all. When night closed, we heard much bustle in the garrison, and soon found that the effectives were removing the invalids relieving them, from which we inferred their intention to attack General Green in the morning or attempt to surprise him before day—being anxious to see the Battle, if one took place, having only a razor blade which allowed us to divide our rations with, I fell to work to cut out a pine Knot, out of a plank nailed over the windows, obstructing the view of Greens encampment, and with the aid of a fellow prisoner, completed my object before day, making an aperture about an inch and half in diameter which gave a full view of Gen. Greens situations. . . . As soon in the morning as objects could be distinguished, the British army was seen drawn up in columns, under cover of the stockade and Col. Kershaws house—a little after sunrise were seen to move a south-east direction, keeping themselves under cover from a view of the Green encampment. It continued in this direction, until it reached the woods, when it wheeled on the left, under cover of the woods, until it reached the Cheraw road; here it received a severe fire from the American picquet and was seen to halt for a moment, when it was again seen to advance and the American picquet retir-ing kept up a brisk fire of musquetry—soon after this, the British were seen advancing in order of Battle up the Hill, and Gen. Green forming on the heights.

"The British supposing Green had no artillery, the officers in front led on their men encouraging them, when Green's battery opened upon with great effect, many horses coming without riders, and many with wounded men upon them and the noncombatants running, helter skelter for safety—soon the small arms were heard and a general action appeared to commence, when the American squadron of horses was seen to charge them on their left and rear, and cut off the retreat of the British from their redoubts—never were hearts more elated than ours, at the glitter of American swords wielded by American arms so successfully which promised immediate release to us, having cut off the left of the British army which as appeared, he had perfectly in his power if Green had been able to sustain himself in his position—how short was our Joy, for soon thereafter the roar of the cannon ceased, the sound of our small arms appeared to be retiring, and the cavalry appeared to be attacked in front vigorously, and his only alternative to cut his way thro the enemy, which appeared to be done with great gallantry and retired out of view. The firing having ceased, Capt. Smith of the artillery (American) was brought in a prisoner and lodged in this room with us, who related to us the disaster of our army . . . Capt. Smith said his command was entirely killed or taken but he saved the pieces. . . ." [53]

Through this pine-knot peephole, Andrew Jackson witnessed a scene which he would never again have to look upon—an American army quitting the field in defeat.

A few days after the battle Jackson and six others were exchanged, after which they examined the battlefield, finding many muskets with their butts up, some barrels out of their stocks— every evidence, in fact, to indicate a sudden and unexpected attack while the Americans were cleaning their arms and making preparations for strengthening their position. Here Jackson learned an important lesson—never permit an army to be surprised.

This he learned, along with other bitter lessons of war, for he had seen the homes of his relatives and friends burned; he had witnessed the sufferings of helpless women and children in the

111

path of the foe; and he had shared personally in such sorrows, for he had lost his entire family—his mother and two brothers. His elder brothers, Hugh and Robert, had died as a result of the fatigues of military service, untended wounds and the dread disease, smallpox, all of which he had, miraculously, been able to withstand. And, as if this were not enough, his gallant little mother, going down to care for friends and kinsmen held on British prison ships at Charleston, contracted smallpox, died and lies buried in an unknown grave in Charleston. These things, and many more, he had learned—and, on March 15, 1781, he was only fourteen years old. His case, in wartorn Carolina, was not unusual.

Although the British were greatly crippled during their invasion of the Carolinas, they were still undefeated and General Greene's calls for aid from the western riflemen continued. It was not possible to answer all of them, because of the critical situation in the West. However, a small group joined Col. Elijah Clarke at the siege of Augusta, and a small number were probably with Greene at the unsuccessful siege of Ninety Six. Finally, the Americans took Augusta, thus ending its years of British occupation. At last, Clarke and his Georgians could return home.

The fall of Augusta, and the loss of British aid supplied them from that post, was felt among the Cherokees and, when they finally arrived at the Long Island for the proposed treaty negotiations during the latter part of July, 1781, Old Tassel was quick to place the blame for the deplorable condition of his people on the late British commandant of Augusta.

To Sevier he said: ". . . You have risen up from a warrior to be a Beloved Man. I hope your speech will be good."

Sevier answered that he did not hate the Cherokees, but had fought them for the safety of his own people.

It was at this treaty that Nancy Ward rose, left the group of women, to stand regally before the commissioners, and said:

"You know that women are always looked upon as nothing; but we are your mothers; you are our sons. Our cry is for peace; let it continue. This peace must last forever. Let your women's sons be ours! our sons be yours. Let your women hear our words!"

Col. William Christian made an eloquent reply to Nancy Ward's speech, and the treaty was, at length, concluded without any effort on the part of the white men to secure additional lands. There was peace between the white settlements and the Overhill towns, but the Beloved Woman's words fell upon a bitter, warring world. The British were still fighting in the East and the Chickamaugas, now strong and independent, made no pretense of coming in to the treaties and openly refused to be bound by any acts of the older chiefs. Their raids continued against both the Holston and the Cumberland settlements.

General Greene, reporting his victory at Eutaw Springs on September 8, called upon the mountain men to come over again and help cut off Cornwallis' retreat through North Carolina to Charleston. Now that a reasonable peace had been made with the older towns, Sevier and Shelby made preparations to join him. Six hundred men—two hundred under Sevier and four hundred under Shelby—soon were on the march, with the avowed purpose of stopping Cornwallis.

In his autobiography, Shelby gives this interesting comment on the campaign:

"To effect this important object, the people on the western waters were induced to volunteer their services—it was for this purpose that they were prevailed upon to leave their homes five hundred miles from the scene of operations to defend a maritime district of country surrounded with a dense population and in comparative quiet, while their own fire-sides were daily menaced by the Chickamauga Indians, who as you know had declared perpetual war against the whites and could never be induced to make peace.

"I was far advanced on my road when I received vague information of the surrender of Cornwallis in Virginia and hesitated whether to proceed. But the men appeared to be willing to serve out a tour of duty which at the time of entering the service I repeatedly assured them would not exceed sixty days absence from their homes. I proceeded on more leisurely to Greene, who observed to me that such a body of horses could not remain in the vicinity of his camp on account of the scarcity of forage and requested me to serve out the tour with Marion, in which I consented, however, with some reluctance, as the men would be drawn seventy or eighty miles further from their homes. . . ." [54]

The mountain men, though deploring the tame action which now replaced their anticipated pursuit of Cornwallis—who had surrendered at Yorktown on October 18—were willing to remain and joined Marion at a place called Ferguson's Swamp. Soon Sevier's and Shelby's mounted riflemen and Mayham's Dragoons captured a British-Hessian post at Monk's Corner and participated in "mopping-up" operations, as a result of which the remnants of the British army were driven into Charleston.

After this, the enemy kept so well within the limits of their lines that little or no blood was spilt, and all active movements seem to have ceased. Shelby then applied to General Marion for a release which would allow him to attend a session of the General Assembly of North Carolina, of which he was a member, while Sevier and most of the mountain men served out the remaining few days of their tour of duty and reached home in January, 1782.

They had fought almost constantly since the outbreak of the Revolutionary War—but their battles were by no means over. Their eastern neighbors might look forward to an early cessation of hostilities, but for them the year of 1782 offered no hope of peace. Farther west, James Robertson's little settlement on the Cumberland River had, only by the narrowest margin, survived the savage warfare of 1781.

CHAPTER III

The Cumberland Settlements

While the settlers on the Holston and its tributaries were alternating between battles east and west of the mountains, many of their number were pushing westward to establish a new frontier. In the spring of 1779, exactly a decade after William Bean had built his cabin on the Watauga, James Robertson led a small party composed of William Neely, James Henley, Edward Swanson, Mark Robertson, Zachariah White, William Overall, a Negro man whose name is not given, and a few others, over the land route to the Great French Lick on the Cumberland River. Their immediate purpose was to clear the land, plant some crops and start building shelters for their families, whom they planned to bring out the following autumn.

During the past decade the Cumberland country had been extensively explored by men from the eastern colonies, as well as by members of the settlements on the Holston and its tributaries.

For some three-quarters of a century prior to that date, however, this territory was known to French traders. A large spring, salt-bearing rocks and luxuriant vegetation, attracted to it every species of wild life found in the section, so the Frenchmen found it not only a hunter's paradise, but a pleasant and convenient place of residence during their long hunting expeditions. The Cumberland River and its tributaries, leading as they do to the Mississippi and to the Gulf of Mexico, provided easy access to markets for their pelts and furs. Among the men known to have made long stays at this place was Charleville, probably as early as 1713 or 1714, and Timothy Demonbreun of Kaskaskia, who eventually became a permanent citizen of Nashville. For several years before the settlements were formed, DeMonbreun at times occupied a cave on the banks of the Cumberland River. He frequently had with him parties of hunters from the Illinois settlements.

Another of these early hunters was Thomas Sharpe Spencer,

115

who came into the Cumberland country with a party of hunters about 1776. They built a few cabins, but soon most of them returned home, leaving only Spencer and a man named Holliday. About the same time another party of French hunters came up the Cumberland River as far as the Bluffs, where they built a few rude cabins and a small trading post. In the spring of 1778 the Spencer party planted a small field of corn.

This cornfield was near Bledsoe's Lick, at the place later known as Castalian Springs. Near it was a large hollow tree in which Spencer settled down and made his home for several months. His companion, Holliday, did not share his enthusiasm for the situation and tried for some time to persuade Spencer to return home with him. Finally, realizing that he could not change his companion's mind, Holliday determined to make the trip alone, in spite of the fact that he had lost his knife. Spencer, realizing that it would be suicidal to attempt the trip without even this simple means of providing food, broke his own knife in half and presented one part to Holliday. Then, generously, he accompanied Holliday as far as the barrens of Kentucky, returning to the Cumberland to spend the winter alone in his hollow tree.

Some historians say that Spencer's tree was a sycamore, others that it was a poplar. It could have been either, for both grow to great size in this and other sections of the country. Spencer's was not the only known example of this unique type of residence. John Lawson, in his rare book on the history of the upper portion of South Carolina, describes one of this species, which, incidentally, is the Tennessee state tree. It is called a poplar, or tulip tree, so known because of its tulip shaped blossoms, and its poplarlike wood. Lawson's description reads:

". . . The Tulip-Trees, which are by the planters called poplars, and are nearest approaching the wood in grain, grow to a prodigious Bigness, some having been found one and twenty foot in Circumference. I have been informed of a Tulip Tree, that was ten foot in Diameter, another wherein a lusty man had his bed and household furniture, and lived in it until his labour got him a more Fashionable Mansion. He afterwards became a noted man in his country for wealth and Conduct. . . ."

116

Spencer was a man of gigantic size, with feet which harmonized with the rest of his magnificent proportions. His tree was, apparently, built on the same generous proportions, for it gave him roomy and comfortable quarters during the bitter winter which was ahead. Here he hunted and lived in solitude, apparently having no contact with the French hunters who came to the area. Certainly they knew nothing of him, for when they found his footprints in the rich alluvial soil about their encampment, they became so terrified at their size that they swam across the river and wandered through the woods until they came to the French settlements on the Wabash.[1]

Spencer was probably the tallest man in Tennessee, and, undoubtedly, he is the subject of some of the tallest tales. So many and so varied are the stories told about him that he has become a hero not unlike those who appear in the ancient Greek and Roman myths, or in the folk tales of various European nations. Fortunately, a number of these stories have been set down in well-authenticated records or in the accounts of persons who actually knew him. One such account appears in the narrative of Gen. William Hall, who, after the resignation of Sam Houston, became Governor of Tennessee.

"Colonel Isaac Bledsoe," General Hall wrote," discovered the Lick, or Sulphur Spring, which, much to the dislike of the old settlers, has been changed; and at the time he first saw it, the locality was so covered with buffalo that he stated to me that 'he was afraid to get off his horse lest they trample him to death.' Thomas Sharpe Spencer afterwards came to the same place . . . (he) was a most remarkable man, a perfect Hercules in form—indeed the most powerful man I ever saw. He was a very peaceable man, withal, and on one occasion I saw him perform a feat which will hardly bear relating, it is so incredible. Being at the house of Elmore Douglas at a muster, two of the boys commenced fighting, and old Bob Shaw, also a very stout man, ran up and insisted on having them 'fight it out." Spencer, however, was of a different opinion, and parting the crowd right and left as if they were children, he seized one of the belligerents in each hand, and pulling them apart with scarcely an effort, told them 'to clear themselves.' Old

117

Bob, hereupon, struck him with all his force upon the forehead right over the eye, but Spencer, wheeling about suddenly, seized him by the collar and waistband of his trousers, and running a few steps to the fence, which was ten rails high, tossed him over it! The poor fellow tumbled upon his head, nearly killing himself by the fall, but quite cured of his fighting propensities for the time. Spencer told me that knowing his own strength he was really afraid to strike a man in anger, for fear he would kill him. Spencer's Hill, in this state, on the road to Knoxville (Near Crab Orchard) was named for him, he having unfortunately been killed there in the summer of 1794. He had been to Virginia after some money and was returning. He generally rode in advance of the rest, and at the gap near the top of the hill the Indians laid in wait and shot him dead. He had one thousand dollars in his saddlebags and these, falling off, the Indians got the money. The horse, a very fine one, fled to the party and was secured. The stories are very numerous which are told about him. . . ." [2]

In the spring of 1779, the Robertson party set to work clearing land, planted a crop of corn and began the building of rude shelters. By the end of the season, when the corn crop was made, they left three of their number to guard it from the depredations of wild animals and began their return journey to the Holston settlements, where they would help complete arrangements for bringing their families to their new homes. On the way back, Robertson visited George Rogers Clark at the Vincennes post in the Illinois to consult with him about cabin rights, still thinking that the bend of the Cumberland River was in Virginia, which, of course, it was not. Settlements were founded, however, on the insecure claim of the Richard Henderson Transylvania Company to these lands.

When they reached Fort Patrick Henry, they found the boat building for the pioneer flotilla to be commanded by Col. John Donelson well under way. His flagship, *The Adventure* and several others under construction, were flatbottomed boats, made of sawed planks, with a shelter which was boarded up at the sides and covered with a roof which extended over half, or, sometimes the whole, length of the boat. Other water craft of every imaginable description were also being built, many of which were the simple,

118

Indian-style canoes, or pirogues made of the trunks of great poplar trees, which were skillfully hollowed out by axe and adze. Women and girls were busy with their household tasks and with their preparations for their journey into the wilderness. Among them was one in particular who was destined for future fame—Colonel Donelson's bright-eyed, vivacious little daughter Rachel, then about thirteen years of age. She would, one day, be the beloved—but much maligned wife of Andrew Jackson.

Why, the question naturally arises, would such people prepare to forsake the comparative safety of the eastern settlements for the still unknown dangers and hardships of a new, entirely unpopulated land? None of them, it is quite certain, were seeking to evade their responsibilities as far as the War of American Independence was concerned, for all of them, by their very presence, as well as their fighting on both sides of the mountains, had already contributed richly to that cause. Perhaps one of the very sound reasons which motivated many of them was that, should the Americans fail to win the war, this remote western settlement would offer a haven to hundreds of their relatives and friends, who would need to escape British rule and, perhaps, British vengeance for their rebellion. Others, undoubtedly, considered the possibility of founding a free state which, by an alliance with Spain or other European powers, through which they might have free navigation of the Mississippi and freedom of deposit at its ports. There was also the tempting prospect of getting into the fertile territory included in the Henderson purchase in time to select choice lands and to establish themselves before some unfortunate turn in the Revolutionary War might make such a move impossible. Whatever their reasons, they were committed to the journey and they went forward with high hopes.

Putnam, the noted historian of Middle Tennessee, has this comment to offer on the importance of their venture:

"It was in the midst of the War of the Revolution, and near its darkest day, that the emigrants came to the Cumberland. They had not made the move to expatriate themselves; they had fought, and would not yield to the common enemy. They came not here to avoid the duties or burdens of faithful citizens, or because they were indifferent to the struggle in which their dearest friends were engaged.

"There was a combination of strong influences impelling to this emigration. To secure this vast extent of country they came. Here they endured the extreme of peril and suffering; and here they rejoiced when the great result was known. But their own triumph, safety, and peace, came not so soon as to citizens 'in the States.' Their toils and sufferings continued for ten years after the acknowledgement of Independence. Then there were added ten or more years of temptations, privations, and conspiracies, instigated by less savage but more crafty foes—Spanish, French, and English, and a few mistaken, disappointed, or ambitious, but unworthy Americans. And yet it must be said, to the praise of the great mass of the people, they were honest and patriotic—ingrained democrats." [3]

So, in the midst of the desperate struggle for American independence, these Cumberland settlers pushed forward the western frontier of the nation yet to be born. Their very presence contributed to the safety of the settlements on the Holston and its tributaries, as well as to the frontiers of eastern provinces. In so doing, they laid their breasts bare to the attacks of Dragging Canoe and his Chickamauga Indians, affording them a closer, more convenient, more vulnerable victim and, to a great extent, thus mitigating their attacks on the eastern settlements. Neither the Cumberland settlers nor their descendants ever failed in their duty to their country, nor neglected any opportunity to fly to its defense.

Before final preparations were completed for the long and difficult voyage of the Donelson flotilla from Fort Patrick Henry to the Great Salt Lick on the Cumberland, and the return, by land, of Robertson's party, it was planned that the flotilla would stop at the upper end of the Muscle Shoals, where it would be joined by Robertson's party and led, by the shorter land route, to its destination. Unavoidable circumstances, however, prevented the carrying out of this plan, which proved to be fortunate. Women and children could scarcely have survived even this shorter land route, because of the extreme cold, lack of food, and excessive hardships.

They were, as future events proved, much safer aboard the crude ships of Donelson's flotilla.

Robertson, in fact, could make no attempt to meet them at Muscle Shoals, for he and his party had only, with great difficulty, survived their land journey. Game was scarce, as was forage for their horses, so both men and beasts arrived at the Lick in an emaciated condition. Then, too, they had no means of knowing whether or not the extremely cold weather had caused Colonel Donelson to postpone his voyage until spring. Once at the Lick, Robertson and the men of his party set to work, as best they could, making ready for the eventual arrival of their families.

An account of the voyage from Fort Patrick Henry on the Holston to the Great Salt Lick on the Cumberland was, fortunately, kept by Colonel Donelson himself, day by day, during much of the journey. Fortunately, it has been preserved and has been printed in full by several Tennessee historians—Ramsey, Putnam and others. A brief summary follows:

On December 22, 1779, the flotilla took its departure from the fort and floated down the river to the mouth of Reedy Creek, but it was stopped here because of the fall of water and ". . . . a most excessive hard frost. . . ." After many difficulties and much delay, the flotilla reached the mouth of Cloud's Creek on Sunday evening, February 20. Here several other vessels joined them and the enlarged flotilla set sail on Sunday morning, February 27—but here, again, there was trouble. Donelson's *Adventure* and the boats of Boyd and Rounsifer struck the Poor Valley Shoal and there they lay ". . . in much distress . . ." until the twenty-eighth, when thirty people where taken off the boats to lighten them and, with the aid of rising waters, they were able to get off the shoal.

On March 2, they passed the mouth of the French Broad River, but here again, disaster struck. Mr. Henry's boat, driven to the point of an island by the force of the current, was sunk—the cargo much damaged and the crew's life endangered. The whole fleet then put ashore and went to their assistance, bailing out and raising the Henry boat and putting it in shape to reload its damaged cargo. During this period one Reuben Harrison went ashore to hunt, but did not return. A searching party, the firing of guns—

121

even a four pounder—failed to bring him in, so, regretfully, the party had to proceed, leaving old Mr. Harrison with some other vessels to continue the search. Reuben was later found down the river, however, and taken aboard Mr. Belew's boat.

The bitter cold continued and there was much suffering. One person, Colonel Hutching's Negro man ". . . being much frosted in his feet and legs . . ." died on March 6.[4]

The bitter weather and the many difficulties and dangers which had plagued the voyage from its beginning seemed minor, however, when compared with the ones which lay ahead as they approached the country of the Chickamauga Indians.

The flotilla got under way early on the morning of March 7, but there was a strong wind which, Colonel Donelson recorded, ". . . occasioned a high sea, insomuch that some of the smaller crafts were in danger. . . ." Fortunately, at this point, they reached the uppermost of the Chickamauga villages, which had been evacuated completely some time before—perhaps because of the Indians' superstitious fear of witches. Here they lay in the afternoon and camped that night and here it was that the wife of Ephraim Peyton, who had gone ahead with Robertson's land party, was delivered of a child.

It was here also that they passed through their most grueling ordeal. Nature and a savage enemy seemed to have joined forces for their destruction. High seas, rough water through the Whirl, or Suck, and the rapids of Muscle Shoals lay ahead and, even though their sturdy crafts and good seamanship might overcome these handicaps, Indians lined the banks of the river, taking advantage of their helpless condition and made merciless attacks upon them.

At ten o'clock on the morning of March 8, the flotilla cast off and proceeded down to an inhabited Indian village on the south side of the river. Here, the Indians made friendly signs to them, called them brothers and invited them to come ashore. John Caffrey and a son of Colonel Donelson, taking a canoe, went over to the village, while the fleet landed over on the opposite shore. The canoe had not gone very far, however, when a half-breed, Jack Coody, with some other Indians, jumped into their canoe and advised them to go back to their boat. They took his advice, carrying him and the others with them, and followed by several more Indians in canoes. Presents were distributed among them, but while this was going on, it was observed that other Indians, embarking in their canoes, wore red and black war paint. Coody made signs to his companions to leave the Donelson canoe, while he and another Indian remained. They sailed with them for some time, but later quitted them, saying that they had passed all of the towns and were out of danger—which, unfortunately, proved to be far from the truth.

Colonel Donelson continues the story:

"But we had not gone far until we came in sight of another town, situated, likewise on the south side of the river, nearly opposite a small island. Here they again invited us to come on shore, called us brothers, and observing the boats standing off for the opposite channel, told us that 'their side of the river was better for boats to pass.' And there we must regret the unfortunate death of young Mr. Payne, on board Captain Blakemore's boat, who was mortally wounded by reason of the boat running too near the northern shore, opposite the town where some of the enemy lay concealed; and the more tragical misfortune of poor Stewart, his family and friends, to the number of twenty-eight persons. This man had embarked with us for the Western country, but his family had been diseased with the smallpox, and it was agreed upon between him and the company that he should keep at some distance in the rear, for fear of the infection spreading; and he was warned each night when the encampment should take place by the sound of a horn. After we had passed the town, the Indians having now collected to a considerable number, observing his helpless situation, singled off from the rest of the fleet, intercepted him, killed and took prisoners the whole crew, to the great grief of the whole company, uncertain now how soon they might share the same fate: their cries were distinctly heard by those boats in the rear. We still perceived them marching down the river in considerable bodies, keeping pace with us until the Cumberland Mountain withdrew them from our sight.

"We are now arrived at the place called Whirl, or Suck, where the river is compressed within less than half its common width

123

above, by the Cumberland Mountain, which juts in on both sides. In passing through the upper part of these narrows, at a place described by Coody, which he termed the 'boiling pot,' a trivial accident nearly ruined the expedition. One of the company, John Cotton, who was moving down in a large canoe, had attached it to Robert Cartwright's boat, into which he and his family had gone for safety. The canoe was here overturned, and the little cargo lost. The company, pitying his distress, concluded to halt and assist him in recovering his property. They landed on the northern shore, at a level spot, and were going up to the place, when the Indians, to our astonishment, appeared immediately over us on the opposite cliffs, and commenced firing down upon us, which occasioned a precipitate retreat to the boats. We immediately moved off. The Indians, lining the bluffs, continued their fire from the heights on our boats below, without doing any other injury than wounding four slightly. Jennings' boat is missing. . . ."

Having at last passed through the Whirl, they found that the river widened and flowed with ". . . a placid and gentle current. . . ." All the company had apparently come through the ordeal except for the family of Jonathan Jennings. Their boat, in coming into the Whirl, had run into a large rock, partly covered by water and, to the great distress of the rest of the party, they had to be left, perhaps, to be slaughtered by the Indians.

During the rest of that unhappy day—March 8—the flotilla proceeded down the river and floated all that night. The following day passed uneventfully, the travelers floating until midnight and pulling ashore to camp for the night. At four o'clock the next morning, somewhere far in the rear, were heard the cries: "Help poor Jennings! Help poor Jennings!"

"He had discovered us by our fires," Colonel Donelson recorded, "and came up in the most wretched condition." He states that as soon as the Indians had discovered his situation, they turned their whole attention to him, and kept up a most galling fire on his boat. He ordered his wife, a son nearly grown, a young man who accompanied them, and his two Negroes, to throw all his goods into the river, to lighten their boat for the purpose of getting her off; himself returning their fire as well as he could,

124

being a good soldier and an excellent marksman. But before they had accomplished their object, his son, the young man, and the Negro man, jumped out of the boat and left them: he thinks the young man and Negro man were wounded.

"Before they left the boat, Mrs. Jennings, however, and the Negro woman succeeded in unloading the boat and shoved her off; but was near to falling a victim to her own intrepidity, on account of the boat starting so suddenly as soon as loosened from the rocks. Upon examination he appears to have made a wonderful escape, for his boat is pierced in numberless places with bullets. It is to be remarked that Mrs. Peyton, who was the night before delivered of an infant, which was unfortunately killed in the hurry and confusion consequent upon such a disaster, being frequently exposed to wet and cold then and afterwards, and that her health appears to be good at this time, and I think and hope she will do well. Their clothes were very much cut with bullets, especially Mrs. Jennings'."[5]

The following day, Saturday, March 11, the flotilla got under way, after having distributed the family of Mrs. Jennings in the other boats. On Sunday, after sailing for a few hours, they passed another town, from which they were fired upon, but without damage. Then, halting on the northern shore, they searched for the signs James Robertson was expected to have made for them at that place.

". . . To our great mortification we can find none," Donelson wrote, "from which we conclude that it would not be prudent to make the attempt (to continue the journey by land) and are determined, knowing ourselves to be in such imminent danger, to pursue our journey down the river. . . .

". . . After trimming our boats in the best manner possible, we ran through the shoals before night. When we approached them they had a dreadful appearance to those who had never seen them before. The water being high made a terrible roaring, which could be heard at some distance among the drift-wood heaped frightfully upon the points of islands, the current running in every possible direction. Here we did not know how soon we should be dashed to pieces, and all our troubles ended at once.

Our boats frequently dragged on the bottom, and appeared constantly in danger of striking: they warped as much as in a high sea. But, by the hand of Providence, we are now preserved from this danger also. I know not the length of this wonderful shoal: it had been represented to me to be twenty-five or thirty miles; if so, we must have descended very rapidly, as indeed we did, for we passed it in about three hours. . . ."

After these ordeals, a comparative peace descended upon the flotilla and Colonel Donelson's entries in his journal are not only more brief, but less frequent. The voyagers, in due time, reached the Ohio River and made their way to the mouth of the Cumberland and upstream to their long hoped for destination. Now and then they had had time to kill a few buffaloes and even a swan, whose meat, Colonel Donelson reported, was "very delicious." Spring was on the way, and on March 29, Colonel Donelson recorded that they proceeded up the river; gathered some herbs on the bottoms of the Cumberland, which some of the company called 'Shawanee salad.' "

Finally, on Monday, April 24, Colonel Donelson made his final entry in the journal of the historic voyage which he had commanded:

"This day we arrived at our journey's end at the Big Salt Lick, where we have the pleasure of finding Captain Robertson and his company. It is a source of satisfaction to us to be enabled to restore to him and others their families and friends who were intrusted to our care; and who, some time since, perhaps, despaired of ever meeting again. Though our prospects at present are dreary, we have found a few log-cabins which have been built on a cedar bluff above the Lick by Capt. Robertson and his company."

But, in spite of the "dreary prospects," it was a happy landing for the weary voyagers and for the men who had waited so anxiously through the long, cold winter months for word of their wives and children who had been entrusted to Colonel Donelson's care. It was also a happy event for the few women and children who had made the land journey with the Mansker, Eaton and Rains parties a few months earlier. The spring of 1780 brought not only great beauty to the Cumberland country, but also a re-

126

newed faith in the great adventure in which all of them had participated.

About thirty families had sailed with the good boat *Adventure*. They, with those who had traveled in other crafts, numbered probably about one hundred and sixty persons. Children, long cooped up in the necessarily close quarters of the boats, must have landed with shouts of joy, and soon have busied themselves with exploring the wonderful new country which was to be their home. Women, enlisting their help, went to work at once to make temporary homes and the men quickly busied themselves with the labors of homebuilding and planting crops, and also with such important matters as establishing land titles, securing tracts of land and organizing a government. There was an early tendency to spread out and build rude shelters on choice tracts of land, rather than to concentrate on forts or stations which would withstand Indian attacks.[6]

According to Putnam, "When the people arrived upon the Cumberland, they saw no Indians, and they knew of no tribe that was settled between its waters and those of the Tennessee, nor of any Indian towns north of them and south of the Ohio. Here seemed to be a vast extent of woodland, barrens, and prairies, inviting human settlement and the improvements of civilization. The Delawares, who had appeared on the headwaters of Mill Creek, and professed to have come only to hunt, had traveled a long distance. The Creeks and Cherokees claimed no lands within the limits of those new settlements; therefore, it is not surprising that some of the people were reluctant to give much of their time and labor to the erection of forts and stations, when all wanted homes; and some had made haste to select the choicest places, thus creating discontent with others.

"But the desire and temptation to mark and blaze, and scatter abroad, and locate as soon as they learned a little of the richness of the country, was repressed by the experienced and prudent among them, sufficiently to agree to give a portion of their time and labor to the erection of a few strong-holds and defences, as also for the deposit of provisions, arms, and ammunition."[7]

By common consent, it was decided that the fort at the Bluffs, which had been named in honor of Gen. Francis Nash,[8] Revolutionary hero, should be the headquarters and principal fortification. Others under construction at the same time were, according to Putnam, "Freelands . . . at the spring in North Nashville; one on the east side of the river, upon the first highland at the river bank, called Eaton's (or Heaton's); others near the sulphur spring, ten miles north, called Gasper's, where now is the town of Goodlettsville; one at Station Camp Creek, about three miles from Gallatin, called Bledsoe's; one at the low lands on Stone's River . . . or Donelson's, [in our day known as Clover Bottom]; and one at Fort Union, at the bend of the river, above the bluffs, about six miles distant; where was once the town of Haysborough."

The fort at Nashborough was erected upon the bluff, between the southeast corner of the Square and Spring Street, so as to include a fine spring which then issued from that point. The water of this spring dashed down the bluff giving much interest and charm to the location.

Like Fort Nashborough, all of the forts were built of logs and were two stories high, usually with the upper story extending over the first story for a few feet on all sides, thus giving the defenders an opportunity to shoot down upon attackers who might attempt to storm the fort at close quarters. All of them had small portholes, through which the barrels of rifles might be inserted, and all were provided with well-placed lookouts. Most of them—as far as the often scant supplies of the settlements would permit—were kept well stocked with ammunition, food and water. They were not entirely invulnerable, but they were hard to take or to starve out.

As to the general appearance of Fort Nashborough and the Great Salt Lick, Putnam wrote:

"The account they [the settlers] gave of the appearance of the bluffs and Salt Lick, when the companies arrived in the winter and spring of 1780, is, that although there was 'open ground,' there was no evidence that it had ever been in cultivation. The open space around and near the Sulphur or Salt Spring, instead of being an 'old field,' as had been supposed by Mr. Mansker at his visit here in 1769, was thus freed from trees and underbrush by the innumerable herds of buffalo and deer and elk that came to these waters. The place was the resort of these wild animals, among which also came bears, panthers, wolves, and foxes. Trails, or buffalo paths, were deeply worn in the earth from this to other springs. Much of the country was covered with a thick growth of cane, from ten to twenty feet high. (Upon the banks of our rivers and creeks and on many plantations in Middle Tennessee, the cane has not yet (1859) been entirely destroyed.) Like the wild beasts who formerly found in its denseness their places of rest and concealment, like the Indians who, 'from the beginning,' hunted the beasts, and traversed these well-stocked parks, and called them all their own; so savage beasts and savage men, have had to retire before the race of white men, and before settlements and agriculture. . . ."

This, then, was the scene which greeted the new breed of men who came to take this land of promise, to establish in it a new way of life and to put its rich lands to new, more fruitful uses. With them they brought another and almost untested form of government. One of their first concerns was to provide for the orderly operation of their public affairs, for the regulation of ordinary business transactions, and for the maintaining of law and order in the community.

Richard Henderson and other members of the Transylvania Land Company, who had just come in from surveying a line to the Tennessee River, as well as such men as James Robertson, John Donelson and many others, were already familiar with the working of the Watauga Association and the provisional governments which had been established east of the mountains after the outbreak of the Revolutionary War. All of them were of the opinion that a government to meet present needs must be set up at once.

Accordingly, they and the other inhabitants of the settlement came together and produced the document known as the Cumberland Compact. Under it, provisions were made for a government to be administered by Judges, Triers, or General Arbitrators, generally called the Government of Notables. This government was to be composed of twelve "conscientious and deserving persons to be chosen by the free men, over twenty-one years of age,

129

by representatives from the different stations: from Nashboro, three; Gasper's, two; Bledsoe's, one; Asher's, one; Stone's River, one; Eaton's, two; Fort Union, one."

These General Arbitrators were given the power to punish at their discretion, having respect for the laws of the country, all offenses against the peace, misdemeanors, and those of criminal nature, provided such Court did not proceed with execution so far as to affect the life or member of the offender. On such cases the prisoner was to be sent to a place where a legal trial could be given.

Much of the document was taken up with the important business of land deals and records. Some authorities, notably Dr. Archibald Henderson, a descendant of Richard Henderson, who wrote extensively on the subject, state that the Cumberland Compact was actually a contract between Henderson, his Transylvania Company and the Cumberland settlers. To some extent this is true, but it was much broader in scope. True, it did provide that Henderson appoint an Entry Taker, but this officer's duties and responsibilities were explicitly defined and, upon violation of any of them he was subject to removal from office, his books to be turned over to the Court of Notables until his successor was appointed.

It also provided that, although no consideration money was to be paid for lands within the claim of Henderson's Company until a satisfactory and indisputable title to their lands on the Cumberland River could be had, the company should be paid something. To provide for this the Compact authorized that a "reasonable and just" amount of twenty-six pounds, thirteen shillings and four pence, per hundred acres, be paid, which transaction would be properly recorded by the Entry Taker.

Although important in paving the way and participating in the founding of the Cumberland settlements, Richard Henderson's part in developing them was confined to the early months of their existence. His Sycamore Shoals treaty was repudiated by Virginia and North Carolina and titles to the lands on the Cumberland were invalid.

In concluding, the Compact declared ". . . we do not desire to be exempt from the rateable share of the public expense of the present war, or other contingent charges of government . . ." and sought the early erection of a county which would include the Cumberland settlement.

These settlers, like the Wataugans, were deeply loyal to the American cause.

They were, Putnam says, "sincere in devotion to the cause of American Independence. They had avowed, sworn, and proven their attachment to the great cause for the success of which patriotic men in all of the Colonies . . . were now fervently praying and heroically contending.

"Although, by their removal across the (Cumberland) mountains, they were the more distant from the very 'battle-fields of the Revolution,' their hearts were in the work; they, as wisely and as well as any other men in that eventful day and struggle, were ordained and trained, sent and stationed, where the invaluable services, which only such men could perform, would be most needed. And they acted their part. They foiled the schemes of diplomacy, they secured the best part of the continent, 'they kept the faith and the country.' " [9]

Richard Henderson is generally credited with the authorship of the Cumberland Compact, which most authorities agree is in his handwriting. It was signed by 256 settlers, only one of whom made his mark instead of signing his name. That these men, like those of many other pioneer settlements of Tennessee, possessed a high degree of literacy is shown by their signatures on early documents. Only two signers of the Washington District petition of 1776 made their mark and those who signed later documents maintained a similar percentage of literacy. This valuable document was brought to light by the historian, Putnam, who discovered it in 1846, in an old trunk which, he said ". . . had evidently belonged to Col. Robert Barton, who, as will be seen, was a useful citizen, one of the Notables of that day, and lost not his character for usefulness while he lived . . . ." So, as Ramsey had discovered and brought to light the Watauga petition of 1776, Putnam found, preserved and perpetuated, the equally important, but neglected, Cumberland Compact. It is dated May 1, 1780.

THE DANGEROUS EXAMPLE

During this critical period the Cumberland settlements were comparatively quiet, as far as attacks by large bodies of Indians were concerned, although, almost from the beginning, one individual after another fell victim to tomahawks and scalping knives. Strangely, a number of apparently unrelated events kept major attacks from being launched by the British and Indians during the year of 1780. The bitter cold of the winter had not only resulted in great human suffering, but it had also destroyed, by freezing and starvation, much of the game on which both the red man and the white man depended for food. The game which did survive was scarce and of poor quality. At the same time smallpox ravaged the Cherokee towns.

This dread disease had originated with the British camps and ships at Charleston and was carried as far as the Chickamauga towns, where these Indians had captured the Stuart boat of the Donelson flotilla, which was lagging behind the rest of the fleet because it had smallpox cases on board. The disease spread throughout their towns, taking a heavy toll of life.

Col. Joseph Brown, who himself had been a captive of these Indians, in his narrative of pioneer experiences, calls this mortality "a judgment upon the Indians." When they took smallpox and when the fever was upon them, they took a heavy sweat in their houses, then leaped into the river, and died by the scores. A large number of them destroyed themselves, or died of the disease.

When spring came, the Indians, who had been quieted only temporarily by these misfortunes, soon resumed their depredations. The British had instigated an attack upon the whole frontier, from Pennsylvania to Georgia. The Shawanee tribe, especially, which had once held the Cumberland Valley, made every effort to help bring all of the northwestern tribes together for a massive attack during the coming summer. Working with them in this plan were the British agents at Detroit, on the Maumee, and elsewhere. Similar influences were in progress among the southern tribes, who were displeased with the building of Fort Jefferson in Chickasaw territory without their consent. Colbert, their chief, prepared to drive out the invaders by force. The nearness of this tribe to the Cumberland settlements was a serious cause of alarm;

132

however, the first assaults upon them were not made by the Chickasaws, but by the Cherokees and Creeks.[10]

These incursions, which had begun as early as the spring of 1780, were in the nature of small, but continuous raids on isolated parties and persons. Putnam tells something of them:

"In the spring of this year, and at a time when the stationers were generally felicitating themselves upon the quiet they enjoyed, the goodly land to which they had been conducted, and the happy homes they were soon to have . . . a gun was heard, whose report was not familiar, yet at the time attracted little remark or notice. . . . Some questions were asked, but not until the next evening was the startling fact made known that 'a man had been shot and scalped!' The first emigrant had been killed; the savages had begun here the work of bloodshed. They had all looked upon the dead; but few, if any, had gazed upon the victims of the scalping knife and tomahawk. There was some curiosity to see the body of Joseph Hay. . . ."

It was a horrible sight, chilling the blood of even those experienced in the extremes to which the Indians could go. Sadly, and with dark forbodings, they buried Hay's body in open ground on the point of land east of the Lick.

John Milliken, who was killed about that time on Richland Creek, may have been the first man in the settlement to be killed by the Indians. It was the body of Hay which was first to be interred in the spot which became Nashville's first cemetery, but other similar casualties followed in rapid succession.

Scarcely a month had passed since the landing at the Great Salt Lick when the killing of settlers by the Indians began. In May, 1780, two men named Mayfield and Porter were shot down in broad daylight at Eaton's Station.

Meanwhile, Colonel Donelson had established his large family and his slaves at an open-face camp on his rich river bottom plantation, on Stone's River, which he named Clover Bottom. Here he planted corn and the first crop of cotton to be raised in this section. Here, also, his daughter-in-law, wife of Capt. John Donelson, gave birth to the first white child to be born in the new settlements. He lived only a short time, however.

133

In July, Stone's River flooded, completely covering the bottom lands where Colonel Donelson had planted his corn and cotton—a major disaster for a man with a large family and thirty slaves to feed. Added to this was the ominous threat of a major Indian attack. Two men at the Bluffs, as well as Jim, a Negro man belonging to Colonel Henderson, who, with a young white man, had been left to take care of Henderson's lands in the Clover Bottom section, were killed. These disasters caused Colonel Donelson to remove his large household to the comparative safety of Mansker's Station.[11] He had neither blockhouse nor stockade and knew quite well that in such an exposed position his whole family would have soon fallen under the tomahawk and scalping knife.

Soon afterwards, however, it was learned that after the flood had receded, his crops of corn and cotton at Clover Bottom had matured, so he decided to risk the danger of harvesting them. For this purpose he organized a party composed of his son Capt. John Donelson, Jr., Abel Gower, Jr., John Randolph Robertson, brother of James Robertson, and several others, among whom was an elderly man named Robert Cartwright.

After meeting at the appointed rendezvous, the party, with two boats, proceeded up Stone's River to the Donelson fields, where, for several days every man—both black and white—worked with a will to harvest the coveted crops. Capt. John Donelson had brought a "slide"—a type of large sled with wooden runners—and a horse to carry the corn and cotton to the boats.

During the early morning of the last day, Colonel Donelson had pushed his boat across the west side of the river, where his cotton lay. He thought that gathering it would delay the party very little and had expected the Gower party to follow him and share the crop with him. It was the first and only cotton crop in the settlement. The Gower party, however, finished its breakfast and immediately launched its boat and began to descend the river. Captain Gower, answering Colonel Donelson, who hailed them from the opposite bank, said that it was getting late and that as they wished to reach the Bluffs before night, they would have to move on.

Colonel Donelson, however, told them he would finish gathering his cotton before he went back to the station. While they were still talking, the Gower boat started and reached the narrow channel between a small island and the western bank of the river. Here a party of Chickamaugas who had hidden themselves on the bank opposite the island opened fire on them, with the result that four or five members were killed in the first volley. One member of the party, Jack Civil, a free Negro, surrendered, and was carried as captive to the Chickamauga towns.

When the firing began, Colonel Donelson ran to his own boat, took up his rifle and fired at the Indians, and then rushed to rejoin his own party. He found them very much scattered, as they, being well trained in the methods of Indian warfare, had fled at once to the surrounding thickets for protection. When they were finally reassembled, it was agreed that they travel by separate routes, in order that they would leave no trail for the Indians to follow, and meet, on the following day at a spot on the Cumberland River some miles above the mouth of Stone's River. Their one horse was given to Robert Cartwright, who because of his advanced age, could not have hoped to escape on foot.

Then, according to their plans, they met at sunset and sheltered themselves in the branches of a large hickory tree which had fallen to the ground. During the night they suffered from the cold, but they did not dare build a fire for fear of attracting the Indians who, they were sure, were still lurking in the neighborhood.

The next morning they attempted to build a raft which would carry them across the river, but for lack of materials, tools and time were not successful. It was then that Somerset, Colonel Donelson's body servant, volunteered to swim the river in order to secure aid. He reached the settlement without injury or interruption and returned with a rescue party and boats to carry his master and the rest of the party to safety. The Gower boat, in the meantime, had drifted down the river to the Bluffs with its tragic burden of dead bodies and the corn which its unfortunate crew had risked their lives to harvest.

It was during this period that William Neely was killed and his daughter, who had accompanied him to the camp he had established in Neely's Bent, for the purpose of making salt, was carried into captivity in the Creek nation. These bold attacks on

135

the infant settlements, as well as the serious shortage of food, forced many families to leave the Cumberland on the approach of winter. Colonel Donelson was among those who removed their families to Kentucky. But James Robertson, setting an example for those who chose to remain, stiffened his backbone and decided to weather the storm.

These are only a few of the stories of the early days in the Cumberland Settlements. Others, equal in drama, in courage and even in humor, occurred almost daily. Miraculous escapes and recoveries, exhibitions of super-human courage—even death—were so frequent that they became almost commonplace.

One tragic incident piled upon another. Nathan Turpin and another man were killed in an attack on Renfroe's Station on Red River. This attack was made in June or July, 1780, by a body of Choctaw and Chickasaw Indians. The Renfroes, who had made the river journey with the Donelson flotilla, had stopped to locate at Red River, instead of going on to the Great Salt Lick with the others. This attack made them realize, however, that they could not continue in their isolated position, so they made immediate plans to go to Freeland's station, where they had friends. They had begun their journey, when some of the party, regretting to part with possessions they had left behind, decided to go back for them—the others wisely proceeded on their journey with all possible haste. The return party reached the deserted settlement in safety and was on its way back when, camping for the night at a creek, later called Battle Creek, it was again attacked. All members of the party—about twenty persons—were horribly slaughtered, except one woman, a Mrs. Jones. She managed to make her way through the heavy underbrush and the forests until she finally reached Eaton's station. Her clothes had been torn almost to shreds and she was in a great state of exhaustion and shock. The members of the first party reached the upper stations in safety.

These incursions, which continued with growing intensity, became so frightening that not only the Donelsons, but many other families, decided to go either to Kentucky or to the Illinois or to

Natchez and there was much gloomy talk of abandoning the entire Cumberland settlement. James Robertson and a few sturdy souls were left, with dwindling supplies of food and ammunition, to defend themselves as best they could against the constantly increasing dangers of starvation and massive Indian attacks.

The Indians now lay in ambush along every path which led from the Cumberland and, so critical had the situation become toward the close of 1780, that James Robertson decided to attempt the dangerous journey to Kentucky to obtain powder for the defense of the settlement. With his usual good fortune, he completed his mission and, on January 11, 1781, reached Freeland's station, where he had left his family—finding that on that very day his wife, Charlotte, had given birth to a son—Felix Robertson, the first white child born in Nashville.

It was by a remarkable coincidence—indeed, a kindly act of Providence—that James Robertson had made the hazardous journey and returned safely at this particular time. The emigration to older and stronger settlements had now stopped, for the simple reasons that, due to the thefts by the Indians, there was a great shortage of horses and on every path along which these people could travel parties of Indians lay in ambush. The hardy few who had determined to stay, at all costs, were thus reinforced by others who stayed from necessity, rather than choice. All of the inhabitants were now concentrated in the two main forts—the one at the Bluffs, where the Robertsons and others were and the other at Eaton's, across the river and some two and a half miles distant. Freeland's was never entirely abandoned, although, at times, it was very scantily maintained. Had it not been that Robertson had been able to return with a new supply of ammunition, they could easily have been destroyed by the Indians, for they were in constant danger of a strong attack.

Long after the rest of the people in Fort Nashborough lay quiet in sleep, James and Charlotte Robertson must of talked softly to each other of the new baby—their sixth child—and of the many things which had happened in James' absence. Then, suddenly, Robertson's alert ears detected a foreign sound. Grabbing his rifle, he dashed out to find that a body of Chickasaws had opened the gates of the fort and were already entering. His shots brought the other men to the rescue and, aided by the bright moonlight, they soon drove every invader out of the fort. The powder he had brought from Kentucky and his own sharp hearing had saved the station. This was the last attack made by the Chickasaws on the Cumberland settlements.[12]

Unfortunately, it was by no means the last Indian attack, for the Chickamaugas, often united with the Creeks, found the new settlements on the Cumberland a weaker and easier prey than those on the Holston and its tributaries. Minor depredations continued and, on April 2, 1781, a strong, well-planned attack was made on the fort at the Bluff, where the Robertson and other families had come together for mutual protection.

The Indians crept up at night and lay in ambush about the fort. Early in the morning, three of their number appeared, fired upon the fort and retreated. Nineteen horsemen dashed out in pursuit and, at a small stream, came upon a large body of Indians. They dismounted to give battle, and their horses, riderless and excited by the noise, ran wildly past the fort in the direction of the Salt Lick. Several Indians, seeing this rich prize, chased after the horses, thus lessening to some degree, the danger from another large body of Indians which lay in ambush, ready to attack from the rear. Now, on foot, between the two bodies of the attackers and completely cut off from the fort, the defenders were in a dangerous position. Suddenly, the gates of the fort, which had been closed behind the horsemen, were opened wide to admit the men who were now desperately fighting their way back to safety—and to loose upon the Indians a large pack of hunting dogs. Charlotte Robertson, seeing the excitement of the dogs when they scented the Indians, conceived the idea of turning them loose to join in the fight. As she had hoped, the dogs made a furious attack upon the Indians and played an important part in winning the hard-fought battle.

Mrs. Robertson lived many years after this historic event and told over and over, for the benefit of the rising generation, the story of this miraculous experience. One of her listeners was the historian, who heard from her the exciting story:

138

"Her mind was clear and her memory distinct," he wrote. "She said she stood by the sentry at the gate as the horsemen passed out and dashed down the hill through the cedars and bushes. She had a glimpse of the Indians upon whom the whites made the attack, heard the crack of every gun, saw some of the movements of the Indians who were in ambush; and then her heart began to fail, for fear that every man who had gone out would be killed, and the station probably fall into the hands of the murderers.

"She, as did some others at the fort, saw the large party of Indians moving from their lair and advancing with evident intention to cut off the retreat of the horsemen, and perhaps attempt an entrance to the fort. She and other women had a gun or axe in hand, resolved to die at the gate rather than admit the enemy there.

"She saw the horses fleeing—the Indians turning in pursuit—and supposed that every man who had gone out was killed or captured. Presently she discovered some of the whites attempting to escape to the fort, hotly pursued, and in utmost peril from the pursuers and those of the ambushed party who had not joined in the chase for the horses.

"There was terrible excitement in the fort. She advanced to the position nearest the retreating party to fire upon the pursuers. The pack of fifty dogs was raving to join the melee and hubbub, and—at her own suggestion—the sentry 'let slip the dogs of war.' They never made such music before; they out-yelled the savages; they ran like mad, and fiercely attacked the advancing Indians.

"She saw how greatly the savages were surprised. They could not pursue the whites, and firing at the dogs wasted the loads they needed to shoot at the white people. These Indians joined in the hunt for the horses. And 'she patted every dog as he came in the gate and thanked God it was no worse.

" 'What a deliverance!' said she."

And, for many years afterward, the settlers often said: "Thank God that the Indians have a love for horses and a fear of dogs!" [13]

Tales of such incredible courage and endurance abound—though in necessarily abbreviated form—in all of the early histories of Tennessee, as well as in newspapers, magazines and still unpublished manuscripts. One of the greatest contributions to the

139

preservation of the history of these times was made in the series of narratives of many Middle Tennessee pioneers published by the *Southwestern Magazine,* located "four doors from the Post Office," in 1852. One, which is especially interesting, was that of John Rains, Jr.

Rains was a son of the John Rains who was a member of Robertson's party which reached the Cumberland late in 1779, and whose cattle were driven across the Cumberland River on ice during the bitter winter of that year. The elder Rains was the first to bring domestic cattle into the settlement. The younger Rains states that his father had many cattle, as well as eighteen to twenty horses, stolen by the Indians during the early months of settlement. This, and the constant depredations of Indians which made the cultivation of crops impossible, to say nothing of the great loss of human life, so discouraged him that he took his family to Kentucky and stayed there for a year, before returning to his holdings in the Cumberland. The older man and a companion named Stull, on their way back to the Cumberland, were attacked by a party of Indians. Rains, turning from the trail, jumped his horse through undergrowth and over a grapevine, thus making his escape. Stull's mount was not such a good jumper and became entangled in the grapevine. The Indians overtook, killed and scalped him.

Another interesting story in the narrative of young Rains is that of the remarkable character, David Hood, wag, philosopher and humorist, to say nothing of being one of the outstanding heroes of those Indian-fighting days.

"One of the most interesting incidents connected with the early history of Tennessee," Rains writes, "is one in which a man named David Hood figured. He was coming up from Freeland's station, the present place of residence of Dr. McGavock below the Sulphur Dell Spring adjoining Nashville, when several Indians gave chase to him, firing upon him as he ran. He, thinking there was no other chance for his life, concluded to try 'possuming it' and so fell flat upon his face in the weeds. The Indians ran up and gathered around him, and one of them very deliberately twisted his fingers into his hair to scalp him. His knife being very dull, he let go, took a better hold, sawed away until he could pull it off; poor Hood bearing it meanwhile without a groan. After the deed was done they stood around a little while, reloaded their guns, and started towards town, one of them giving him a few stamps on the back. After a while, Hood raised his head cautiously, peeped out under his arms and at last finding the coast clear, got up and started towards town. Mounting the ridge above the Spring, what was his dismay to find himself once more right in the presence of the whole gang. Again he started, but they fired upon him as he ran, one of their bullets cutting him deeply across the breast, but finally after getting so close as to pull one of the skirts off of his coat, the Indians abandoned him. When quite spent, he dropped behind a log in the cornfield nearby, after facing around to get one fire at them and was rescued by some of the whites who came out at the sound of the firing. . . ."

After his rescue, Hood was placed, by his friends, in an outhouse, where they cared for him, although none of them thought he would live more than a few hours. But he was still alive the next morning, and when General Robertson visited him, he said, when asked how he felt, that he thought if he had half a chance he could live. Robertson then took the case in hand and Hood recovered. Rains stated that he had often seen General Robertson making rolls of lint for the wounds he treated.

It is interesting to observe that James Robertson had this apparent natural aptitude for surgery, and that it was, apparently, inherited by his son, Felix, who became one of the leading physicians and surgeons in this part of the country.

Another scalping patient whom General Robertson treated successfully was the little Dunham girl.

The Dunhams had settled on the land later improved and cultivated by General William G. Harding. Still later, under the management of the Confederate General W. H. (Red) Jackson, it became known as the Belle Meade estate, famous for its fine horses and elegant social life. In late 1780 and early 1781 the Dunhams, like others who had outlying stations, were forced to take shelter in the fort at the Bluff. In a period of comparative quiet, Mrs. Dunham had instructed her little daughter to go outside the fort to a place where some wood had been cut and to bring in an armful of sticks and chips.

141

The pile of wood was not more than three or four hundred yards from the Fort. The tops of the trees which had been cut down were imprudently left as they fell among the small cedars and privet bushes, which grew thickly all over the ground south of the Square and the branch. In or near this wood and tree-tops, Indians were concealed. As the little girl approached to gather wood, they grabbed her and carried her with them screaming at the top of her voice. Her mother, without a moment's hesitation ran out to her rescue and being in advance, was shot by the Indians and quite dangerously wounded.

As the mother was shot down, some Indians caught the little girl by the hair, held her screaming and in terror, and were trying to scalp her. However, seeing armed men from the fort rushing to the rescue, they succeeded in taking only a part, about six inches in diameter, from the top of her head, leaving a rough, irregular wound. Fortunately, both she and Hood eventually recovered and lived many years. The little girl, another of General Robertson's patients, joined with Hood and others in the all too rapidly growing number of settlers who had had the harrowing experience of being scalped.

"At a later day," Putnam relates, "when the number of these cases was multiplied, 'the said Hood,' with his imperturbable humor, would select a position by the side of others who had suffered like himself, and do this with the intention of making some reference to his 'select company.' Besides the soubriquet by which he was usually known, he was often called 'O'possum.' Little Miss Dunham called him 'Possum.' But nothing offended him—he could not get mad. He never swore or threatened upon any provocation. Indeed, we may presume he prayed for the savages who tried to kill him."[14]

General Robertson's treatment of scalp wounds, learned, it is said, from a traveling French surgeon, was most unique. The method was to take a pegging awl, or some other sharp instrument, and perforate thickly the whole open space. The purpose of this was to permit natural granulation to come up through the awl holes and, eventually spreading, to form a covering to the denuded skull before it could deteriorate and thus expose the brain. There were persons in every station who learned to perform this and other operations for the treatment of gunshot and tomahawk wounds. Many of them lived scalpless to a ripe old age.

The cause of these and other hostilities was the erection by George Rogers Clark, of Fort Jefferson,[15] a few miles below the mouth of the Ohio River. Building of this fort was ordered by Thomas Jefferson, then governor of Virginia, who supposed the location to be on lands owned by the Cherokees. The Chickasaws, however, held undisputed claim to the entire territory west of the Tennessee River—now the western portions of Kentucky and Tennessee.

Resenting this encroachment, the Chickasaws, led by their chief, James Colbert, laid siege to the fort and for six days fought desperately to destroy it. Finally, they were driven back by the fort's swivel guns. The hungry, exhausted survivors were rescued by Col. John Montgomery and carried to the Illinois settlements. Fort Jefferson was abandoned. During the engagement Colbert, who was carrying a demand for surrender, was seriously wounded as he approached the fort. The neutral policies which had been followed by the Chickasaws until this time were abandoned and the Chickasaws became open allies of the British.

Similar conditions prevailed in the Holston settlements and, when John Sevier and his western riflemen reached home early in 1782, after participating in the final battles of the American Revolution, they found themselves still at war. The Chickamaugas, defiant and scornful of the pacific attitude of their older chiefs, were steadily reinforced by restless young warriors from the over-hill towns of the Cherokees and similar elements from the Creek nation.

But the ancient towns of the Cherokees grew weaker and weaker each year. Some time around 1780, Attakullakulla, their chief orator and statesman and friend of the white man, died. In the fall of 1782, Oconostota, their chief warrior, realizing that he could hope to live but little longer, made the difficult trip upstream to the home of Joseph Martin, near the Long Island, where he resigned as chief in favor of his son and begged Martin to aid in assuring the succession. He spent the winter with him and, in the spring, knowing that the end was near, begged to be carried to the sacred town of the Cherokees to die. Martin himself made the canoe trip with him and remained at his side until his death. It was to Tassel, a more able chief, not to Oconostota's son, however, that the leadership fell. This portion of the nation never regained its former strength and glory, but continued to disintegrate until its people became little more than objects of pity to the white settlements and to those Cherokees who had moved down country to the south and west.

As the power of the old towns waned, Dragging Canoe's villages grew strong. They now boasted some one thousand warriors who, with each passing moon, grew more warlike and audacious. This was their only hope, for, being seceders, they had no lands to barter with the white men; even the inaccessible coves into which they had fled were held only by force of arms. No American state nor Indian nation could treat with them, for they possessed nothing but their unhappy skill in battle and constant harassment. Their very existence depended upon continued hostilities, so they fortified themselves in their wild country and followed, relentlessly, with the aid of the British and the Spanish, the only trade they knew.

The only remedy for their atrocities was the torch of an invading army, and John Sevier, convinced of this, called upon his troops to rendezvous at the Big Island of the French Broad River in September, 1782. On the twentieth of that month, they set out for the Chickamauga towns, going by way of the Elijah, Little River, Nine Mile Creek, and crossing the Little Tennessee at the town of Citico on the third day of their march. Here they held a council with the friendly chief, Hanging Maw, and the deceptive John Watts, who was rising to power under Dragging Canoe's tutelage. On the seventh day, they crossed the Hiwassee River, on which they had encamped the previous night, and entered the hostile territory. They struck first at Vann's towns, which they burned, and passed on to Bull Town, at the head of Chickamauga Creek. Thirty miles further on they reached the Coosa River and entered a village where a British sergeant was killed. They continued their march to Spring Frog Town and Estanaula, which they destroyed, and returned home through the Old Hiwassee towns to Chota, on the Tennessee River.[16]

The salutary effect of this campaign, while not permanent in the Holston settlements, was of even shorter duration in the Cumberland country. The Chickamaugas, now assured of swift and terrible punishment from the older settlements, turned with greater frequency and ferocity toward those which were not yet strong enough to defend themselves. The Cumberland people lived also in danger of invasion by the Chickasaws, for that nation had not yet been won over by the diplomatic James Robertson. His opportunity to establish permanent friendly relations with them after the unfortunate Fort Jefferson incident and the invasion of the Cumberland, came in a way he did not welcome, but which he skillfully turned to the advantage of these settlements. Their attack on Freeland's Station January 15, 1781, however, was their last attack on the Cumberland settlements.

Col. John Donelson who, with his family, was still in Kentucky, now turned his eyes, not only toward his lands in the Cumberland settlement, but also toward the vast tracts in the great bend of the Tennessee River. He, and perhaps others, persuaded the Virginia authorities to finance a treaty with the Chickasaws and chose Nashville as the treaty grounds. The commissioners named to conduct the negotiations were Donelson, Joseph Martin and Isaac Shelby. The youthful John Reid of Virginia was sent out to make advance arrangements for the holding of the treaty.

James Robertson, however, refused permission for Reid to travel among the Chickasaws and withheld his consent for holding the treaty in Nashville until a vote was taken in the stations. Robertson's own station voted against the treaty, but in the total vote of the stations, eighty-four were in favor of it and fifty-four were against it. The chief objectors, Robertson among them, opposed it because they realized the danger of allowing such a large body of Indians to see the weakness of the settlement. Robertson may have feared, also, the consequences of land speculation in the Indian country. Certainly, he knew from experience the danger of clashes between irresponsible persons on both sides. His position was well taken, but he bowed to the will of the majority and the ultimate

145

success of the treaty was due largely to his skill in handling the Indians.

This treaty, which was conducted in June, 1783, was unusual in many ways. As Judge Williams points out ". . . it was held by Virginia's commissioners, on North Carolina soil, and Virginia's money was spent in negotiating it. It did not accomplish the acquisition of Western Kentucky, but it did result in clearing the Chickasaw claim from a boundary of very fertile land, south of the Tennessee ridge, for the North Carolinians. . . . For their part, leading North Carolinians east of the mountain were at that time working strenuously in parceling out a part of the domain of the Chickasaws (the present West Tennessee) to 'insiders' and . . . without even the leave of the Chickasaws." [17]

This treaty, however, was later rendered null and void by the fact that Virginia did not have the right to negotiate. It is often overlooked by historians and omitted from lists of treaties through which the United States obtained Indian lands.

At that time, however, the most important treaty to all parties concerned was that between the United States and Great Britain, which was concluded at Paris in 1783. By it the independence of the American republic was formally established, although the loosely knit Confederation which attempted to perform the functions of a national government was in no way prepared to guarantee immediate enjoyment of the hard-won freedom which it had secured. While it groped for a permanent structure, the states were unruly and jealous of their rights, and citizens in both legislative halls and private life constantly questioned and debated each step made toward the forming of a permanent national government. The miracle was that, after seven years of war and a complete change in the type of government, the American people experienced so few of the disorders which commonly follow revolutions.

The money system was chaotic; the policy for the disposition of public lands, which was of paramount importance in the West, was uncertain; Congress, under the Articles of Confederation, was practically powerless; many terms of the treaty with Great Britain were vague and incapable of enforcement; foreign trade and foreign relations were uncertain and confused; and the people, in

146

general, were unwilling to accept anything without prolonged debate. Vast distances contributed to misunderstandings and mistrust; yet, in spite of all of the difficulties and diverse interests, a united nation finally emerged. The astonishing thing is that it came as quickly as it did.

In the West, where, for more than a decade, an independent government had existed, the people were extraordinarily sensitive on the subject of their rights. Any steps which threatened their freedom or hindered their development met vigorous resistance. The conservative east, like the British colonial governments, soon found their lusty self-reliance both irritating and disturbing. There was always the threat that they would break away and become a completely separate state, or a subsidiary of whatever European nation happened to be in power in the lower south. Free and unrestricted navigation of the Mississippi River and of free ports and deposit at its mouth were more important to them than alliance with the people of the East, who, by the nature of things, could not engage in commerce with them.

There was also the threat of international complications. Spain feared that the unruly backwoodsmen might descend the Mississippi and take by force any rights of navigation and deposit which might be denied to them. The two portions of the Treaty of Paris which concerned them most were those which dealt with the surrender of Britain's western posts and the free navigation of the Mississippi. While both were provided for in the treaty, Britain's deliberate procrastination and our own fumbling diplomacy prolonged their execution until, at certain critical stages, it came near to causing the separation of the western settlements from the East.

CHAPTER IV

The State of Franklin

At the close of the Revolutionary War the impoverished national government looked for aid toward the states with extensive western lands. Virginia, with her holdings, which, harking back to the original grants, reached to a legendary "south sea"; and North Carolina, which claimed a similar extent of territory, were, at once, the target and the envy of the less landed states. They were pressed for cession of their western lands to the central government, and, after several stormy years, were at last prevailed upon to give up this rich domain.

The final cessions were due, however, quite as much to pressure from the western inhabitants of this territory, who favored the creation of separate states, as to that of the federal government. Kentucky's separatist movement, which began at Danville in 1784, was similar to a simultaneous one in the Tennessee country.

"In Kentucky," Judge Williams states, "the movement for a separate government, begun at Danville in 1784, renewed in January and May, 1785, was carried to the point of 'confirming a decree of separation from Virginia,' in August, 1785. An immediate erection of the district into a new State was asked of the Virginia legislature, which body, in January, 1786, stipulated that a new convention should be held in the district in September, 1786; and that, if it declared for independence, a separate state should come into being after September 1786; provided, however, that Congress, before January, 1787, should consent and agree to its admission into the Union. Kentucky was, during the year of 1786, in turmoil, produced by this action of Virginia, deemed as it was by many of the leasers of the district to be purposely and needlessly dilatory." [1]

This arrangement was vastly superior, however, to that made for the Tennessee country in North Carolina's poorly conceived cession of her western lands, passed at the April, 1784, session of

149

its General Assembly. According to its provisions, the land was ceded to the national government and a period of two years was allowed for its acceptance or refusal. During that time North Carolina laws were to be in effect; but, significantly, the land office was to be closed, ". . . with minor exceptions having relations to the reservations for the military." [2] This was the final blow. The western settlements were in the habit of managing their own affairs and protecting themselves and their interests, but they could make no further progress if they were not free to continue their land deals. This unhappy situation resulted in open rebellion, which was followed by immediate separation from North Carolina and the creation of the Independent State of Franklin.

It was a drastic step and one which, even at its inception, failed to meet unanimous approval. That it was popular with the majority of the inhabitants of the western settlements is proven, however, by the fact that they sustained it through the four stormy years of its existence.

The late Judge Samuel K. Heiskell, eminent attorney, jurist and historian, makes a strong case for the Franklinites.

"North Carolina," he points out, "at no time exercised any real control of the Western people . . . but they put up with the situation from 1777 to 1784, when, patience ceasing to be a virtue, they organized the State of Franklin. . . . It was justifiable from any standpoint from which it can be viewed. The mistake was that they ever petitioned the State of North Carolina for annexation; if that had never been done, the right to organize the State of Franklin would have been just as unquestionable as their right to organize the Watauga Association; but for all practical purposes they were in the same condition when they organized the State of Franklin, and this movement, like their first efforts at government, was the product of necessity.

"King's Mountain forever settled the fact that the Watauga people were much better able to protect and assist North Carolina, than North Carolina was to assist and protect the Watauga people. . . . John Sevier and Isaac Shelby redeemed North Carolina when they organized the pioneers, and by a bold and masterly stroke, went in search of Ferguson and conquered him, instead of waiting for Ferguson to carry out his threat to come to the Western waters and hang their leaders and burn their homes. Annexation had been in force for three years when King's Mountain was fought, and notwithstanding, the pioneers knew that they had saved North Carolina, they tolerated the weakness of that state and its total inability to be of any service to the Western people for four years before they organized, as a matter of necessity, the State of Franklin. Neither the State of Franklin nor any of the men who brought it into existence need any apology for what was done. . . ." [3]

Another important legal defense of the State of Franklin was made by Hugh Lawson White, son of Knoxville's founding father, James White, brilliant lawyer, jurist and long time member of the United States Senate.[4] Senator White, on March 24, 1838, joined in the fiery debate on the subtreasury bill, one of the important measures sponsored by the Van Buren administration, in which Daniel Webster of Massachusetts and Robert Y. Hayne of South Carolina were leading, and extremely bitter, contenders. Webster had made an unflattering reference to the early history of Tennessee and the State of Franklin, to which Senator White, apparently with his tongue in cheek, replied:

"The senator from Massachusetts, at the close of his reply to the senator from South Carolina, 'for his special benefit,' in very good temper, and in a most happy manner, referred to the early history of that portion of my State, now called East Tennessee, once known as the State of Franklin. He read us a part of one of her acts of assembly, which fixed the salaries of some of her officers, and directed the *species of currency* in which they were to be paid.

"I always feel gratified when I know, or hear, that my State has done anything which benefits any portion of my fellow-man.

" 'Blessed are the peace-makers,' is the language of Holy Writ. On this occasion the two honorable and distinguished senators had assumed an attitude so belligerent, that I really feared it might end in something worse than words. But no sooner were the labors of my State fifty years ago brought to the notice of this grave body, that we all forgot that any of us had ever been out of temper, and so soon as we could recover composure enough to adjourn, we

151

separated like a band of brothers—no two leaving the chamber in better temper with each other than the two honorable senators.

"But, sir, the senator knew nothing of the practice under the State law; therefore we have not had the full benefit which we ought to derive from this reminiscence. He could have related the whole incident so much better than I can, that I regret he did not mention this subject to me before he addressed the Senate; if he had I would have given him the additional facts, that the whole might have been detailed in the Senate in his good tempered and felicitious manner.

"It will be remembered that the governor, chief justice, and some other officers, were to be paid in deer-skins, other inferior officers were to be paid in raccoon-skins. Now, at that day, we were all good whigs, although we had some of the notions of the democrats of the present day.

"We thought these taxes might safely remain in the hands of the collectors, as subtreasurers, until wanted for disbursement. The taxes were, therefore, fairly collected in the skins and peltry pointed out in the law. But the collectors, as the report says, knew that although raccoon-skins were plenty, opossum-skins were more so, and they could be procured for little or nothing. They, therefore, procured the requisite numbers of opossum-skins, cut off the tails of the raccoon-skins, sewed them to the opossum skins, and paid them into the general, or *principal* treasury, and sold the raccoon-skins to the hatters.

"The treasurer had been an unlucky appointment, although a worthy man; he was a foreigner, knew nothing of skins or peltry, and was, therefore, easily deceived by the subtreasurers. When this imposition was discovered, the whole system went down, and we have never had a great fancy for leaving the taxes in the hands of subtreasurers or collectors, from that day to this.

"But, sir, these old proceedings more clearly developed the true character of my State than almost anything of the present day. . . ."

Senator White then continued, telling, from his own recollections and those of his pioneer father, some of the history of Tennessee during these early days. He explained that the state of

Hugh Lawson White, son of
James White, founder of
Knoxville. Engraved by T. B.
Welch from a painting by
E. C. Leutze.

Daniel Webster, portrait
drawn from life and engraved
by James B. Longacre.

Franklin had been composed of four counties of North Carolina—Washington, Sullivan, Greene and Davidson—which were completely separated from the mother state by great, almost impenetrable mountain ranges; that when the Revolutionary War with Great Britain was terminated in 1783 it was still continued west of the mountains; and that North Carolina was not in a position to furnish aid or protection to these western outposts. North Carolina sought a solution by ceding her western lands to the national government. But Senator White concluded:

"North Carolina discovered her error, and before Congress could act on the subject, repealed her act of cession. But it was *too late*. We had been disposed of without our consent. Though but a handful, with a powerful savage enemy infesting our whole frontier, and without a dollar to begin with, we set up for ourselves. We would not brook the indignity; we had begun the fight for liberty, and liberty or death we would have. We continued the controversy until 1789, when an accommodation with our parent State took place; and with our own consent, and upon terms thought just, we, with other portions of territory, were ceded, in 1789, to the United States. . . ."

Thus two outstanding legal authorities of East Tennessee explained and defended the position of men on the western waters who organized the independent state of Franklin and who refused to abandon it when North Carolina revoked her act of cession. But no one has yet been able to do full justice to the vivid drama of its brief, tempestuous existence, though many men have written excellent reports on its legal aspects and have related stirring narratives of its personal conflicts.

The state of Franklin should not be considered as an isolated incident. It was, undeniably, one of the major manifestations of the separatist movement in the West and it grew from natural causes which were common to the entire region. On the one hand were Georgia, Kentucky, the Cumberland settlements and the state of Franklin, all bordering on rich, undeveloped lands and inhabited by a sparse, but vigorous, ambitious and rapidly increasing population. On the other was a timid, and, as yet, ineffective federal government, which was swayed mercilessly by

153

the vagaries of groups within its as yet ununited states. Self-interest had not yet been subdued sufficiently to permit a workable union.

Vast distances, rugged terrain, and the inadequacy of primitive transportation systems removed any hope of profitable commercial relations between the East and the transmontane, or, as Thomas Jefferson sometimes termed it, the ultramontaine country. At the same time, the opening up of vast areas of cheap, fertile lands, threatened to depopulate some of the eastern states. To these disadvantages, eastern statesmen added the gloomy prediction that the center of political power would shift toward the rapidly growing West, threatening the domination of the East in national affairs. Long after the state of Franklin had had its day, these natural problems remained to vex the nation.

The first step in organizing the new state was taken when two from each captain's company were chosen to meet in county conventions, which, in turn chose representatives to meet in a general convention. These delegates, accordingly, met at Jonesboro on August 23, 1784, elected John Sevier president, and Landon Carter, secretary. The next step was to arrange for a constitutional convention and the establishment of a permanent government. Such a convention was called to meet at Jonesboro on September 16, but, Ramsey states:

"For some reason not now distinctly known, the convention did not meet until November, and then broke up in confusion. . . . Some preferred a longer adherence to the mother state, under the expectation and hope, that by the legislation of North Carolina, many, if not all, of the grievances which had disaffected the western counties, would be redressed. Her Assembly was then in session at Newbern, and repealed the act for ceding her western territory to Congress. During the same session, it also formed a judicial district of the four western counties and appointed an assistant judge and attorney-general for the Superior Court, which was directed to be held at Jonesboro. The Assembly then formed the militia of Washington District into a brigade, and appointed Col. John Sevier the brigadier general." [5]

Had these steps been taken earlier, or had the cession act provided better terms for the transition into statehood, the state of

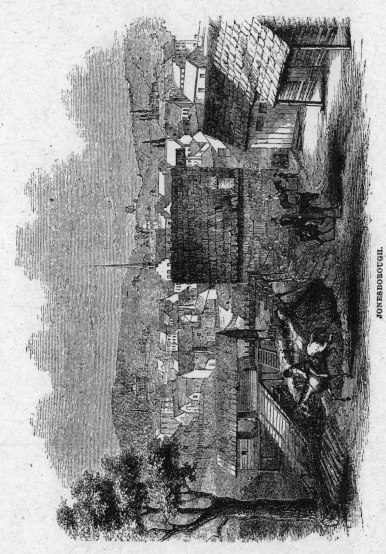

JONESBOROUGH.

Sketch of Jonesborough, site of the Constitutional Convention of 1784. Taken from an engraving in *Harper's New Monthly Magazine*, October, 1857.

Franklin movement might never have sprung up, but once started, it proved too attractive for the freedom-loving westerners to relinquish. John Sevier himself, speaking after news of the repeal of the cession act had been received, recommended continued allegiance to North Carolina, but when his friends would not yield, he cast his lot with them, although he had promise of a brilliant future under the government of the old state.

However, the constitutional convention was held at Jonesboro on December 14, 1784, before news of North Carolina's action had been received in the West. Here an intelligent approach to constitution-making for the new state was demonstrated by the numerous and vigorously debated suggestions which were brought to the floor during both the December, 1784, convention in Jonesboro and that of November, 1785, which was held in Greeneville. Many of the controversial points were set forth by three clergymen—the Reverend Samuel Houston, [a cousin of Sam Houston] who made the keynote address at the first convention, and two other ministers of the gospel, William Graham and Hezekiah Balch, who engaged in verbal battles at the second.

Houston, in his speech before the convention which framed the temporary constitution, Ramsey says: ". . . arose and addressed the convention on the importance of the meeting, showing that they were about to lay the foundation on which was to be placed, not only their own welfare and interest, but, perhaps, those of posterity for ages to come; and adding that, under such interesting and solemn circumstances, they should look to Heaven, and offer prayer for counsel and direction from Infinite Wisdom. . . ." [6]

The temporary constitution drafted by this convention was presented to the people for a six months period of study, after which it was to be replaced by a permanent constitution, made after they had had this opportunity for serious reflection.

"The document," Judge Williams says, "was unique in that it was prefaced by a Declaration of Independence, in which was set forth the 'reason which impels us to declare ourselves independent of North Carolina.' . . . There follows the usual Bill of Rights, under the 'Declaration of the State of Franklin.' Next in order is the governmental scheme, the latter closely modeled after the North Carolina constitution of 1776. . . ." [7]

155

John Sevier was thoroughly familiar with the constitution of North Carolina, for he, with three other Wataugans, had been a member of the North Carolina assembly which drafted it.

The advantages of the proposed new government were set forth in the report of William Cocke and Joseph Hardin:

"If we should be so happy as to have a separate government, vast numbers from different quarters, with little discouragement from the public, would fill up our frontiers, which would strengthen us, improve agriculture, perfect manufactures, encourage literature and everything truly laudable. The seat of government being among ourselves, would evidently tend, not only to keep a circulating medium in gold and silver among us, but draw it from many individuals living in other states, who claim large quantities of lands that would lie in the bounds of the new state. . . ." [8]

During the early part of 1785, John Sevier appears to have made an earnest effort to reconcile the differences between the old state and the West; but was able neither to turn the Franklin people from their course, nor to persuade himself that his place was not among them. During this period, he used every possible means of delaying final action until the people had had ample time to consider fully and earnestly the serious step they were contemplating. Judge Williams says on this point:

"In reviewing the conduct of Sevier, the North Carolina Assembly of 1789 found that Sevier did in 1784 oppose efforts made to subvert North Carolina's authority 'in such manner as actually to prevent elections being held under the new government in two of the counties.'

"This indicates that the first attempt to hold an election for members of the Assembly of Franklin under the Constitution was frustrated by Sevier, in efforts initiated in his Jonesboro speech and Kennedy letter; and also explains why the Assembly did not meet until March, 1785." [9]

At long last, Sevier, with William Cocke, Landon Carter, David Campbell, Samuel Houston, Joseph Hardin, William Cage, and many others, became completely involved in the affairs of the new state and, once having made his decision, followed its course to the bitter end. He did this, knowing full well that identification

156

with the Franklin movement sounded the death knell to his brilliant prospects for advancement under the state of North Carolina; but, in the years to come, his loyalty to his friends was richly rewarded.

During the delayed March session of the Assembly, Sevier was elected governor of the free state of Franklin.

Information concerning the meeting place of the March, 1785, General Assembly, detailed records of many of its actions, and even a full roster of its members, are often lacking, thereby causing considerable confusion among historians of later periods. One subject of debate has been the actual meeting place of this and other General Assemblies. Judge John Allison was of the opinion that this session was held in Greeneville,[10] while Judge Williams, states:

"The Assembly met early in March and did not adjourn until near the end of the month, though it is probable that there were recesses taken in order that the committees charged with the drafting of a series of legislative acts might mature the same for report and passage.[11] The Assembly was held at Jonesboro, as Ramsey correctly states;[12] though Allison states that the meeting was at Greeneville. This fact entitles the county site of Washington county to the honor of having been, in the fullest sense, the first capital of the Commonwealth."

While most of this historic session was devoted, necessarily, to the intricate details of state-making, there was time for the Franklin legislators to engage in a lively running battle with North Carolina authorities. Nor was North Carolina itself exactly idle in this regard. Governor Alexander Martin, hearing rumor after rumor of the goings-on beyond the mountains, decided to send a personal emissary to go to the Western waters and find out just what was happening. For this mission he chose Maj. Samuel Henderson, brother of Richard Henderson, who had negotiated the Transylvania purchase. He provided Henderson with a letter for John Sevier, whom he addressed as "brigadier-general" and a detailed set of instructions for his own activities, which read in part as follows:

". . . You will make yourself acquainted with the transactions of the people in the Western Country such as holding a convention; and learn whether the same be temporary, to be exercised only during the time of the late cession act, and that since the repeal thereof do they mean to consider themselves citizens of North Carolina; or whether they intend the same to be perpetual; and what measures they have taken to support such government. . . . That you be informed whether a faction of a few leading men be at the head of this business, or whether it be the sense of a large majority of the people that the State be dismembered at this crisis of affairs, and what laws and resolutions are formed for their future government; also, where the bounds of their new State are to extend, and whether Cumberland or Kentucky, or both, are to be included therein. . . ." [13]

Martin also instructed Henderson to get a copy of the constitution of the new state, the names of its leaders, and to learn ". . . the temper and disposition of the Indians. . . ." Furthermore, he cautioned him to conduct himself with prudence, being careful not to use any language which might serve ". . . to irritate persons concerned in the above measures. . . ."

Sevier, upon receipt of Governor Martin's letter which Henderson brought to him, laid it before the General Assembly for consideration and reply. This it did—promptly and to the point. Among other pertinent points, their reply, dated Jonesboro, March 22, 1785, stated:

". . . We humbly thank North Carolina for every sentiment of regard she has for us; but we are sorry to observe that it is founded upon principles of interest, as is apparent from the tenor of your Excellency's letter. We are therefore doubtful, when the cause ceases which is the basis of your affection, we shall consequently lose your esteem.

"Sir, reflect upon the language of some of the most eminent members of the General Assembly of North Carolina at the last spring session, when the members from the Western Country were supplicating to be continued as a part of your State. Were not these their epithets: 'The inhabitants of the Western Country are the offscourings of the earth, fugitives from justice, and we will be rid of them at any rate.' The members of the Western Country, upon hearing these unjust reproaches and being convinced it was the sense of the General Assembly to get rid of them, consulted each other and concluded it was best to appear reconciled with the masses in order to obtain the best terms they could, and were much astonished to see North Carolina, immediately on passing the act of cession, enter into a resolve to stop the goods that they, by the act of the General Assembly, had promised to give the Indians for the lands they had taken from them and sold for the use of the State. . . ." [14]

And so, at some length, they recounted grievance after grievance, finally reminding the mother state that her own constitution provided for erection of new states to the westward whenever the Legislature consented. This section of the North Carolina constitution was probably suggested, or written, by the members of the delegation which represented the Wataugans in this historic session—John Sevier, John Haile, John Carter, and Charles Robertson.

Continuing, they set forth in great detail the position of the westerners and requested that their reply be laid before the General Assembly of North Carolina. That body was to be assured ". . . that, should they ever need our assistance, we shall always be ready to render them every service in our powers, and hope to find the same sentiments prevailing in them towards us. . . ."

Furthermore, they stated, ". . . we are induced to think that North Carolina will not blame us for endeavoring to promote our own interest and happiness, while we do not attempt to abridge hers; and appeal to an impartial world to determine whether we have deserted North Carolina or North Carolina deserted us. . . ." The signers were William Cage and Landon Carter, speakers, respectively, of the Franklin House of Commons and Senate, and Thomas Chapman and Thomas Talbot, clerks.

At the same session, William Cocke was chosen to act as agent for the State of Franklin in negotiations with the Congress of the Confederation concerning an early admission to the Union.

Governor Martin's answer to the Western country was in the form of a manifesto, drawn up after a hasty meeting called on April 7, 1785, to consider the emergency created by the secesssion of the western counties. In this document, he explained at length

North Carolina's position, not only in regard to her western counties, but on the general subject of cession of her western lands.[15]

"But," Martin continued, "designs of a more dangerous nature and deeper die seem to glare in the western revolt . . . facts evincing that a restless ambition and a lawless thirst for power have inspired this enterprise, by which the persons concerned therein may be precipitated into measures that may, at last, bring down ruin, not only on themselves, but our country at large.

"In order, therefore, to reclaim such citizens, who by specious pretenses and the acts of designing men, have been seduced from their allegiance, to restrain others from following their example who are wavering, and to confirm the attachment and affection of those who adhere to the old government, and whose fidelity hath not yet been shaken, I have thought proper to issue this Manifesto. . . ."

And, again, the back water men were setting a *dangerous example* for, Martin warned, ". . . by such rash and irregular conduct a precedent is formed for every district, and even every county of the state, to claim the right of separation and independence for any supposed grievance. . . ."

The Westerners were also admonished by him to ". . . tarnish not the laurels you have so gloriously won at King's Mountain and elsewhere, in supporting the freedom and independence of the United States, and in this state in particular, to be whose citizens has been your boast, in being concerned in a black and traitorous revolt, by solemn oath, you are still bound to support. Let not Vermont be held up as an example on this occasion. Vermont, we are informed, had her claims for a separate government at the first existence of the American war, and, as such, with the other states, although not in the Union, hath exerted her powers against the late common enemy. . . ."

On the fourteenth day of May, 1785, John Sevier's proclamation, happily brief and to the point, stated that Martin's manifesto, ". . . thinking . . ." to destroy that peace and tranquility that so greatly abounds among the peaceful citizens of the new happy country, "had deliberately tried to create sedition and stir up an insurrection." He called upon the citizens of the state of Franklin for continued loyalty and reminded North Carolina ". . . that their own acts declare to the world that they first invited us to separation . . . and . . . if in their power, would now bring down ruin and destruction on that part of their late citizens, that the world well knows saved the State out of the hands of the enemy, and saved her from impending ruin. . . ."

The plain, unadorned fact is that neither in her cession act nor in its repeal did North Carolina consider either the wishes or the well-being of the western country. The repeal was due largely to the fact that the cession of the western lands had caused great dissatisfaction in the eastern parts of the state, although the prompt separation of the western counties was a contributing factor. It was a critical period in national history, for the weak, loosely held Confederation had already demonstrated its inability to serve the needs of the American republic and a better way had not yet been found. The habit of separation was a dangerous one, however, and one which, if carried too far, would have been disastrous.

At this time Governor Martin was succeeded by Gov. Richard Caswell, who was not only a close personal friend of John Sevier, but who, with his family, had found refuge in Sevier's own home when North Carolina was overrun by the British. Sevier put the entire situation before him and, in his reply, dated June 17, 1785, Caswell explained his difficulty in serving, at one and the same time, his state and his friends in the West. Until the next meeting of the North Carolina General Assembly, he said, "Things must rest as they are with respect to the subject matter of your letter. . . . In the meantime, let me entreat you not, by any means, to consider this as giving countenance, by the executive of the state, to any measures lately pursued by the people to the westward of the mountains. . . ."

Caswell had considered delivering the goods promised by North Carolina to the Indians by crossing the mountains in person to attend to the matter. However, he pointed out, "A man may submit to these things in a private character, he may be answerable to the people, at least they may judge it so, in a public situation. Therefore, without your assurance that the officers and men under your command being subject to my orders in this case, as matters stand, I think it would be imprudent in me to come or send commissioners to treat with the Indians. . . ."

This failure to deliver the promised goods was blamed for the Indian hostility in the west during the early days of the new state. However, the Franklin authorities soon took matters into their own hands and negotiated a treaty with the Cherokees at Henry's station, the home of Maj. Samuel Henry, at the mouth of Dumplin Creek, on May 31, 1785. In this treaty of "amity and friendship" the Cherokees relinquished ". . . the tract of country lying south of the French Broad River and north of the watershed which divides the waters of Little River and the Little Tennessee River."

John Sevier served as commissioner and the white men who witnessed the treaty were: Lew Boyer, Alexander Outlaw, Joshua Gist, Ebenezer Alexander, Joseph Hardin and Charles Murphy, who served as "inguister." The Cherokee chiefs were: The King, Ancoo, chief of Chota; Abraham, chief of Chilhowee; the Bard, head warrior of the Valley Towns; the Sturgeon, from Tallassee; the Leach, from Settico; the Big Man Killer, from Tallassee; and thirty warriors, or more.[16]

Old Tassel, the Beloved Man of Chota, repudiated this treaty and asked for removal of the white settlers who had flocked to the lands south of the French Broad River after it was signed. Previous plans for participating in the Hopewell Treaty, November, 1785, had kept him from attending the Dumplin Treaty.

"Your people," he complained, "have built homes in sight of our towns . . . We are very uneasy, on account of a report that is among the white people who call themselves a new people, that lives on French Broad and Nolechuckey; they say they have treated us for the lands on Little River. . . . Some of them gathered on the French Broad, and sent for us to come and treat with them; but as I was told there was a treaty to be held with us, by orders of the great men of the thirteen states, we did not go to meet them, but some of our young men went to see what they wanted. They first wanted the land on Little River. Our young men told them that all their head men were at home; that they had no authority to treat about lands. They then asked them liberty for those that

162

were living on the lands, to remain there, till the head men of the nation were consulted on it, which our young men agreed to. Since then, we are told that they claim all the lands on the waters of Little River . . . and call it their ground." [17]

Old Tassel then requested the governors of North Carolina and Virginia, to whom his talk was addressed, to remove the settlers south of the French Broad, and suggested that if they had not the power that "the Great Council of America" be requested to do it.

The Cherokee Nation was probably as fairly represented at the Dumplin Treaty as it was at most similar negotiations, although it is true that some of the older chiefs with whom the white men had been accustomed to do business were not present. Still, the Franklin men were not at fault for the ever widening breach between the younger warriors and the old men who had been so long in power. The Cherokees, naturally, were under the influence of Col. Joseph Martin, North Carolina's agent to their nation and whose Indian wife was the daughter of Nancy Ward. Martin, who wrote from Chota on September 19, 1785, the date of Old Tassel's talk, said that he had no part in the new state, but considered himself under direct orders as the agent of North Carolina.

"I am now," he said, "on the duties of that office, and have had more trouble with the Indians, in the course of the summer, than I ever had, owing to the rapid encroachments of the people from the new state, together with Talks from the Spaniards and the Western Indians. . . ." [18]

There was always an element in the Indian nations which was willing to listen to "talks" from new sources, just as there was usually one, or more, who refused to accept the action of the chiefs who represented them in their treaties. This was due partly to the nature of the Indians and partly to the fact that their nations were so loosely organized that no contracts with them were actually binding. The attempt to treat them as "nations," in the sense of the term as applied to the nations of Europe, was one of the greatest errors in the early American negotiations with the various tribes.

Spain was now beginning a long drawn out effort to withhold free navigation of the Mississippi River from the men of the western waters, who considered both free navigation of that vitally important stream and the right of deposit at its mouth as their inviolable right. This, and the constant danger of Indian hostilities gave both the North Carolina and the Virginia statesmen some rather bad moments, for they had long considered both the Tennessee and the Kentucky settlements as effective bumper states between them and any foe who might approach from the west. They also relied upon the fighting power of the frontiersmen.

Patrick Henry, when governor of Virginia, was greatly disturbed by Col. Arthur Campbell's activities which affected the territory of that state contiguous to the State of Franklin and even he, the great protagonist of liberty, grew timid at the spectacle of free men making free governments for themselves in defiance of the old, established order. He, too, feared the influence of the "dangerous example." In transmitting to the legislature of Virginia information concerning ". . . a memorial to Congress from sundry inhabitants of Washington County, praying the establishment of an independent state," he commented:

"The proposed limits include a vast extent of country, in which we have numerous and very respectable settlements, which, in their growth, will form an invaluable barrier between this country and those who, in the course of events, may occupy the vast places westward of the mountains, some of whom have views incompatible with our safety. Already, the militia of that part of the state is the most respectable we have, and by their means it is that the neighbouring Indians are awed into profession of friendship. But a circumstance has lately happened, which renders the possession of the territory at the present time indispensable to the peace of Virginia; I mean the assumption of sovereign power by the western inhabitants of North Carolina. If the people who, without consulting their own safety, or any other authority known in the American constitution, have assumed government, and while unallied to us, and under no engagements to pursue the objects of the federal government, shall be strengthened by the accession of so great a part of our country, consequences fatal to our repose will probably follow . . . information has come to me, stating that several persons, but especially Col. Arthur Campbell, have used

164

their utmost endeavours, and with some success, to persuade the citizens in that quarter to break off from this commonwealth, and attach themselves to the newly assumed government, or to erect one distinct from it. . . . If this most important part of our territory be lopped off, we lose that barrier for which our people have long and often fought; that nursery of soldiers, from which future armies may be levied, and through which it will be almost impossible for our enemies to penetrate. . . ." [19]

The grandiose plan for the Virginia free state included territory which embraced Kentucky, the state of Franklin, and parts of the present states of Georgia and Alabama—an area which might, based upon long-accepted usage, be claimed as the results of western military campaigns. This particular movement was short-lived and had little substantial support; but the free state idea in Kentucky was by no means abandoned. It merely took a more conservative turn.

Meanwhile, the state of Franklin flourished, in spite of considerable opposition from adherents of the old state. Lively and often bitter debates over the proposed constitution had been in progress for some months and, by the time the delegates to the second constitutional convention were elected, feeling in some quarters— particularly among the clergymen—ran high.

The Rev. Samuel Houston, who had been "keynoter" at the first constitutional convention, continued his labors and, at the opening of the second one, which convened at Greeneville on November 14, 1785, had a new constitution drafted and ready for consideration. It provided, in detailed theological terms, among other things, that none but believers in God and a future state of rewards and punishment should be allowed to vote. In fact, this document would have placed every portion of the government in the hands of only those whom its authors considered strictly orthodox churchmen.

When Houston presented the proposed constitution and was speaking in its behalf, the Reverend Hezekiah Balch, who was only a spectator, sought, and was given, recognition on the floor of the convention. He launched into a forceful defense of religious freedom and succeeded in crystalizing the already existing oppo-

165

sition to Houston's constitution with the result that it was rejected by the convention. The North Carolina constitution, which Sevier himself had had a hand in drafting, was then adopted.

The Houston element did not accept defeat quietly, and soon, by means of a pamphlet in which its constitution was printed, took the case to the people. They did not succeed in having their ideas incorporated in the new government, although they did create a long and violent public argument. Governor Sevier, who was noted for his skill in handling Indians on the warpath, was unable to quiet two quarreling clergymen.[20]

On November 19, 1785, after the second constitutional convention of the State of Franklin had convened, the General Assembly of North Carolina took notice of the recent events in her revolting western countries and held out an olive branch.

". . . the Assembly are ready to pass over, and consign to oblivion, the mistakes and misconduct of such persons in the above mentioned counties, as have withdrawn themselves from the government of this state; to hear and redress their grievances, if any they have, and to afford the protection and benefits of government, until such time as they may be in condition, from their numbers and wealth, to be formed into a separate commonwealth, and be received by the United States as a member of the Union." [21]

But the Franklinites, admitting neither mistakes nor misconduct, continued their course, ignoring the offer to consign their acts to "oblivion."

Early in 1786, attacks by the Cherokees on the exposed portion of the Franklin frontiers made it necessary for Governor Sevier to organize an expedition to quiet them. He, at the head of one hundred and sixty horsemen, left Houston's Station on Little River, crossed the Tennessee River at the Island Town, passed Tellico Plains, and crossed the Unaca Mountains to the Hiwassee River, where they destroyed three villages, called the Valley Towns. Spies and advance troops, following a wide trail, approached a body of possibly one thousand warriors led by John Watts, whose adroit and wily diplomacy had raised him to leadership in both the old villages and the Chickamauga Towns. Fearing

166

that his small body of horsemen would be trapped, Sevier led them quickly back to the settlements. The campaign was successful, however, in bringing at least temporary quiet to the frontiers.

The situation in the Cumberland settlements was becoming more acute all of the time. Writing to Governor Caswell, Col. Joseph Martin said:

"I left Chota the fourteenth of last month when two or three parties had gone out towards Cumberland and Kentucky . . . The 17th of last month (April) the parties of Indians returned with fifteen scalps, sent several letters to Gen. Sevier . . . they informed the general that they had now taken satisfaction for their friends that were murdered, that they did not wish for more war, but if the white people wanted war, it was what they would get." Martin further stated that there was a great preparation making by the Creeks, to carry on an expedition against the Cumberland—that they were about to erect a post at or near the Muscle Shoals—that several packhorses had already passed Chickamauga.—"They say," he continued, "that the French and Spaniards that are settled there are to furnish them with arms and ammunition—the Indians told me I might depend that the Creeks would endeavor to break up the Cumberland in this manner. . . ." [22]

Commenting on the new state of Franklin, Colonel Martin informed Governor Caswell that, in his opinion, two-thirds of the westerners were still for the old state and would probably send delegates to the next General Assembly. He also reported that the Franklinites had held an assembly lately and had appointed Cocke a member of Congress; had authorized Charles Robertson to establish a mint to produce their own coin; and had provided a coat of arms.

Apparently, Colonel Robertson's mint did not materialize, but if it did produce either gold or silver coins, none have yet been brought to light. While awaiting the establishment of the proposed mint, however, the Franklinites provided for a unique currency of their own. By act of their General Assembly, on October 15, 1785, they provided that salaries of their officers be paid as follows:

"His excellency, the governor, per annum, one thousand deer

skins; his honor, the chief justice, five hundred do.do.; the treasurer of the State, four hundred and fifty otter do.do.; secretary to his excellency the governor, five hundred raccoon do.do.; each county clerk, three hundred beaver do.; members of the assembly, three do.; justices for signing a warrant, one muskrat do.; to the constable for serving a warrant, one mink do. . . ."

During the summer of 1786 the state of Franklin negotiated its second treaty with the Cherokees, this time bringing both Hanging Maw and Old Tassel in to answer for the killing of two young white men and for other hostile acts. The treaty talks were blunt and to the point. They cited not only the killing of the two young men, but also the recent killings of Col. John Donelson and Colonel Christian, who, the Indians were reminded,

". . . were always your friends when you were brothers, and were great warriors and counsellors; and that you may not be any more deceived, we now tell you, plainly, that our great counsellors have sold us the lands on the northside of the Tennessee to the Cumberland Mountains, and we intend to settle it and live on it, and if you kill any of our people settling there, we shall destroy the town that does the mischief; and as your people broke the peace you made with Congress and us, and killed our men, it was your fault that we come out to war. *We have the right to all the ground we have marched over,* but if you wish to live as brothers, and be at peace, we will let you live in Coytoy, as brothers, in your old home, if you will agree to give up the murderers when you can get them. . . ."

Right or wrong, the white settlements continued to push westward. Along with claims based upon direct purchase of land was offered the ancient right of conquest, which was thoroughly understood and practised by the Indians. If both the Kentucky and Tennessee lands could have been laid out in separate states and taken into the Union at this time, it is possible that a consistent plan for the occupation of these western lands and for dealing with the Indians might have been worked out, thereby avoiding much bloodshed. But the federal government, in those last struggling days of the Confederation, was probably less able than the state of Franklin to handle such problems.

The new state continued to look forward hopefully to admission

Benjamin Franklin, for whom the State of Franklin was named, had little to offer it beyond the most casual and noncommital advice. Portrait from Bancroft's History of the United States, 1840 edition.

to the Union, but William Cocke, who was selected a second time as its would-be representative in Congress, did not attempt to attend the 1786 session. Instead, he wrote to Benjamin Franklin, who had returned to America from an extended stay in Europe, advising him of the creation of the new state which had been named for him.

". . . I make no doubt you have heard that the good people of this country have declared themselves a separate state from North Carolina, and that, as a testimony of the high esteem they have for the many important and faithful services you have rendered your country, they have called their State after you. . . ." [23]

Explaining that he had set forth to present himself to Congress, but had learned that it would soon adjourn, Cocke asked Franklin to inform him concerning the date of the next sessions, and, continuing, said:

". . . I will thank you to be so kind as to favor me with a few lines by the bearer, Mr. Rogers . . . and shall be happy to have your sentiments and advice on so important a subject. . . ."

Franklin replied promptly, stating that Congress would probably "sit out the year" and that if Cocke decided to make the journey, he would be glad to see him as he passed through Philadelphia. He stated that, having been so long in Europe, he knew little of the details of the controversy between North Carolina and the State of Franklin, but advised submitting the matter to Congress.

A year later, writing to Governor Sevier, Franklin advised that "there are two things which humanity induces me to wish you may succeed in; the accommodating of your misunderstanding with the government of North Carolina, and the avoiding of Indian war by preventing encroachments upon their land. . . ." These were both noble, humane desires, but showing a total lack of understanding of the true situation in the West.

Clearly, Benjamin Franklin had little to offer the State which had been named for him beyond the most casual and noncommittal advice, clearly tilted toward the interests of North Carolina.

Thomas Jefferson, on the other hand, had a clearer understanding and a deeper sympathy for, as he called them, "the ultra-montane" settlements. While he viewed the separation of the

Kentucky and the Tennessee country from the Union as a misfortune, he sanctioned their early statehood and separation from the mother states of Virginia and North Carolina.[24]

"Whenever the people of Kentucky shall have agreed among themselves," he wrote from Paris in September, 1785, "my friends write me word, Virginia will consent to their separation. They will constitute the new State on the south side of the Ohio, joining Virginia. North Carolina, by an act of their Assembly, ceded to Congress all their lands westward of the Allegheny. The people inhabiting that territory, thereon declared themselves independent, called their state by the name of Franklin, and solicited Congress to be received into the Union. But before Congress could act, North Carolina (for what reasons I could never learn) resumed the cession. The people, however, persist; Congress recommended to the State to desist from their opposition and I have no doubt they will do it. It will, therefore, result from the act of Congress laying off the western country into new States, that the States will come into the Union in the manner therein provided, and without any disputes as to their boundaries. . . ."

Another letter, written from Paris on January, 1786, gave Jefferson's broad and sympathetic view concerning western expansion.

". . . I fear from an expression in your letter," he wrote A. Stewart, "that the people of Kentucky think of separating, not only from Virginia (in which they are right) but also from the confederacy. I own I should think this a most calamitous event, and such a one as every good citizen should set himself against. Our present federal limits are not too large for good government, nor will the increase of votes in Congress produce any ill effect. On the contrary, it will drown the little divisions at present existing there. *Our confederacy must be viewed as the nest, from which all America, North and South, is to be peopled.* We should take care, too, not to think it for the interest of that great continent, to press too soon on the Spaniards. Those countries could not be in better hands. My fear is that they are too feeble to hold them till our population can be sufficiently advanced, to gain it from them, piece by piece. *The navigation of the Mississippi we must have.* This is all we are, as yet, ready to receive. . . ."

170

While North Carolina continued to withhold her western lands and factions in Congress, fearing the growing power of the west, refused to hear its plea for admission to the Union, the state of Franklin continued in complete independence. It was not what its leaders or its people wanted, but there was no alternative. Meek submission to North Carolina might delay statehood indefinitely.

It is to John Sevier's credit that he continued his efforts to bring about an orderly separation from North Carolina and early admission to the Union.

Writing to Governor Caswell on October 28, 1786, he said:

"Our Assembly have again appointed Commissioners to wait on the parent state, who, I hope, will cheerfully consent to the separation as they once before did . . . Our local and remote situation are the only motives that induce us to wish for a separation. Your constitution and laws we revere, and consider ourselves happy that we had it in our power to get the same established in the State of Franklin, although it has occasioned some conflict among ourselves. We do, in the most candid and solemn manner, assure you that we do not wish to separate from you on any terms, but on those that may be perfectly consistent with the honour and interest of each party; neither do we believe there is any among us who would wish for a separation, did they believe the parent state would suffer any real inconveniency in the consequence thereof. We would be willing to stand or fall together, under any dangerous crisis whatever. . . .

"However inconsiderable the people of this country may appear at this day, reason must inform us that the time is not far distant, when they will become as consequential in numbers, if not more so, than most of the Eastern States, and when your Excellency will be pleased to view the many advantages arising from the fertility of our soil, and the moderate salubrious climate, you cannot, I presume, differ in sentiments on this head. . . .

"As to my own part, I have always considered myself happy under the government of North Carolina, and highly honoured with the different appointments they have been pleased to confer. . . ."[25]

The commissioners to whom Sevier referred were David Campbell and William Cocke, but Campbell, because of ill health, was not able to serve in person. However, he addressed an eloquent appeal to Governor Caswell.

". . . If we set out wrong, or were too hasty in our separation," he said, "this country is not altogether to blame; your state pointed out the line of conduct, which we adopted; we really thought you in earnest when you ceded us to Congress. If you then thought we ought to be separate, or if you now think we ought to be, permit us to complete the work that is more than half done; suffer us to give energy to our laws and force to our councils, by saying we are a separate and independent people, and we will yet be happy. . . . Our leaders were induced to engage in the present revolution, but from pure necessity. We are getting into confusion, and you know any government is better than anarchy. . . ."

Cocke, however, went on to Fayetteville, where he presented his appeal in person, to the North Carolina General Assembly. His magnificent appearance—for he was a tall, handsome, well-proportioned man, with dark skin, black hair and flashing black eyes—captured the attention of his audience even before his masterful appeal was heard.

"Immediate and pressing necessity," he told the North Carolina House of Commons, "calls for the power to concentrate the scanty means you possess of saving yourselves from destruction." A cruel and insidious foe was at their doors. Delay was but another word for death. They might supinely wait for events, but the first of them would be the yell of the savage through all their settlements. . . . The hearts of the people of North Carolina should not be hardened against their brethren, who have stood by their sides in perilous times, and never heard their cry of distress when they did not instantly rise and march to their aid. . . . "When driven into the late war, by the presence of that enemy, from your homes, we gave many of you a sanctified asylum in the bosom of our country, and gladly performed the rites of hospitality to a people we loved so dearly. Every hand was ready to be raised for the least unhallowed violation of the sanctuary in which they reposed. . . ."

But neither Cocke's presence and eloquence, nor Sevier's and Campbell's masterful arguments to Governor Caswell, persuaded North Carolina from her stubborn course.

The state of the nation, at the beginning of the year 1787, like that of the Franklin people, was one of confusion; but out of it was born the federal constitution, which offered, among other benefits, a definite plan for the admission of new states. The plan, while admittedly disappointing to the West, did, however, give hope for the future. But the dissatisfaction was not confined to the West; the East was disturbed and doubtful about the formation of new states, and their admission, their rank and their representation in the national Congress, were the subjects of long and bitter debates.

The general tenor of the arguments concerned schemes which would perpetuate the power of the Atlantic states, and, at the same time, reduce the proposed new states to inferior rank and privileges. Some argued that the new states, having less experience in government, should have less power; others that, since their lands were worth less, they should have fewer representatives; that the formation of western states would deplete the population and wealth of the East; that the western country, thus built up by emigration, would usurp the power of the eastern states. The state of Franklin not only had no representatives to plead her cause, she had the adverse attitude of most of the North Carolina delegation to combat, both at home and in the councils of the nation.

George Washington, although he had openly expressed his agreement with Thomas Jefferson in regard to the western states, could not descend from his lofty position as presiding officer of the constitutional convention actively to espouse their cause. On this subject Washington Irving says:

"We forbear to go into the voluminous proceedings of this memorable convention, which occupied from four to seven hours each day for four months; and in which every point was the subject of able and scrupulous discussion by the best talent, and noblest spirits of the country. Washington felt restrained by his situation as president of the convention, from taking a part in the debates, but his well-known opinions influenced the whole. The result was the formation of the constitution of the United States, which (with some amendments made in after years) still exists." [26]

Judge Williams, who made an able and a detailed study of the

173

debates of the constitutional convention, sums up their effect on the development of the West, as follows:

". . . The result sealed the fate of the state of Franklin, in that it placed her recognition and admission securely at the option of North Carolina. It remains only to be observed that in this convention of patriots no voice was raised to urge an equitable right to self-determination on the part of the western people, since they by their bravery and fortitude had conquered the western wilderness and given it value in the esteem of the claimant States; and more, had turned to aid in prizing the foot of the British invader from the seaboard soil, which the invader was determined to claim on the basis of *uti possidetis.*"

Within the state of Franklin, the year of 1787 was characterized by dual governments, personal conflicts, and lively arguments, from every stump or public speaking place between the adherents of the "Old State" and the Franklinites. On June 27 of that year, John Sevier met with representatives of the "Old State" group and attempted to bring about a truce, but his efforts were of no avail. Early in July, it was announced that elections would be held in August to choose members of the North Carolina General Assembly, with the result that the opposing parties tore into each other with renewed vigor. The Franklinites met this effort to assert North Carolina's authority by a unique strategy. They put up their own candidates to oppose the "old state" men in their elections!

The Franklin candidates had little trouble in defeating the "Old State" men in their southern counties, Blount, Sevier and Caswell, but in Spencer (Hawkins, under North Carolina,) where Stockley Donelson, a Franklinite, opposed Thomas Amis, the situation was tense. The North Carolina sheriff announced, when he opened the polling place, that only those who had paid taxes to the old state could vote; but, after the appearance of a number of men, some of whom were said to be from Greene County, the sheriff, fearing a riot, closed the polls until the next day. The threat of violence continued, however, so the polls never reopened and Donelson was declared elected. The North Carolina sheriff gave him a certificate of election, but the North Carolina Assembly refused to recognize it and declared the election null and void.

majority of the western people, whose idol he was and continued to be down through the years.

After this unfortunate incident, Sevier and his men returned to the settlements, but there was no rest on the frontiers. Communications from Georgia advised of dangers of another Creek invasion and sought his aid in a joint expedition against them. However, Gen. Joseph Martin, reluctantly putting aside his title as Indian agent, took over and, assuming his military duties, conducted a rather unsuccessful campaign against the Chickamaugas.

James Robertson, in the beleagured Cumberland settlements, despairing of help from North Carolina, appealed desperately to the Kentuckians and to Sevier for aid. Since neither was in position to help him, Robertson himself raised one hundred and thirty men and set out with them to follow the trail of a party which had lately invaded the Cumberland and had killed, among others, his own brother, Mark Robertson. Pursuing them to the town of Coldwater, near the lower Muscle Shoals, they attacked and killed about twenty—among them a Creek chief, a Cherokee chief, three Frenchmen, and a French woman, killed by accident in one of the boats. Nine Frenchmen, Robertson reported to Governor Caswell on July 2, 1787, chiefly from Detroit, had joined the Indians against them.

"This spirited invasion of the heart of the Indian country," Ramsey states, "and the success that attended the assault against Coldwater, were followed by a short respite from savage aggression. Heretofore, there had not been an hour of safety to any settlers on the waters of the Cumberland, and offensive measures were adopted and energetically executed. The vengeance so long delayed, had, at length, fallen with the most fatal effect upon those who most frequently provoked it. At Coldwater, Colonel Robertson discovered the sources from which the Indians were supplied with materials which enabled them to make inroads upon the Cumberland settlements; the means by which, and the channels through which, they received them; and the practicable modes of cutting them off. . . ." [29]

The settlers on the Cumberland had not, of course, affiliated with the state of Franklin, but had continued their allegiance to

179

North Carolina. The Cumberland settlements, however, received very little aid or comfort from that distant commonwealth, as they struggled for existence.

Richard Caswell, meanwhile, had been succeeded as governor of North Carolina by Samuel Johnston, under whom the last unhappy chapter of the mother state's persecution of John Sevier was written. On July 29, 1788, Johnston, from Hillsborough, wrote the following instructions to Judge Campbell:

"Sir:—It has been represented to the Executive, that John Sevier who styles himself as Captain-General of the State of Franklin, has been guilty of high treason, in levying troops to oppose the laws and government of this state, and has with an armed force put to death several good citizens. If these facts shall appear to you by the affidavit of credible persons, you will issue your warrant to apprehend the said John Sevier, and in case he cannot be sufficiently secure for trial in the District of Washington, order him to be committed to the public gaol." [30]

Campbell did not obey the order, however, and the warrant was finally issued by Judge Spencer, a prominent judge of North Carolina. Meanwhile, tension mounted and tempers flared, but the arrest of John Sevier was delayed. Sevier made no effort to evade the order, but appeared about his business in Jonesboro as usual until, having decided to leave town, he was pursued by John Tipton and a small body of eight or ten men. He had taken a night's lodging at the home of a Mrs. Brown, and it was here, after searching several other places, that Tipton sought to take him into custody.

At dawn, Tipton and his party rushed forward to the entrance door of the house. Mrs. Brown, who had already risen, saw them and, knowing Tipton's disposition, was determined that he should not enter and take Sevier. She simply sat down in her front doorway and refused to move. This, Ramsey recounts, "caused a considerable bustle between her and Colonel Tipton."

While this was going on, Sevier, who had been sleeping in a room near the end of the house, rose, looked out and, seeing his friend Colonel Love, who had been lodging nearby, went to the door and put out his hand to Love and said: "I surrender to you."

Tipton, pistol in hand and in a towering rage, threatened to

180

shoot Sevier, and Sevier, knowing well the temper of the man, was not at all sure he would not carry out his threat. Tipton was eventually satisfied, however, to put handcuffs on Sevier and take him into custody like a common criminal.

Colonel Love accompanied Sevier and the party back to Jonesboro and, when the prisoner asked him to try to arrange to have his trial held in Jonesboro instead of over the mountain in North Carolina, Love advised him to go on to Morgantown. His reason was that, should Sevier be imprisoned under heavy guard in Jonesboro, his friends, determined to rescue him, might be involved in heavy bloodshed. He also advised Sevier to influence his friends to be calm and take peaceable measures to accomplish his escape.

Sevier, yielding to his advice, asked Love to send word to his wife, telling her to prepare a few necessities for him to carry with him, and was sent under guard by Tipton's order, to Morgantown.

There are many versions of the dramatic events which followed. Some are taken from the writings of eye-witnesses, and others were handed down by word of mouth until the stories themselves have become legends. One version of Sevier's rescue is given in the manuscript of William Smith which is quoted by Ramsey as follows:

"They had suffered with him; they had fought with him; with them he had shared the dangers and privations of frontier life, and a savage warfare; and they were not the spirits to remain inactive when their friend was in danger. The chivalry of the country gathered together; a number of men were selected to fly to the rescue; armed to the teeth, those dauntless sons of the woods crossed the mountains, determined to rescue their beloved commander, or leave their bones to bleach upon the sand-hills of North Carolina. . . . Their plan was to obtain his release by stratagem, and if that failed, to fire the town, and in the hurry and confusion, burst the prison doors by force, and make their escape. . . ."

Smith's version continues, stating that the rescue party, bringing with it Sevier's celebrated race mare, saddled and ready to ride, entered Morgantown quietly, one by one, and sauntered calmly into the court room, where they found Sevier "arraigned at the bar, as firm and undaunted as when charging the hosts of Wyuca at Lookout Mountain."

181

Meanwhile, a member of the party, named Evans, had brought the racehorse to a place which could be seen from the courtroom door, and, catching Sevier's eye, let him know that his rescuers had come and were ready to ride. Sevier, so the story goes, immediately dashed from the room, jumped into the saddle and, with his party, made a mad dash for the mountains—and home.[31]

There are other more prosaic and, perhaps, more accurate accounts of this exciting incident; but even the most cautious and blasè historian can not discount the simple fact that the over-the-mountain men rescued their beloved "Nolichucky Jack" from the hands of an enemy determined to destroy him.

"The capture and brief expatriation of Sevier," Ramsey concludes, "served only to awaken in his behalf a higher appreciation of his services, and a deeper conviction of his claims to the esteem and consideration of his countrymen. His return was everywhere greeted with enthusiasm and joy."

For the time being, however, Sevier was still outlawed in North Carolina, although its General Assembly had extended an act of pardon and oblivions "to such of those who had taken part in the Franklin revolt" except "that the benefit of this act should not entitle John Sevier to the enjoyment of any office of profit, of honour or trust, in the State of North Carolina, but that he be expressly debarred therefrom. . . ."

The people of Greene County soon elected Sevier to represent them as senator in the North Carolina General Assembly and, on November 2, 1789, he presented himself at Fayetteville to assume this office. After a few days, he was sworn in and seated, in spite of the fact that the act by which he was disqualified had not yet been repealed. He was also elected as a member of the convention chosen to reconsider the ratification of the Federal Constitution, which North Carolina had failed to approve the previous year. Also up for consideration before the General Assembly at this time was the question of recession of her western lands. It was John Sevier's privilege, although still disbarred by law, to vote in the affirmative on both of these questions, thus giving him an active part in establishing a stable national government and bringing his western country into it.

Soon, he was to have another honor. North Carolina, in order to provide for its representation in the Congress of the United States, apportioned itself into four districts—the westernmost of which included all of its territory beyond the mountains. This district promptly elected Sevier as its member of Congress and, by so doing, conferred upon him the signal honor of being the first member of that body from the Mississippi valley.

Congress formally accepted the cession of North Carolina's western lands and formed them into a territory to which it gave the rather cumbersome official title: "The Territory of the United States of America, South of the River Ohio." For the sake of brevity, it was often called the Southwest Territory.

John Sevier's vindication was complete when President Washington appointed him as brigadier-general of the territorial forces, thus making it clear that he and his friends were the acknowledged leaders of the new Territory. John Tipton and his adherents also received honorable recognition, but it was obvious that the Sevierites were in the ascendancy.

"It is singular," says Ramsey in his final tribute to the men of the state of Franklin," and well worthy of remark, that not one of the master-spirits of Franklin, perhaps not one of its officers, in a long life of usefulness or distinction afterwards, ever forfeited the esteem, or lost the confidence, of his countrymen. They became the officers under the Territorial Government, and, soon after, the leading spirits of the proud State of Tennessee; a beautiful comment on the purity of their principles, and the loftiness of their patriotism—a fit tribute of respect for their public services and their private virtue."

William Blount, first governor of the Southwest Territory. Prior positions held were as member of the old Congress and the Constitutional Convention of the United States in 1787, and member of the Constitutional Convention of North Carolina. Photo courtesy of State of Tennessee Tourism Development Division.

CHAPTER V

The Southwest Territory

The long-delayed cession of her western lands by North Carolina and the establishment of the new territory brought some degree of stability to the West, although it did not, unfortunately, bring peace with the hostile Indians. It would be a decade and a half before the last major Indian engagement was fought within the limits of the present State of Tennessee and more than a quarter of a century before the rich territory which is now known as West Tennessee was acquired by treaty.

Meanwhile, the westerners went about the business of forming a permanent government with one hand and defending themselves against the Indians with the other. Probably realizing the difficulties of building a new government and, at the same time, handling the Indian problems, President Washington, in his selection of a governor for the new territory, chose William Blount of North Carolina, who was skilled in both areas, to be superintendent of Indian affairs, as well as governor. In addition, Blount had an attractive personality, a gift for handling people tactfully, and was personally popular in the west.

Theodore Roosevelt, in his *Winning of the West*, says of him:

"Blount was the first man of leadership in the West who was of Cavalier ancestry; for though so much is said of the Cavalier type in the southern states it was insignificant in numbers, and comparatively few of the southern men of mark have belonged to it. Blount was really of Cavalier blood. He was descended from a Royalist baronet, who was roughly handled by the Cromwellians, and whose three sons came to America. One of them settled in North Carolina, near Albemarle Sound, and from him came the new governor of the southwestern territory. Blount was a good-looking man, with cultivated tastes; but he was also a man of force and energy, who knew well how to get on well with the backwoodsmen. . . ."

185

Among the important positions held by Governor Blount before he came to the new territory were: service in the military with the rank of colonel; member of the old Congress and the Constitutional Convention of the United States in 1787; member of the state Constitutional Convention of North Carolina; and, both prior to the Revolutionary War and following it, an important member of legislative bodies of North Carolina. When Tennessee's Constitutional Convention was held, he served as its president and was responsible for a number of important passages which were framed in it—notably that regarding free navigation of the Mississippi River.

Governor Blount's commission as territorial governor was signed by President Washington on June 8, 1790. It read, in part:

"To all who shall see these Presents—Greeting.

"Know ye, that reposing special Trust and Confidence in the Patriotism, Integrity, and Abilities of William Blount, Esquire, a citizen of North Carolina, I have nominated, and with the Advice and Consent of the Senate, do appoint him Governor in and over the Territory of the United States South of the River Ohio, and do authorize and empower him to execute and fulfill the Duties of that Office according to Law. . . ." [1]

Justice James Iredell, of the U.S. Supreme Court, administered the oath of office to Governor Blount at Alexandria, Virginia, on September 20, 1790.[2]

Blount had been formally notified of his appointment by Thomas Jefferson, Secretary of State, on August 1, 1790, to which he replied:

"Washington (N.C.), August 20th, 1790.

"Sir, on the 18th instant I had the Honor to receive your letter of the 1st with the Inclosures. On the 24th I leave this for the ceded Territory of the United States South of the River Ohio from whence I will embrace the first Opportunity of Writing you after I have fixed my residence which I now suppose will not be far distant from Judge Campbell's.—I am very happy to hear that friendly arrangements are like to take place with Colonel McGillivray and the Creek chiefs, there will then be little or Nothing to apprehend from the other Tribes to the Southward. Would it not be best to direct letters for me to the Care of the Governor of Virginia, he will have frequent Opportunities to forward them—I thank you for your Promise of a Copy of the Laws of the United States and shall be glad to receive it as early as conveniently may be. I have the Honor to be with great Respect—

"Your most Obedient Humble Servant

"Wm. Blount."

Blount arrived in the "ceded Territory" on October 10 and, from "Mr. Yancey's", on the following day wrote to Daniel Smith, who had been appointed secretary of the Territory:

"I arrived here yesterday, My servant was sick on the Road or I should have been here five days sooner.—I find it necessary to fill all Commissions for the civil officers on this Side of Cumberland Mountain before I come over to your part of the state, this I shall do as soon as I can and then come on.—I shall much need your assistance but shall do the best I can without you taking it for granted that you will have no Objection to authenticating my executive Acts upon my record of them. When I shall be over I can form no positive Opinion but it shall certainly be as soon as Business here to be done will permit. . . ." [3]

On the same day he wrote a similar letter to James Robertson, assuring him that he would come on to Nashville as fast as possible and fill all appointments for the counties of Davidson, Sumner and Tennessee. Concluding, he requested that if Major Farragut (father of Adm. David G. Farragut) was in Nashville to ask him to wait there to see him.

By February, 1791, Governor Blount had established a temporary seat of government at the home of William Cobb, near Jonesboro. Cobb was one of the early settlers of Watauga and was not only a man of considerable property, but also a highly respected, leading citizen of the area. His home still stands and is one of Tennessee's greatly esteemed shrines. The headquarters of the territorial government remained here until early 1793, when Governor Blount founded the city of Knoxville, made it the permanent capital of the territory, and built his home there.

Much of the important business of the territory was transacted, however, while the Cobb home was his official residence. Here he began to familiarize himself with matters of local interest, to make appointments, and to organize counties. His first official act, after taking the oath of office, September 20, 1790, was the laying off and organization of Washington County, which took place on October 22, 1790. The organization of Sullivan, Greene, Hawkins, Davidson, Sumner and Tennessee counties followed in rapid succession. Military organizations and courts were established in each county, and the machinery of government, in Blount's experienced hands, was soon operating smoothly.

A list of his early appointments to various offices is especially interesting for the well-known names it contains. Among the men he selected were many young men—like Andrew Jackson—who were destined to serve not only the territory, but the future state of Tennessee and the nation in important capacities.

Among these early appointments to office were: James Winchester, Landon Carter, James Allison, David Allison, John Rhea, Charles Robertson, James Robertson, Edward Tate, James White, Stockley Donelson, Joseph McMinn, F. A. Ramsey, John Rains, Andrew Ewing, Isaac Bledsoe, Kasper Mansker, Ezekiel Polk (grandfather of President James K. Polk). Luke Lea, Charles McClung, Howell Tatum and many others.

As his secretaries, Governor Blount chose Hugh Lawson White, Richard Mitchel and Willie (pronounced Wiley) Blount, his half-brother. Francis Alexander Ramsey (father of the historian Ramsey) was made clerk of the Supreme Court for the District of Washington, and the clerk and master in equity for the same district was Andrew Russell. Thomas King, lieutenant-colonel; George Farragut, second major; and Francis Ramsey, first major, were chosen as officers in the Washington District Cavalry.

The courts existing in the Mero (now Middle Tennessee) and Washington judicial districts prior to the creation of the Territory were continued and lower courts were organized for each of the counties. The higher court was called "The Superior Court of Law and Equity," and the lower courts the "Inferior Court of pleas and Quarter Sessions."

Andrew Jackson was named Attorney General for Mero Dis-

188

trict. David Allison was made clerk and James Sitgreaves, clerk and master in equity.

Appointed to practice in the several courts of law and equity in the territory were: Archibald Roane, Joseph Hamilton, Waightstill Avery, James Rees, John Rhea, Josiah Love, John Overton, Andrew Jackson, David Allison, Howell Tatum, James Cole Mountflorence and James White.

Andrew Jackson received his first military appointment when, on September 10, 1792, he was made judge advocate for the Davidson County regiment.

By the early part of 1791 several major offices had been filled by presidential appointment, among the most imortant appointments being David Campbell, Joseph Anderson, and John McNairy as judges, and Daniel Smith as territorial secretary.

The new territory, with its rich promise of becoming an important asset to the entire nation, was considered with great interest in the East and was the subject of much correspondence concerning its value and its possibilities. Benjamin Hawkins, at that time United States senator from North Carolina, writing from New York, on June 10, 1790, to the new territorial secretary, Daniel Smith, offered some sound advice:

"Let me advise you to impress as early as possible on your citizens the necessity of attending to their home manufactures, your relative situation with the commercial part of the United States is such that this is indispensable to your prosperity. You can raise fruit trees of all sorts, grapes of all sorts for wine, salt, Iron, clothing of cotton, flax, wool and silk. You can never have much money but you have facility in acquiring the necessaries and comforts of life from the richness of your soil and mildness of your climate unknown to any other country in my recollection. Recommend therefore by your own example the raising of nurseries of fruit trees and having them planted throughout your whole country. I have often lamented the unaccountable inattention of our people to the raising of the comforts of life. One hour devoted only weekly to the planting of vines, trees and garden stuff is quite sufficient to start any plantation with an abundance of these things." [4]

Hawkins, in 1796, became Indian agent for all of the tribes

189

south of the Ohio River. For many years he had an important part in the relation of the western people to the federal government in regard to Indian affairs.

Governor Blount and other territorial leaders agreed that the development of agriculture and manufacturing should be prime objectives of the territorial government, but they realized also that, while laboring to bring this about, they must take steps to establish a satisfactory relationship with the friendly Indian tribes and to quiet the hostile ones. One of Governor Blount's first steps, therefore, was to arrange for holding a treaty with the Cherokee Indians. The place he chose for this important event was a gently sloping hillside overlooking the Tennessee River and the beautiful countryside beyond it. This spot lies, roughly, between the present Knox County Courthouse and the well-preserved home built by Governor Blount only a few blocks beyond it.

Here he prepared to entertain and negotiate with the ruling chiefs of the Cherokee nation. He was well versed in official protocol—both colonial and Indian. Knowing the love of the Indians for colorful ceremonies, he made elaborate preparations which, he hoped, would impress them with the dignity and the power of the young American Republic with which they were now to deal. It was, undoubtedly, a wise gesture, for there were among the Indians a few who still remembered stories of the splendor of the British court, brought back by Attakullakulla and his companions who accompanied Sir Alexander Cummings to England in 1730, where they placed the crown of Great Tenassee at the feet of His Britannic Majesty.

It was in this dramatic and picturesque setting in the heart of the wilderness that in 1791, the Treaty of the Holston was negotiated. Governor Blount, recognizing the Indian love of splendor and formality, appeared in full dress uniform, complete with sword, gold lace, and much gold braid. He chose as master of ceremonies, Trooper James Armstrong, who was well acquainted with the Indians. Each of the forty-one chiefs who participated in the treaty was presented, by his aboriginal name, to Armstrong by an interpreter who was attired in Indian dress. Armstrong, in turn, presented each of the chiefs to Governor Blount, who had placed himself in an imposing seat of honor. Among them were Squollecuttah, Auquotague, Ninetooyah, Chuquelatague, and others with equally complicated names.

The late Judge Heiskell, in his vivid description of the treaty, said:

"Trooper Armstrong had seen service in Europe and was familiar with foreign manners, and seems to have acquainted himself on this occasion to the satisfaction of both the Governor and the Indians; but posterity will never cease to wonder just how he pronounced . . . those Indian names."

Governor Blount was pleased, not only with the success of the treaty negotiations, but with the delightful site upon which it took place. It was here, he decided, that he would make his home and official residence.

Writing to John Steele on July 22, 1791, he said:

"I have determined to make the Place where the Treaty was held the place of my future Residence and shall honor it with the name of Knox-Ville. It is on the North Bank of the Holston about four Miles below the Mouth of French Broad, in lat. 35.42 distance from Chota about forty Miles. . . ." [5]

Blount's choice of name for the territorial capital, which also became the name of Knox County, was a gesture of respect to Henry Knox, secretary of war. It was, perhaps intentionally, designed to enlist the aid of the War Department in the defense of the western frontiers. For several months after selecting the permanent seat of the territorial government, Governor Blount continued to conduct territorial affairs from the home of William Cobb. By the latter part of 1792 and early 1793, however, he had built a two-story frame house—the first west of the Alleghenies—had furnished it and had brought his family west to make their home. Here he and his gracious wife, Mary Grainger Blount, presided, entertaining with an easily flexible formality distinguished visitors, pioneer citizens and Indians.

The influence of Governor Blount and his family on the social, cultural, and educational life of the territory was important, but they made no effort to impose artificial standards upon the society of the West.

"The older citizens still refer to the last years of the Territorial Government as furnishing models of refinement and etiquette, of gentility and polish, seldom seen in a new community. . . ." Ramsey states. "The court of Governor Blount was thronged by strangers and gentlemen, visiting the seat of government from all parts of the Union on business, or for curiosity and pleasure. Levees and entertainments became frequent and crowded. . . ." [6]

John Sevier and other western leaders were frequent guests. He often jotted down in his diary, ". . . dined at the governor's house," or, ". . . drank tea with Mrs. Blount. . . ."

An important member of the household was the daughter, Barbara Gray Blount, whose beauty and wit were famous. She, with three or four other young ladies, attended Blount College, established by the Territorial Legislature in 1794 and evolving, eventually, into the present University of Tennessee. It is claimed, so far without satisfactorily documented contradiction, that she was the first woman in the United States to receive a degree from an institution of higher learning and that she and her friends were the first "co-eds." It is certain that in those days higher education for women was still in its infancy and that coeducational institutions were unheard of. The hill upon which the main buildings of the University of Tennessee now stand was called Barbara Hill in her honor and, many years later, one of the girls' dormitories was named Barbara Blount Hall. She was married to General Edmund P. Gaines and, after gracing social, military and political circles in the far south for several years, died and was buried in Mobile, Alabama.

Cultivated speech and civilized dress were not necessary for entrèe to the governor's mansion, however, for even the most unmannered Indians who ate at its lavish table were treated with the kindness and courtesy accorded distinguished guests.

Among the most remarkable visitors at the Blount mansion were the Indian chief, Unacata, who was later wounded in the 1792 attack on Buchanan's Station, near Nashville, and his wife, who were guests of the Blounts for a ten-day period, only a short time before this battle.

Governor Blount, in a letter to the Secretary of War, reported on this visit of the deceitful Unacata:

"This Unacata mentioned above, among the wounded (at Buchanan's Station) left Pensacola the day Watts arrived there, and making very little halt at his own house, came with his wife to this place, and stayed with me ten days immediately preceding the time he set out with Watts for war, and made the strongest professions of friendship during his stay and at his departure. . . ."[7]

Social duties and the gentler, more cultivated aspects of life, composed, however, only a small part of Governor Blount's services to the new territory. There was unceasing friction between the white men and the Indians—men, women and children were constantly being killed within the settlements, as well as along the more exposed frontiers, and thousands of dollars worth of property in horses, cattle, and household goods were lost each year to thieving red men. The federal government counseled moderation and patience. But the frontiersmen demanded action and the swift, unrelenting retaliatory measures which John Sevier had found to be the only language which the red warriors could understand. The Indians, meanwhile, continued to wage war against the settlements, with complete disregard of the consequences. The frontiersmen, restricted by the government to an inadequate defensive warfare, were no longer allowed to go out to meet their enemy and fight him on his own lands—so the frontiers continued to be drenched in the blood of helpless women and children, and the dim paths of the forests bore the footprints of captives being dragged into the Indian towns.

As much as this policy was detested, such men as Sevier and Robertson attempted to sustain Governor Blount in carrying it out—but all of them kept watchful eyes upon the frontiers and, in cases of extreme danger, took the course they deemed necessary and explained to the government later.

Throughout the greater portion of the territorial period William Blount was under a constant fire of criticism from the secretary of war with regard to the protection of the western frontiers. He was also caught between the determination of the westerners to have free navigation of the Mississippi River and free deposit at its mouth and that of certain elements of the federal government to surrender that right to Spain. Here were the seeds of the so-called conspiracy which led later to his expulsion from the United States Senate and the attempt to impeach him.

Blount's sympathies, however, were with the settlers, but he and they well knew that the only real solution to their problems was early statehood, which would give them a permanent form of self-government and would strengthen them by encouraging emigration. So, as far as was possible without sacrificing the interest of the West, Blount and other western leaders used tact and moderation. There were many times when neither were possible and then William Blount did not hesitate to place himself staunchly behind the westerners. His correspondence with various branches of the federal government is filled with strong statements written in defense of the West.

One of the most interesting of these documents is a letter written in Knoxville, January 14, 1793, which appears in Volume one of American State Papers, Indian Affairs. It not only explained the situation on the frontiers, but also gave important information on both the Cumberland (or Mero) and the Holston settlements.

"I am called upon to assign reasons for ordering and continuing in service the militia command by Brigadier-General Sevier," he wrote. "The time when ordered into service, and when discharged, I have already informed you; their greatest number, as appears by General Sevier's monthly report, was eight hundred and thirty. My reasons for ordering them into service were that I had received authentic information . . . that the five lower Cherokee towns had declared war against the United States; that they would be joined by a large number of Creeks, and that, with their united force, they would immediately attack the frontiers of this territory, and that both were supported by the Spaniards.

"My reasons for continuing them in service, were to give protection to the people of this territory, which had been confided to me in their persons and property, against a numerous body of Indians, who had declared war against them, not only in words, in a more formal manner than Indians ever did, to my knowledge, before, but by a powerful invasion of a part of the territory, by at least seven hundred warriors, headed by the bold and enterprising John Watts, and by many other acts of hostility. Let it be supposed I had discharged the militia, and the party who had declared war, and from whom I had no right to expect anything but war, had fallen on the unprotected citizens, should I not have deserved, and received, the heaviest censure of the Federal Government, and the execrations of the people?

"It will, no doubt, be observed, that General Sevier's brigade of militia is not equal to a regular regiment in numbers, consequently, that there must have been an over-production of officers. In reply to this I have to inform you, that the militia were called out under the militia law of North Carolina, and I conceived it essential to form them into a brigade, otherwise I could not have had the services of *General Sevier, whose name carries more terror to the Cherokees, than an additional regiment could have done."*

In the same communication, Governor Blount gave a vivid description of conditions in the Cumberland settlements: —

"The settlements of Mero district extend up and down the Cumberland river, from east to west, about eighty-five miles, and the extreme width, from north to south, does not exceed twenty-five miles, and its general width does not exceed half that distance, and, not only the country surrounding the extreme frontier, but the interior part . . . is covered generally with thick and high cane, and a heavy growth of large timber, and where there happens to be no cane, with thick underwood, which afford the Indians an opportunity of laying days and weeks in any and every part of the district, in wait near the houses, and of doing injuries to the inhabitants, when they themselves are so hid or secured, that they have no apprehensions of injuries being done in return, and they escape from pursuit, even though it be immediate. This district has an extreme frontier of at least two hundred miles.

"The protection of that district, the most difficult to protect in the Union, of its size, as well as every other part of the territory south of the Ohio, was confided in me by the President. This placed me between the Government and the people of the territory, answerable to the Government that I did not incur too great an expense in giving protection to the frontier inhabitants, nor yet

195

suffer them to be killed or robbed of their property; and to the people themselves, who looked to me, from the nature of my appointment, that I should not suffer them to be murdered and robbed. . . . Besides the example of the protection given to other frontiers by the Federal Government, and a knowledge of the sufferings of the people of Mero district, was the clamor of the people against the Government for not giving protection, which alone appeared to render the degree of protection I gave this district indispensable. I can truly say, all faith appeared to be lost in Government until Sharp's battalion was ordered into service. . . ."

Conditions in Mero District kept going from bad to worse, however, and Congress, failing to authorize a punitive expedition against the hostile Chickamauga towns, not only left the people at the mercy of almost daily marauding parties, but also in danger of an immediate large-scale invasion. Governor Blount was in a difficult situation.

"With respect to the lower towns," he wrote to the secretary of war, "however vigorous such a measure might be, or whatever good consequences might result from it, I am instructed, specially, by the President, to say, that he does not conceive himself authorized to direct such a measure, more especially, as the whole subject was before the last session of Congress, who did not think proper to authorize or direct offensive operations. . . ." [8]

Fortunately for Mero District, James Robertson, its brigadier-general, did not sit and wait for Congress to take action. His long experience with the Indians made him realize the gravity of the situation, for he had received reliable information that a large party of Creeks and Cherokees had organized in the lower towns for the purpose of invading Mero District. He assembled openly, for the defense of the frontiers, a body which finally reached a total of some five hundred and fifty men. It was composed of about seventy men detached from the United States troops of Hamilton District, and dispatched under the command of Major James Ore, for the protection of Mero District; the Mero District militia, ordered out by General Robertson; and a body of Kentucky militia under the command of Col. William Whitley.

Both the Tennessee and Kentucky troops were eager to reach

Blockhouse at Knoxville, Tennessee, from the painting by Lloyd Branson.

the Chickamauga towns, for many of them had relatives who had been killed or carried into captivity by these warriors. They were also convinced that their frontiers could never be made safe until these towns were subdued. Major Ore, who entered wholeheartedly into the plans, was placed in command, and was openly ordered by General Robertson to destroy the towns.

The troops held their rendezvous at Brown's blockhouse on September 6, 1794, and began their march on Sunday, September 7. Their particular destination was the town of Nickajack and the famous Tallassee, or Nickajack, Cave where the Creek, Cherokees and a mixed banditti of Spaniards and renegades of the wilderness had their retreat.

One of the leaders of this expedition was Joseph Brown, who, as a boy, had been held captive in these towns. His father and brothers had been brutally murdered there and his mother and sisters had been captives for a long while. In returning to destroy the towns, he fulfilled the prophecy of an old squaw who declared, when his captors spared his life, that he was old enough to remember the murders of his father and brothers and that some day he would return with an army and "cut them all off."

When the towns of Nickajack and Running Water were taken on September 12, 1794, Brown was recognized by some of the Indian women who, remembering the old squaw's prophecy, thought he had returned to kill them in revenge for the sufferings of his family.

Andrew Jackson served as a private under Major Ore on this expedition, and so gained valuable experience for the future battles which were to be fought under his command, although certain historians have maintained that he did not participate in it. The historians Putnam and Parton take the position that he did not, while Ramsey, basing his statement on the correspondence of Willie Blount, gives competent proof that he did. A Blount letter to Jackson, dated January 4, 1830, acquired some twenty or more years ago by the Tennessee State Library gives additional proof of his participation. In this letter the former governor of Tennessee spoke of:

"The pleasurable feelings I experience in the knowledge I

197

possess of the motives and conduct in the various promotions of my friend yourself and the result of your efforts since the battle of Nickajack, commanded by Orr: where, as Sampson Williams says, our friend, the Mountain Leader, the friend of man, was at that never to be forgotten good day's work, in which you lent an active useful hand, that gave peace to our frontier, never to be forgotten by me." [9]

Among others of this expedition who were destined for future fame were William Pillow, later a colonel under General Jackson at Talladega, and John Gordon, of the famous "Gordon's Spies," who served Jackson faithfully during the Creek War, 1813-14.

This expedition was the last major engagement against the Indians within the boundaries of the present state of Tennessee. James Robertson, gratified by its success, willingly shouldered the blame for violating the orders of the federal government. He had not the brilliance and dashing bravery of John Sevier; nor the cultured diplomacy of William Blount; but he was not inferior to either of them. His strong hands, his deep, unfailing wisdom, and his quiet courage, had an important part in building all three grand divisions of the future state of Tennessee. He, more than any other, truly deserves the title, "Father of Tennessee."

While this struggle for survival was going on and the frontiersmen, largely by their own efforts, had quieted the hostile Indians, they also, through Governor Blount and their members of the Territorial Legislative Council, had gone about the business of state-making.

On November 28, 1795, Governor Blount was able to issue a proclamation providing for taking the initial step toward admission to the Union.

"Whereas," he announced, "upon taking the enumeration of the inhabitants of the said territory, as by the act directed, it does appear that there are sixty thousand free inhabitants therein, and more, besides other persons; now I, William Blount, Governor &c., do recommend to the people of the respective counties to elect five persons for each county, on the 18th and 19th of December

198

next, to represent them in a convention to meet in Knoxville, on the 11th day of January next, for the purpose of framing a constitution or permanent form of government. . . ." [10]

Twenty-seven days after the convention opened on February 6, 1796, the first constitution of Tennessee was completed, engrossed and placed, for safe keeping, in the hands of Governor Blount, to be held by him until the proper state officials could be elected. Governor Blount, who had been elected president of the Constitutional Convention, was instructed to have a copy made for transmission to the secretary of state, by "express," at the earliest possible moment. He was further authorized to call an election of state officers and members of Congress—which he did promptly under the date of February 6, without awaiting the sanction of the federal government. This circumstance soon caused friction between the federal officials and the impatient citizens of the newest commonwealth, with the result that the state election held on March 28, 1796, was later repudiated by the federal government.

These early Tennesseans were no novices at government, nor were the leaders of their first constitutional convention inexperienced in the making of basic laws. Governor Blount, who served as president of the convention, had been a member of the convention which drafted the Constitution of the United States. He was also a member of the Constitutional Convention of North Carolina, had served often as a member of North Carolina legislative bodies and, in many other ways, was skilled in the making of laws. William Cocke was an eloquent orator, was possessed of a brilliant legal mind and was destined for an important career in the new state. Andrew Jackson, then twenty-nine years old, was on the threshold of his career. James Robertson, who at times served as presiding officer, was near the meridian of his long, useful life, and had, long since, established the fact that not only in Indian negotiations and the founding of settlements, but also in legislative halls, his sagacity and experience far outweighed his scant schooling.

John Sevier, easily the most popular man in the West, being a member of the Territorial Legislative Council was not a delegate to the Constitutional Convention. He was present in Knoxville, however, during its sessions and exerted a powerful influence upon its acts. His diary records, with tantalizing brevity, something of his activities and surroundings during this history-making period.

"Fry. 1 day of Jany. 1796 a warm and pleasant day . . . Mon. 4 warm, the violets in the garden bloomed. Tues. 5 very warm & pleasant in the night snowed. Wed. 6 snowed all day. Thurs. 7 clear and windy set out for Knoxville. . . ."

The weather, his various business transactions, visits and contacts with relatives and neighbors, are recorded along with such important items as:

". . . Fry. 15 the committee reported on the bill of rights. Sat. cold. . . ."

Finally, sandwiched in with reports of mundane affairs: ". . . Feb. 6—Convention adjourned. . . ." [11]

But in spite of his seemingly casual interest in the convention, Sevier had worked with the many other able men who had come together in a truly brilliant and representative body to draft Tennessee's first constitution. After twenty-seven days of joint deliberations they brought into being the free, independent state for which they had been laboring and experimenting for twenty-seven years. The system of government which they produced, Thomas Jefferson pronounced, was "the least imperfect and most republican" yet adopted by an American state.[12]

Self-government, in those days, was a new and vital subject. That it was considered carefully by the men who framed the Tennessee constitution is evident from the deep interest which they showed in writing their bill of rights. The omission of such provisions in the federal constitution had caused Thomas Jefferson, then in Paris, France, to insist that full definition of the basic rights of men be included in it.

". . . Let me add," he wrote to James Madison on December 20, 1787, "that a bill of rights is what the people are entitled to against every government on . . . earth; and what no just government should refuse, or rest on inference. . . ."

The first ten amendments to the federal constitution, adopted by Congress in 1789, ratified by the states, and made a perma-

200

nent part of that document in 1791, satisfied the demands of Jefferson that the rights of the people be clearly stated in the nation's basic law.

The bill of rights in the Tennessee constitution begins by stating that

"all power is inherent in the people, and all free governments are founded on their authority, and instituted for their peace, safety and happiness. For the advancement of those ends, they have at all times an inalienable right to alter, reform, or abolish the government in such manner as they may think proper. . . ."

Continuing, it describes in detail such basic rights as freedom of the press, freedom of assembly, freedom of religion, trial by jury, and other matters pertaining, in general, to human freedom. Then, having taken care of these basic freedoms, the authors of the constitution looked to local rights, and specified that ". . . the people residing south of French Broad River and Holston, between the rivers Tennessee and Big Pigeon, are entitled to the right of preemption and occupancy in that tract. . . ."

Furthermore, they declared emphatically "that equal participation in the free navigation of the Mississippi is one of the inherent rights of the citizens of this State; it cannot, therefore, be ceded to any prince, potentate, power, person or persons whatever. . . ."

These provisions relating to navigation of the Mississippi, as well as the premature setting up of the state government, were resented by Congress and resulted in many lively and, often, acrimonious debates between branches of the federal government and representatives of the new state. The fact that at the time the Tennessee constitution was being written, the United States was on the verge of bartering away to Spain the navigation rights to the Mississippi for a period of twenty-five years, caused more hard feeling than any other subject related to the entrance of Tennessee to the federal Union. On several occasions, the people on the western waters had become so aroused on the subject that they threatened to march down and take for themselves not only the river, but the ports at its mouth.

It was fitting that James Robertson should act as presiding officer of the convention while the momentous questions involved in the Bill of Rights were considered. The manner of its presentation and the submission of the final draft of the constitution are described by Ramsey as follows:

". . . Mr. Smith, Chairman, presented to the Convention a draft of the Bill of Rights. It was considered in Committee of the Whole, Mr. Robertson in the chair. In like manner, a draft of the constitution was, on the 27th of January delivered to the Committee of the Whole, and considered and amended until the 6th of February, when the engrossed copy of the Constitution was read and passed unanimously. . . ." [13]

While the convention, generally speaking, had been harmonious, it had been preceded by considerable opposition, particularly in the Cumberland settlements, which had voted overwhelmingly against the formation of a new state. This was due to various reasons, the chief of which was that both leadership and government still centered in the almost inaccessible eastern Tennessee settlements. In this portion of the state the large followings of Blount and Sevier were strongly in favor of early statehood. Davidson County, however, sent an able representation and took an important part in the convention. Tennessee County, at the suggestion of Andrew Jackson, willingly surrendered its euphonious name to the new commonwealth, and other portions of the "far west" of those days contributed able and useful members to its deliberations.

The name, Tennessee, goes back to the dim, unwritten history of the Cherokee Indians, and its meaning is as vague and mysterious as its origin. It does not mean "river of the Big Bend," nor "river of the great spoon," as some writers who would link it with the great Moccasin Bend, near Chattanooga, have suggested; nor does it mean "river of the great waters." The euphonious sounds, interpreted in various ways by the white men who first visited the Cherokee nation, have been applied from time immemorial, not only to the river, but to a principal village of the Over-hill Cherokees.

It is generally conceded that Lieut. Henry Timberlake was the first to give the name its present spelling, Tennessee, although he was not always consistent in adhering to this form. Both the Tennessee River and Tennessee Town, however, have this spelling on the map of the Cherokee country which was made by Timberlake after his extensive travels in 1762.

Other early travelers and writers spelled the name according to their individual whims—Tenassee, Tunisse, Tunassee, and many others. These widely varied forms persisted for many years, as did other place names, for explorers found it difficult to translate the spoken words of the Indians into the French or English language. The French, in documents and maps dated as early as 1701, called the Tennessee River the "Riviere des Casquinampo," and also "Riviere des Cheraquis." Some of the British called it the Cussato, after a tribe of Indians of that name. Others called it the Hogo-hegee.

The remote village of Tenasse was visited as early as 1725 by Colonel George Chicken, of South Carolina, and five years later by a Scotchman, Sir Alexander Cummings, who spent some time in the principal towns of the Cherokees and succeeded in securing from them a "Tender of Submission and Obedience" to the British king. The town of Great Tennassie, played an important part in this remarkable story, and one of its young warriors, known as Atta-kulla-kulla, or "The Little Carpenter" was chosen by Sir Alexander to accompany him and other Cherokee head men to London, where, as a symbol of submission, "The Crown of Great Tannassie" was laid at the feet of the British King.

The decision to take this step was made after Sir Alexander and his companions had been entertained with great ceremony and after serious consultation with Jacob, the Conjurer and the chief Moytoy. After the elaborate ceremony at the Town-House, Sir Alexander records that he made a great friend of the King of "Tannassy", made him do homage to King George II, on his bended knee and, that night departed for Great Telliquoe. Here, too, a great entertainment was staged. The Indians sang songs, danced and ". . . stroaked Sir Alexander's head and body over with eagle's tails."

Returning soon to Charleston, Sir Alexander carried with him Atta-kulla-kulla and the six other Cherokee chiefs, whom he wished to present to His Majesty as "evidence of the truth of what had happened."

On May 4, they set sail for England on the *Fox,* man of war and, on June 22, the strange visitors from the Tennessee country, were presented to George II.

The Cherokees later repudiated this action of the seven chiefs, but their story makes a charming chapter in the history of the great state which perpetuates the memory of the "Crown of Great Tennassee."

But what was it like—this new state of Tennessee? Only twenty-seven years had elapsed since William and Lydia Bean had lighted the hearth fire in the first white man's home west of the Appalachian Mountains. Yet, in this brief time a new state had come into being and a new way of life had been established. The niceties of the cultural and social life which these western emigrants had left behind them were not forgotten, however, either in their homes or in public affairs. They were fortunate in having among them many well-educated teachers and preachers, who from the beginning, turned their attention to the education of the young. These men paved the way by establishing small private schools which formed the nucleus of several of Tennessee's outstanding educational institutions.

Samuel Doak's private school which was opened in Washington County about 1780, was the forerunner of Martin Academy, established by North Carolina in 1783, and named for Alexander Martin, Governor of that State. Thomas Craighead's academy in Nashville, became officially Davidson Academy in 1785, then the University of Nashville and later George Peabody College for Teachers. Samuel Carrick's private school in Knoxville preceded the establishment of Blount College in 1794, which eventually became the University of Tennessee. Hezakiah Balch's academy, also established in 1794, became Greenville College.

The late Dr. Robert H. White, pays a fitting tribute to these pioneer ministers of the gospel, who were also the leading pioneer educators:

"The pioneer preachers were deeply and genuinely interested in education. Many of them were teachers as well as preachers, and occasionally a preacher-teacher was also a physician. . . . These early preachers and teachers knew the value of turning the attention of the settlers toward religion and education, and their influence was from the first felt in the frontier settlements. So great was the influence of the minister and teacher that churches and schools received some attention almost from the very beginning of the first settlements." [14]

Neither in their cultural life nor in material things were these western settlers actually separated from the great centers of commerce to the north and the south of them. They were fortunate in having access to great waterways and the early traders and trappers, as well as the Indians and the emigrants who came to make permanent homes in the west, all followed the courses of their many navigable streams from their sources in the mountains, to the broad waters of the Holston, French Broad, Tennessee, the Cumberland and the Ohio to the Mississippi.

Light, swift Indian canoes, made of bark, well-cured skins or the trunks of trees, as well as the larger flatboats, keel boats, rafts and all manner of crude watercraft dotted the bosoms of these streams long before the steamboats were invented. Fur traders and later, farmers of the western settlements, all carried their produce to the markets of the lower south with comparative ease. When they returned, however, they had to abandon their heavy boats and travel on foot or horseback. The Natchez Trace, first used by the Indians, was for many years the most traveled of the land routes. It reached from Nashville, Tennessee, to Natchez, Mississippi, and until the days of steamboats, was the major trade route. Much trading was done, even in the earliest years, between Nashville, Knoxville, Philadelphia and New Orleans. By contact with these excellent markets a surprising number of luxuries, as well as necessities, were brought into the pioneer settlements of Tennessee. Stores were established in Knoxville, Nashville and other settlements in the early days, among them those of Andrew Jackson at Gallatin, Hunter's Hill and Clover Bottom. Account books of these Jackson stores are among the most valuable, and most revealing, of the manuscripts in his library at the Hermitage, for they record, not only details of the articles brought in for sale, but give long lists of purchases by James Robertson, the Donelsons and many others. They included such things as china, silks, broadcloths, morocco shoes, ladies' hats and books. As the population increased and the trade routes were better protected, greater varieties of luxuries, as well as necessities, were brought in by the storekeepers.

Most of the people, including such leading men as James Robertson, John Sevier and Andrew Jackson, lived in log houses for many years after Tennessee became a state—sometimes in a single cabin, but usually in a cluster of log buildings, among which were slave quarters. In the earliest days of settlement the houses were usually located within reach of such major strongholds as Fort Watauga, the James White fort in Knoxville, and Fort Nashboro on the banks of the Cumberland River. Later, the population spread out through the countryside, large plantations were cultivated and the log cabins were supplanted by handsome brick mansions of the more prosperous planters. Andrew Jackson's home, until 1819 was, however, the log cabin Hermitage, two buildings of which are still in a good state of preservation.

Dress, for the most part, was limited to garments made of cotton, flax and wool. The spinning, the weaving and the sewing were done by the pioneer women and girls. Occasionally, however, a few of the most elegant materials, such as silks, satins and broadcloths, were brought in by the early storekeepers, or by men who traveled to Philadelphia, New Orleans or Charleston. John Sevier, William Blount, Andrew Jackson and others who went to such places on matters of personal business or affairs of state, wore the conventional dress of the times—knee pants, silk stockings, silver buckles on their shoes and powdered hair. It is reasonable to suppose that when they returned home they brought with them a few fine materials and "pretties" for the ladies of their families.

With the establishment of the territorial capital in Knoxville, Governor Blount and his wife, Mary Grainger Blount, held a fashionable court at their new frame house in the midst of the wilderness and within the actual sound of the war-whoop of hostile Indians. Strange that from the Governor's mansion should come the sound of minuets and quadrilles, played and danced much as they were in Philadelphia and New Orleans, while only a few miles

The log cabin Hermitage which formed the Jackson dwelling from 1804 to 1818. Building in foreground was once a portion of the two-story blockhouse owned by Nathaniel Hays, from whom Jackson bought the Hermitage estate in 1804.

away might be heard the music of the Indians as they celebrated their various feasts, or made ready for war on the white men!

Tonight, gentlemen with powdered hair, knee breeches and silken hose, might dance with ladies almost as fashionably gowned as those in Philadelphia, but tomorrow, perhaps before the dawn, they might be called upon to don the rough hunting shirt, coonskin cap and leggins of the frontier and ride with John Sevier to subdue hostile Indians. Tonight the ladies, in their gay silks, might dance and forget, for the moment, the dangers which surrounded them; but should one of them venture beyond the immediate confines of the settlement, she would face the possibility of instant death, torture, or, perhaps, long years of captivity in the Indian nations. Yet, neither the constant presence of danger, nor the hardships of the frontier, kept them from observance of the little amenities which, from the beginning, have made the social life of the South so gracious and charming. High spirits, laughter and song were parts of the life of these heroic men and women, as well as work, privation and even death. Such were the pioneers who founded the state of Tennessee.

CHAPTER VI

The State of Tennessee

After framing their constitution, Tennesseans lost no time in setting up their state government and proudly assuming what they believed to be their rightful place among the sisterhood of states. The popular John Sevier, having been elected governor, appeared before the first state legislature on March 30, 1796, to make his inaugural address. It was brief—a matter of two short paragraphs, in the first of which he expressed his appreciation of ". . . the high and honorable appointment conferred upon me by the free suffrages of my countrymen . . ." and in the second voiced his confidence in the legislators elected to serve with him.

"Gentlemen," he said in his concluding paragraph, "accept my best wishes for your individual and public happiness; and, relying upon your wisdom and patriotism, I have no doubt but the result of your deliberations will give permanency and success to our new system of government, so wisely calculated to secure the liberty and advance the happiness and prosperity of our fellow-citizens." [1]

The next day, March 31, 1796, the legislature promptly elected William Blount, the retiring territorial governor, and William Cocke to represent the new state in the Senate of the United States. These two gentlemen, who were among the most brilliant and popular men in the West, were also unusually handsome and were possessed of cultivated manners which would easily win for them a place among the most cultured gentlemen they might encounter in the nation's capital.

Blount and Cocke arrived in Philadelphia during the first week of May and promptly presented their credentials to the Senate. Instead of being welcomed with open arms as representatives of a new, rich addition to the national Union, they had the door literally slammed in their faces.

This action had something of a precedent, for in the fall of 1794, James White, under the then existing law, was elected and sent as a delegate to represent the territory south of the River Ohio. The Congress, after a long debate, permitted White to take a seat in the House of Representatives ". . . with a right of debating, but not of voting. . . ." [2]

The debate which the appearance of Blount and Cocke precipitated in the United States Senate was much more bitter and of longer duration than those which preceded the eventual seating of James White in the House of Representatives.

Although credentials of the Tennessee senators had been presented prior to that date, the senate took no action until May 9, 1796, when it acknowledged receipt of ". . . a paper purporting to be the appointment of William Blount and William Cocke, respectively, to seats in the Senate. . . ." [3] That body agreed to a motion to read the paper, but promptly postponed any action until the following day. After that date, minor actions were taken on the report of the committee which had been appointed to consider President Washington's message of April 8 on the subject of admission of Tennessee, but no definite action on seating the Tennessee senators was taken until May 23, when the following motion was passed:

"That Mr. Blount and Mr. Cocke, who claim to be Senators of the United States, be received as spectators, and that chairs be provided for that purpose until the final decision of the Senate shall be given on the bill proposing to admit the Southwestern Territory into the Union."

Time was running out, however, and it began to appear that the debates in both houses would continue until it would be too late to secure Tennessee's admission before adjournment. That, most of all, was feared by the impatient Tennesseans.

While there was apparently little danger of failing to gain admission to the Union, there was a serious threat that, had certain members, especially in the House of Representatives, had their way, it might have been delayed for a long while, quite possibly until the Territory had been divided and admitted as two or more states. Each of these divisions would have been required to have a minimum of sixty thousand inhabitants, which could have continued the territorial status for a period of years. Should this have

210

happened there is no doubt that the steady stream of emigrants then pouring into Tennessee would have slowed down materially. This, of course, was exactly what many eastern Congressional leaders, fearing the growth of political power in the West, wanted.

One of the most dangerous speeches on this subject was made in the House of Representatives by Samuel Sitgreaves, of Pennsylvania:

"By act of cession of the State of North Carolina, accepted by Congress, it is provided that the ceded territory should be laid off into one or more States. . . . They have no other or greater privileges than the inhabitants of the North-western Territory; and it cannot be pretended that these would be entitled to admission into the Union as one State, so soon as their whole number shall amount to sixty thousand, because the ordinance itself divides that country into three separate and distinct States, each of which must contain sixty thousand free inhabitants before it can claim to be received.

"The actual circumstances and situation of the South-western Territory evinced the reasonableness and propriety of the construction; it is composed of two settlements, the Holston and the Mero districts, separated from each other by the Cumberland Mountains and a wilderness of two hundred miles in width, which has always been inhabited by the Indians, and the soil and jurisdiction of which have been actually ceded to them by the United States, by late Treaties; and by an examination of the documents on the table it would appear, that when, agreeable to the act of the Territorial Legislature, the officers who took the census put to the people of the Territory the question whether they were desirous of admission into the Union; the inhabitants of the Western or Mero district almost universally answered in the negative. . . . It looked somewhat absurd to connect under one permanent Government, people separated from each other by natural barriers, by a distance of two hundred miles, and by a foreign jurisdiction. . . ." [4]

Had Mr. Sitgreaves' argument prevailed it would have been the death knell of the infant state of Tennessee. At that time, of course, Mr. Sitgreaves did not take into consideration the magnificent territory between the fringes of the Mero district and the Mississippi River, which was claimed and partially occupied by the Chickasaw

Indians. This, totally unlike the Holston and Mero districts in geography, soils, and natural resources, might well have been used as an argument for making three states of the Tennessee country. In fact, for most of the entire period of Tennessee's history there have been those who have argued that three states, instead of one, should have been created. It was destined, however, that in spite of the natural, as well as political differences which developed through the years, Tennessee was to be one state.

There were others, however, who spoke forcefully and courageously for Tennessee's early admission into the Union. Among them were such men as James Madison and Robert Rutherford of Virginia; Thomas Blount of North Carolina; Albert Gallatin of Pennsylvania, and many others.

On May 6, 1796, the House of Representatives ". . . resolved itself into a Committee of the Whole on the report of the Committee to whom was referred the Message of the President, relative to the Territory south of the river Ohio. . . ."

Mr. Rutherford, speaking on the question, said that he hoped the committee would concur in the report, that he himself had no idea of confining the territory to the strict legal line—that he did not wish to cavil with this brave, generous people. He would have them taken out of leading-strings, as they were now able to stand alone; it was time to take them by the hand, and to say, we are glad to see you stand on your own feet. We should not, he said, be too nice about their turning out their toes, or other trifles; they soon would march lustily along. They had complied with every requisite for becoming a state of the Union—they wished to form an additional star in the political hemisphere of the United States—they have erected a state government, and wished to come into the Union, and to resist their claim would be out of character.[5]

Jonathan Dayton, of New Hampshire, then arose to say that he could never give his assent to any proposition which expressly or even impliedly admitted that the people inhabiting either of the territories of the United States could, at their own mere will and pleasure, and without the declared consent of Congress, erect themselves into a separate and independent state.

As the opposition continued its arguments, Thomas Blount of North Carolina rose to the defense.

"Do the gentlemen," he asked ". . . wish to re-establish a temporary Territorial Government there?" If they did their wish would not be easily accomplished; for the people there believed, that in changing their government, they only exercised a right which had been secured to them by sacred compact; and under that belief, they would be disposed to defend it. That right was, in his opinion, recognized by the government of the United States, when Mr. White was permitted to take his seat in the House of Representatives as the representative of the territory; and from that circumstance they had reason to expect to be a member of the Union.

Mr. Gallatin was of the opinion that the people of the Southwestern Territory ". . . became *ipso facto* a State the moment they amounted to 60,000 free inhabitants, and that it became the duty of Congress, as a part of the original compact, to recognize them as such, and to admit them to the Union. . . ."

While all of this was taking place in the House of Representatives, the Senate was also engaged in lively debates on the subject. Finally, on Thursday, May 26, the bill laying out into one state the territory ceded by the state of North Carolina to the United States, and providing for the enumeration of inhabitants thereof, was read for the third time.[6] Several amendments were introduced, debated and some of them incorporated into the bill, the most important of which being the amendment providing that as soon as:

". . . it shall appear to the President of the United States that the territory by this act laid out, and formed into a State, doth contain sixty thousand free inhabitants, then it shall be lawful for the President, by his Proclamation, to declare the same . . . and, until an enumeration shall be made, under the authority of Congress, for the purpose of apportioning Representatives, the said State of Tennessee shall be entitled to choose one Representative. . . ."

The Senate on May 31, withdrew its nonconcurrence with the legislation passed by the House of Representatives, thereby approving the admission of the State of Tennessee to the Union—the first to be erected out of a territory.

213

President Washington signed the bill on June 1 and Tennessee became the sixteenth state to enter the union.

As a final gesture, on ". . . Wednesday Evening, 5 o'clock, June 1 . . ." the Senate resolved ". . . That the Honorable William Blount and William Cocke, Esquires, who have produced credentials of being duly elected senators for the State of Tennessee, be admitted to take the oath necessary for their qualification, and their seats accordingly." [7]

Admission to the Union was an important step toward the eventual solution of many of Tennessee's problems, but it neither removed nor greatly reduced some of its most serious troubles. The fact that it consisted of two major settlements, separated from each other by two hundred miles of wilderness, still held by the Indians, represented one of its greatest difficulties. It was true also that these two settlements possessed wide differences of opinion on many subjects and that both of them, not trusting the weak federal government during the period of the Confederation, had received and had made overtures to representatives of the Spanish government in the lower south. The Cumberland settlements had gone so far as to honor the Spanish governor by naming their district Miro, [Mero] in his honor. Both John Sevier and James Robertson had dealings with Miro and with Don Diego de Gardoqui, who came to the United States to represent the Spanish government in 1785.

Another serious matter, which Governor Sevier took promptly to the first General Assembly for consideration, was the unfortunate condition in which settlers south of the French Broad River found themselves. The Dumplin Treaty, which had been negotiated by the state of Franklin, was ignored, leaving these people, in the eyes of the federal government, as trespassers on Indian lands.

In his message of April 11 to the General Assembly, Governor Sevier called attention to the fact that Tennessee's senators were about to depart for Philadelphia and suggested that, before leaving, they be instructed to present the plight of these settlers to the Congress.

"In my humble opinion," Governor Sevier declared, "it is a matter of great public importance, and particularly interesting to the state and to individuals, to either have the Indian claims extinguished, or the adventurers compensated for those lands. . . ." [8]

The Assembly acted promptly to carry out the Governor's suggestion, but, as its members, the two senators and the governor himself, soon learned, none of the acts performed by them and none of the persons elected by the premature legislature of the state of Tennessee were considered by the federal government to have any legal standing. Therefore, it became necessary, after Tennessee was admitted to the Union, to hold new elections and to reenact certain measures already passed by the first General Assembly, which had convened on March 28 and adjourned on April 23, 1796. It was at this time also that Andrew Jackson was elected a member of the House of Representatives, under provisions of the section of the bill admitting Tennessee to the Union.

During the years which intervened between the formation of the Cumberland settlement and Tennessee's admission to the Union in 1796, much of its history and that of the distant Holston settlements ran along parallel lines. Both took early steps toward forming independent governments, and both fought desperately to avoid being completely overrun by hostile Indians.

After its first setback, caused by the fact that the new state of Tennessee had set up a complete organization and had begun operations *before* it had been admitted to the union, the affairs of government began to function smoothly. During the called session of the General Assembly, which convened on July 30, 1796, steps were taken to harmonize its legislation with that of the federal government and to send duly elected senators and its one member of the House of Representatives to the Congress of the United States. Having attended to these matters of national concern, Governor Sevier then turned his attention to two pressing subjects of local interest—the plight of the settlers south of the French Broad River and the building of roads.

Action regarding the building of a road which was suggested in Governor Sevier's message to the Legislature on April 1, 1796, placed before it a communication from Governor Vanderhorts of South Carolina, suggesting that the two states cooperate in the ". . . making of a waggon road over what is commonly called the western mountains. . . ." [9]

"I need not point out to you," Governor Sevier continued, "the

215

general utility and advantages that would be derived to the citizens of this State in consequence of such a road and I flatter myself that in your deliberations you will not hesitate to provide ample and necessary means to effect the same."

The dream of a network of "waggon" roads uniting major points of interest in the South was still a long way in the future, but the proposed road from South Carolina would be a beginning step. These first roads were, themselves, scarcely more than mere trails, but they at least blazed a way through the wilderness, giving men a chance to bring their families and their belongings west on wheels, instead of on packhorses.

However, of far more concern than roads was the continuing problem of the settlers south of the French Broad. The late Dr. White comments: "Inasmuch as 'the line of experiment' run by the United States Commissioners had proved to be quite objectionable to Tennessee citizens and officials, for the reasons set out in their remonstrance, it will be noted that the way out for the President of the United States (John Adams) was to call for another treaty with the Cherokee Indians. Meanwhile, Tennessee citizens were forcibly removed from their homes by Colonel Butler's military detachment, and passports from the Governor were necessary for citizens to be permitted to return to their former homes in order to gather their crops or attend to business matters. . . ." [10]

These complicated matters, like other dealings with the federal government and the Indians, were years in being settled and many unnecessary inconveniences were suffered on the part of Tennesseans. It did not help matters any that President Adams realized that Thomas Jefferson had a strong following in the new state. In fact, Tennessee's three electoral votes were cast for Jefferson and Aaron Burr.

Governor Sevier, who had been elected chief executive of the state in 1796, 1797 and 1799, could not, under the constitution, serve another consecutive term. During his six years in office he had, however, set the new commonwealth well on the way to success and his popularity had increased rather than diminished. Many important events, entirely out of his jurisdiction as governor, had taken place during this six year period. One of the most unfortunate was the expulsion of William Blount from the United States Senate on the charges of treason and provisions for his impeachment trial. He was the first man to be expelled from this august body, but, instead of going home in disgrace, he returned to Tennessee to receive a royal welcome by its citizens!

The story is long and complicated, but, briefly, it was this: A letter, said to have been written by Blount to James Carey, stated that he was attempting to engage in a conspiracy with England to bring about an armed invasion of Florida and Louisiana; that he was trying to discredit the President of the United States and his agents among the Indians; and that he was attempting to swindle the Indians themselves. It was never proven that he had written the letter or, if he had, that he had actually committed any of the offenses with which the senate charged him.

The late Judge Samuel G. Heiskell of Knoxville explains the legal details as follows:

". . . We are forced to conclude that as a matter of law the . . . charges preferred . . . absolutely broke down, and it follows that if the senator was not guilty in law he could not be guilty at all. His expulsion, therefore, can be charged up as a political outrage committed by the Adams administration, members of the cabinet of which brought all of the influence of the administration to bear to expel Senator Blount from the senate." [11]

Soon after Blount's return to Tennessee, however, the sergeant-at-arms of the United States Senate, James Matthers, appeared in Knoxville to arrest him and take him back to Philadelphia for trial. Matthers was received politely, permitted to serve papers on Blount, and was entertained with apparently sincere hospitality for several days. When he decided it was time to leave with his prisoner, however, things took on another look. A body of horsemen appeared and told him pleasantly that they would ride out with him to start him on his way—but that he could not take William Blount off of Tennessee soil. They did just that and Matthers made the rest of his return journey alone. Eventually, for a variety of legal reasons, the impeachment charges were dismissed.'

This refusal to surrender Blount to federal authorities was but one of the manifestations of the confidence which his fellow Tennesseans felt in him. James White, who was at that time Speaker of the State Senate, promptly resigned this position as well as his membership in the senate, leaving both positions vacant. Blount was immediately elected without opposition to succeed White and, at a called session of the State Legislature, he was, on December 3, 1797, made Speaker of the Senate. His premature death at the age of fifty-three, March 21, 1800, prevented any additional expressions of gratitude for his services during the territorial period and the formation of the state of Tennessee. He was buried in the historic cemetery of the First Presbyterian Church in Knoxville.

In addition to the legal facts, which are a matter of official record, there were other aspects of the Blount case. Too little attention has been paid to the real possibility that William Blount, rather than being a conspirator, was himself the victim of a conspiracy—principally on the part of representatives of the Spanish government. It should be considered also that the federal government during the period of his administration as territorial governor, was deliberately negotiating with Spain to surrender free navigation of the Mississippi River for a period of twenty-five years in return for an alliance and favorable trade agreements. Furthermore, the national government was placating eastern politicians and tradesmen by attempting to force the trade of the western settlements to the Atlantic states, rather than to the far South.

William Carmichael and W. Short, representatives of the United States in Spain, writing to Thomas Jefferson, Secretary of State, on May 5, 1793, stated that Don Diego Gardoqui, Spanish Minister to the United States, had conversed with some individuals in America who wished to see the navigation of the Mississippi limited, in order to have western produce marketed through the Atlantic states and to limit the growth of these settlements. There was also fear among the eastern politicians that the growth of population in the west would threaten their control of the national government.

"From hence he has formed the opinions," Short and Carmichael continued, "which he has not concealed from us, that the United States does not desire this navigation and the limits we ask, or at least do not desire it so generally as that they could be brought to make any general effort to obtain it, and also that the western

218

inhabitants, whenever they shall acquire force, will separate from the Atlantic states. . . ." [12]

Gardoqui, who was sent to the United States as charge d'affaires in 1785, had himself been busily engaged, especially in regard to the Cumberland settlements, in a conspiracy to win the westerners into a separation from the United States and an alliance with Spain. Spanish authorities in Louisiana were constantly on the alert for possible attacks from the north and were greatly alarmed when M. Genet, Minister of the French Republic, with which Spain was then at war, began his activities to organize and finance such an expedition. Genet sought the aid of inhabitants of Kentucky and the Cumberland settlements, many of whom were already on the point of raising their own troops and going down to take by force the Mississippi and its ports, which were about to be denied them by action of their own government. To this end, he appointed several willing westerners as officers in the French army and authorized them to raise troops.

Strangely enough, this willingness of many inhabitants of the Cumberland, who had, in 1784, chosen to honor the Spanish governor and intendant, Don Esteban Miro, by giving their district his name—Miro (or Mero) District, seems highly contradictory. Then, they were accused of participating in a great "Spanish Conspiracy" to separate this area from the United States—now they were charged with plotting against Spain! It was a period of charges and counter charges and apparent contradictions—but it was actually quite consistent when it is realized that these westerners had but one major aim—free navigation of the Mississippi River and free ports of deposit at its mouth. To achieve this end they used any tools which might come to their hands.

But, if Spain was alarmed by M. Genet's activities, John Adams, president of the United States, and his government were even more so. Thomas Jefferson, in a letter dated August 29, 1793, to Governor Isaac Shelby of Kentucky, sent him official verification that certain persons in Philadelphia were ". . . taking measures to excite the inhabitants of Kentucky to join an enterprise against the Spanish dominions in Mississippi . . . I have it, therefore, in charge from the President to desire you to be particularly attentive to any

219

attempts of this kind among the citizens of Kentucky, and if you shall have reason to believe any such enterprise meditated, that you put them on their guard against the consequence, as all acts of hostility committed on nations at peace with the United States are forbidden by law and will expose them to punishment. . . ." [13]

Continuing, Jefferson reminded Shelby that such an expedition would not only be a threat to the peace of the general union, but that ". . . nothing could be more inauspicious to them than such a movement, at the very moment when those interests are under negotiation between Spain and the United States. . . ."

Jefferson's letter met a cool reception from Shelby, for at that very moment the federal government was attempting to barter away the free navigation of the Mississippi—the very life-blood of western commerce and expansion. On October 5, 1793, he replied briefly that he knew of no such movement and assured Jefferson that ". . . the citizens of Kentucky possess too just a sense of the obligations they owe to the general government to embark on any enterprise that would be injurious to the United States. . . ."

However, by late 1793, or early 1794, two Frenchmen, La Chaise and Delpeau, appeared in Kentucky for the purpose of carrying out Genet's plan. Shelby then assured the secretary of state in a letter dated January 13, 1794, that, if the president sent him specific orders he would attempt to carry them out—if they were consistent within his constitutional powers.

"I have great doubts," he continued, "even if they attempt to carry their plan into execution . . . whether there is any legal authority to restrain them or punish them, at least before they have accomplished it. I shall also feel but little inclination to take an active part in punishing or restraining any of my fellow citizens for a supposed intention only to gratify or remove the fears of the minister of a prince who openly withholds from us an invaluable right, and who secretly instigates against us a most savage and cruel enemy. . . ."

This, in brief, was the state of affairs in the West during the years William Blount served as territorial governor. In the early 1790s he was the target of accusations made by two of Spain's charges d'affairs, Joseph Ignatius Viar and Joseph de Jaudennes.

They, in a document dated January 12, 1793, protested to Thomas Jefferson, Secretary of State, against Blount's presentation of gold and silver medals bearing the likeness of George Washington to chiefs of the Chickasaw and Choctaw nations.

"We do not pretend to impeach the character of governor Blount," they wrote, "nor would we produce evidence against him if we were not persuaded that since they declaim so bitterly against the governor of New Orleans in words, it is very just that we vindicate his proceedings, and show those of Governor Blount and others, not only in words, but in palpable facts. . . ." [14]

In another communication, dated June 18, 1793, they accused Governor Blount of sending supplies to the Chickasaws by a son of General James Robertson and asked:

"Does it argue good faith, or sincerity toward the Creeks, to succor the Chicasaw nation with a portion of corn, that they with more convenience pursue war, which the son of General Robertson carried with him; and moreover a piece of artillery, the use of which the Indians never knew and always feared?"

They concluded this lengthy communication with the threat:

"Recapitulating all the proceedings of the United States and of their agents with respect to our nation and the various nations of Indians, our friends . . . we foresee, with no small sensibility, that the continuation of the peace, good harmony, and perfect friendship which have so happily prevailed till now between our nation and the United States, is very problematical for the future, unless the United States shall take more convenient measures and of greater energy than those adopted for a long time past. . . ."

In the face of threatened international complications, the Adams administration sided with Spain and left the West to fend for itself. William Blount fought shoulder to shoulder with them and—finally—they won the great Mississippi valley for their nation as well as for themselves.

Many other important matters took place during the first six-year period Sevier served as governor of Tennessee. Among them were the creation of Robertson county (named for James Robertson) and Montgomery County (named for Col. John Montgomery) from Tennessee County, which had surrendered its name to the new state.

THE DANGEROUS EXAMPLE

In 1796, Landon Carter was commissioned brigadier-general of the Hamilton District and James Winchester brigadier-general of Mero District.

During the years immediately following Tennessee's admission to the Union, curiosity about this new part of the country led many visitors, as well as prospective settlers, to make extensive tours of the major settlements. Among the most interesting were Louis Philippe, later to claim the throne of France, and his two brothers, sons of the Duke of Orleans, who began their visit to Tennessee in the spring of 1797. They first traveled in East Tennessee, visiting Governor Sevier and other leading citizens, and spending some time among the nearby Indians. Among both the Indians and the pioneer citizens they were introduced to such native foods as wild turkey and bear meat, as well as to the crowded and often quite crude, sleeping conditions at the taverns they found on their way. There are lengthy and sometimes highly amusing accounts of the reaction of these young men, fresh from one of the most elegant courts of Europe, to pioneer fare and customs. From Knoxville they came to Nashville, crossing the Cumberland Mountains, sometimes swimming their horses across rivers and enduring the everyday hardships of such travel. En route to Nashville they passed through Dixon Springs, Bledsoe's Lick and other places of interest in the present Middle Tennessee.

During these years Governor Sevier, the state legislative and judicial bodies, and the various county and town governments, organized and took on the duties of administering public affairs. These men were no novices in government. Most of the older leaders were well educated; many of them in the law and had had valuable experience in the writing of constitutions and the drafting of laws in the eastern settlements before coming West. The young men, like Andrew Jackson for instance, learned from them and added much knowledge and practical experience to any prior schooling they might have had. Although it is a fact too often overlooked, many of these men had brought surprisingly complete libraries with them and, as the years went on, men like Jackson and his friend John Overton acquired excellent collections of books for their day and time.

CHAPTER VII

Tennessee and the War of 1812

John Sevier, after serving three terms as governor, was limited by provisions of the Tennessee Constitution from running for a fourth consecutive term, although, had it not been for this impediment, his great popularity would easily have swept him into office again. His successor was Archibald Roane, an able, scholarly lawyer and jurist, who was well qualified to serve as the state's chief executive.

Roane was born in Lancaster County, Pennsylvania, about 1760, although according to some authorities, it may have been as much as five years earlier. At his father's death, he was placed under the guardianship of an uncle, the Reverend John Roane, who saw to it that his nephew had a good education. Sometime in late 1787, or early 1788, both he and Andrew Jackson arrived at Jonesboro, as is shown by the fact that their names were signed to a December, 1787 petition praying separation of the western territory from North Carolina. Soon both Roane and Jackson were admitted to the bar and, again, in 1790, when William Blount entered into his duties as territorial governor, both were granted the right to practice as attorneys in the several courts of law and equity in the territory. From these early days their names frequently appeared on the same legal documents and official records. Both were delegates to the 1796 convention which drafted the constitution of Tennessee, both served as judges, and both participated in politics. Jackson, however, soon became involved in military organizations, while the greater part of Roane's life was devoted to the judiciary.

However, in 1801, Roane was elected to succeed John Sevier as governor of Tennessee. In many ways, in his brief two years as chief executive, Roane could do little more than carry out and extend various movements which were already under way for the development of the new state.

The fact was that John Sevier, in his last legislative message of his third term, delivered the day before Roane's inauguration, had not only reviewed Tennessee's achievements in the first six years of her existence as a state, but had outlined many measures for further consideration.

Calling attention to this fact, Roane added in his inaugural address:

"You will permit me, however, to repeat that it is essential to the interest of the state that a market be found for the produce of our farms, and the impediments in our roads and rivers removed as speedily as circumstances will permit. I observe with pleasure that our domestic manufactures have considerably increased, and yet a large surplus of provisions and raw materials remain for exportation. If houses of inspection shall be early established under proper regulations, and conducted by persons suitably qualified for the task, the credit of those articles in the foreign markets will be enhanced, a spring will be added to industry, and we shall soon be a wealthy people."

Sevier, in concluding his address, had congratulated the people of Tennessee that Thomas Jefferson had assumed the office of president, and that he had been the choice of Tennessee.

As Roane's term neared its conclusion, John Sevier again became candidate for governor. Though scholarly and, by nature, not fitted for the political arena, Roane, supported by Andrew Jackson and many others allied with him, fought with full strength for reelection. But he, even with such strong support, proved no match for Sevier's popularity. He was elected to begin what proved to be another three terms as Tennessee's governor.

This campaign was so bitter and so ruthless, however, that many long lasting enmities resulted from it. Sevier was accused of fraudulent land deals, purportedly involving actual theft of papers from county records and other irregularities which, had they been true, would not only have ended the popular Sevier's political life, but would have put him in prison. As it turned out, the charges were never proven and none of the testimony offered ever had to stand up to court trial. Andrew Jackson, as well as many other anti-Sevier men, was a lawyer, yet he took the charges against Sevier

224

at face value and in his impetuous, high-tempered way, did his best to prove Sevier guilty. The Tennessee House of Representatives was anti-Sevier, but the senate was pro-Sevier and its members supported him wholeheartedly and fought gallantly for his vindication, finally succeeding in obtaining a much modified report on the affair.

Certain comparatively recent writers on the subject, who have accepted the pseudoevidence presented by the anti-Sevierites in 1803, have been effectively corrected by one of Tennessee's most eminent historians, Dr. Robert H. White.

With the acceptance of the modified report by the General Assembly, the matter was officially ended and the final decision as to Sevier's innocence or guilt left up to the people, who voted overwhelmingly to place him once more in the governor's chair. But Roane and the anti-Sevierites were not through; they injected the subject into the 1805 campaign when Roane again ran for governor. Again Sevier was victorious; and, according to Dr. White, judged innocent of wrong-doing by his own people:

"If votes received be a valid criterion, Sevier was fully vindicated in his political triumph over Roane by a vote of 10,730 to 5,909, or a margin of almost two to one." Sevier was reelected governor in 1807, though William Cocke offered weak and futile opposition until he withdrew from the race. In 1809, Sevier, being ineligible to the governorship for another term, was elected to the State Senate, and in 1811 he became a member of Congress and remained so until his death in 1815." [1]

Roane was an able man, a good governor, and a great scholar and jurist. It is unfortunate that he became embroiled in the political conflict with Sevier, for not only his personal services, but his influence and assistance to young men just obtaining an education and coming into the legal profession and public life, were of inestimable value to the state and the nation. One of the many examples of his contributions to promising young men was shown in his teaching of Hugh Lawson White, who became a lawyer and jurist, and was for many years a United States Senator and a candidate for the presidency. While Roane, in his one term as governor, made no spectacular contributions to the state, he made and would have continued to expand, had he been reelected, all current measures designed for its progress and development, as well as of the nation which was already beginning to extend its western frontiers.

It was his privilege to announce in his farewell address that Thomas Jefferson, he understood, had concluded a treaty with France, by which New Orleans and all of the vast, fertile province of Louisiana, would soon pass into the possession of the United States.

John Sevier, soon after his fourth inauguration, in his message opening a special session of the General Assembly (July 23, 1804) was able to verify and give further details on this important subject:

"Suffer me to observe our warmest acknowledgments are due and justly owing to the federal administration; an almost boundless territory by the late Treaty with the French Republic is added to the United States, an acquisition of incalculable value, securing to the Western Citizens free and unmolested use of one of the finest and longest rivers in the known World and object of the greatest magnitude and importance to our commercial rights and advantages which we very recently did not expect would be obtained for ages to come are already possessed and engaged.

"Many flattering prospects are opened and progressing in this State and the Western Hemisphere which ought to inspire every benevolence and sincere acknowledge of Gratitude to the great and Almighty disposer of all earthly enjoyments. . . ."

Many other important matters claimed Governor Sevier's attention as he entered into his fourth term, among them the question of making certain sweeping changes in the British code of laws which the American colonies as well as the new American states had adopted and used with little change through the years. In his inaugural address of October 7, 1803, Sevier had emphasized this subject, declaring that the laws of Great Britain being enacted and having their original existence under "a monarchical, and I may say, tyrannical government, a government that is in no manner similar to that of our own, neither in policy, liberty, property, toleration or religion or situation" were seriously in need of alteration.

A special legislative committee was appointed to consider this matter and, after due deliberation, its chairman, Sen. Thomas A. Claiborne, reported to the governor, assuring him that the legislature would cooperate fully in guarding the citizens of Tennessee against any injustices which might arise from the application of the British law.

"Some of the statutes of Great Britain," he admitted, "it is true, were enacted in an age of tyranny and usurpation; yet having been in a great measure ingrafted into the American code of laws, will require the most accurate investigation to separate them from our civil code. Happily our wise constitution has guarded against their influence in religious concerns; equally happy for America is it, that the constitutions of the several states are founded upon republican principles, and that grand bulwark of all, the constitution of the United States, has guaranteed these invaluable blessings to them. The legislature is proud to say that the shackles of British common law are as little felt here as in any state in the union; and this legislature pledged themselves, that the sons of Tennessee will be foremost in breaking all such improper barriers to freedom." [2]

With the acquisition of the Louisiana Territory the westerners stood poised and ready to cross the Mississippi at the first opportunity and to push their frontiers into this land of promise. Thomas Jefferson, realizing the eagerness with which they and, indeed, the entire United States, looked forward to settling the new territory, turned his attention immediately to the subject of thorough exploration, a matter in which he himself had long been interested.

As John Sevier's fourth term ended he was elected to serve another two years as governor. By this time, the dispute between the United States and Great Britain, which chiefly concerned illegal attacks upon American vessels on the high seas, the impressment of American seamen, and related matters was increasing in intensity. Actually, there was a much broader and more far-reaching aspect to the controversy, for British claims to American territory persisted and were a constant threat to the United States in spite of the treaty which followed the Revolutionary War.

In his inaugural address, September 24, 1807, Governor Sevier called the attention of the General Assembly to the threat of war

227

with Great Britain, citing the recent unprovoked attack by the British warship, *Leopard,* on the U.S. frigate *Chesapeake.* Knowing that his hearers, like the rest of the nation, were familiar with and greatly disturbed by the incident, he did not dwell at length upon the subject, but informed the legislators that the request of the president for the state's quota of militia had already met the prompt response characteristic of Tennessee volunteers. He commented also that while the country's foreign relations presented a gloomy aspect, it appeared that the federal government was making a sincere effort to reconcile the differences between the two countries without recourse to actual war.

But the international situation did not show the hoped-for improvement. On December 2, 1807, in a brief message to the legislature, Governor Sevier reported on the rapidly deteriorating state of international affairs and the deplorable condition of the state arsenal.

"The prospects of peace in every quarter of the United States appear to be very much menaced," he declared, and the arsenal did not possess for public use "one pound of powder and ball, nor a single musket wherewith to defend our country; should the president call for the whole or any part of this state's quota of volunteers. . . ."

". . . It seems," commented Dr. Robert H. White, "that a slingshot was about all that was available." [3]

The matter was soon remedied, however, for before adjourning the legislators authorized the governor to purchase for the militia of the state, should he deem it necessary, any quantity of powder, not exceeding fifteen hundred pounds and any quantity of lead, not exceeding three thousand pounds. Immediately following this resolution an act was passed for the purpose of encouraging the raising of additional volunteer companies.

In his address to the legislative session in April, 1809, Governor Sevier was able to report that responding to ". . . a requisition from the president of the United States for this State's quota of militia, the proper officers have been called upon for their proportions, and I have the pleasure of informing you that there is exhibited by our fellow citizens such a spirit of patriotism, in defense of our country's cause, as evinces that they will very soon be in complete readiness to take the field, should they be called upon. . . ."

Governor Sevier also assured the legislators that, in obedience to their resolve of the last session, he had procured the powder authorized and had also made arrangements to obtain the lead and would deposit an equal quantity of the same, unless otherwise directed, in East and West (now Middle) Tennessee.

The Creek Indians, he informed them, had exhibited ". . . some disaffection and contempt for the government of the United States." They had stopped and placed in confinement for some days a public post rider on his route to Camp Stoddart and forbade him to return on the same errand. He prophesied that should war break out between Great Britain and the United States ". . . we shall, as heretofore, find them an implacable enemy."

Problems of people residing south of the French Broad and Holston Rivers, of debtors, banking, and the scarcity of money were also brought to the attention of the legislators at this time. Concluding that "under the propitious hand of Providence, the productions of our farms . . ." and, amazingly, "as to political sentiments, there does not seem to be any divisions or factions among us. . . ."

At the conclusion of Sevier's sixth term, he was succeeded by Willie Blount, half-brother of the brilliant and popular territorial governor, William Blount. There is no doubt but that in appearance, personal charm, and spectacular achievements, the younger brother lost by comparison. He was a good governor, however, and was elected without difficulty by the people of Tennessee to serve three consecutive terms—1809, 1811 and 1813. In the beginning of his first term he was overshadowed by the outgoing governor, John Sevier, who, in spite of the efforts which had been made by Jackson, Roane and others to prove him guilty of land frauds, was still the idol of the people. So much so, in fact, that Sevier, having again served the constitutional limit of three successive terms, was immediately elected to the state senate. Having heard his last gubernatorial message on September 19, 1809, the Senate *Journal* on the following day, just before adjournment, recorded that "Mr. John Sevier, a member from Knox County, appeared, produced his credentials and took his seat." His fellow legislators, voicing their appreciation and pledging their continuing loyalty to him, not only paid tribute to him, but promised to carry out his policies:

"The various subjects which you have recommended to our consideration demand and will receive our serious attention, and we trust that no exertions on our part will be withheld to promote the interest of our constituents.

"In taking leave of your excellency on the present occasion, permit us to express the grateful sense, which, in common with our constituents, we entertain of the various and important services you have rendered to your country, both in your civil and military capacity. These services have evinced an extent and a purity of patriotism which have justly secured to you the confidence of your fellow citizens." [1]

It was evident that Sevier's glamòr and popularity with the people of Tennessee overshadowed the in-coming governor. Governor Blount, fully realizing it, said in his brief inaugural address:

"My predecessor in office, of whom it might become me to speak in terms of respect for his past meritorious services in support of the rights of the citizens of this state, having so recently made a communication to the legislature touching on points material and interesting to the state, together with the short time afforded me to make this address (having been so lately informed of my election) will supercede the necessity of a more full communication at this time, and will, I trust serve as apology for the brevity of this."

The imprint of Sevier's personality and undoubted ability, from the time he became governor in 1796 until he finally relinquished that position in 1809, influenced strongly the legislation and also the material progress of the state. Under his leadership, Tennessee had emerged from the hunting and trapping era and was already well on the way to great progress in the fields of agriculture, commerce and education. His influence would continue briefly in the state senate, but in 1811 he was elected to membership in the United States House of Representatives, where he served three consecutive terms. It was during his third term that he, serving as a member of the Committee on Military Affairs, was appointed by President Madison as a commissioner to run the boundary line of the territory ceded by the Creeks to the United States. Leaving his home in Knoxville in June, 1815, he went into the Creek country, where he later contracted fever and died on September 24 of that year. He was buried near Fort Decatur, Alabama, with full honors of war, by the troops commanded by Captain Walker, U.S.A.[5] In 1889 the remains of Tennessee's own "Nolichucky Jack" were brought home and reinterned on the grounds of the Knox County Courthouse.

Governor Blount's first administration and, to some extent, his second, were occupied largely by routine subjects related to internal developments which had been initiated during the Sevier administrations. There was no question, however, of Blount's ability and fitness for the job, for since the beginning of the territorial period, when he served as a secretary to his brother, William Blount, he had had the opportunity to gain a thorough knowledge of the country, its progress and its needs. During this period he had been acquainted with the leading men of Tennessee, as well as many national figures, who, from time to time, were associated with the Tennessee government. His full worth, his courage and patriotism were not fully recognized, however, until war in the Indian country and with the British broke out.

On September 7, 1812, at the call of Governor Blount, the legislature of Tennessee assembled in Nashville at a small building located at the site of the present Hume Fogg High School, Eighth Avenue and Broadway.[6] It was the first time that a legislative session had been held outside of East Tennessee. In his message, delivered September 7, 1812, the governor expressed gratification at the full attendance of the legislators and appreciation of the preparations made for the accommodation of the members and, having done this, launched at once into the serious business which had caused him to call the session.

"At this interesting crisis in American affairs," he began, "requiring the exertions of the regularly constituted authorities both of the United States Government, and of the governments of the several states, as well as the people at large . . . it is a circumstance of peculiar gratification to witness the punctual attendance of the members composing the Legislature upon this executive call. . . ." [7]

The governor referred, of course to the declaration of war, on June 18, 1812, by the United States government against "Great Britain and Ireland and the dependencies thereof."

Urging a diligent and harmonious course, he presented to the legislators a letter, dated June 19, 1812, enclosing a copy of the president's message to both houses of Congress, recommending the measure, along with a copy of the report of the committee on foreign relations of the House of Representatives. Along with these documents was a copy of his letter, dated July 4, to the secretary of state:

"I trust that the assurances therein given will meet with your approbation," he said. "Our cause is a good one—I feel satisfied that the people will rally around the standard of the government of their own choice . . . determined to afford every aid in their power, in support of American liberty; which is the birthright of the people of the United States; given to us by our fathers, many of whom stamped the true value thereon by their actions in the revolutionary struggle, and sealed it with their blood, for this their act we should be grateful. I am so and believe you are."

Needless to say, the legislature, as well as the people of Tennessee lived up to Governor Blount's highest expectations. The people at large were already fully acquainted with the declaration of war and their leaders kept step with the governor and legislative body in preparation for their speedy participation in the nation's defense. William Cocke, Andrew Hynes and William Carroll, on the second day of the session, presented a memorial requesting authority to organize a regiment of militia to aid in the subjugation of Canada. The memorial was enacted into law.[8]

In Congress the war spirit of Tennesseans was also demonstrated by Felix Grundy and "Nolichucky Jack" Sevier, who declared that the United States had only two choices—one, to submit to Great Britain, the other to fight. But Andrew Jackson, anticipating the early outbreak of war, had already replied to the nation's

Tennessee's capitol—1812. In this small building, which stood on the site of the present Hume-Fogg High School at Eighth Avenue and Broad Street, the first state legislative body to meet outside of East Tennessee assembled on September 7, 1812, to plan for Tennesse's participation in th War of 1812. Illustration from Crews' History of Nashville, published circa 1880.

call for fifty thousand volunteers, by a stirring call to arms, written at the Hermitage on March 7, 1812.

"Citizens! your government has yielded to the impulse of the nation. Your impatience is no longer restrained. . . . A simple invitation is given to the young men of the country to arm for their own and their country's rights. . . . Shall we, who have clamoured for war, now skulk into a corner the moment war is about to be declared?

"But another and nobler feeling should impell us to action. Who are we and for what are we going to fight? Are we the titled Slaves of George the third? The military conscripts of Napoleon the great? Or the frozen peasants of the Russian Czar? No—we are the freeborn sons of America; the citizens of the only republic now existing in the world; and the only people who possess rights, liberties, and property they dare call their own. . . ." [9]

Jackson was not alone in his enthusiasm for war with Great Britain, though memories of his boyhood days as a soldier of the American Revolution could well have caused him to feel more deeply than others who had not had such experience. Governor Blount, writing to United States Senator, George W. Campbell, said that "the people of Tennessee would use their pocketbooks for gun wadding and melt their silver into bullets, if necessary, rather than submit to the insults and injuries of Great Britain. . . ." [10]

With this spirit so openly manifested throughout the state, General Jackson had no difficulty in raising twenty-seven hundred volunteers who were soon ready and waiting for a call to service. But neither he nor his volunteers were called, nor was his offer to march against Canada at once accepted. Finally, in October, 1812, the War Department requested Governor Blount—not General Jackson, commanding officer of the volunteers—to send fifteen hundred men to reinforce Gen. James Wilkinson at New Orleans, which, at that time was thought to be threatened by a British invasion of the Gulf coast. Jackson immediately recognized this action of the War Department for what it was—a deliberate and undisguised snub. Governor Blount fully realized the situation and was greatly embarrassed when blanks for the selection and commissioning of officers were sent to him—not Jackson. Since the

233

request sent to Blount referred only to "volunteers who might offer themselves," the governor could not call on Jackson's volunteers who were already organized and had offered themselves for immediate service to the government of the United States. After considerable thought and competent legal advice, Governor Blount took the matter into his own hands, placed Jackson's name on one of the blanks sent to him, and announced that Tennessee was ready for action.

Jackson was fully aware of the insult which had been dealt to him, but, letting his patriotism and his desire to serve his country triumph, for the time being, over his notoriously high temper, he accepted the situation. He did not hesitate, however, to speak frankly in his letter of November 11, 1812, to Governor Blount:

"I have read the orders of the Secretary of War which you had the goodness to show me. . . . I am clear in the opinion, if the Secretary did intend to embrace the volunteers tendered by me that the order recd. by yesterday's mail, was either to exclude me from command, or if I did command by an apparent willingness and condecension of my part to place me under the command of Genl. Wilkinson. I cannot disguise my feelings, had the Secretary of war directed you to call me and my volunteers into the field, and had confined my compensation to that of sergeant or private soldier I should have been content. . . . But Sir, viewing the situation of our beloved country at present, should your Excellency believe that my personal service can promote its interest in the least degree, I will sacrifice my own feelings, and lead my brave volunteers to any point your excellency may please to order. . . ." [11]

Twenty-seven hundred and fifty brave volunteers, Jackson reminded the governor ". . . under my order, stepped forward and enlisted under the banners of their country, resolved to protect their own and their country's rights or nobly die in the glorious struggle. These brave men had chosen me to lead them to the field, and required me thro' your excellency to make a tender of their and my own service to the President of the United States. . . ."

This tender was made, he continued, reminding Blount that it was not accepted by the president or the War Department. The matter was soon corrected, and Governor Blount informed Gen-

234

Andrew Jackson in full dress uniform.

eral Jackson that ". . . the Volunteers under your command, whose services with yours have been tendered to and accepted by the President . . . you will command them." [12]

No time was lost, either by the governor or Andrew Jackson, in readying the Tennessee volunteers for their departure for the lower South. On November 23 Jackson issued his general orders from the Hermitage. In these orders the rendezvous date was fixed as December 10, after which the departure was to be made "without delay." The cavalrymen were to provide themselves with pistols and sabres, the infantry, "as far as it may be convenient," with rifles. With his field officers, Jackson decided that the detachment would "appear in uniforms of dark blue, or brown . . . homespun . . . at the election of the wearer . . . hunting shirts or coats at the option of the different companies, with pantaloons and dark colored socks . . . white pantaloons, vests, etc., may be worn on parade. . . ." Winter clothing, as well as lighter garments for wear in the spring and summer were also ordered. The field officers, however, were to appear in the uniform prescribed for officers of the same grade in the army of the United States.

Governor Blount's orders to Jackson were brief, but they, too, left to the volunteers the responsibility for arming and clothing themselves.

"The Volunteers," he said, "will be expected to arm and equip themselves with their own Arms including rifles and to furnish themselves as fully as may be conveniently practicable and to furnish themselves as fully as may be conveniently in their power to do with ammunition. . . ." [13]

The looms, the sewing needles and knitting needles of the women of Nashville and Middle Tennessee must have been very, very busy in the short time which elapsed between the general orders and the final departure of the flatboat fleet on January 10.

On November 21 the governor had commissioned, under orders from the president, twenty-one captains, and three regiments of infantry were being organized. A fourth, which Jackson called one of the finest regiments of cavalry he ever saw, had chosen John Coffee to command them. Since pistols were not to be had at that time in Nashville, Coffee equipped his regiment with swords—

235

and they had supplied themselves with uniforms "homespun, blue, with caps complete." Coffee, himself a handsome commanding figure, with his almost equally handsome command in their blue uniforms and riding fine horses were soon dispatched to New Orleans by a land route. Meanwhile, the fleet of flatboats on the Cumberland at Nashville was being readied for the infantry regiments and the commanding general—as well as their own chaplain-soldier, the Reverend Gideon Blackburn.

Jackson, on November 14, in an announcement to his soldiers, gave final instructions for their preparation, not only in organization and supplies, but in morale. Telling them that their state was about to act in the ". . . honorable contest of securing the rights and liberties of a great and rising republic," he reminded them of their duty to preserve the freedom which their fathers had won for them and cited a real and present need for their services in preserving their rights to the great Mississippi river, which they had so lately obtained.

"Every man of the western Country," he said, "turns his eyes intuitively upon the mouth of the Mississippi. He there beholds the only outlet by which he can reach the markets of foreign or the Atlantic states: blocked up, all the fruits of his industry rots upon his hand—open it and he carries on a trade with all the nations of the earth. To the people of the western country is then peculiarly committed by nature herself the defense of the lower Mississippi and the city of New Orleans. At the approach of an enemy in that quarter, the whole western world should pour forth its sons to meet the invader and drive him back into the sea. Brave Volunteers! it's to the defense of this place, so interesting to you, that you are now ordered to repair. . . ."

The people of Nashville, entering wholeheartedly into equipping and supplying their volunteers, glowed with pride as they followed them to the banks of the Cumberland to see them embark on January 10, 1813, on their flatboats for the long, winter journey to New Orleans. A journal of their voyage was kept, quite probably, by Robert Searcy, aide to General Jackson, from the morning of their embarkation until their arrival in Natchez, February 16, 1813. This journal records that the morning of the

236

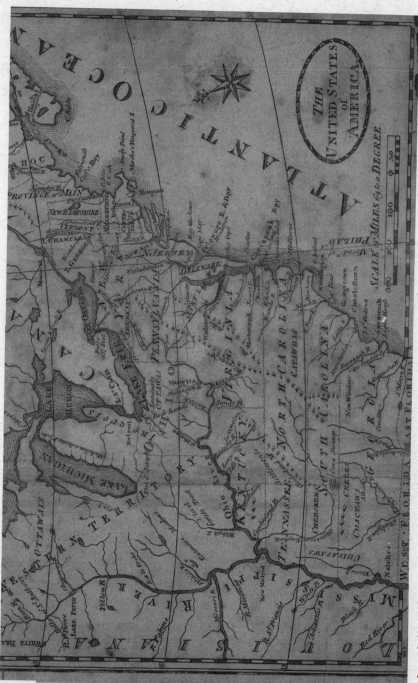

Map of the United States, 1813, showing the boundaries of the United States before Jackson's Indian Campaigns of 1813-1814.

departure was solemn, as, of course, all partings with soldiers destined for combat, are. Yet, there was an overwhelming sense of pride in the vigorous and courageous young men who had volunteered to serve in their country's defense. There was also a feeling of satisfaction from the government officials and the citizenry that they, too, had contributed by outfitting these men and sending them to the service of their country.

"The concourse of Spectators were unusually great," the author of the journal narrates. "All the distinguished characters of the country attended. When the Nashville Company of Volunteers, whom the Gen'l. had chosen as his Guards, arrived at his headquarters, the march commenced from town to the place of embarkation, attended by Governor Blount and his secretary. The Judges of the Superior Courts; The Genl. was attended by his principal Officers attached to the Army. . . ."

Reaching the fleet of flatboats which were to carry the troops to their destination by way of the Cumberland, Ohio and Mississippi Rivers, there was a slight delay, while additional military supplies were being placed on board. Citizens mingled with the troops; wives, children and sweethearts were bidding sad, but brave, farewells to their men until the final moment of departure was signaled by a few taps of the drum and the firing of a cannon. Soon the cables were loosened and as many as seventeen rounds were fired by minute guns.

"Four beautiful standards of Colours waved in the air, added to the grandeur of the scene," wrote the journalist. "Each round of cannon shot was responded to with three cheers. The huzzas made the shores of the Cumberland resound and the high cliffs re-echo'd the melancholy of the parting scene."

Day by day, the journal was kept faithfully and, on Sunday, January 17, it was recorded that the Reverend Mr. Blackburn "preached this morning on the roof of the General's Guards' Boat; and afterwards attended other boats for the same purpose. . . ." [14]

While the Reverend Blackburn was performing divine service on board Captain Williamson's boat, the collection (of men) being great, the roof gave way, and about a dozen men fell through, to the great astonishment of the preacher and others: But Preacher

Blackburn was not to be disturbed by minor things like a roof falling in; he visited the men from boat to boat, conferred with them in private, preached to them publicly and, on some occasions, when they halted for exercise, or were delayed by bad weather, he followed them ashore and spoke to them earnestly of the importance of obeying orders and respecting military discipline.

On January 19 the weather changed from moderate to excessively cold and by the following day, when the fleet approached the mouth of the Cumberland, it was found that ice was running in great masses in the Ohio. Before attempting to enter the Ohio, General Jackson decided to encamp on the river bank, where it was convenient to obtain wood. It was not until dawn on January 23 that it was found that but little ice was afloat on the Ohio and preparations for immediate departure were made. By eight o'clock that morning all of the boats were underway, but it was discovered, on entering the main part of the Ohio, that the ice was present in much larger quantities than expected. Arriving at Fort Massac by night, the boats could not land because of the ice and, against a strong head wind, they had to make for the opposite shore. Here a storm prevented their continuing the voyage.

They were able to take off again, however, by the morning of January 25, but it rained, hailed and snowed all day. The next day they started out early, the author of the journal being aboard Colonel Bradley's boat, where they amused themselves by putting on a mock trial of Chaplain Blackburn, Major Carroll and the Reverend Mr. Schermerhorn. The amount of their fines were some chickens for the use of the boat. The snow was deep that day and some of the men who went ashore to hunt killed nine or ten deer.

On January 27, at daylight, the Mississippi River was sighted, but the morning was excessively cold and the men sent by Jackson to examine the situation at the mouth of the Ohio found that great masses of ice were running in the Mississippi. Unable to make further progress, the fleet found a good harbor at the lower end of a sand bar, which, incidentally, proved to be a fine parade ground for the men. General Jackson, irked at the delay, decided to make use of the lost time by ordering his brigade instructor to have them perform maneuvers and to exercise for about three hours. They

238

also found time for hunting parties, and brought in several deer and wild turkeys.

On January 29, the journal records continued delay, but observes that the troops were improving under the drilling and military instruction order by the general:

". . . It is a pleasing circumstance to observe their rapid progress in the science of Tactics. They are emerging from a state of ignorance, to the honourable qualifications of soldiers. The appearance of our army on the field, their order, discipline and marching entitle them to the praise of regular Troops. . . ."

The waters of the Ohio were still rising and, on Saturday, January 30, it was still cold, but the ice had almost disappeared, apparently not from a changing temperature, but from the rising water. At any rate, the fleet set sail and soon entered the Mississippi. In describing the scene, the journalist waxed poetic:

". . . who can withhold his emotions while viewing the beauties of this august River—the Father of the waters! it is the grand Reservoir of the streamlets from a thousand hills! Rivers from every latitude of our country pay their tribute to this mighty Water. The Productions of every climate are destined to float on its bosom! It is the grand high way to wealth for the people of Western Columbia." [15]

On that day they had a good sail and landed about forty miles below the mouth of the Ohio. On February 3 they passed the second Chickasaw Bluff, but the going was rough as they came in sight of Island No. 35. Here there were snags, and Captain Wallace's boat, attempting to pass through a channel which was free of them, was on the point of sinking. A boat commanded by Captain Newland, which was nearest them, moved away instead of going to their rescue, but Captain Martin and his men managed to reach the wreck and take some of the men aboard. As this lightened the load, the boat rose and was towed to shore, but its men were distributed among other boats for the rest of the trip. By February 4 there was a noticeable and pleasant change of climate. The next day was clear and pleasant and, except for a wind which impeded the progress, things were going well.

General Jackson, however, was determined to make up for lost time in a manner which was not particularly attractive to his crews. The journal commented, apparently with the writer's tongue in his cheek ". . . the morning star, the Harbinger of day, shone with delightful splendor. Indeed, the General appears anxious that we should contemplate its beauties every morning."

Every morning thereafter the journal reports that the fleet started before day, or before five o'clock, or by break of day—but one day the general arose at half-past two o'clock in the morning and gave orders for starting. By three o'clock the fleet was underway, but, breaking all his previous records, on February 15, the men were awakened at half-past eleven and by midnight, they were moving rapidly toward Natchez. That night the general, being informed that there was a good landing three miles above Natchez, ordered the fleet, a little after sundown, to pull in for the night.

Early on the morning of February 16, accompanied by Majors Carroll and Hynes, General Jackson took a skiff and went down to Natchez, where the firing of a small field piece announced his arrival. Breakfasting at Thomas M. Winn's, he and his escorts greeted local citizens and examined letters which had been awaiting him there. One was from General Wilkinson, telling him to disembark his troops, encamp at Natchez and await orders from the government there, instead of coming on to New Orleans as he had been ordered. Wilkinson cited as his reason for this order the fact that it would be difficult to provide accommodation for Jackson's troops, or to obtain forage for his horses at New Orleans.

Jackson replied to Wilkinson and dispatched his letter promptly before returning to his transports. Arriving at the landing, he gave orders to drop the boats down to Natchez and prepare for encampment. Early on the morning of the seventeenth, the order for disembarkation and for marching the troops to the cantonment at nearby Washington was given. Forming in line on the hill, the Tennessee volunteers, with their baggage wagons behind each regiment, began their march through Natchez.

"When passing thro' the city of Natchez," the journalist recorded, "we excited very general attention of the inhabitants, by whom we were treated with distinguished politeness; and also by all the officers, both civil and military, whom we met with. . . ."

Just before they reached the cantonment, they were met by John Coffee's dashing, blue clad cavalry, which escorted them to the place chosen for their camp. However, it proved that the first site did not please the general, so he soon changed to a more desirable place, the remaining baggage was brought from the boats and the troops settled down to drill and to enjoy the admiration, the courtesies and the hospitality of Natchez, while they awaited orders from their government. They were in good spirits and good health and, constantly drilled, exercised and instructed by such able young officers as Hynes, Carroll, Benton and Coffee, were rapidly developing into excellent soldiers.

But things were not going so well with their general. From the day he arrived in Natchez and received Wilkinson's first dispatches, there was constant friction concerning the authority of command. Wilkinson was exceedingly jealous and resented Jackson's independence.

"I must regret," he wrote, "that you have not done me the honor to communicate with me; I could have better forwarded your views than any other person . . . But under orders which direct my conduct, my personal honor, my public obligations and the national interest forbid that I should yield my command to any person, until regularly relieved by superior authority. . . " [16]

After further investigation, however, Wilkinson admitted that Jackson was not under his authority, stating that "Your orders clearly justify you in acknowledging no authority but that of the President of the United States."

But the worst was yet to come; orders came from John Armstrong, secretary of war, announcing that the British threat to the Gulf coast had not materialized, therefore:

"The causes for embodying and marching to New Orleans the Corps under your Command having ceased to exist, you will on receipt of this letter, consider it dismissed from public service and take measures to have delivered over to General Wilkinson all articles of public property."

With blood in his eye and fire in his pen, Jackson wrote letter after letter to everybody from President Madison, John Armstrong, James Wilkinson, Governor Blount, his personal friend in Nashville, William B. Lewis, and to any others he considered necessary, announcing his determination to disregard completely the orders of the secretary of war and to march his men back to their homes in Tennessee before he disbanded them. Furthermore, he announced his intention of retaining such government property as his sick needed for the long homeward march and such medical supplies as he could not obtain otherwise, he secured by pledging his personal credit.

His fiery and eloquent letter to President Madison—though far from perfect in its spelling—reviewed, somewhat at length, the background of the situation and stated bluntly:

"On this day I received the Inclosed astonishing order. I cannot Beleave this thing was ever written by your directions or Knowledge. Why I cannot beleave it is after inviting us to rally round the Standard of our country in its defence, accepting our Services as tendered and ordering us to the lower Mississippi (an inhospitable clime) you would Dismiss us from Service Eight hundred miles from our Homes, without Money without supplies and even strip our sick of every covering and surrender them victims to Pestilence and famine, and if any of my Detachment escape this there arms to be taken from them, They have to pass thro' a Savage wilderness and subject to all these Depredations. I cannot beleave you would reward thus, the tendered support of the purest patriots of America, to beleave it would be to beleave you were lost to all sence of humanity and Country. . . ."

Concluding the letter, General Jackson informed the president that he had determined to march his men directly to Nashville and discharge them near their homes, adding that he hoped he would find in Nashville funds provided for the discharge of his detachment on its arrival.

And that is just what he did. By March 30 he had arrived at the Choctaw Agency, where he wrote the secretary of war announcing that he had gotten that far "tolerably well" with his sick and expected to reach Nashville in twenty or thirty days. He had not lost heart nor patriotism, for on April 8, from the Chickasaw Agency he wrote again to Armstrong informing him that his sick were mending fast, although without any medical supplies other than those he himself had provided. They were being conveyed in eleven baggage wagons, a few packhorses and horses belonging to officers of the line.

To his friend William B. Lewis, he wrote: "I have not rode 20 miles, the field and Staff have been on foot and the sick mounted on their horses. . . ."

It was a long, weary way and a disillusioning one for the enthusiastic young volunteers who, such a short time ago, had set sail under Jackson's command to defend their country. But they made it and neither their loyalty to their government nor that of their commanding general suffered as a consequence of their treatment. He had defied even the President of the United States, he had shared their hardships, had walked beside them and had gone hungry with them. He was tough as a hickory limb—and so they began calling him "Old Hickory."

Spring was well on the way as the tired men approached Tennessee, but each step brought them closer to home and before long they were on their own soil. Now it was truly spring, and there is nothing lovelier than April in Tennessee—except, of course, in that particular April it was excelled by the brightness of the smiles and the warmth of the embraces of their own people. At Columbia, on April 20, there was a great welcoming celebration and the men of that vicinity were dismissed by General Jackson. The rest of the forty-five miles to Nashville, which they reached on April 22, was a march of triumph. Here, too, they received a royal welcome.

Jackson's morale and that of his men was still high and they were still ready to march on a moment's notice to the defense of their country. Jackson had written Secretary of War Armstrong that his sick were mending fast and that he still had ". . . a few standards bearing the American Eagle, that I would be happy to place on the ramparts of Malden. . . ."

One of the first matters of business attended to by General Jackson after he reached Nashville was to report to David Holmes, governor of the Mississippi Territory. Stating that when he had left Natchez he had intended to keep him notified of his progress,

243

he explained that ". . . the want of Candles in the night and the attention to the sick in the day, prevented me. . . ."

He reported also on a solution to his problems with the War Department, saying:

"This moment I have recd advices from the war department, which goes to show that if we were for a moment neglected by the government we were not forgotten, and that the return of my detachment to Tennessee, as I have marched them fully, meets the wishes of government. They are directed to be paid all the expenses of the return march. This will surprise your D.q. master, and astonish the officer who ordered recruiting officers to my encampment, to enlist my brave fellows, then in the service of their country. . . ." [17]

Early in May, Colonel Benton, one of Jackson's most promising young protegés, who had served well with him on the Natchez expedition, went to Washington for the dual purpose of obtaining authority to raise a regiment and also to expedite the payment of the Tennessee troops for their services. He carried with him a letter to John Armstrong from General Jackson:

"This will be handed to you by Colo. Thos. H. Benton, commandant of the second regt. of Tennessee volunteer Infantry, who having been detained here, on the further service of the Detachment of Volunteers under my command, from the delay of communications on this subject a belief has arisen that our services to the northwest will not be called for by the president. Colo. Benton having abandoned a profitable profession, for the tented fields, having determined during the continuation of the present war to continue in the field of Mars, if Government will give him employ in her armies, goes with this view to the city of Washington. . . ." [18]

Jackson, after recommending Benton highly, continued, telling Armstrong that the quartermaster at Natchez had refused to pay the wagoners employed to haul the sick from that place to Nashville and reciting other indignities. Concluding, he warned:

"If the agents of governments are thus permitted to act with impunity, the disgust will become so general in the west, that the administration will lose that united support that it uniformly recd. in this state. . . ."

Benton went on to Washington and, although his request to raise a regiment at that time was not granted, he made a favorable impression and found a generally favorable atmosphere. He was to be sent back to Tennessee to help recruit a new regiment, of which John Williams of Knoxville would be colonel and he would be lieutenant-colonel. On June 15 he reported at length to Jackson on his own affairs, as well as the Natchez business.

The president, Benton told him, ". . . enquired after your health in terms of particular kindness. . . ." The Tennessee Volunteers, he assured him, were spoken of at the nation's capital in the most honorable terms; reports on their conduct from influential people in Natchez bearing testimony to their conduct and competence as soldiers had been received in Washington. Benton also reported that Jackson's friends were ready, at the first suitable opening, to push Jackson's name for a brigadier generalship.

Unhappily, while Thomas Benton was on this mission, his younger brother, Jesse, became involved in a disagreement with William Carroll, with the result that a duel between them was threatened. Andrew Jackson, being an older man and a friend of both, tried to intercede as a peacemaker, but the interference of trouble makers who sought to use the affair as a means of involving and embarrassing Jackson, made it impossible to bring about a reconciliation. Carroll did not want the duel, but, finally forced into it, asked Jackson to serve as his second. Regretfully, he accepted and was present when the duel took place.

The eminent Jackson historian, James Parton, gives a lively account of the affair—based, no doubt, on firsthand information from older persons whom he interviewed when he was in Tennessee gathering material for his valuable three-volume work. According to Parton, the two men were placed back to back, at the accepted distance apart, and, at the word, wheeled and fired.

"Benton fired first," Parton states, "and then stooped or crouched, to receive the fire of his antagonist. The act of stooping caused a portion of his frame, that was always prominent, to be more prominent still. Carroll fired. His bullet inflicted a long, raking wound on the part exposed, which would have been safe but for the unlucky stoop. . . ."

Jackson then ran up to his principal and asked if he had been hit. Carroll thought not, but noticing that his hand was bleeding, found that a thumb had been shot. Otherwise, there were no injuries. Benton was taken home, and his wound, which was more embarrassing than serious, dressed. He was unable to sit down for some weeks, however, and remained in seclusion.

"The incidents of the duel," Parton remarked, "were so ridiculous that they are still (1859) a standing joke in Tennessee." [19]

The events which followed, however, were no laughing matter. The Bentons went back to their home in Franklin, and Jackson to his Hermitage, but his enemies and the town busybodies would not let the matter rest. Tom Benton, as well as his brother and their friends, further inflamed by the malicious gossip, made threats against Jackson, who for a time, tried to ignore them. But his temper was finally aroused to the point where he declared he would give the young upstarts a sound horse-whipping. At last, the two parties, armed to the teeth, appeared in Nashville—Jackson and his party to their accustomed stopping place, the Nashville Inn, on the Public Square, the Bentons and their friends at the City Hotel, just across the Square. There was much going back and forth by members of both parties and curious onlookers, with the result that a bloody encounter was soon underway at the City Hotel. It was a rough and tumble affair, and the tragic result was that, at length, Andrew Jackson lay on the floor, his left shoulder and side gushing blood, and very, very near to death.

Every doctor in Nashville rushed to the scene, working frantically to staunch the blood and, if possible, to save Andrew Jackson's life. He was carried to bed, where it is said, two mattresses were wet by his blood. Slowly the physicians began to have some hope of his survival and soon, though still prostrate from the wounds and loss of blood, he was carried home to his Hermitage, to be nursed by his devoted wife and sustained by her prayers. This tender care, with the aid of his physicians and his own indomitable will, made it reasonable to expect that, in time, he would recover. But there was to be almost no time at all. Before he was able to

246

leave his bed, news of the massacre at Fort Mims reached Nashville.

Never in the annals of American history has there ever been a more tragic and blood-curdling story. Fort Mims was actually the fortress-home of Samuel Mims, who had built a commodious one-story home on the shores of Lake Tensaw, near Mobile in the present State of Alabama. He had surrounded the acre of ground of which it was the center, with heavy, upright logs which were pierced with five hundred portholes. Heavy gates were placed at the two entrances and, to all appearances, it should have been impregnable.

With the declaration of the War of 1812 there was increasing unrest evident in Indian tribes of the lower South, particularly in the Creek country. Governor Claiborne of New Orleans sent 175 volunteers to protect the fort, to which were added seventy militiamen. They, with a group of friendly Indians who had come to the fort, 160 Negro slaves and the people from more exposed neighboring settlements, brought the total number of persons in the fort on the day of the attack, August 30, 1813, to 553.

Although, on the day before, two Negro men who had been sent out to bring in cattle reported that they had seen Indians nearby, the commandant, Maj. Daniel Beasley, scoffed at their story. The people in the fort, weary of the crowded conditions and inconveniences, relaxed and, with both gates wide open, went about their usual affairs. Lurking all around, from early morning, were one thousand warriors with their chief, William Weatherford, whom they called Red Eagle. Also with them were five prophets, with blackened faces, medicine bags and magic rods, who were supposed to be invulnerable. Hundreds of the warriors lay so quietly in nearby ravines that their presence was not suspected, awaiting the sound of the noon drum which was always beat to announce dinner at the fort. At this sound, which Weatherford had designated as the signal for attack, the inhabitants were assembling for their usual noon meal when the wild cry, "Indians! Indians!" went up. There was not even time to close the gates when the Indians came pouring in.[20]

Major Beasley, belatedly trying to shut one of the gates, could

247

not move it because sand had drifted against it. He was struck with clubs and tomahawks and trampled to the ground. Dying, he exhorted his men to continue resistance. The carnage continued without respect to women, little children or the aged—no one was spared except some of the Negroes who were carried into the Indian nation as slaves. After three hours the bloody attack seemed to slacken, partly, perhaps, because some marksmen had succeeded in killing the five prophets who, like Weatherford's warriors, were supposed to be invulnerable. Weatherford, himself, soon rode up, however, on a great black horse, and persuaded them to go back into the fort and set fire to it. In a short while the flames were consuming it and a small group of women, children, old people, Negroes and wounded soldiers who, huddled together in an effort to escape the flames, were brutally murdered.

"At noon that day," Parton states, "five hundred and fifty-three persons were inmates of Fort Mims. At sunset four hundred mangled, scalped and bloody corpses were heaped and strewn within its wooden walls. Not one white woman, not one white child, escaped. Twelve of the garrison, at the last moment, by cutting their way through two of the pickets, got out of the fort and fled to the swamp. . . . A Negro woman, with a ball in her breast, reached a canoe on lake Tensaw, and paddled fifteen miles to Fort Stoddart, and bore the first news of the massacre to Governor Claiborne. . . ."

Parton, continuing, gives an interesting resumé of Weatherford's effort to secure the aid of the Spanish governor of Florida, Maxeo Gonzalez Manxique, in an attack on Mobile, which, at that time, was in a deplorably weak condition. However, he failed in this and Mobile was spared a massacre which could well have been more terrible than that at Fort Mims.

The nation as a whole, however, was not aware of the precarious situation in the South. News traveled slowly in those days and it was a full month before even a small item appeared in a New York paper mentioning the Fort Mims massacre. But the north and east were rejoicing over Perry's victory in Lake Erie and the triumph of Harrison over Proctor and Tecumseh at the Battle of the Thames, where the latter was killed.

248

The South, from Tennessee to Mobile, was aflame with the horror of the massacre and also with the knowledge that immediate steps must be taken to prevent the recurrence of such atrocities. The settlements near the Tennessee border, like, for instance, Huntsville, in the present state of Alabama, but at that time the last white settlement before entering the Indian country, were in an extremely vulnerable condition.

While Perry and Harrison, returning from their victories, were being feted and praised in the East, Parton comments:

"In a room in Nashville, a thousand miles from these splendid scenes, lay a gaunt, yellow-visaged man, sick, defeated, prostrate, with his arm bound up, and his shoulders bandaged, waiting impatiently for his wounds to heal, and his strength to return. Who then thought of *him* in connection with victory and glory? Who supposed that *he*, of all men, was the one destined to cast into the shade those favorites of the nation, and shine out as the prime hero of the war?"

The primitive means of transportation and the appalling disstances which intervened between Governor Claiborne, the former Congressman and citizen of Tennessee, who was then governor of Louisiana, made it impossible for him to undertake any immediate retaliatory measures against the Indians, or, for that matter, even to provide defense for the exposed portions of Alabama, which were also a part of his territory. New Orleans was two hundred miles away from the posts in lower Alabama, Washington a month's journey, Georgia's capital three hundred miles away and Nashville, four hundred miles. The swiftest express riders were promptly dispatched to all of these places, but it was, naturally, from his friends in Tennessee that he expected the greatest help.

Breaking all records for speed, his express rider reached Nashville on September 18, 1813—only nineteen days after the massacre. A mass meeting of citizens was called at once. Rev. Thomas B. Craighead was asked to preside and the following day, which was Sunday, this pioneer minister made an eloquent appeal to the assembled citizens, who passed the necessary resolutions unanimously and appointed Col. John Coffee to confer at once with Governor Blount and Andrew Jackson. His report was expected the following day, for the aroused citizens of Nashville meant to lose no time in going to the aid of their friends in the lower South.

A committee of citizens went immediately to the Hermitage to see if there was any hope that General Jackson would be able to lead his volunteers into the Creek country. Reaching there, they found him still confined to his bed, but, propped up on pillows, he assured them that he could—and would—take command of his troops.

From his sick-bed, on September 19, he issued general orders:

"The late attack of the Creek Indians on the almost defenceless frontier of Mobile settlements, the taking of Fort Mims, and the indiscriminate murder of all the inhabitants, amounting upwards of three hundred, not even sparing the women and helpless children found therein call aloud for retaliatory vengeance. Those distressed citizens of that frontier who have yet escaped the Tomahawk implored the brave Tennesseans for aid. They must not ask in vain. . . . They are our brethren in distress and we must not await the slow and tardy orders of the General Government. . . ." [21]

Colonel Coffee's regiment of cavalry was ordered to proceed promptly to Huntsville, which was then the last white settlement before going into the Indian country, and, should he find this place reasonably well protected, to cross the nearby Tennessee river.

Maj.-Gen. John Cocke, who commanded the militia in East Tennessee, was fortunately in Nashville when news of the Fort Mims massacre was received. He was ordered by Governor Blount to return to Knoxville and to march his troops to Ditto's landing, on the Tennessee River near Huntsville. War was, indeed, on Tennessee's doorstep.

Jackson's volunteers were ordered to rendezvous at Fayetteville, a village located some eighty miles south of Nashville and a little over thirty miles from Huntsville. The general himself arrived at the encampment, which he named Fort Blount, late in the afternoon of October 7, beginning at once, preparations for a march into the enemy country. Though still in a weakened condition, he proved himself fully capable of taking active command. The day after Jackson's arrival at Fort Blount, Coffee informed him that a large force of Indians was in motion on the Coosa and was threatening the borders of Georgia and Tennessee.

Jackson then hurried forward to join Coffee and, near Huntsville, at Ditto's Landing, they established Fort Deposit. Coffee, who was ordered forward with seven hundred cavalrymen, established Camp Coffee and, later, at Ten Islands, he and Jackson established Fort Strother, which was his base of operations. He had expected to be joined here by troops from East Tennessee under General White, but neither they nor expected provisions had yet arrived.

Back in Nashville, Governor Blount was doing his utmost to support Tennessee's army in the field. Upon receiving news of the Fort Mims massacre, he had made a call upon the state legislature for authorization of 3,500 volunteers and, for putting them into the field, a sum of $300,000. In these and other actions for prosecuting the war he had the full cooperation of an enraged citizenship and, eventually, approbation of the federal government.

Jackson's first step toward retaliation for the Fort Mims massacre was on November 2, when he ordered Colonel Coffee—who had now been promoted to the rank of brigadier-general—forward to meet a large body of Indians at Tallushatchee, on the south side of the Coosa, about thirteen miles away. The Indians fought desperately, but Coffee won an outstanding victory, in spite of his modest report that he had had ". . . a small skirmish with the Indians and a part of my Brigade, where we killed two hundred and took eighty prisoners. . . "

Jackson, meanwhile, had his army busily engaged in strengthening and fortifying Fort Strother and in making preparations for pushing deeper into the Indian country. In the late afternoon of November 7, 1813, a runner came into camp with word that the friendly Indians at the Talladega fort were under siege by a body of more than one thousand hostile Indians. General Jackson knew that help must reach them immediately or they would be destroyed, so he began at once to make preparations to go to their relief. First he sent a message by express to General White, who, with his East Tennesseans, were supposed to be on the way to join him, requesting him to come on to Fort Strother at once and remain there for its protection. He then gave orders for taking up the line

251

of March with a force composed of eight hundred cavalry and mounted gunmen, and twelve hundred infantry. He left behind his sick and wounded, all of his baggage and a small force which he considered adequate for the protection of the fort until General White arrived.

Knowing that the friendly Indians at Talladega were in their present predicament because of their determination to show their friendship for the United States, Jackson was determined to reach them before they were destroyed. He had his troops ready to march before midnight and, by one o'clock in the morning, they were crossing the river, which, at that place was six hundred yards wide. This, naturally, consumed several hours, but the fatigued men did not pause to rest after they had landed on the other side. Pushing forward with all possible speed, they came within six miles of Talladega fort by late afternoon and at once dispatched two friendly Indians to reconnoitre. They returned about 11:00 p.m. with the news that the enemy was posted within a quarter of a mile of the fort, but they had not been able to get close enough to judge their exact number. In less than an hour a runner came in with the news that General White, instead of proceeding to Fort Strother, had, under orders from General Cocke, changed his line of march and had gone on to the mouth of the Chattauga creek. This alarming news convinced General Jackson that he must attack at once and return as rapidly as possible to Fort Strother, which he had, unavoidably, left in a seriously vulnerable position.

Arriving about a mile from the Talladega fort at seven in the evening, the troops were formed in order of battle, with about 250 of the cavalry placed in the rear as reserves. William Carroll, then with the rank of colonel, and later to become Governor of Tennessee, led the advance, which was composed of a company of artillerists, with muskets, two companies of riflemen, and one of spies.[22] The advance, which had been ordered to commence the action and then fall back, so as to draw the enemy with them, arrived within about eighty yards of the Indians at about eight o'clock. Finding the enemy partially concealed in the undergrowth along a small stream, the advance opened a heavy fire upon them. This brought the Indians out into a screaming, yelling attack and the action became general. There was a brief setback, due to some misunderstanding on the part of Colonel Bradley's command and the reserves had to be dismounted to correct their error, but after some fifteen minutes the Indians began fleeing in every direction. General Jackson ordered his men forward in a rapid pursuit, which lasted for three miles—when the mountains were reached. The Indians later placed their loss at not less than six hundred. Fifteen Americans were killed and eighty wounded.

White's failure to go on to Fort Strother prevented General Jackson from taking advantage of his victory by pushing forward, so, burying his dead and starting his wounded on the return march, he turned back to strengthen his rear before starting a major forward movement. In spite of this necessary retrograde movement, his victory was a significant one. He had not only freed the frontiers of Tennessee and Georgia from the danger of a powerful Indian invasion, but he had also made the first step in his march to New Orleans and the freeing of the entire South from both British and Indian attacks.

As he turned back to Fort Strother, winter was beginning to settle down and an enemy whom Jackson had never met before was soon confronting him. For stark drama, for courage and wisdom and sheer tenacity far beyond the capacity of ordinary men, this cruel chapter of Andrew Jackson's life is without parallel.

When he got back to Fort Strother, he found that even the scant food supply which he had left behind him was all but exhausted. Only a few biscuits left from his own private stores remained and these he ordered at once to be given to the sick and wounded. His army contractors, particularly those who had been engaged to send bread, by way of the river, down from East Tennessee, had failed completely to deliver them. Others failed to deliver beef and other foodstuffs, or sent shipments forward in such small amounts that they fell far short of feeding the large body of hungry men. There was desperation in camp, for it was impossible for a body of men of that size to maintain itself in the wilderness.

One morning a hungry soldier, seeing General Jackson sitting on the root of a large tree and eating something with apparent relish, approached him and asked for food.

253

" 'I will most cheerfully,' Jackson said, 'divide with you what I have,' and putting his hand in a pocket drew forth a few acorns, on which he had been feasting, adding that it was the best and only fare he had.' "

Another story is that one day the general invited some of his officers to dine with him and, when they arrived, offered them a cup of water and a platter of acorns.

It was not like Jackson, however, to sit and wait for something to happen, or to consider a retrograde movement.

"What," he had thundered, "retrograde under those circumstances? I will perish first!" [23]

He was fully aware of the dangerous situation which confronted him, however, and with characteristic vigor, took prompt action to remedy it. He wrote a frank letter to Governor Blount, who, it appeared, had begun to lose his courage. Jackson was, however, soon reassured and received his full cooperation. He also dispatched Carroll, Coffee and others to the settlements to recruit and get supplies moving forward. Then he appealed to his friend, the Presbyterian preacher at Franklin, Tennessee, the Rev. Gideon Blackburn.

"Dr. Genl.," Blackburn wrote him on November 20, 1813, "do not risk too much until you should be recruited. West Tennessee has souls who would fly to your relief if they knew you needed their assistance. I would myself commence the office of recruiting officers and march to your encampment. . . ." [24]

And he did just that! He preached and recruited faithfully and, with the men he had helped organize, marched out under Colonel Carroll to join Jackson in the field.

But while the Rev. Blackburn, Hugh Lawson White, and others were recruiting and Governor Blount was putting his full strength behind the contractors and the war effort in general, Jackson's army was threatened with complete disintegration. Even after the hunger was assuaged by food brought in so tardily by the contractors, open mutiny was threatened. Major Reid describes one of the most serious scenes as follows:

"Almost a whole brigade had put itself into an attitude for moving forcibly off. A crisis had arrived; and feeling its importance,

254

he [Jackson] determined to take no middle ground, but to triumph or perish. He was still without the use of his left arm; but seizing a musket, and resting it on the neck of his horse, he threw himself in front of the column, and threatened to fire on the first man who should attempt to advance. For many minutes the column preserved a sullen, yet hesitating attitude, fearing to proceed in their purpose, and disliking to abandon it. In the mean time, those who remained faithful to their duty, amounting to about two companies, were collected and formed at a short distance in advance of the troops and in rear of the General, with positive directions to imitate his example in firing if they attempted to advance. At length, finding no one bold enough to advance . . . they abandoned their purpose, and turning quietly around, agreed to return to their posts. . . ." [25]

Actually, as General Jackson had pointed out many times, he had no authority to dismiss them before their terms of service had ended. It was not long, however, until legal expiration of enlistment periods had practically stripped him of his army. But, at last, the contractors were moving food stuffs and other supplies and Parson Blackburn and an army of wholehearted volunteers from Tennessee were on the march to join him.

But Jackson did not harbor resentment toward the men who deserted him. In his correspondence of the period he spoke of ". . . the meagre monster Famine . . ." and, in the midst of his trials, he wrote to his friend, Gideon Blackburn:

"I left Tennessee with the bravest army, I believed, that any general ever commanded. I have seen them in battle; and my opinion of their bravery is not changed. But their fortitude—upon this I relied, but it has been too severely tested. You know not the privations we have suffered, nor do I like to describe them. Perhaps I was wrong in believing that nothing but death could conquer the spirits of brave men. I am *sure* I was, for my men I know are brave. But privations rendered them discontented: that is enough. The Campaign must nevertheless be prosecuted and brought to a successful termination. Gladly would I have saved these men from themselves, ensured them the harvest which they themselves had sown. But if they *will* abandon it to others, it must even be so. . . ." [26]

General Jackson was sufficiently reinforced and supplied by the first of the year to renew his invasion of the Creek country, although at that time he was not strong enough to undertake a major movement against Weatherford's chief stronghold. On January 15, he sent a force across the Coosa and, on the following day, crossed to lead them. His objectives were the hostile towns on the Coosa and Tallapoosa rivers, near the mouth of Emuckfa Creek.

He returned to Fort Strother on January 27, 1814, and on the next day wrote reports to various authorities and, to Mrs. Jackson, a deeply revealing personal account. The battle, he told her, had begun at six o'clock in the morning on January 22, the enemy's spies having located them before they had started their attack. He was prepared, however, and his troops, though raw, met the bold and ferocious attack with firmness and undaunted resolution.[27]

". . . The battle raged," he continued, "until it was sufficiently light to discover and to distinguish our enemies from our friends, when I was informed that that part of the line where the battle waxed hottest was very much thinned, there being many wounded. I immediately ordered the only reserve I had Capt. Ferrell commanding about forty raw infantry to repair to the spot. They were led briskly by Colo. Carroll to the weak point, and Genl Coffee ordered and led on the charge, with Colos. Carroll and Higgins. The enemy gave way at all points. The friendly Indians entered the pursuit which was continued about two miles. . . ." [28]

Concluding the letter, General Jackson said, "accept my blessing kiss my little andrew (their adopted son) for me, I will send him Lyncoya." Lyncoya was the little Indian boy Jackson found near the body of his dead mother and, when he could not get any of the Creek mothers to accept him, took him in his own arms and saw that he was cared for. He lived as a member of the Hermitage household, was educated and taught a trade, but died in early manhood of tuberculosis, it is said.

Jackson, with his limited and badly punished force, did not attempt to continue punitive measures by burning the town. He had a great number of wounded and both his men and his horses were sadly in need of food. All that he could do was to turn back to Fort Strother. He prepared litters for the wounded men and made ready for the return march, knowing that the Indians were preparing another attack. By the morning of January 24, he took up the line of march and had succeeded in getting the last litter bearing a wounded man to safety before the second battle—Enotachopco— broke upon him. It was such a hard fought battle that the right and left columns of his rear guard, with a part of the center, broke and ran. Jackson himself stopped the rout by riding into their midst.

"I attempted to draw my sword," he wrote in a letter to Mrs. Jackson, "but it had become hard to draw, and in the attempt I had like to have broke my left arm, or I should have halted the fugitives. . . ."

However, the effect of his stern command and the force of his personality prevailed, sparing him actual use of his sword, and his seasoned officers, by their own gallant conduct, helped him save the day.

"Colo. William Cocke 65 years old had advanced to the front and joined in the chase and killed an Indian," he continued. "Capt. Gordon who was in front at the head of his spies rushed to the fight, and entered the pursuit, which was continued for two and a half miles with considerable slaughter . . . ."

Returning to Fort Strother, he began preparations for the final push into the Creek country. Back in Tennessee, Governor Blount and leading citizens in both East and West Tennessee were energetic in recruiting. Even Judge Hugh Lawson White, of the Tennessee Supreme Court, patriotically joined in the effort and traveled all the way to Jackson's wilderness camp to talk with him. In a short time, some five thousand men were raised and marched to join Jackson—two thousand under General John Cocke, two thousand five hundred raised for a three months term of enlistment by Governor Blount, and the remainder under Col. John Williams, of the thirty-ninth Regiment, United States Army.

With this body of men Andrew Jackson started out once more— this time in great enough force to assure a final victory over Weatherford and his fanatical warriors. It took him eleven days to march his army through fifty-five miles of swamps and cane and forests which stretched between Fort Strother and the strongly fortified position of the enemy in the bend located about midway

between the source and the mouth of the Tallapoosa river. Here
Weatherford and his warriors, whom Tecumseh had whipped up to
a state of half madness, securely entrenched and imbued with the
belief that they were on holy ground and could not be defeated,
waited, confident that the victory would be his.

Tohopeka was the Indian name of this bend, but the Americans
called it the Horseshoe. It consisted of an area of some one
hundred acres of fertile land in a kind of isthmus formed by a sharp
bend of the river. The distance across the neck of this U-shaped
isthmus is about three hundred and fifty yards. Andrew Jackson
himself, in his report of March 31, 1814, to Governor Blount, describes the fort and its location:

"I took up the line of march from this place (Fort Williams)
on the morning of the 24th inst. & having opened a passage of
fifty-two & a half miles, over the ridges which divide the waters of
the two rivers, I reached the bend of the Tallapoosa . . . on the
morning of the 27th. The bend resembles, in its curvature that of
a horse-shoe & is thence called by that name among the whites.
Nature furnishes few situations so eligible for defence; and bar-
barians have never rendered one more secure by art. Across the
neck of land which leads into it from the north, they had erected
a breastwork, of the greatest compactness & strength, from five
to eight feet high, & prepared with double rows of port-holes very
artfully arranged . . . The area of this peninsula, thus bounded by
the breast-work, I conjecture, eighty or a hundred acres . . . ." [29]

On the night of March 26, General Jackson camped about six
miles from the Bend and, early the next morning, detailed General
Coffee, with almost his whole force of Indians, to cross the river at
a ford about three miles away and surround the bend so that there
could be no escape by crossing the river.

". . . at half past ten oclk A.M.," General Jackson continued in
his report to Governor Blount, "I had planted my artillery on a
small eminence, distant from its nearest point about eighty
yards . . . from whence I immediately opened a brisk fire upon its
centre . . . With musquetry & rifles I kept up a galling fire whenever
the enemy shewed themselves behind their works, or ventured to
approach them. This continued, with occasional intermissions, for

258

about two hours, when Capt. Russell's company of spies & a part of the Cherokee force, headed by their gallant Chieftain Col. Richard Brown, & conducted by the brave Col. Morgan, crossed over to the extremity of the peninsula in canoes & set fire to a few buildings which were there situated. They advanced with great gallantry towards the breastworks, & commenced firing upon the enemy who lay behind it . . . ."

In spite of the hundreds of cannon balls and rifle bullets which were fired into the fort, comparatively little damage was done. They entered the soft wood of the logs and the earth of which its walls were constructed, burying themselves and not shattering the logs. Realizing that the stronghold could not be reduced in this manner, General Jackson ordered that it be taken by storm.

He describes this action and its effect:

"Having maintained for a few minutes a very obstinate contest, muzzle to muzzle, through the port-holes, in which many of the enemy's bullets were welded to the bayonets of our musquets, our troops succeeded in gaining the opposite side of the works. The event could no longer be doubtful. The enemy altho many of them fought to the last with that kind of bravery desperation inspires, were at length entirely routed & cut to pieces. The whole margin of the river which surrounded the peninsula was strewed with the slain."

Colonel Coffee stated that his command had counted 557 dead on the ground, besides about three hundred who were shot and sank in the river—making a total of something like eight hundred or more killed and about five hundred prisoners—mostly squaws and children. Jackson lost twenty-six of his men killed and 106 wounded, and among the friendly Indians who fought with him, twenty-nine killed and forty-seven wounded.

The carnage was indeed dreadful. The Indians, who with increasing desperation, fought from mid-morning until darkness ended the battle, had been so indoctrinated with the belief that they would meet a more terrible death if they fell into the hands of the white men, gave no quarter and accepted none. Many of them kept fighting long after they were wounded and struggled

259

wildly against the surgeons who tried to help them, until they learned they would not be killed by them.

Sam Houston, then a young ensign in his twenty-first year, was among the most striking of the soldiers who marched down from East Tennessee to join Jackson's forces. He was tall, handsome, powerfully built and of a personality which even then attracted favorable attention. He and his family in Blount County were already well known to General Jackson.

When General Jackson gave the order to storm the breastworks at Tohopeka, he was among the first at the portholes with his rifle, but, seeing this effort fail, he, with a number of others, scaled the breastworks and dropped down among the Indians to engage in hand-to-hand fighting. Unfortunately, as he mounted the breastworks, he received a barbed arrow in his thigh and, being forced to have it removed, asked a lieutenant to pull it out. After two attempts, the lieutenant failed, but Houston, in pain and desperation, shouted for him to try again and, if he failed this time, he'd knock him down! Once more the lieutenant, summoning all of his strength, pulled and the arrow came out—leaving a great, gaping wound which was bleeding so profusely that Houston was forced to go back to a surgeon to have it bandaged. As he was lying on the ground under the care of the surgeon, General Jackson came by and, recognizing him, ordered him not to go back into action.

Later in the day, when General Jackson called for volunteers to dislodge the Indians who had barricaded themselves beneath the bluffs by the river, Houston was the first to step forward. Calling to his platoon to follow, he immediately dashed toward the riverbank—only to receive two bullets in his right shoulder. Now completely disabled and already weak from loss of blood, he was carried from the field. His condition was serious and his recovery was dangerously slow, but his magnificent constitution finally responded to treatment and he recovered and was spared to play his part in great events which were yet to come.

David Crockett, who also participated heroically in the Creek campaign, was of a different personality and entirely different nature. He, too, gained early political prominence in Tennessee and became a member of Congress. For a time, he was a supporter

David Crockett, "peerless bear hunter of the West," with rifle and attired in hunting shirt. Photo courtesy of State of Tennessee Tourism Development Division.

David Crockett as a young statesman. Photo courtesy of State of Tennessee Tourism Development Division.

of Andrew Jackson, but, in his last years in Tennessee, he affiliated himself with the Whig party and became one of Jackson's liveliest opponents. His untimely death at the Alamo cut off what might have been a brilliant political career in Texas. That he was able and intelligent, his official actions and records show, but it is seldom for these that he is now remembered. Such a wealth of folklore and legend has grown up about him that it is sometimes difficult to find the real person. One of the most interesting descriptions of him during the Creek war period is given by Parton, the Jackson biographer, who pictures him as a member of the expedition which had paused on the Tennessee river, near Huntsville, Alabama, just before they pushed on into the Creek country:

"There they were, twenty-five hundred of them, in the pleasant autumn weather, upon a high bluff overlooking the beautiful Tennessee, all in high spirits, eager to be led against the enemy. There were jovial souls among them. David Crockett, then the peerless bear-hunter of the West (to be member of Congress by and by, to be national joker, and to stump the country against his present commander) was there with his rifle and hunting-shirt, the merriest of the merry, keeping the camp alive with his quaint conceits and marvelous narratives. He had a hereditary right to be there, for both his grandparents had been murdered by the Creeks, and other relatives carried into long captivity by them. 'Perfectly a child of nature,' observed his biographer, 'and thrown by accident among men raised, like himself, on the frontiers . . . he was perfectly at home. Naturally a fine person, with a goodness of heart rarely equalled, and a talent for humor never excelled, he soon found his way to the hearts of his messmates. No man ever enjoyed a greater degree of personal popularity than did David Crockett while with the army; and his success in political life is mainly attributable to that fact. I have met with many of his messmates, who spoke of him with the affection of a brother, and from them have heard many anecdotes, which convince me how much goodness of heart he possessed. He not unfrequently would lay out his own money to buy a blanket for a suffering soldier; and never did he own a dollar which was not at the service of the first friend who called for it. Blessed with a memory which never forgot anything, he seemed

261

merely a depository of anecdote; while, at the same time, to invent, when at a loss, was as easy as to narrate those which he had already heard. The qualities made him a rallying point for fun with all his messmates, and served to give him that notoriety which he now possesses." [30]

Fortunate indeed, that Davy Crockett was along to liven things up, for his commanding officer and the officers surrounding him were weighed down with the difficulties and the awful realities of the days ahead when they, with these rollicking, high-spirited young men, would be pushing into the wilderness against a barbaric foe. Jackson, from the time he was a child, knew war and had no illusions about it. Many of his soldiers, even if he were victorious, would find their graves in the Indian country—and he felt a deeply paternal responsibility for them.

Following the victory at Horseshoe Bend, Jackson moved down into the Creek country to the junction of the Coosa and Tallapoosa Rivers, where he built Fort Jackson. Halting there, he sent word to the fleeing Creeks that their Chief, Red Eagle, must be brought in to him. Shortly after sending this message, Jackson was surprised to have that proud chieftain walk quietly into his tent—unattended, unarmed and unannounced. Jackson was impressed by his manly bearing, but considerably surprised that he had come in of his own free will, instead of waiting to be captured and brought in as a prisoner of war. However, both retained their poise and their dignity—Jackson, as a stern military officer, and Weatherford as a proud chieftain, though now in the hands of the victor.

Explaining, in a firm and formal manner, the terms upon which the Creeks might make peace with the United States, Jackson made it clear that Weatherford would have to submit to them. There are many versions of Weatherford's reply, but all of them convey the general tone of his speech. He informed Jackson bluntly that there had once been a time when he would have scorned the terms of the treaty and would have continued fighting, but that now he had no choice. Sadly, he continued, the warriors whom he could once have led into battle were dead—their bones now rested on the battlefields of Talledega, Tallushatchee, Emuckfa, and Tohopeka—and his people were wandering, destitute and starving in the forests.

His one wish, he said, was to spare them further suffering, so he accepted Jackson's terms and agreed to bring his leaders together to negotiate a formal treaty. Rising, and it is said, handing him a cup of brandy General Jackson bade him a formal, but not un-friendly farewell, allowed him to leave his tent as he entered it—unbound and free.

It was a remarkable and tragic discourse, but it contained not one word on the part of Weatherford of repentance or regret for the slaughter at Fort Mims! Jackson had not forgotten it, as is shown in his proclamation to his soldiers at Fort Williams on April 2, 1814:

"The fiends of the Tallapoosa will no longer murder our women and children, or disturb the quiet of our borders. Their midnight flambeaux will no more illuminate their council-house, or shine upon the victims of their infernal orgies. In their places, a new generation will arise, who will know their duty better. The weapons of warfare will be exchanged for the utensils of husbandry and the wilderness, which now withers in sterility, and mourns the desola-tion which overspreads her, will blossom as the rose, and become the nursery of the arts. But before this happy day can arrive, other chastisements remain to be inflicted. It is indeed lamentable, that the path of peace should lead through blood, and over the bodies of the slain; but it is the dispensation of Providence, and perhaps a wise one, to inflict partial evils, that ultimate good may be pro-duced . . . ." [31]

When news of the victory at Horseshoe Bend reached Nashville, cannons roared forth the news of the great event. Rachel Jackson, waiting eagerly at Nashville for word, heard them.

". . . once more you have been Led from The feild of battle in safety," she wrote to her husband on April 12, "murcifull God how he has Smiled on us and Crowned your patriotic Zeale with unequaled successes and Glory and Honour for your self and Country . . . I received the News with so much pleasur . . . when I heard the first Cannon oh never can I describe . . . but when there was nineteen or twenty I was sure you wer safe and one of the most Splendid victoryes of all. . . ."

The roar of the cannon was followed by great rejoicing of the entire population of Nashville and surrounding areas and the beginning of preparations for a great welcome home celebration for Jackson and his volunteers. Many citizens hurried toward the little frontier town of Huntsville, eager to be the first to welcome them—among them were Rachel Jackson and the adored "little Andrew," whom the general mentioned so often in his letters. Soon they were rewarded by the sight of the volunteers, who were quite as eager to be back home as their families were to have them. Joining the triumphal homeward progress at Huntsville, they accompanied the victorious general and his troops back to Nashville and to the greatest celebration of all. First, there was a public meeting at the courthouse, then a banquet at which many speeches were made, a sword was presented to Jackson and every mark of respect was shown to his officers and men. At long last, Rachel and little Andrew, along with many friends and relatives, took him home to the Hermitage, where he was showered with comforts and attention—although it is hardly probable that he had very much time for rest.

Almost at once, he was involved in local military matters and in correspondence with John Armstrong, secretary of war, and others of the national government. On June 8, he wrote to Armstrong accepting the rank of Brigadier-General in the regular army and, on the twentieth, wrote another accepting that of Major-General, succeeding Major-General Harrison, who had just resigned.

Then, there was a treaty to be negotiated with the Creeks, so, under instructions from Armstrong, he set out from Nashville for Fort Jackson on June 25 and reached that place on July 10. Calling the starving, but still proud, Creek chiefs together, he succeeded in closing negotiations on August 9. In discussing the treaty, Secretary Armstrong had advised that it be altogether military in character and suggested that it should be a capitulation, which would place the whole authority for its negotiation in the hands of the commanding general. Acting upon these instructions, Jackson conducted and concluded the treaty by which a tract of some twenty-two million acres of land, which included the whole of Alabama and certain valuable territory on the Coosa and Cahaba, was acquired. Quietly and modestly, he presented this rich acquisition to his country. As a precaution against additional uprisings, he separated the Creek nation from easy intercourse with Pensacola by running a piece of the ceded lands through their nation. Having enforced these harsh terms, Jackson then took up the matter of relieving the sufferings of the Creeks. While it is true that Andrew Jackson was a hard fighter and was stern in enforcement of the terms of peace, it is also true that he was capable of great sympathy and compassion. In his appeals to the secretary of war and to the national government for relief of the unfortunate nation, he also emphasized, however, the military necessity of meeting their needs at once and warned that, otherwise, they would have no alternative but to seek aid from the British.

It was fortunate indeed that the Creek uprising had occurred and been settled before the British turned their attention to the invasion of the Gulf coast. The situation in Europe had changed materially since Napoleon, on March 31, 1814, had signed the treaty of Fontainebleau, abdicating his throne and renouncing all rights for himself and his family. Being freed of this menace, Great Britain then turned her attention to intensifying her war against the United States, launching strong attacks against the Southern coast, as well as on the nation's capital city itself. She left Washington in ashes, after setting the torch to it on August 24. With this victory, she felt assured of a swift and successful conquest of the South.

It was fortunate, too, that Andrew Jackson was in the far South at this particular time. While he was negotiating the treaty with the Creeks he was reliably informed that the British, with the aid of the Indians, would, at an early date, attack some portion of the Gulf coast, more than likely Mobile. Deciding to investigate the situation for himself, he sent his famous spy, Capt. John Gordon, to Pensacola to report to him. As early as July 12 writing to the Spanish commandant at Pensacola, he questioned him about the landing of a British frigate bearing guns and ammunition ". . . for the avowed purpose of enabling the vanquished Creeks to renew a Sanguinary war . . . ." [32] Captain Gordon confirmed this and many other disturbing rumors.

Soon Jackson himself was on the way and it was indeed fortunate that at this crisis and in the low ebb of national morale, that he was in the field, ready, not only to redeem his country's pride, but to drive the British forever from her shores.

Writing to Secretary Armstrong from Fort Jackson on August 10, 1814, he announced: "I shall on the 16th inst. leave this territory with the 3d Infantry for Mobile."

On August 22, he was within four miles of Mobile and, soon arriving there, he began at once to send letters and reports to Governors Blount, of Tennessee; Claiborne, of Louisiana; and Holmes, of Mississippi—as well as to his own officers and many others, urging upon all of them the necessity for raising troops and supplying them for the invasion which he was now convinced was impending.

To Holmes, on September 30, he wrote:

"I had received the degrading news of the burning of our capital by the enemy previous to the receipt of your letter, and although I like every American fealt much mortification at an event so well calculated to show the embecility of our military preparations and I might add the general measures adopted for the protection of the country as well as the general apathy which had pervaded the greater part of the Union, Yet I am well assured that it will have a happy tendency to arouse the people, to a vigorous, and united effort, in the defence of the country. That it will render the war popular . . . We may then look forward to a termination of the war upon terms honorable and advantageous to our country and not until then . . . ." [33]

Immediately after writing this letter, General Jackson became so ill with fever that his aide de camp, Thomas L. Butler, with an explanatory note, signed the letter. For several days the general remained too ill to attend to his correspondence, but on October 7, he wrote a forceful letter to Governor Blount in which he pled earnestly for the recruitment of Tennesseans to meet the emergency which, even then, was upon him.

"I shall be very thankful for any volunteers, in any shape, which your Excellency may be pleased to send. Our country needs them. I had hoped, and do still hope to see you stand forward in a patriotic appeal to the citizens of Tennessee on this subject; inviting

266

them to the field to save their country for subjugation and ruin. We have too long rested on feelings unsupported by proper action. By a careless, misplaced confidence our Capital has been lost; and we shall not recover the national disgrace, unless energy becomes the order of the day." [34]

Soon General Jackson informed Secretary Monroe, who had succeeded Armstrong, that militia from Tennessee was on the march to him, and that he had decided to go over to Pensacola, drive the British and Indians out, and take possession of the place.

"As I act without the orders of government, I deem it important," he continued, "to state to you my reasons for the measure I am about to adopt. First I conceive the safety of this section of the union depends upon it. The Hostility of the Governor of Pensacola in permitting the place to assume the character of a British Territory by resigning the command of the Fortresses to them, permitting them to fit out an expedition against the U.S. and after its failure to return to the Town refit, and make arrangements for a second expedition."

Jackson continued, listing many other grievances against the Spanish governor, then, as soon as he could get his force organized, proceed to march on his unauthorized expedition. As he approached Pensacola, he began carrying on a lively correspondence with Gonzalez Manxique, the governor, but not being able to come to any agreement with him, carried out his promise to take the place and chase out the British and Indians.

In a lengthy report written on November 14, 1814, to Secretary Monroe, he announced:

". . . Thus Sir I have broken up the hot bed of the Indian war and Convinced the Spaniards That we will permit no equivocation in a nation professing neutrality, while we most scrupulously respect national, neutral and Individual rights. . . ."

It was a high-handed, colorful and typically Jacksonian affair— but it proved highly beneficial to the American cause. By November 20 he was back in Mobile and reported to Secretary Monroe:

"I flatter myself that I have left such an impression on the mind of the Governor of Pensacola, that he will respect the American Character, and hereafter prevent his neutrality from being infringed. Should he suffer the British again to occupy his Town, and the Indians to return, This District cannot be protected unless they are (as you have expressed in your letter of 7 September) promptly expelled."

But the British invasion was fast approaching and there was much speculation as to where they would strike first. Jackson was of the opinion that they might attempt a landing at Pascagoula, which had an excellent harbor, penetrate the country of that locality and thus be able to cut off his supplies from New Orleans.[35] General James Winchester was on the way to relieve Jackson of the command at Mobile, and Jackson advised him, in a letter written November 22, 1814, that he was to take immediate command of the section of his district from Pascagoula to the eastern limits of the district and as far north as the Tennessee River. This freed Jackson to move on to New Orleans.

On the same day that he wrote this letter to Winchester, General Jackson ordered Coffee to move by easy marches toward New Orleans, choosing the roads and the course which offered most forage. Also on that day he himself started out toward New Orleans, having informed Secretary Monroe that he would leave on that day and ". . . travel by land to have a view of the points at which the enemy might effect a landing." [36]

It was a remarkable and arduous journey for a high-ranking officer and particularly so for one who had been but lately confined to bed with a violent attack of fever and was still suffering from wounds he had received in the Benton affair. In fact, he had written to Rachel from Mobile, on September 22, that since, a bone, which he had sent to her, had come out of his arm and that it was healing and strengthening very fast.

"I hope," he said, "that all the loose pieces of bone is out, and I will no longer be pained with it . . . ." [37]

Only a man with Jackson's indomitable will could have taken and kept the field in his weakened and painful condition. Yet he did and, with no escort except his own small staff, he mounted his horse on the morning of November 22 and rode off in the same direction Coffee's troops had taken. He had ahead of him a journey of 170 miles, through rough and sometimes swampy roads—

Washington Street in Pascagoula, Mississippi, the "Singing River" in the distance. This is the area examined by Jackson in November 1814 on the supposition that the British might land here rather than at New Orleans.

British cannon captured in the Mobile area by Jackson in 1814, now on the grounds of the Old Spanish fort, built in 1718 at Pascagoula. Photo courtesy of Mrs. Henry M. Gautier, director of the Old Spanish Fort.

or no roads at all—but, by riding about seventeen miles a day, he reached New Orleans on the first day of December.

He camped at night at strategic points along the way and compared the terrain with a map which Governor Claiborne had sent to him and, by the time he reached New Orleans, he knew the country well. He was still of the opinion that the enemy might wisely choose to make a landing at the mouth of the Pascagoula, or "Singing River" and he may, as he carefully observed this beautiful, storied country, have heard the mysterious "music" which gave this river its name. An old legend tells the story of a tribe of local Indians who, hopelessly outnumbered by an enemy, walked singing—every man, woman, and child of them—into its waters, preferring this death rather than to submit to defeat and enslavement by the enemy. Some freak of Nature now and then produces, so local residents say, echoes of their singing. With its luxuriant vegetation and great live oak trees, festooned by wispy, gray Spanish moss, it is a lovely, romantic country—but passing through, Andrew Jackson was concerned chiefly with evaluating its importance as a strategic position which might, all too soon, be occupied by the enemy.

Early on the chilly, misty morning of December 1, General Jackson and his staff urged their horses to trot briskly along the road which followed the course of Bayou St. John, which emptied into Lake Pontchartrain and, as Jackson knew, offered the enemy a convenient entrance to the city. Halting at the gates of the palatial residence of J. Kilty Smith, probably the wealthiest and most prominent merchant of New Orleans, they tossed their bridles to the little Negro stable boys who were awaiting them, dismounted, and walked to the old Spanish villa which was the home of their host. Mr. Smith welcomed them in his handsome marbled hall. Though he was a bachelor, his household was in perfect readiness, for he had solicited the aid of a neighbor, a distinguished Creole lady, who knew the niceties of New Orleans society and was thoroughly familiar with the mysteries of Creole cookery. She had spared no effort—and had seen that Smith's servants spared none—to have everything in readiness to entertain the famous and

269

widely heralded General Jackson and his party in a style which she considered suitable for such an occasion.

She was thoroughly shocked and much annoyed, however, when the great general was presented to her. At the first opportunity she managed to draw the host aside and whisper to him:

"Ah! Mr. Smith, how could you play such a trick on me? You asked me to get your house in order to receive a great General. I did so. I worked myself almost to death to make your house *comme il faut,* and prepared a splendid *dejeuner,* and now I find that all my labor is thrown away upon an ugly, old Kaintuck-flatboatman, instead of your grand General, with plumes, eqaulettes, long sword, and moustache."

Her reaction was typical for, at first sight the citizens of New Orleans could not reconcile Andrew Jackson's appearance with his already established fame. Men like Governor Claiborne, who knew both the frontiers and the more sophisticated society of older settlements, knew well, however, that he was capable of appearing at ease in both. However, such superficial matters were not thought of on that crucial morning of December 1. Jackson, knowing the urgency of the moment, and his own impaired health, ate only a little boiled hominy and conversed with his host on the state of affairs in New Orleans, while his young staff members did full justice to the elegant meal which the Creole lady had planned in their honor. But even the host was a little annoyed because, at the earliest possible moment, Jackson made it clear that he must proceed to New Orleans at once.

Carriages were brought around immediately and the entire party was on the old Bayou road and would soon be in the city, where Daniel Clark, Louisiana's first representative to the Congress of the United States, had prepared his elegant home to receive them. Immediately upon their arrival Jackson was visited by military officers, city officials, prominent citizens and Governor Claiborne, who had known him well back in Tennessee. General Jackson still wore his threadbare uniform, his high and still muddy leather boots, a short blue Spanish coat and a leather cap—but his appearance did not disturb the leaders who knew his record well, appreciated him for what he had already accom-

270

plished, and hailed him as the "Saviour of New Orleans." A public meeting was held at once, at which citizens of all walks of life had the opportunity to see him, to greet him and to hear his urgent plea for harmony, for the ceasing of all differences and for uniting in the preparations to repel the invasion which was almost upon them.

The city rang with the news, Parton says:

"Jackson had come! There was magic in the news. Every witness testifies to the electric effect of the general's quiet and sudden arrival. There was a truce at once to indecision, to indolence, to incredulity, to factious debate, to paltry contentions, to wild alarm. He had come, so worn down with disease and the fatigue of his ten days' ride on horseback that he was more fit for the hospital than the field. But there was that in his manner and aspect which revealed the master. That will of his triumphed over the languor and anguish of disease, and every one who approached him felt that the man of the hour was there." [38]

Jackson called immediately upon all of the military organizations and the citizens of Louisiana, asking for their support. Among those responding at once was Jean Lafitte, who generously tendered his services and those of his pirate band. They were accepted promptly and without question, but, fortunately, the Legislature of Louisiana had, in this emergency, already passed resolutions granting amnesty to Lafitte and his band, who were under indictment for violation of revenue laws and other offences. The British had been making overtures to Lafitte, in order to obtain the benefit of his valuable knowledge of the waters, the swamps and the bayous around the city. He led them on skillfully for some time, always relaying information which he was able to get from them to the authorities at New Orleans. Jackson gratefully accepted the proffer of aid and found it, not only throughout the brief period of preparation, but also during the battles, of great military value.

To the "free men of colour" Jackson addressed an urgent appeal:

"Through a mistaken policy, my brave fellow Citizens, you have heretofore been deprived of participation in the glorious struggle for National rights, in which our Country is engaged. This shall no

271

longer exist; as sons of freedom, you are now called upon to defend our most estimable blessing! As Americans, your Country looks with confidence to her adopted children for valorous support . . . ." They, as was proved throughout the campaign, offered valuable support.

Turning then to his own forces, he found that Coffee had arrived from Mobile with his command; that Thomas and his twenty-three hundred Kentuckians had set sail on December 8 from the mouth of the Cumberland and were expected to arrive soon; and that William Carroll, with the West Tennessee militia, had arrived at Natchez on December 14. The backwoods riflemen, in their picturesque hunting shirts, were looked upon at first with curiosity and then with genuine appreciation.

As for the backwoodsmen, they were naturally and, sometimes boisterously unawed by the fashionable dress and stilted manners of the city folks they had come down to defend against the British. They sang their songs, among them "The Hunters of Kentucky", with lusty enthusiasm and bowed their knees to no one, except, of course, as their song went, to the ladies. As for themselves, they'd let their rifles do their talking for them! Their general was at home with them in their camps—and quite as much at ease in the stately drawing rooms of the city, which were enthusiastically opened to entertain him and his almost invariably handsome officers.

In the midst of his heavy duties in preparation for the British invasion someone found time to have Jackson provided with a new uniform, befitting his high rank. Social activities and lavish entertainments continued, even in the midst of the feverish preparation for the impending battle. Now, however, Jackson would be able to make a creditable appearance at the few such things as he could find time to attend. One day his aide, a brilliant New Orleans lawyer, Edward Livingston, whose services he had secured shortly after his arrival in the city, announced to his wife that he was bringing General Jackson home to dinner. Mrs. Livingston, gay, beautiful and acknowledged leader of both the French and American social circles, was flabbergasted. The lovely young Creole belles who fluttered around her in the crisis, cried: "But what shall we do with this wild General from Tennessee?"

The answer was soon forthcoming. Mrs. Livingston, seated on a sofa at the head of her drawing room, says Parton, was "anxiously awaiting the inroad of the wild fighter into the regions sacred hitherto to elegance and grace." The young ladies, seated around the room, were also waiting breathlessly. General Jackson was announced and, pausing a moment in the doorway, he entered ". . . Erect, composed, bronzed with long exposure to the sun, his hair just beginning to turn grey, clad in his uniform of coarse blue cloth and yellow buckskin, his high boots flapping loosely about his slender legs, he looked, as he stood near the drawing room door, the very picture of a war-worn noble warrior and Commander. . . ." He made a magnificent bow to the ladies, all of whom arose, it is said, as much from amazement and delight, as from politeness. Mrs. Livingston stepped gracefully toward him and ". . . with a dignity and grace seldom equalled, never surpassed, he went forward to meet her, conducted her back to her sofa and sat by her side. The fair Creoles were dumb with astonishment. . . ." [39]

Dinner soon followed, during which the general conducted himself with the most polished manners and chatted pleasantly with the ladies, assuring them that they need have no worry about the British taking the city—he and his men would attend to that!

The affair ended soon, for the general had to excuse himself and get back to the serious business of making his promise good. As he departed, the girls clustered around their hostess in great excitement: "Is this," they asked "your backwoodsman? Why, madam, he is a prince!"

Quite a contrast to the impression received by the Creole lady who had assisted Mr. Smith in entertaining the general and his staff! Strangely, both of them were true, not only in the case of Andrew Jackson, but of most of the western leaders. They had crossed the mountains and necessarily lived the rough life of the frontiers for a time, but they did not leave their manners and their culture behind them. Still more, they set an example for a gracious social life in the communities west of the mountains.

More than social amenities occupied the commanding general's attention, however, for the British fleet had arrived in the waters in front of New Orleans. The people were alarmed by all sorts of rumors and disaffections. Sailors thronged the streets, but Commodore Patterson could get none to man his two armed vessels. Governor Claiborne, at the commodore's appeal, requested the legislature to suspend the habeas corpus act, in order that men might be pressed into service—but it refused. The American gunboats were captured and the situation grew more serious each day. General Jackson, disgusted at the lukewarm support of the legislature, took things into his own hands and, on December 16, 1814, declared martial law, demanding that every individual entering the city report to the adjutant general's office. Failing to do this he would be subject to arrest and questioning. No person could leave the city without permission in writing from either the general or a member of his staff; no vessels would be permitted to leave New Orleans or the Bayou St. John without a passport from the general, a member of his staff, or the commander of naval forces. Street lights must be extinguished at nine o'clock, after which time any one not having written permission or the proper countersign, would be apprehended as a spy and held for examination. To sum it up, the civilian population of New Orleans was made subject to the same rules which governed the military in the presence of the enemy. It was a stringent and not completely popular measure, but it restored confidence and cooperation on the part of most of the people. The legislature now took firm steps toward cooperation in this and other measures. Jackson, by sheer force of his own personality, in less than a month, had organized his military forces and placed the city under effective martial law.

The first clash of arms between the opposing forces occurred on the night of December 23. The enemy had landed early that morning on the banks of the Mississippi about two and a half leagues below New Orleans, according to General Jackson's report to Governor Holmes on Christmas Day. Telling him that this was a critical moment, in which the stoppage of supplies could have the most dangerous consequences, he urged Holmes to order all vessels carrying provision articles, whether under order of the contractor or not, to descend to New Orleans immediately.

Two days later, General Jackson sent a report to Secretary Monroe, informing him of the arrival of the enemy and of his night attack upon him. He had reached the British encampment about seven o'clock and immediately made preparations to open fire, choosing the strongest point in the enemy's line as his target. Commodore Patterson, with the schooner *Carolina*, had dropped down the river and he also opened fire. This being the signal for attack, General Jackson continued, General Coffee's men, with their usual impetuosity, rushed on the enemy's right and entered their camp, while our right advanced with equal ardor. Had it not been for a thick fog, Jackson believed, his men, even with their smaller force, would have succeeded in capturing the enemy. Under the circumstances, he did not think it wise to continue the night attack, so he remained on the field that night and at five o'clock the next morning took a stronger position about two miles closer to the city. Encamping here, he awaited the arrival of the militia from Kentucky and other reinforcements.

"As the safety of the city will depend on the fate of this army," he concluded, "it must not be incautiously exposed." [40]

At last the Kentucky militia arrived. General Adair, who was acting as Adjutant-General, reported to General Jackson that they had been left at Lafourche, but that not more than one-third of them were armed and those very indifferently. But the general had not yet received the expected arms and ammunition.

On January 1, the enemy had opened a tremendous cannonade, General Jackson wrote to Secretary Monroe on the following day. They had erected several batteries during the night, but their surprise attack was met successfully by the American troops.

"It was sustained by every corps under my command with a firmness which would have done honor to veterans," Jackson told him. "The enemy still occupy their former position; and whether they will renew their attempt today or ever, I am not able to judge. Whenever they do, however, I perswade myself, from the spirit of my troops, I shall be able to render a good account . . . ."

Each day it became more obvious that the enemy was actively engaged in preparations for a major attack on General Jackson's lines. For some time they had been widening and deepening the canal on which they had disembarked and, by the night of the seventh, they succeeded in getting their boats across from the lake

275

to the river. General Jackson wrote Secretary Monroe that he was aware of these movements, but had been unable to impede the activities of the enemy because he considered it unwise to attempt an offensive in open country against a numerous and well-disciplined army.

Meanwhile, he was getting everything in his encampment in shape for action and, on the morning of January 8, when the enemy, after throwing a heavy shower of bombs and Congreve rockets against them, began advancing on his right and left, he was ready to receive them.

". . . I cannot speak sufficiently in praise of the firmness and deliberation with which my whole line received their approach," he wrote to Monroe. "More could not have been expected from veterans inured to war. For an hour the fire of the small arms was incessant and severe as can be imagined. Yet the columns of the enemy continued to advance with a firmness which reflects upon them the greatest of credit. At length, however, cut to pieces, they fled in confusion from the field, leaving it covered with their dead and wounded."

Among the slain were Sir Edward Pakenham, major-general in command of the British forces, and Major-General Gibbs. Major-General Keane was seriously wounded, upon which the command devolved upon Maj. Gen. John Lambert, who conducted the necessary negotiations concerning the wounded, the killed and the prisoners with General Jackson following the battle.

There have been many accounts of the losses of the contending armies, the most dependable of which is probably that given in the Reid and Eaton history of Andrew Jackson, which places the total British loss at twenty-six hundred—seven hundred killed, fourteen hundred wounded and five hundred taken prisoners. The American loss was seven killed and six wounded.[41]

Down through the years, military experts have analyzed this historic battle and have advanced many theories to explain the tremendous disparity in the British and the American casualty figures. Wellington himself trained these troops; many of them were already veterans of Napoleonic wars; Great Britain outfitted them and equipped them with an abundance of arms and ammuni-

276

The Battle of New Orleans, January 8, 1815.

tion; yet, a greatly inferior body of raw troops from the furthermost frontiers of the United States mowed them down like wheat before a scythe. It was after this defeat that Wellington himself was to lead survivors of the Battle of New Orleans to final victory over Napoleon at Waterloo, on June 18, 1815, so they certainly lacked nothing in the skill or the will to fight. Why? Some say it was because the British foolishly charged in the mass formation approved by European military experts; others point out that the Americans were better shots; still others hold that the American guns, with their long, rifled barrels, were superior to the smoothbore guns which the British were said to have used. Yet none of these things really explain it.

Andrew Jackson, on January 19, willingly and humbly attributing the victory to the intervention of Divine power, sent his request to the Abbe Guillaume Dubourg to call for a public service of thanksgiving:

"Revd. Sir, The signal interposition of Heaven; in giving success to our arms against the Enemy, who, so lately landed on our Shores, an enemy as powerful, as Inveterate in his hatred, While it must excite in every bosom attached to the happy Government under which we live, emotions of the liveliest gratitude, requires at the same time some manifestation of those feelings.

"Permit me therefore to entreat that you will cause the service of public thanksgiving to be performed in the Cathedral in token at once of the great assistance we have recd. from the ruler of all Events and our humble sense of it." [42]

In spite of the war, however, Jackson's men seemed to be thoroughly enjoying their sojourn in New Orleans. Especially after the victory, the attentions of the people were showered upon them. They responded by giving the city a taste of the frontier, its dress, its manners and its music. They attended the great public functions staged in honor of their general. They saw little children and pretty young ladies strew flowers in his path and, at the great cathedral services presided over by the Abbe' Dubourg, the citizens sang poems written in his honor. Then, returning these courteous gestures, the frontiersmen gave the citizens of New Orleans some of their own music—such as their own song, "The Hunters of Kentucky."

Ye Gentlemen and Ladies fair,
Who grace this famous city,
Just listen, if you've time to spare
While I rehearse this ditty.

I s'pose you've read in all the prints, how Packenham
attempted
To make Old Hickory Jackson wince, but soon his schemes
repented,
For we with rifles ready cock'd, thought such occasion lucky,
And soon around the general flock'd the hunters of
Kentucky . . .

They found at length 'twas all in vain to fight where lead was
all the booty
And so they wisely took to flight, and left us all the beauty.
And now if danger e'er annoys, remember what our trade is;
Just send for us Kentuck boys, and we'll protect you Ladies!

O, Kentucky, the hunters of Kentucky,
O, Kentucky, the hunters of Kentucky.

While the men were being so royally entertained, the general
and his staff were being feted in the most elegant drawing rooms
of the city. Jackson, for all of his rugged camp life, had charming
manners which took the ladies of New Orleans by storm. He was
a superb horseman, a graceful dancer and, whether riding through
the streets on horseback, or appearing at social functions in his
honor, he made a striking appearance. New Orleans was surprised
and delighted. Even the horse he rode on the day of the great
battle played his part in the glamorous scene.

Uncle Alfred, the general's body servant, who, as a boy had
been with him at New Orleans, told a story of Duke, the horse
the general rode on the memorable January 8.

"General is ridin' Juke (Duke) dat day; he warn't ridin' dat ar
white horse standin' in de parlor . . . He's ridin' Juke. An' Juke he

dance Yankee Doodle on three legs; and he dance it so plain dat de ban' struck up and play 'Jackson, Jackson Yer's de man fo' me. . . .'" Uncle Alfred referred to the portrait by Ralph Earl showing General Jackson riding Sam Patch, the beautiful white horse presented to him later by the citizens of Philadelphia.[43]

Such stories are entirely in keeping with Jackson's character. He not only liked music, but at home he participated in it and in camp he encouraged it. He also had the opinion that it was necessary for the training of troops and, from the heart of the Indian country, in February, 1814, he ordered a man named Hunt, who was imprisoned on some minor charge, to be released and sent at once to help train some of his recruits:

"It is impossible that raw troops can be disciplined without good music, and in a short time Hunt can instruct such raw music, as is with the 39th. and the Regt. can be progressing in their discipline . . . ."[44]

Victory was not all a series of social affairs, parades and sacred services in the great Cathedral. Following the military victory there were other matters—some of which were most troublesome— to occupy the general's time and attention. One of them was the Judge Hall incident. With the advent of peace, some of the citizens of New Orleans, chafing under the restrictions of martial law, demanded its immediate removal. General Jackson, although peace between the United States and England had been announced, refused to lift the restrictions until he received satisfactory official documents on the subject. One of the cases brought to the attention of the court over which Judge Dominick Hall presided became the center of heated debate in the courtroom as well as throughout the city. Finally, General Jackson had both the plaintiff and Judge Hall put into jail. Shortly, peace having been assured, the judge, as soon as he was restored to his bench, had Jackson appear before him, upon which, in a manner quite as high-handed as Jackson's action in putting him in jail, Judge Hall fined him one thousand dollars—stating that the question was, ". . . whether the Law should bend to the General, or the General to the Law." Jackson, of course, became more of a hero than ever and the people of New Orleans raised a fund to reimburse him for the payment of the fine. General Jackson, expressing his appreciation of the act, declined, asking that the fund be applied to some charitable purpose.

About this time Rachel Jackson realized her long delayed wish to join her husband in the South. It was General Jackson's desire and intention to bring her and their little Andrew down much earlier, but the fortunes of war made it impossible. As early as August, 1814, he had written to her, saying that he had instructed a nephew, John Hutchings, to get a fine pair of horses for her and telling her either to have her carriage repaired, or go in to Nashville and order a new one. She must also, he told her, supply herself with a wardrobe suitable for the position she now had—the wife of a major-general in the service of the United States—something elegant, but simple and not too extravagant.[45]

But it was not until January 19, 1815, that she with her niece, Rachel Butler, wife of Colonel Robert Butler, and little Andrew, set sail from Nashville. The successful termination of the war between the United States and Great Britain made it fitting that the wife of the conquering general should be properly attended and sent down the river in fine style. Colonel Robert Hays, brother-in-law of General Jackson, made arrangements for Mrs. Jackson and her party, with a suitable crew and escort, to make the trip. A part of the cargo would be meat, meal, corn and other products of the Butler and the Hermitage plantations to be sold in New Orleans, and to be used on the trip. Colonel Anderson, with twenty of the handsomest men in his command, properly outfitted in new uniforms, and his "musick" would accompany the party.

"I do not want to hear of Mrs. Jackson going down to you without some sort of a military escort," Colonel Hays wrote to Jackson on December 20, 1814.

He reported also that he had found a very handsome keel boat of 30 ton burden, which would cost more than a flatboat, but that it would go down much faster and they would get off much sooner than they could by waiting to build a flatboat. Harman Hays, son of Nathaniel Hays, from whom Jackson had bought his Hermitage property, would also accompany the party, and, to speed the passage even more, the owner of the boat had agreed to double man the oars.[46]

Portraits of Rachel and Andrew Jackson. Mrs. Jackson's likeness is from the miniature which General Jackson carried constantly, and his is from the well-known portrait by Earl.

In this fine style, and with her "elegant, but plain" dresses, Rachel Jackson and her party set out on their journey and arrived safely in New Orleans twenty-five days later—in time for the great dinner given in honor of George Washington's birthday—and also in honor of a new star on the national horizon—Andrew Jackson.

But the "elegant but plain" dresses which Rachel had brought from Nashville did not seem quite the style in New Orleans—a matter which was promptly and efficiently remedied by the beautiful Madame Livingston. She hurriedly assembled French seamstresses and more stylish dresses were soon completed. They did not transform Rachel Jackson's appearance—after all, she was forty-seven, more than a little plump, and browned from the days when she rode over the Hermitage plantation, superintending the work and caring for the many people who formed her household, while the master was absent winning the wars. She was still beautiful, but in a placid, comfortable, matronly way—and to her distinguished husband, still the loveliest woman in the world! She and Madame Livingston became fast friends and other Creole ladies, who had first smiled behind their fans when they gossiped about her, learned to love her. Others were not so kind, for the anti-Jackson element, which, since the victory was won now dared to show their true nature, made her the victim of their attacks and their ridicule. One of the New Orleans papers published a caricature, showing Rachel Jackson standing on a table, while Madame Livingston, behind her, using all of her strength, was pulling the laces to a corset, trying to make a waistline where there was none. Others, like the writer, Vincent Nolte, used the old French saying that she demonstrated how far the skin could be stretched. Nolte also gave the ridiculous picture of the long, lean general and his plump little wife giving the guests at the Washington birthday ball an exhibition of a pioneer "hoe-down" to the wild tune of "Possum up de Gume Tree"—dancing opposite each other "like two half-drunken Indians."

But such things mattered little to Rachel Jackson now—the war was over, her general was being crowned with laurels, but, best of all, they'd soon be going home to the Hermitage. On the whole, however, they had far more genuine friends in New Orleans than enemies.

The anti-Jackson group, however, did not cease their efforts to discredit him and, for that matter, to question the significance of his victory at New Orleans. Although it is true that the United States and Great Britain had signed the treaty concluded at Ghent, Belgium, on December 24, 1814, fifteen days before that battle was fought, news of the treaty in many instances, was not received in the centers of government until a month after it was concluded. Some historians have dwelt at length on what they term the uselessness and futility of this battle, not taking into consideration the difficulties of travel and communication.

More competent students know, however, that during the 1814 negotiations, the British had insisted that the United States relinquish valuable territory on its northern frontiers, establish a permanent Indian reservation in the northwest, and make other undesirable concessions. Although the American victory caused many of these stipulations to be withdrawn, the final treaty was far from advantageous to the United States and left several dangerous loopholes to the British. The part of the treaty most dangerous to this country was that which provided for commissioners from both sides to be appointed to settle ownership of all disputed claims about the boundaries. Had it not been for Jackson's decisive victory at New Orleans, Great Britain, as well as France and Spain would have undoubtedly been more aggressive about extending their boundaries and making additional settlements in regard to their lands in America.

And so it was to be through all the years of Andrew Jackson's life. From one side he would continue to receive the most enthusiastic approval and from the other—which was usually in the minority—the most scathing criticism. Knowing his devotion to his wife and his sensitiveness to the conditions of her divorce from Lewis Robards, his worst opponents used this subject deliberately in attempts to arouse his own ungovernable temper. But, in spite of the unpleasant side, the path of victory was strewn with flowers and the brilliant light of fame was already upon him.

At the earliest possible moment, he concluded his business in

New Orleans and with his Rachel and their party, started home. Their route was over the old Natchez Trace, now so much improved that a carriage could travel over it, but still very rough and still passing through an almost unbroken wilderness.

From the time they reached the first settlements north of the Tennessee River, the welcome home celebrations began, continuing into Nashville, where they were greeted with the greatest of joy and excitement. On May 24, a little more than a week after they reached home, a great public dinner was given for Nashville's own "Hero of New Orleans." A contemporary report states that the assembly was large and that every act of the company "evinced the satisfaction and joy which each one felt in the return, in victory and peace," of their beloved and distinguished country-man.[47]

There were toasts—many toasts, always accompanied by enthusiastic cheers. One, to Jackson who had returned "crowned with well-earned laurels; he has the best reward, the thanks of a free and enlightened nation. . . ."

Following this toast, Governor Blount, who was now nearing the end of the third term of his eventful administration, presented to General Jackson in the name of Governor Holmes of Mississippi "a superb and elegant sword, which was voted by the legislature of Mississippi Territory to the general at their last session."

Then followed many more toasts, among them "The American Fair—Humane and grateful to the hero, he is proud of their smiles."

Proud of their smiles, it is true—gallant and dashing in his acceptance of the honors which they bestowed upon him—but with eyes only for the plump little middle-aged woman beside him. Now, and forever, she filled his heart, his mind, his very existence.

At last for a time, they could go back to their modest log Hermitage, but they never had been and never would be alone. Relatives, friends, the great and the near-great, flocked to their humble abode. But there was a little time before Jackson was again involved in government business. There was also the demand that, at his earliest convenience, he visit the nation's capital, so, in the early autumn of 1815, he, with his lady started on a triumphal trip to Washington. Here, too, they were welcomed with great celebrations.

This visit had been postponed until early autumn, chiefly because General Jackson was called upon to go again into the Creek country to settle questions about boundaries which had been stipulated in his treaty with the Creeks. It was also true that the later trip would avoid traveling in the heat of summer, and make it more pleasant for Rachel, who would accompany him.

The period after Andrew Jackson's victory at New Orleans was of tremendous importance in the extinguishment of Indian titles to lands in Tennessee and the lower South. In this work he was closely associated with Joseph McMinn, who had succeeded Willie Blount as governor of Tennessee. His administration was notable for accomplishments in this important phase of the nation's growth.

General Jackson, on October 16, 1816, reported to Governor McMinn that all of the disputed territory on the south side of the Tennessee and all of the Chickasaw claim north of that river had been obtained. McMinn, passing this information on to William H. Crawford, secretary of war, stated that the military significance of these lands to the nation at large, as well as their importance to the citizens of Tennessee and the western portions of Virginia in providing easier access to markets for their produce, were of great importance to the entire nation.

In November, 1816, General Jackson, reporting to the secretary of war, announced that the whole southern country from Kentucky and Tennessee to Mobile had been opened by the late treaties. He emphasized especially the advantages of the lands at the end of the Muscle Shoals of the Tennessee River, for location of a large depot of munitions of war, stating also that the falls of the shoals should be diverted into any channel and adapted to machinery.

"But what constitutes the chief advantage of this position is its being at the very point where the military road contemplated to be opened must cross Tennessee, and, consequently, on the very route troops moving from the upper to the support of the lower country. Hence, the troops may rendezvous at the depot, receive all their arms . . . and transport themselves and on their return march can re-deposit their arms received . . . ."

One of the most important treaties in the history of Tennessee, however, was the one negotiated by General Jackson and Gov. Isaac Shelby of Kentucky, with the Chickasaw Indians in 1818.

"We have just closed a treaty with the Chickasaw Indians," he wrote to the editors of *The Nashville Whig* on October 18, 1818, "for all their claims in the states of Tennessee and Kentucky, containing about seven million acres, of the best land in the western country, and washed by the Tennessee, the Ohio and the Mississippi Rivers, for at least three hundred and fifty miles; for an annuity of twenty thousand dollars for fifteen years. . . ." [48]

And so, with one majestic gesture, he added to the richly varied domain of Tennessee, the entire western portion of its territory! The whole state was thrilled and, a month later, a great celebration of the treaty was staged in Nashville.

"A tribute of respect," the *Whig* reported. "A splendid ball was given to General Jackson and staff at the Nashville Inn, last Evening, in honor of the late Chickasaw Treaty."

General Shelby was not able to attend in person, but his portrait, painted a few weeks earlier by Ralph E. W. Earl, a young artist who had recently come to Nashville, was prominently displayed at the ball.

"I can, in truth, say that there never came from the hands of an artist a better likeness," General Jackson wrote to Governor Shelby.

These magnificent acquisitions of land were a fitting conclusion to Tennessee's first quarter of a century, and a sound beginning for the great period of expansion and development of the nation's western frontiers. Many of its more restless and ambitious citizens had already begun pushing across the mighty river which now formed its most western boundary to satisfy their own curious eyes and to examine the territory beyond it. Within two decades they would have a strong foothold in Texas and from there they would go on and on until they reached the distant Pacific. With them they would carry, not only their brains and brawn, and their well-tested courage, but also their independent government by free men, for which their grandfathers, back in Watauga, had set "the dangerous example."

CHAPTER VIII

Jackson: The Later Years

During the decade which intervened between his victory over the Creeks in 1814 and the presidential election of 1824, Andrew Jackson was called upon to negotiate a number of important treaties. He, like others in the executive, legislative and military branches of government, was confronted with the necessity of attempting to reconcile the interests of the advancing white men and the receding Indians. State papers of the period are filled with records and reports of their theories, their successes and their failures. Beyond a doubt, much progress was made by both the officials of government and the Indians themselves, but the problem is still, even today, far from a satisfactory solution.

Andrew Jackson's writings have countless references to this subject, one of the most interesting being that contained in his letter written to President James Monroe on his inauguration day, March 4, 1817:

"Circumstances have entirely changed, and the time has arrived when a just course of policy can be exercised toward them [the Indians]. Their existence and happiness now depend upon a change of policy in the Government. The game being destroyed, they can no longer exist by their bows and arrows and Gun. They must lay them aside and produce by labour; from the earth a subsistence; in short they must be civilized; to effect which their territorial boundary must be curtailed; as long as they are permitted to roam over vast limits in pursuit of game, so long will they retain their savage manners, and customs. Good policy would therefore point to just and necessary regulations by law, to produce this grand object, circumscribe their bounds, put into their hands the utensils of husbandry, yield them protection, and enforce obedience to those just laws provided for their benefit, and in a short time they will be civilized. . . ." [1]

It was not long, however, until Jackson was involved in more

Indian fighting—this time against the Florida Indians. There was much debate as it became apparent that this expedition had involved the Spanish authorities and that Jackson, as he had been accustomed to doing, had taken the matter into his own hands. He was convinced, and rightfully so, that Pensacola was the hotbed of the Indian uprising and had been supported, if not actually instigated, by the Spanish governor there. Jackson's high-handed action, however, and the validity of President Monroe's orders became the subjects of long and hairsplitting arguments. Whether President Monroe did, or did not know of General Jackson's intentions and approve them—or whether the general proceeded entirely upon his own responsibility, the fact remains that, for a second time, he took possession of Pensacola. Eastern sticklers for strict adherence to laws governing international relations were shocked, but the settlers, who were being threatened with the same fate of those whose fresh scalps were found in Indian villages by Jackson and his men, felt that he had taken a reasonable course and had exhibited great forbearance.

Jackson, as usual, stated his opinion frankly and with force:

"I am but little versed in the etiquette or punctillios of these matters; and I must take the liberty of adding, that whenever I shall be entrusted with the defense of an important section of my country I am quite sure it will not be *sacrificed* by too strict attention to them . . . ."

The authorities in Washington were left to argue the matter with Spain and to negotiate a treaty which would eventually lead to the possession of the Florida territory by the United States. When this was finally accomplished, General Jackson was appointed governor of the Florida Territory and, in early July, 1821, appeared once more in Pensacola.

"Thrice have I seen the Spanish colours lowered and the American colours waving over this place," Jackson wrote to John Coffee on July 18, 1821, "and my fatigue has been greater this time, than at any other period. . . ."

Arguments over the formal transfer of Florida from Spanish to American rule had been long and annoying. Neither General Jackson nor Mrs. Jackson, who had accompanied him, had desired the governorship, and they were both eager to get back to the new brick Hermitage which they had built only two years earlier. But Jackson, never one to leave an important job unfinished, went down to see that this time the United States would finally come into possession of the territory which he had twice offered it on a silver platter. He remained only long enough to establish government and get it into operation. They were back in Nashville by early November, 1821.

The years 1822 and 1823 were politically significant ones in the Jackson story. With each passing month the general was being pressed closer toward the time when he would no longer be addressed by that title—but would be called "Mr. President." The Tennessee legislature, in session at Murfreesboro, on July 20, 1822, passed a resolution, put forward by Representative Pleasant M. Miller of Knoxville (son-in-law of William Blount), nominating him for the presidency. It read, in part:

"The members of the general assembly of . . . Tennessee, taking into view the great importance of the selection of a suitable person to fill the presidential chair . . . have turned their eyes to *Andrew Jackson*, late major-general in the armies of the United States. In him they behold the soldier, the statesman, and the honest man; . . . calm in deliberation, cautious in decision, efficient in action.

". . . Therefore, Resolved . . . that the name of major-general Andrew Jackson be submitted to the consideration of the people of the United States. . . ."

" I have never been an applicant for office," Jackson wrote to a friend. "I never will . . . I have no desire, nor do I ever expect to be called to fill the Presidential chair, but should that be the case . . . it shall be without exertion on my part . . . ."

From this time forward, however, his friends pressed his candidacy vigorously and enthusiastically. Wisely, the Jackson men decided that it was important to have their candidate appear on the national scene and, accordingly, the Tennessee legislature elected him to the United States Senate.

Soon, the presidential campaign was in full swing with four popular and well-qualified men in the race—John Quincy Adams, Henry Clay, William H. Crawford and Andrew Jackson, But, regardless of the undeniably high character of the three candidates opposing Jackson, he and his wife became the targets of an un-scrupulous and slanderous campaign. Seizing upon the unhappy circumstances of Mrs. Jackson's marriage to Lewis Robards, their divorce and her marriage to Andrew Jackson, they sought not only to defeat Andrew Jackson, but to bring about his permanent ruin by exciting his sensitive temper in regard to any derogatory remark about his "beloved Rachel." Yet, when the campaign was ended, it was found that Jackson had received a plurality of the popular vote of the American people. Victory was denied him, however, for the electoral college, hopelessly confused by its own diverse opinions, could not come to a decision. As a result the election was thrown into the House of Representatives. Here, Henry Clay yielded his substantial following to Adams, thereby giving him the victory.

But the Jackson men did not know how to accept defeat. There would be another presidential election in four years, and they'd make themselves heard! Accordingly, the presidential campaign of 1828 had its official beginning in October 1825, when the legislature of Tennessee again submitted Jackson's name to the people of the nation as a candidate for the highest office within their gift. With a resounding battle cry, they flocked again to his standards and their leaders assembled at Rachel Jackson's pleasant Hermitage to outline plans for the attack and for invasion of the enemy country. This time the victory was theirs and, in 1828, Andrew Jackson was elected President of the United States. But a terrible price was paid for their success. Never in the history of American political campaigns has a candidate for president been subjected to such ruthless and unprincipled attacks—and never has a woman been crucified as was Rachel Jackson by the cruel and untruthful charges of his enemies.

Victory was soon turned into mourning, for the gentle, kindly Rachel died suddenly on December 22, 1828, leaving her husband to make his lonely way to Washington without her at his side and without being able to place her in the White House as its mistress, where her gracious hospitality and well-bred manners would for-ever disprove the ridiculous charges which had been made against her. Through eight long years he lived there without her, devoting

Andrew Jackson, president-elect, in 1829. From a painting by J. Wood, engraved by J. W. Steel. This engraving appears as the frontispiece in The Jackson Wreath, published in 1829.

The Hermitage in 1834, after the final remodeling. From a drawing dated 1856, the original of which is in the Hermitage museum.

himself to his country and to what he believed to be its best interests.

Among the many things he accomplished during his eight years in the presidency were: payment of the national debt, collection of the long overdue debt from France, prevention of nullification threatened by his native state of South Carolina, and, perhaps, most of all, proof that the American people could, by their vote, have a hand in government and could choose their own leaders. Always a loyal supporter of the Union, Andrew Jackson believed with equal sincerity in the rights of the states. While he is remembered especially for his famous toast: "The Federal Union—it must be preserved!", he was equally staunch in his defense of the protection of the rights of the states. There are numerous passages in his writings on this subject, such as the following, taken from his Farewell Address:

"It is well known that there have always been those among us who wish to enlarge the powers of the general government; and experience would seem to indicate that there is a tendency on the part of this government to overstep the boundaries marked out for it by the constitution. Its legitimate authority is abundantly sufficient for all the purposes for which it was created, and its powers being expressly enumerated, there can be no justification for claiming anything beyond them. Every attempt to exercise power beyond these limits should be promptly and firmly opposed. For one evil example will lead to other measures still more mischievous . . . . From the extent of our country, its diversified interests, different pursuits, and different habits, it is too obvious for argument that a single consolidated government would be wholly inadequate to watch over and protect its interests; and every friend of our free institutions should be always prepared to maintain unimpaired and in full vigor the rights and sovereignty of the states, and to confine the action of the general government strictly to the sphere of its appropriate duties." [2]

During Andrew Jackson's long absence from Tennessee, the state, for the most part, was controlled by his adherents. In 1829, William Carroll, elected to succeed William Hall, who had filled out the few remaining months of Sam Houston's unexpired term, began his fourth term as governor of the state of Tennessee. During this and two succeeding terms. Carroll sponsored and supported many improvements, among them the constitutional convention of 1834. This constitution, while retaining, for the most part, the greater portion of the 1796 constitution, made important and necessary changes in regard to taxation, the judiciary, property qualifications for officeholders, the election of certain officials and other matters which had to do with current needs. It was not, however, a new constitution in any sense.

Whig strength was constantly growing in Tennessee and, as Carroll's sixth term as governor approached its final days, they were already grooming the popular Newton Cannon to succeed him. This tremendous increase in Whig power caused Tennessee Democrats to plan for returning Carroll for a fourth consecutive term, basing his eligibility for office on the theory that the constitution of 1834 had completely abolished the 1796 constitution and, with it, the provision making it unconstitutional for a man to serve more than three consecutive terms as governor. The Whig candidate contended, however, that the 1796 constitution, with a few revisions and amendments, was still in effect.

Carroll finally consented to run, knowing that the Whigs were already waging an active campaign to place the able, intellectual and popular Hugh Lawson White in nomination, in opposition to Jackson's choice for his successor, Martin Van Buren. As a result of the strong Whig influence in Tennessee, Cannon defeated Carroll, and White carried the state against Van Buren—even in Andrew Jackson's own Hermitage District. To say the least, Jackson was shocked and humiliated.

"What has happened?" he asked James K. Polk. "The once Democratic Tennessee, apostate from the republican fold, and the only state in the Union unrepresented at the national republican (democratic) convention at Baltimore by members fresh from the people . . . How strange; how humiliating to every real friend of democracy of our beloved country . . . . If my hands were free, if I was a mere citizen of Tennessee again and wanted everlasting fame, I would ask no other theatre to obtain it than before the people of Tennessee. . . ." [3]

Van Buren was elected without the vote of Tennessee, greatly to the satisfaction of the tired old man in the White House, who, having chosen and having been largely responsible for Van Buren's election, was ready and eager to return to his Hermitage to spend the rest of his days.

But the Whigs still held sway and Newton Cannon was elected to serve a second term as governor. One of the important events of this administration was the removal of a major portion of the once powerful Cherokee nation to the West. The subject, which had been debated for many years had, by this time, become a serious issue in political circles of both the American government and the Cherokee nation. The latter was divided into two political camps, led by John Ross and Maj. John Ridge, the most powerful chiefs of the nation. The Ross party, which was bitterly opposed to the removal, was supported by such opponents of Andrew Jackson as Daniel Webster, Henry Clay, Edward Everett and others. The Ridge party, which agreed to the far-seeing policy suggested by Andrew Jackson and others, felt that removal to the West was the only possible solution to the problem.

At length, on December 29, 1835, the treaty of New Echota was negotiated between the Cherokees and Gen. William Carroll and John F. Schermerhorn, commissioners for the United States. By its provisions the Cherokees ceded to the United States, for a consideration of $5,000,000, all of their lands east of the Mississippi River. In turn, the United States ceded to the Cherokees 15,000,000 acres of land in the Indian Territory, with the agreement that it should never be included in the government of any state or territory. The United States also agreed to pay all of the expenses of the removal and to allow a two-year period for it to be accomplished. In addition, it agreed to furnish one year's subsistence, to pay for improvements on the land, for tools and other equipment and to add $150,000 to the existing permanent school fund. It also agreed to pay debts owed by the Cherokees to Americans, amounting to about $60,000. In 1836 a supplementary treaty provided for the addition of $1,000,000 to the amount paid to the Cherokees, as well as many minor benefits included in both treaties, among them being the provision that all of the Cherokees who wished to remain where they were might do so and, becoming citizens of the state, were to be entitled to preempt 160 acres of land.

The followers of John Ross arbitrarily rejected these treaties and protested bitterly against them, but the United States refused to recognize their authority and conducted all of its negotiations with the Ridge party. During the two years which had been allowed for the removal, John Ross, with strong support from the anti-Jackson men in Washington, waged a bitter and powerful battle against it.

It is said that Junaluska, another great chief of the eastern Cherokees, exclaimed bitterly when the treaty at New Echota was signed:

"If I had known that General Jackson would drive us from our homes, I would have killed him that day at the Horseshoe."

He referred, of course, to the Battle of Horseshoe Bend, in which he had served with a large band of Cherokees and helped defeat Weatherford's powerful force of Creek warriors.

Jackson, who was president when the New Echota treaty was signed, had negotiated an earlier treaty with the Cherokees in 1817, which had begun the trek of the nation to the West. He believed then, and still believed, that relocating the Indian tribes in the western territory was the only possible solution of the problem. His attitude toward the Indians, which has generally been misunderstood and often deliberately misrepresented, is shown in the following excerpt from his message to Congress, delivered late in 1829. He by no means exempted the white people and the government of the United States from the charge of wrongdoing.

"The condition and ulterior destiny of the Indian tribes within the limits of our states," he said, "have become subjects of much interest and importance. It has long been the policy of government to introduce among them the arts of civilization, in the hope of gradually reclaiming them from a wandering life. This policy has, however, been coupled with another wholly incompatible with its success. Professing a desire to civilize and settle them, we, at the same time, lost no opportunity to purchase their lands and thrust them further into the wilderness. By this means they have not only been kept in a wandering state, but have been led to look upon us as unjust and indifferent to their fate. Thus, though lavish in its expenditures upon the subject, government has constantly defeated

294

its own policies and the Indians, in general, receding further and further to the West, have retained their savage habits. A portion, however, of the southern tribes, having mingled much with the whites, and made some progress in the arts of civilized life, have lately attempted to erect an independent state within the limits of Georgia and Alabama. These States, claiming to be the only sovereigns within their territory, extended their laws over the Indians, which induced the latter to call upon the United States for protection . . . ."

So it was that controversy upon controversy developed on the Indian question and finally resulted in removal by military force of that portion of the Cherokees who refused to go willingly, to the West. Before this final removal Andrew Jackson had completed his second term as president and had retired, as a private citizen, to his Hermitage. In spite of his sincere and constructive interest in the Indians, expressed in many of his writings as well as by his humane consideration shown on many occasions, he was still pictured as a brutal Indian fighter and Indian hater.

Early in 1838, Gen. Winfield Scott, a Virginian, who had distinguished himself in the Black Hawk and Seminole wars, as well as in the War of 1812, was ordered to the Cherokee country to hasten the transportation of these Indians to the West.

"This," one of his biographers states, "he did so as to win the approbation of the government and the affections of the unfortunate Cherokees. To this distinguished man . . . belongs the rare honor of uniting with military energy and daring the spirit of a philanthropist. His exploits in the field, which placed him in the first rank of our soldiers, have been obscured by the purer and most lasting glory of a pacificator and a friend of mankind. In the whole history of the intercourse of civilized, with barbarous or half-civilized communities, we doubt whether a brighter page can be found than that which records his agency in the removal of the Cherokees. As far as the wrongs done this race can be atoned for, General Scott has made the expiation." [4]

In spite of Scott's efforts to minimize the sufferings of the Cherokees during this long, heartbreaking trek, it has been properly called "The Trail of Tears."

THE DANGEROUS EXAMPLE

But General Scott, no matter how sincere his efforts and how genuine his good intentions, could not control the harsh actions of some portions of his command. Especially was this true of the units ordered to find and bring in the stubborn Cherokees who refused to leave their native land and who hid themselves in the vastness of the Great Smoky Mountains. About one thousand of them were never captured and carried to the West, but remained and formed what later came to be the Qualla Reservation, on the borderline of Tennessee and North Carolina. Many residents of this reservation became well-educated citizens who took their place in the outside world, but some of their descendants have remained and are known throughout the nation today for their accomplishments in perpetuating the history of their nation, of demonstrating for thousands of visitors the artifacts and way of life of their ancestors.

General Scott organized the Cherokees for their long journey at Charleston, Tennessee, passing from there south of Pikesville, through McMinnville to Nashville and from thence to Hopkinsville, Kentucky. They crossed the Ohio River near the mouth of the Cumberland, but winter had set in and their sufferings became acute. They did not reach their final destination until March of 1839.

According to *The Nashville Union,* of November 30, 1838, they had not reached Nashville until winter was well on its way.

"The last detachment of the emigrating Cherokees, numbering 1,700 or 1,800 persons, is now at Mill Creek, about four miles from this city. Winter is now approaching so rapidly that some of the detachments will be compelled to halt far short of their ultimate destination. A point upon the Ohio, convenient to navigation, will probably be selected for their winter quarters. When the navigation becomes good in the spring, they can easily be transported to their future home."

General Scott arrived in Nashville on November 21, a few days in advance of the emigrating band, and took quarters at the City Hotel. On November 23, *The Nashville Union* stated that the removal contract was being debated again and, in its columns from day to day, recorded details of the tragic story which was being enacted.

296

Old Block House at Old Fort, Tennessee, before the fort was removed to the high school grounds in Benton and restored. This is part of Marr's Fort which was important in the removal of the Cherokees and the "Trail of Tears."

When, at long last, the weary band reached the Indian Territory, they found their nation still embroiled in the Ross-Ridge controversy and, not until Major Ridge was killed, was it possible for them to obtain even a semblance of harmony. There was a long struggle before the nation was able to adjust itself to its new home and to resume the upward trend of progress in the arts of civilization which it had already begun to enjoy in its eastern home.

One of the outstanding accomplishments of the Cherokees was the invention of an alphabet by one of their number, generally known as Sequoyah, but often referred to as "George Guess, or Gist." His father was Nathaniel Gist, an officer in the Revolutionary War and his mother a member of the Cherokee tribe. He was crippled from youth, a condition which gave his studious and inquiring nature full play, since he could not participate in the sports and the hunting expeditions enjoyed by other Indian boys. An account of his invention is given in a letter written on December 13, 1825, by Thomas L. McKenney, superintendent for Indian trade, to Hon. James Barbour, secretary of war.

"The success which has attended the philological researches of 'one in the nation,' and whose system of education has met, among the Cherokees, with universal approbation, certainly entitles him to great consideration, and to rank with the benefactors of man. His name is Guess, and he is a native, an unlettered Cherokee. Like Cadmus, he has given to his people the alphabet of their language. It is composed of eighty-six characters, by which, in a few days, the older Indians, who had despaired of deriving an education by means of their schools, and who were not included in the existing school system as participants of its benefits, may read and correspond! I have the honor to accompany herewith, in paper marked C, this alphabet, together with an example in the word, 'friend,' and also the sound of each character from 1 to 86."

While the great removal of the Cherokees had its heartbreaks, its sufferings and its tragedies, it also produced many long lasting benefits to that nation and to the America of which so many of its citizens became a part. They learned to be self-sustaining and law abiding and made amazing progress in adopting the arts of civilization. Many of them were prosperous and, not a few of them owned slaves and operated large plantations. Their lands increased in value and several of them achieved great wealth. Schools and churches contributed to the education and moral training of the rising generations and, as time passed, many of them became citizens of Oklahoma and other western states. The same conditions prevailed in many other Indian tribes located in the West. This did not, of course, solve all of their problems, but it was sufficient to raise the standards of living enough to enable those who wished to do so to participate successfully in the life of the white man's world.

While the Indian question was being debated another question destined to be quite as controversial was claiming national attention. Texas, with all of its possibilities for settlement and development had long been a tantalizing subject for restless and ambitious men, particularly those in states which bordered on the eastern side of the Mississippi River. As early as the 1820s a small trickle of the stream of emigrants which would soon follow was seen, so, as the Indians were moved unwillingly, at great expense by the American government, white men were moving westward voluntarily, at their own expense and on their own responsibility. Their land titles would be insecure, their relations with Mexico precarious, and their ability to enter and hold the land uncertain. Yet they kept coming.

Sam Houston was already on the scene. Since 1829 he had been living among the Cherokees in what is now Oklahoma, and in 1833 had moved on into Texas. Here, by some strange turn of Fate, he was situated as the growing conflict between the Mexican government and the Texans increased in intensity.

The Texan leader, Stephen Austin, went to the Mexican capital, seeking to solve the problem by annexation to that government as a separate state. He was detained there for some time without an answer to his plea. Finally, giving up hope, he dispatched a letter to his people, advising them to go ahead and erect their province into a separate state without delay.[5] The message was intercepted and Austin was thrown into a dungeon, where he remained for nine months, not being informed of any charge against him .

In the meantime, Santa Anna, after several military campaigns, fought his way to leadership of the Mexican government, and, by

1835, had established a military dictatorship. In September of that year he sent General Cos into Texas to enforce his arbitrary laws. Cos was defeated at the Alamo fortress where he had retired with his garrison, after earlier engagements with the Texans, who then occupied the fortress. Gen. Sam Houston, who commanded the little Texan army, had ordered his scattered men to retire toward the American border to reorganize and await reinforcements, but the Texans at the Alamo, feeling themselves secure, did not obey this order, although they were not sufficiently supplied to undergo a long siege.

After the defeat of Cos, Santa Anna, determined to earn new laurels for himself by heading a large and well-equipped expedition into Texas, crossed the Rio Grande and marched into Texas, arriving at Bexar on February 21, 1836. He immediately launched a surprise attack on the Alamo. For ten days Santa Anna poured shot and shell into the fort, only to have his men mowed down by the withering fire from the unerring rifles of the Texans, many of whom were descendants of the men who won their reputation for expert markmanship at King's Mountain, in the Indian wars and at New Orleans. The total number of the gallant defenders of the Alamo was only one hundred and fifty, thirty-two of whom had arrived shortly after the beginning of the siege. Each day their food became scantier and each hour the men became weaker and weaker from hunger, but their deadly aim at the enemy lost none of its effectiveness. At last Santa Anna, giving up hope of forcing them to surrender, on the night of March 5, decided to take the Alamo by storm, regardless of the cost. Placing his scaling ladders against the walls, he ordered his men to make a hand-to-hand attack. The Mexicans poured into the fort in such great numbers that the little garrison was soon overpowered. They took a heavy toll of the Mexicans until they were reduced to only seven men, huddled helplessly in a corner of the fort. At this point they asked quarter, but it was denied them and they were slain to the last man. It is often said that Thermopylae had one messenger to tell its story—the Alamo none.

David Crockett was there, but who can say that he was more courageous, or more of a hero, than any of the others of that band

299

of immortals? They had, every man of them, given their lives for a cause they believed in and, in their sacrifice, they gave to their fellow Texans the battle cry: "Remember the Alamo!"

But Santa Anna paid a dear price for his victory; hundreds of his men were killed in the attack.

General Houston and his army, thoroughly aroused by the disaster at the Alamo, were now well supplied, strengthened by new recruits and ready to march to avenge their heroic comrades. The Mexicans, now organized in three divisions, were moving in their direction, General Houston chose as his own personal target the center division, commanded by Santa Anna himself. A skirmish took place at once and the Texans were pushed back, but Santa Anna, confident of his ability to crush the Texans at will, did not push his advantage and decided to wait until the following day to make his attack. Meanwhile, General Cos arrived with the rear guard, which brought the Mexican force up to approximately fifteen hundred men. Houston had seven hundred infantry and sixty-one cavalry. Describing the battle of San Jacinto, which took place the following day, Frost says:

"The Texan infantry charged the line of the enemy till within a few yards, when they delivered their fire with dreadful effect, shouted their war-cry, 'Remember the Alamo,' and rushed upon the foe with the bayonet. The battle was decided at once. The Mexicans lost six hundred and thirty killed, two hundred and eighty wounded, and seven hundred and thirty prisoners. Almonte was captured the day of the battle (April 21st), Santa Anna on the 22nd, and General Cos on the 24th. Santa Anna now offered his services to put an end to the war, and, as president of Mexico, signed a treaty on the 14th day of March, 1836, binding himself solemnly to acknowledge, sanction, and ratify the full, entire, and perfect independence of Texas. The Rio Grande was, by this treaty, defined to be the western boundary of the new republic . . . ." [6]

In accordance with the terms agreed upon, Santa Anna was to be returned to Mexico as early as possible, in order to put the stipulations of the treaty into effect. This plan, unfortunately, was interrupted. Santa Anna, writing to President Jackson from Colum-

Sam Houston. Photo courtesy of the State of Tennessee Tourism Development Division.

bia, Texas, on July 4, 1836, explained the situation and sought his aid in obtaining an early return.

"Regarded Sir, in fulfillment of the duties which a public man owes to his native country and to honor, I came to this soil at the head of six thousand Mexicans. The disasters of war which circumstances rendered inevitable have reduced me to the situation of a prisoner, as you will no doubt have been informed.

". . . the President and cabinet had taken measures for my return to Mexico, to enable me to complete the other stipulations, and I had, in consequence, embarked on board the Schooner *Invincible,* which was to convey me to the Port of Vera Cruz, but it unfortunately happened that some indiscreet persons raised a tumult, which obliged the authorities forcibly to land me and again to place me in close confinement. . . . The excitement has gathered strength with the return of the Mexican Army to Texas . . . . The duration of the war and its disasters are therefore necessarily inevitable, unless a powerful hand interposes to cause the voice of reason to be opportunely listened to . . . ." [7]

He then asked Jackson's aid in arranging his early return to Mexico.

From the Hermitage, on September 4, 1836, where he had come for a brief visit, President Jackson replied, assuring Santa Anna of his desire to aid in putting an end to "the disastrous cruelties of the civil war now raging between Mexico and Texas and asking the interference of the United States, to aid in the accomplishment of so humane and desirable an object . . . ." [8]

Replying to a communication from Sam Houston on the same day, President Jackson assured him that he would cut short his visit to the Hermitage and hurry back to Washington to attend to the matter, at the same time approving the course Houston had taken in regard to Santa Anna.

". . . I have seen a report," President Jackson told him, "that Genl St. Anna was to be brought before a military court, to be tried and shot. Nothing *now* could tarnish the character of Texas more than such an act at this late period. It was good policy as well as humanity that spared him . . . his person is still of much consequence to you. He is the pride of the Mexican soldiers and the favorite of the Priesthood and whilst he is in your power the priests will not furnish the supplies necessary for another campaign, nor will the regular soldiers *voluntarily* march when their reentering Texas may endanger or cost their favorite Genl his life . . . ."

Other letters were exchanged by this interesting trio during the ensuing weeks and, during the latter part of November, 1836, General Houston—or, Don Samuel Houston, as Santa Anna called him—sent Santa Anna to Washington to confer with President Jackson. He placed in the Mexican general's hands a letter of introduction, written in his most flamboyant style, and quite equal in courtliness to any of the Mexican general's communications.

"Allow me the pleasure," he wrote, "of introducing to the notice and kind attention of your Excellency, General Antonio Lopez de Santa Anna, the President of the Republic of Mexico.

"The distinction, and the character of Genl Sant Anna will supersede the necessity of my saying anything in his favor, so far as his reputation is a portion of the history of mankind! As an individual, I claim leave to recommend him to your manly, and generous regard. Not unaware that many circumstances connected with the prejudices of the present time may be calculated to influence most minds; and create a feeling which if indulged in might be injurious, to the reception which I claim to solicit for Genl Sant Anna in Washington; I feel confident, that with you, he can at times realize, a just estimation of his worth, as a soldier and a Gentleman. As such, I hope you will allow me to recommend him to your attention and regard.

"With perfect respect and regard, Your friend . . . ." [9]

The newspapers of the period recorded at length and in great detail the progress of the Mexican president to Washington and engaged in many-sided arguments on the questions which the situation provoked. Eventually, in 1837, Santa Anna's return to Mexico was arranged.

Meanwhile, Sam Houston, commander-in-chief of the Texan Army, and soon to be the president of the Texas Republic, occupied himself with the momentous affairs connected with the establishment of the government and ending the Mexican hostilities. From this time forward, the story of Sam Houston was to be the

story of Texas. But he did not stand alone, for he had the friendship, the advice and support of two Tennessee presidents of the
United States, James K. Polk, who was destined to hold that high
office when another war had to be fought for the possession of
Texas, and Andrew Jackson, who, concluding his second term as
president, returned to the Hermitage and continued his fight for
the annexation of Texas.

On March 1, 1845, during the final days of the Tyler administration, Congress passed a resolution providing that the territory
". . . rightfully belonging to the republic of Texas, should form a
part of the American Union. . . ." President John Tyler signed the
document at once, but it was not until several months later and
after long legislative debates that it was ratified by Texas, a state
constitution formed and "the Lone Star State" finally became a part
of the Union. This did not settle the matter, however, for Mexico
still refused to relinquish her claim to Texas, as she had agreed to
do in her treaty with the United States. It was left for the in-coming
president, James Knox Polk, to shoulder the responsibility of asserting the rights of his country and finally establishing the right of
Texas to be a full-fledged state of the union.

President Polk came from a steady, substantial and gifted family
which had served its country with patriotic zeal from the earliest
days of its struggle for independence. Back in North Carolina, his
grandfather, Ezekiel Polk and other members of the family participated in the Mecklenburg declaration of independence in 1775
and in events leading up to it. He was born in Mecklenburg
County on November 2, 1795, the son of Samuel Polk and his wife,
Jane Knox, whose father, James Knox, served as a captain during
the Revolutionary War. About 1806, the Polks—Colonel Ezekiel,
Major Samuel and their families—moved to Maury County, Tennessee. Samuel, who had a large tract of land about six miles from
Columbia, built a log house in which he and his family lived for a
few years. He then built the handsome brick home in Columbia
which is still preserved as a shrine and as a memorial to his son who
became president of the United States.

As a boy, James Knox Polk was rather frail, but not to the extent

303

that his health was seriously or permanently impaired. Of his youth and early education, Polk wrote on October 18, 1848:

". . . It happened to occur to me, and I therefore record it, that 30 years ago this day I arrived at my father's house in Tennessee on my return from the University of North Carolina, where I had graduated in the month of June preceding. I closed my education at a later period in life than is usual, in consequence of having been very much afflicted and enjoyed very bad health in my youth. I did not commence my Latin grammar until the 13th of July, 1813. My instructor was the Rev. Robert Henderson, of the Presbyterian church, who taught an academy two or three miles south of Columbia, Tennessee . . . ."

Soon after his graduation from the University of North Carolina, where he won the highest honors, he went to Nashville, entered the office of one of Tennessee's most distinguished lawyers, Felix Grundy, and began his legal studies. After serving as chief clerk and as a member of the Tennessee House of Representatives, he was elected, in 1825, as a member of the United States House of Representatives, where he was destined to serve continuously for fourteen years. During the terms of 1835 and 1837 he was chosen as speaker of that body.

In 1839, Polk's career took an entirely different turn. His friend and ardent champion in his political campaigns, Andrew Jackson, now retired to his Hermitage, but, by no means from politics, urged him to come home and run for governor against Newton Cannon, a powerful and firmly entrenched Whig, who was expected to run and to win his third consecutive term. Concurring with Andrew Jackson in this request were other leading Democrats, whose candidates for governor had lost to the Whigs in the races of 1835 and 1837. They were still smarting, of course, from the blow dealt them by Hugh Lawson White when he carried Tennessee by some ten thousand votes over Martin Van Buren, whom Jackson had chosen as his successor. Polk knew quite well that Cannon, with his strong Whig backing, would be difficult to defeat, but, ever faithful to the call of the Democratic party and to its aged chief, he came home to try his luck against Cannon.

Most of the newspapers of the state were controlled by the Whigs,

James K. Polk, governor of Tennessee from 1839-1841 and President of the
United States from 1845-1849.

but the Democrats strengthened Jeremiah Harris' *Nashville Union,* making it a tri-weekly, and established E. G. Eastman as editor of the Knoxville *Argus.* Both were excellent newspapermen and both were New Englanders, but both were also experienced political promoters and something of veterans in Democratic politics.[10] The Whig press of the period lacked nothing in brilliance or ability, so the battles in the printed pages were quite as lively as those of orators who were "stump speaking" from one end of the state to the other. This participation in political campaigns was nothing new in the history of Tennessee newspapers, for they have played an important part in public affairs from 1791, when George Roulstone established the *Knoxville Gazette,* to the present day.

Polk, abandoning his customary manner of quiet, serious oratory, engaged in a rough and tumble battle with his opponent, ridiculing him and amusing large crowds by his humor, to almost everyone's surprise, won the election. When he took office as chief executive, the state, as well as the entire nation, was in the midst of a severe financial panic, but, with his sound policies and long experience in public affairs, he was well fitted to serve in such a crisis.

The Whigs had their revenge in 1841, however, when they chose as their candidate James Chamberlain Jones, then thirty-one-years-old and with but little experience in politics. His very appearance was amusing, for though he was over six feet tall, he weighed barely 125 pounds, had shaggy eyebrows, a prominent nose and, when he chose, an awkward way of moving about. He had a melodious, flexible voice which he had great skill in manipulating to express his feelings, whether they were serious or highly humorous. Pitted against him was the cultured, splendidly educated Polk, himself a master at "stump oratory.

". . . Never before and probably never again," wrote the late Dr. Robert H. White, Tennessee State Historian, "will Tennessee experience such a rousing spectacle as the Polk-Jones contests of 1841 and 1843 . . . a deluge of mimicry, joke-telling, and burlesque was let loose upon the swelling and sweltering crowds that thronged to places of speaking where they were regaled from three to four hours with the wisecracks, taunts, and ridicule of the two chieftains in the art of 'stump speaking.' With all his art and mastery in public speaking, Polk was never quite able to 'hem in' his opponent . . . ." [11]

One of Jones' droll tricks, when Polk was discussing some serious issue, was to pull from his pocket an old coonskin—emblem of the Whig party—stroke it gently and ask solemnly of the audience: "Did you ever see such fine fur?"

Jones defeated Polk in the race of 1841, and again in 1843. He was the first native-born governor of Tennessee. However, when he assumed the governor's chair, he found that the hard-fought campaign had split the state and the legislature so seriously that he could accomplish practically nothing. It became actually impossible for the Whigs to elect United States Senators, although they had a small majority in the House of Representatives. There were thirteen Democrats and only twelve Whigs in the Senate, so the Democrats, who became known as the Immortal Thirteen, by refusing to meet in joint session made an election impossible, with the result that Tennessee, for two years, did not send members to the United States Senate. Governor Jones did not fill the vacancies by appointment. Among the Democrats who fought to prevent the election of senators, was Andrew Johnson, destined not only to be governor of Tennessee, but also, like James K. Polk, to be president of the United States.

Among the actions of this session of the state legislature were the passage of a resolution favoring the annexation of Texas and the enacting of legislation which fixed Nashville as the permanent capital of the state. Governor Jones and the legislature took immediate steps to have a suitable statehouse built and, after considering other architects—Gideon Shyrock among them—settled upon a noted architect from Philadelphia, William Strickland. The new capitol building, which was nearing completion at Strickland's death in 1854, was considered by him to be his greatest masterpiece, and, as he had requested, he was buried in a vault in its walls. It was completed in 1855, under the supervision of Francis Strickland, the architect's son. The first meeting of the legislature in the new building had been held, however, in the year 1853. At this time, and for many years afterward, Tennessee's Greek temple capitol was considered the most beautiful public building in the United States.

Governor Polk, as he retired from public office delivered a brief valedictory at the inaugural ceremonies, October 14, 1841, in which he paid tribute to the state of Tennessee and to Andrew Jackson, now retired from public life, but still a powerful figure in national politics:

"She does indeed occupy an enviable reputation among her sisters of the confederacy. Her fame in our military annals is unsurpassed by that of any other State. She was the first of the States after 'the old thirteen' that furnished a chief Magistrate to the Union—a chief Magistrate who left the indelible impress of his character and of the patriotism and wisdom of his administration upon his country; and to whose fame and eminent public services, but imperfect justice can be done until after he shall have been gathered to his fathers . . . ." [12]

The Whigs, jubilant over their victory, crowded into Nashville to see "lean Jimmy" take the gubernatorial chair which had been vacated by Polk, whom they had dubbed "Little Jimmy." Retiring at once to his home in Columbia, ex-Governor Polk, resumed the practice of law. Except for his unsuccessful effort in the 1843 campaign, when he sought to defeat Jones for his second term, it appeared that he would make no further effort to return to public life. But the retired "Sage of the Hermitage" and his powerful Democratic following had different ideas. As the presidential elections of 1844 approached they began grooming him for the vice-presidency and forming an effective political organization to present him to the Baltimore convention.

However, when the Baltimore convention met, Polk was not chosen as a candidate for the vice-presidency, but for the presidency itself—a fact which has caused him to be called the first "dark horse" in the history of American politics. This turn of events was brought about by the hard campaigning and adroit manipulations of his friends and the support of powerful Jackson men in such states as Pennsylvania. To emphasize his close connection with Andrew Jackson, he was immediately dubbed, Young Hickory. George M. Dallas was nominated for the vice-presidency.

THE DANGEROUS EXAMPLE

One interesting bit of campaign literature, prepared by Bidlack, of Pennsylvania, in his reply to attacks on Polk and Dallas, made an impassioned appeal for his support in Pennsylvania:

"Will not," he pleaded, "the state that gave her fifty thousand for General Jackson, 'the noblest Roman of them all,' spurn from her his accuser, and rally round the gallant Polk who so nobly defended him? The people of Pennsylvania know right well, sir, the friendship and the confidence that always existed between the defender of New Orleans and the present Democratic nominee, who is a worthy son of a worthy sire; and whose ancestors, it has been well said, they took up their arms in defense of their country six months before the war commenced and did not lay them down again until a year after its termination. No wonder that 'Young Hickory' is in favor in Oregon and the lone star of Texas, too. He comes honestly by his aversion to British encroachment and British aggression. . . ."

A paramount issue of the campaign for the presidency was the admission of Texas, which was strongly opposed by the antislavery forces of the North and East. Polk, who was highly in favor of bringing Texas into the Union, was bitterly attacked by the abolitionists; but he was elected and westward expansion was soon to become a reality.

CHAPTER IX

Heroes in the Winning of the West

The actual winning of the west had begun with the Lewis and Clark expedition.

Even before final negotiations for the Louisiana Purchase had been completed, Thomas Jefferson began setting on foot plans for extensive exploration of this territory and for acquiring information regarding the position and extent of the dividing lines between Mexico, on the south, and the British and Russian holdings on the north.[1] He had long been convinced of the importance to the United States of ascertaining the extent, the boundaries, physical aspects and resources of the vast territory between the Mississippi River and the Pacific Ocean and, as early as 1792, when he was in France, had suggested to the American Philosophical Society that it solicit subscriptions for this purpose. As the years passed, his convictions of the subject were strengthened and, at last, as president of the United States, it finally became possible for him to realize this dream.

His confidential message to Congress on January 18, 1803, recommending that an overland exploring expedition to the Pacific Ocean be taken at once, was given immediate approval, along with an appropriation adequate to finance it. He had pointed out in his arguments favoring such action that the United States could be justly censured by the rest of the world if it delayed further such an essential project. More important, however, was the fact that a more accurate knowledge of this western country was necessary to its own citizens, who were one day destined to inhabit it. From the early days of the controversy with Spain over the navigation of the Mississippi River, Jefferson had cherished the hope that, in due time, this desirable country could be acquired by the United States. He had also seen, in acquisition of this territory west of the Mississippi, a future home for the now hard-pressed Indian tribes still east of that stream.

Now that he had secured support for prosecution of this long hoped for project, he set to work immediately in organizing for its realization. To head the expedition he chose his private secretary, Capt. Meriwether Lewis, a young man who had been reared in his neighborhood in Virginia and who, in Jefferson's estimation, was admirably fitted for the undertaking. Another member of the party was a young Virginian, Capt. William Clark, brother of George Rogers Clark. This young man came from a family which had, long since, learned to endure the hardships and brave the dangers necessary to blaze the way through unknown wildernesses. The president himself prepared instructions for these young men and sent them on their way to prepare for their great adventure.

On December 20, 1803, the tri-colored flag of France was slowly lowered and the Stars and Stripes raised to half-mast, where it rested briefly, until it was passed by the descending French flag. Then it rose triumphantly to the summit of the flag-staff, and was greeted by wild cheers from the Americans and saluted by a full military band which played "Hail, Columbia" and other patriotic airs.

At this ceremony, which was held at New Orleans, William C. C. Claiborne, governor of the Mississippi Territory, and Gen. James Winchester were the American commissioners for this important event and Governor Claiborne had been authorized to exercise provisionally all civil authority.[2] He, in a brief address, congratulated the people of Louisiana on being placed beyond the constant danger of changes which had threatened for many years and assured them that the people of the United States welcomed them as brothers. Citizens of the French Republic were assured that if they wished to come under the government of the United States they were absolved from their allegiance to France. At last, Americans not only had possession of the navigation rights of the Mississippi River, but they were also owners of the rich, but still unknown territory which stretched far to the westward. It is significant that both Claiborne and Winchester, as citizens of Tennessee, had played important parts in its history.

It was not until the middle of May, 1804, however, that the Lewis and Clark party got underway. By late October they had

James Winchester, who played an important role in western expansion. Photo courtesy of State of Tennessee Tourism Development Division.

William C. C. Claiborne, governor of Louisiana when Jackson fought the battle of New Orleans.

reached the country of the Mandan Indians, where they made camp for the winter. Here they employed a Frenchman, Toussaint Charbonneau, as an interpreter and guide. With him was his wife Sacajawea, sister of a Shoshone chief, whose valuable services made her the true heroine of the expedition. During this winter encampment, she gave birth to a baby boy, whom Charbonneau promptly wrapped and placed on her back, Indian-style, and she carried him the remainder of the trip.

Another less known member of the Shoshone tribe was an old man, who happened to be the first of his people to see the white men. Never having seen men with such pale faces, nor the sticks they carried which made thunder and lightning, he was terrified. When he told his story to his tribe, no one believed him, but, when the party approached and they saw such men and their guns with their own eyes, they believed him and he became a great hero among them. Lewis and Clark, making friends with them, persuaded some of the Shoshones to accompany their party. The old man lived to be over eighty years old and was a frequent visitor to Fort David Crockett, where he was cared for and never allowed to want for anything.[3]

The trip lasted twenty-eight months and ten days, after which the party returned to receive the plaudits of the nation. Thomas Jefferson, felicitating them upon their success, said:

"They have traced the Missouri nearly to its source, descended the Columbia to the Pacific Ocean, ascertained with accuracy the geography of that interesting communication across the continent, learned the character of the country, of its commerce and inhabitants; and it is but justice to say that Mssrs. Lewis and Clarke and their brave companions have, by this arduous service, deserved well of their country." [4]

Tennessee has a unique claim to this party of heroes, for in its soil lie the bones of its courageous leader, Meriwether Lewis, and with him is buried the tragic story of his mysterious death, which brought an abrupt end to his promising career. Many writers are content to end his story with the statement that he met his death at his own hands, but the truth of the matter is that documentary proof to support this statement has not yet been produced.

THE DANGEROUS EXAMPLE

The facts are, briefly, that Meriwether Lewis, who had been appointed governor of the Louisiana Territory, was on his way to Washington and had stopped at Grinder's Tavern on the old Natchez Trace near the present town of Hohenwald, Tennessee. Sometime during the night he was mortally wounded and, after hours of agony, died and was buried in this lonely spot. Until this day there has been no satisfactory explanation of the cause of his death. One of the most interesting accounts of this tragedy is that of the noted ornithologist, Alexander Wilson, who, at that time, was traveling through Tennessee, studying and painting its birds. It is a tragic, blood-curdling narrative and, although it would seem to indicate suicide, there is still no actual evidence that the fatal shot was fired by Lewis himself or by some unknown person, either at Grinder's tavern, or by some of the banditti who infested the Natchez Trace at that time.

Wilson, who had left Nashville on May 4, 1809, wrote:

"Next morning (Sunday) I rode six miles to a man's of the name of Grinder where our poor friend Lewis perished. In the same room where he expired I took down from Mrs. Grinder the particulars of that melancholy event, which affected me extremely. This house, or cabin, is seventy-two miles from Nashville, and is the last white man's as you enter the Indian country . . . ." [5]

Mrs. Grinder told Wilson that Governor Lewis had arrived about sunset and, dismounting and carrying his saddle with him, asked to spend the night. When asked if he was alone, he told Mrs. Grinder that there were two servants behind who would soon be there, and he called for spirits, of which he drank very little, seeming greatly disturbed. He kept walking back and forth, talking to himself. This situation, described in great detail by Mrs. Grinder, continued for several hours, interspersed with times when he would make some pleasant remark and sit smoking quietly for a time, until he started his restless walking and talking again. Finally, leaving him, Mrs. Grinder said that she retired to her kitchen which was in a small cabin very near his room. Later at night she heard pistol shots, after which Lewis called for help, but since her husband was not at home and she was frightened, she did not go to him, leaving him until dawn begging for help and crying for water.

When daylight came she sent her children to the barn to bring her servants. They came, but could do nothing for his terrible wounds and, after a few hours, he died in the greatest agony.

Wilson, leaving money with the Grinders to build a fence around Lewis' lonely grave, departed, carrying his notes with him to publish later for the benefit of posterity, the gruesome story of Lewis' passing. Almost a half-century after his death, the state of Tennessee erected a monument at his grave and named Lewis County in his memory. A tragic end for a great American!

A little more than a year after Lewis and Clark began their expedition up the Missouri River, Zebulon Montgomery Pike was selected to head a similar party to ascend the Mississippi River to its headwaters and explore the adjacent territory. With a party of twenty men, he set sail from Saint Louis on August 9, 1805, in a large boat well stocked with food and supplies, supposed to last for about four months. Soon, however, they were forced to abandon this large boat and proceed on up the narrow streams by land, carrying with them their light canoes for use when they found navigable waters. During this trip, under the greatest handships, Pike kept an interesting and most valuable record of his travels and observations, as well as accounts of the hardships his party suffered during the winter. Unfortunately, not having information on the climate and general nature of the country, the party had not been supplied with sufficiently warm clothing, proper cover and adequate food, so they were often for days at a time on the point of starvation and suffered greatly from the extreme cold. It was under such conditions that Pike managed to keep his journal on his travels and scientific observations, often working by firelight on bitter winter nights. He also took responsibility for ranging far in search of food for his men, as well as for information for his journal. This trip, which was eminently successful in spite of the difficulties which the party encountered, lasted eight months and twenty days.[6]

Two months after he had returned from his first expedition, Pike was selected by General Winchester for a second expedition, the purpose of which was, like the first, to explore the interior of the Louisiana Purchase. He was also instructed to return to their native village a party of some forty Osage Indians, whom he had rescued from their enemies, the Potowatomies and to visit "the different savage nations and to endeavor to assuage animosities . . . ." [7] Having performed these duties, he was instructed to continue his explorations of the Mississippi and its tributaries, especially the Arkansas and Red Rivers. On this second journey, Pike and his party were subjected to dangers and hardships far greater than those of his first expedition. During the bitter winter they struggled through snow two and a half to three feet deep and, their food having been exhausted, they were actually in danger of dying from starvation.

At one time Pike and the doctor who was with him on this trip left the party in camp and went out on a desperate search for food. Coming upon a herd of buffalo, they fired, wounded one three times, but he was still, to their great disappointment, able to run away. After this failure, they decided that it was futile to attempt to return to camp and add to the gloom of their men, so, sheltering themselves as best they could among some rocks, they spent a sleepless night without cover and in clothing totally unsuitable for such a climate.

The next day they crawled about a mile through the snow and, at last, were fortunate in killing a large buffalo. They dressed the animal and each of them, carrying a large load of meat, returned triumphantly to camp, where the hungry men—all of whom had been without food for four days—had a luxurious feast. Pike, however, dizzy from exhaustion, came near to falling as he put his load of meat down. Upon his return from this trip Pike was thanked by the government for his "zeal, perseverance and intelligence" and was immediately made a captain and soon afterwards, major. When the army was enlarged in 1810 his rank was raised to a colonel of infantry. Between this time and the outbreak of the War of 1812 he prepared for publication narratives, maps and charts of his two expeditions, which made available to an eager people important information on the rich territory which they had acquired.

With the outbreak of the war of 1812, Pike was promoted to the rank of brigadier-general and selected to command the land forces in an expedition against York, the capital of upper Canada. In the

314

attack on this place he received a serious wound; but, still living as the surgeons carried him from the field, he heard a great shout of triumph from his men and a soldier told him that the British union jack was coming down and the stars were going up. Smiling, he said:

"Push on, brave fellows and avenge your general!"

Carried aboard the command ship, he lingered a few hours and died just as the flag of the defeated British was placed in his arms.

Pike's great contributions to knowledge of the western country, like those of Lewis and Clark, were of inestimable value to the hordes of Americans who were already planning to occupy it. The great mountain peak bearing his name towers as a lasting memorial above the lesser peaks which surround it.

No parts of the United States have a more dramatic and exciting history than those of the Lower South and the Old Southwest. That Tennesseans and Kentuckians, being nearest them, contributed a large part toward the drama and excitement of their interesting history, is a matter of well-documented records. In the case of that spectacular soldier of fortune, Peter Ellis Bean, however, the facts read so much like romantic fiction that it is difficult to realize that most of them are true.

Bean, a native Tennessean, in 1780, when he was only seventeen years old, joined the band of adventurers organized by Philip Nolan for the purpose of taking Texas and establishing an independent government there. This Texan interlude seems to have lasted until the Mexican Revolution, in which Bean and his associates participated. Meanwhile, he had become prominent in Mexican political affairs, had achieved quite a reputation and had married a beautiful young Mexican girl, Senorita Anna Gorthas, a member of an aristocratic family which owned a large hacienda at Jalapa and had considerable wealth..

In 1812, Bean was sent, as a representative to the United States, to plead Mexico's cause and to seek aid for the revolutionists. While on this mission he lingered for a time in New Orleans, taking part in the battles which led to the victory of Jackson's army on January 8, 1815. At this time he was about thirty-five years old and near the peak of a successful career in Mexico. He decided,

315

however, to go back to White County, Tennessee, to visit relatives. He did not seem at all concerned about getting back to Mexico and his lovely wife, although then—and through the years—he carried with him a silk mantilla, which she had given him.

While in White County, he met and began courting Candance Metcalf, daughter of one of the prominent citizens of that county. Soon, completely disregarding the fact that he had a wife in Mexico, he married her and, sometime in 1819, with his wife, her father and perhaps others of their family, he moved to Arkansas. Living there until about 1821, when his father-in-law died, Bean moved his family to Texas, where he settled at Mound Prairie, near a group of Cherokee Indians who had already moved west. Here he became friendly with the leading chiefs and, in a short while, became Indian agent for the Mexican government. He did not take part in the battle of San Jacinto and, in fact, seemed to lean toward the Mexicans rather than the Americans.

As the years passed, Bean achieved the rank of colonel, became prominent in public affairs, as well as owner of considerable property. He and Candance had three children—two sons, Ellis and Isaac, and a daughter, Susan, but he still kept his silk mantilla and when Candance asked him about it, he always told her it was given to him by a friend who had died in Mexico, long, long ago. As far as he was concerned, it appeared, his first marriage was a closed incident—until, one day, he met a traveler who said he had just come from Jalapa, Mexico. Bean questioned him about Jalapa and learned that his Mexican wife was still living and was now owner of the family hacienda. Here, she lived in complete retirement, grieving for the husband whom she thought had been killed in the revolution of 1810-1814.

Bean returned home and, the next morning, rose, saddled his horse and told his family that he was going away for a few days on a business trip. Candance and the children were not unduly disturbed until several days passed without his return. After weeks of futile search, they decided that he must have been killed by the Indians. The years went on, the family prospered when, one day, a traveler stopped at their home. Seeing one of the boys he asked if they had relatives in Mexico, to which they replied that they had not. He then said that he was well acquainted with a Colonel Bean who was living with his Mexican wife in a large hacienda near Jalapa and commented on the boy's remarkable likeness to his friend. The next day the boy started on the long journey to Jalapa, only to find, when he got there, the grave of his father who had died a few days before his arrival. The fact that Candance had never been legally married to him threw the settlement of his property into the courts of Texas, where the full story still remains a matter of official record.

More realistic and of greater importance in the winning of the western country were the exploits of another Tennessean, James Long, who went out to Texas in 1819 at the head of an expedition which had as its goal setting up an independent government—entirely regardless of the opinion of either the Spanish or American governments. Long and acrimonious debates had preceded the settlement of a boundary line between the United States and Texas. Finally, on February 22, 1819, the Sabine River was agreed upon as the dividing line between Louisiana and Texas. Spain relinquished its Florida territory to the United States, which in turn, surrendered to Spain its claims to Texas. A great many people, considering Florida far less valuable than Texas, accused the American negotiators of bartering away the more valuable Texas lands and thereby halting the rapidly increasing flow of emigrants to that territory. Henry Clay, on the floors of Congress, called their action unconstitutional and many others insisted that it was a violation of the 1803 treaty with the French, which guaranteed to the inhabitants of Louisiana citizenship and the protection of the United States.

Feelings ran high on both sides, for there were many who hailed the acquisition of Florida as a great victory, but, regardless of all opinions, the cry that Texas had been "bartered away," increased in intensity. A group of indignant citizens of Natchez, Mississippi, took matters into their own hands and a large mass meeting was held early in 1819, at which they openly and deliberately made plans for invading Texas. A former citizen of Tennessee, Dr. James Long, was offered command of an expedition to carry out this plan

317

and arrangements were made for outfitting it and putting it in the field at once.

Dr. Long, who had served as a surgeon in General William Carroll's brigade in the War of 1812, and, following the war, had moved to Natchez, where he continued to practice his profession, accepted his fellow citizens' offer of the command of the expedition and set to work at once to recruit his men. He left Natchez about the middle of June, 1819, with about seventy-five men. As his party progressed it received many more volunteers and, by the time it had reached Nacogoches, his force was about three hundred strong.

Here, he and his leaders set up a provisional government, to be controlled by a supreme council, which Long himself was chosen to head. This council immediately issued a proclamation declaring Texas to be a free and independent republic. It then provided for such essential laws as those providing the raising of revenues, the sale of public lands, and law enforcement.

Dr. Long, as head of the Council, soon entered into negotiations with the famous pirate, Jean Lafitte, and received from him assurances of his best wishes. Unable to meet Long in person, he arranged for his New Orleans lawyers to have an interview with him at an early date. Apparently, Lafitte looked forward to co-operating with the new Texan government, but, citing his own experiences in waging an eight-year war, advised that the conquest of Texas not be undertaken without a strong force.

"I am entirely disposed to unite my efforts to yours and fully prepared to enter into any arrangement relative to the organization of the Mexican authorities in the port of Galveston," he wrote Long on September 30, 1819.[8]

Lafitte concluded by stating that he would have been very happy to have a personal interview with Long, but his brother was away in New Orleans and it was out of his power to absent himself from Galveston. He assured Long, however, that his lawyers, Messrs. Davis and Lacase, would cooperate with him.

The correspondence between Long and Lafitte, which is both lengthy and interesting, constitutes a fascinating chapter in the history of Tennessee. Perhaps, if Dr. Long could have obtained the

318

larger force which Lafitte advised, Texas could have had her independence many years before she acquired it.

It is probable these two adventurers knew each other when they helped another Tennessean, Andrew Jackson, win the great victory at New Orleans. The Jackson-Lafitte correspondence is also most interesting.

Unable to raise an army large enough to accomplish his objectives, however, Long continued his courageous, colorful campaign—but it, like other efforts to regain Texas, was doomed to failure. Not until Sam Houston's victory at San Jacinto in 1836, the establishment of the Lone Star Republic, and the Mexican War, did Texas win her place in the Union.

Following closely upon the heels of the James Long expedition, other Tennesseans were migrating to Texas, with the intention of forming independent settlements. Many of them were members of adventurous families which had settled the Tennessee country, had participated in the Revolutionary War, the Creek and earlier Indian wars and in the victory over the British at New Orleans. Among the most prominent of them were Sterling Robertson and his nephew, George Childress.

Robertson, eldest son of Elijah Robertson, brother of James Robertson, went out to Texas about 1822 and soon founded the Robertson, or Nashville colony. Its capital was the town of Nashville, named for Nashville, Tennessee, which the Robertsons had played an important part in founding. Childress was the son of Elizabeth Robertson, a sister of Sterling, and John Childress, who was also descended from a prominent pioneer family of Tennessee. It was this family which was soon to see one of its members—Sarah Childress Polk, wife of President James K. Polk—serve with grace and distinction as mistress of the White House. While these settlements did not solve the problem of Texan independence, they took an important step toward this goal, as well as helping push the American frontiers to the Pacific Coast.

Both Robertson and Childress were members of the 1836 convention which declared the independence of the Texas Republic and adopted its first constitution. George Childress is credited with authorship of this constitution, a task which by education, legal experience and writing ability he was well qualified to perform. Born in Nashville, Tennessee, January 8, 1804, he was educated in the law, was a gifted orator, and possessed unusual writing ability. On September 22, 1834, he became editor of the *National Banner and Tennessee Advertiser,* Nashville's first experiment in publishing a daily newspaper. He held this position until November 9, 1835, when he was succeeded by Allen A. Hall, when the publishers had decided, after three years of experience, that a daily paper could not succeed in Nashville. During his editorship, Childress had taken a strong position in behalf of the Texas colonists and was effective in influencing emigrants to join the Robertson colony. Early in January, 1836, he went out to Texas himself, where he promptly applied for a grant in this colony.

It was during his career as an editor that a disastrous, but not entirely destructive fire, at President Jackson's Hermitage aroused a generous impulse on the part of many Americans to raise a fund for rebuilding it. Childress, eager to sponsor the movement in Nashville, wrote to Andrew Jackson on November 16, 1834, telling him that the New Orleans papers reported that a movement to restore "the President's historic Mansion House" had already started in that city and requested that he be permitted to announce and publicize such a movement in Nashville. The plan was to offer to citizens who wished to do so an opportunity to contribute fifty cents—but no more—to such a fund. Jackson's reply was characteristic:

"I respect as I ought the feelings that dictated the generous feeling in the proposition but cannot accept that boon. I am able to rebuild it, and hope whatever the good people of New Orleans intended to bestow on me as a memento of their regard for my public services may be applied to some charity . . . ." [9]

That, of course, was just what Jackson did and his rebuilt Hermitage stands today as a memorial to him and his beloved Rachel.

It is not strange, considering the long-standing friendship between George Childress and his family and Andrew Jackson, that the leaders of the Texan Republic decided to send him to Washington as their emissary to plead their cause with the president and to solicit his support. The Childress correspondence on this and other subjects related to the history of the Texas Republic has been

320

preserved and published, at least in part. His writings, in Nashville newspapers, as well as his correspondence and other papers related to the Texas period, are of great importance. Unhappily, the life of this gifted citizen of Tennessee and Texas was cut short prematurely. He died in 1841 from Bowie knife wounds inflicted by his own hands. Much of his story and his writings have been preserved by the people of Texas. Many publications dealing with his papers, his colorful life and his valuable services to the young Republic have been published and may be found in Texas historical collections. They offer a rich field for further research.

Another of Tennessee's heroes in Texas was Colonel John Coffee Hays, popularly known as Jack Hays, the Texas Ranger, who won for himself an important place in Texas history. He was born in Wilson County about 1818, the son of Harman Hays and his wife, Elizabeth Cage, daughter of William Cage, a member of one of the most prominent pioneer families in Middle Tennessee. He was also the grandson of Nathaniel Hays, who, in 1804, sold to Andrew Jackson his two-story log blockhouse and the broad, fertile acres included in the present Hermitage estate. Like many other Texas leaders, he came from a family distinguished for their services in the Revolutionary War, the Creek and other Indian wars, and the War of 1812.

He was named for Gen. John Coffee, one of Jackson's favorite and most trusted officers and a popular member of his "military family." Having married a niece of Mrs. Jackson, Coffee had an even closer relationship with the Jackson household.

Before Jack Hays was of age, his parents died within a few days of each other in an epidemic of fever. He, with six brothers and sisters, were taken to his uncle's plantation in Mississippi, where he remained until he reached the age of nineteen. Feeling that the load of his younger brothers and sisters was hard on his uncle, he decided to go out into the world and make his own way. Leaving a note on his pillow one morning, he left for Texas. He arrived in San Antonio sometime in the early part of 1837 and was soon appointed captain of a scouting party. It was not long until he became superintendent of the entire border, with the rank of major. Even before the beginning of the war between the United States and Mexico, he had to

his credit many heroic encounters with the Indians and, so successful had he been that the red men were convinced that he was
superior to ordinary men and had a charmed life.

However, in real life, Jack Hays' appearance had little resem-
blance to his warlike reputation. One of his soldiers described him
in 1849 as "a delicate looking young man, of about five feet eight
inches in stature . . . ." He was dressed very plainly, and wore a
thin jacket, with the usual Texan hat, broad-brimmed, with a
round top, and loose open collar, with a black handkerchief tied
negligently around his neck. "His dark brown hair, and large, brilliant hazel eyes are restless in conversation, and speak a language
of their own, not to be mistaken. He has very prominent arched
eyebrows and a rather thoughtful, careworn expression, from the
constant exercise of his faculties, and the responsibilities of a commander. He wears no whiskers, which gives him a still more youthful appearance, and his manner is bland and very prepossessing,
from his extreme modesty." [10]

Yet, his contemporaries testified, he insisted on rigid discipline
and his word was law among his men. This sternness was relieved,
however, by his pleasant manner, and his men familiarly called him
"Jack," although it was said that there was something about him
which prevented one from taking the slightest liberty with him. . . .
This, then, was the Tennessean who became one of the most celebrated heroes of Texas.

Among the best known Tennesseans who took part in the war for
Texan Independence were Sam Houston and Davy Crockett. Both
have long been the subjects of exciting narratives, as well as serious,
well-documented history. Crockett, however, is remembered chiefly
as one of that gallant band who sacrificed their lives at the Alamo,
and, in almost a legendary fashion, as a hunter, trapper and rip-
roaring frontiersman, who was the hero of many tall tales—both
real and imaginary. That he was also showing great promise of a
brilliant and spectacular career in politics is frequently overlooked.

Crockett was first elected to Congress in 1827, by the Whig
party, which was bitterly opposed to Andrew Jackson, but was
rapidly gaining strength in Tennessee. Elected again in 1829, on
the Whig ticket, he continued his opposition to Andrew Jackson,

but, in 1831, he was defeated. In 1833, however, he made a comeback and, once more secure in his seat in Congress and exulting over his victory, on January 28, 1834, he wrote:

"After all this, the reader will perceive that I am now in Congress . . . and that, what is more agreeable to my feelings as a freeman, I am at liberty to vote as my judgment dictates to be right, without the yoke of any party on me, or the driver at my heels with his whip in hand, commanding me to gee-wo-haw, just at his pleasure. Look at my arms, you will not find there any collar with the engraving: 'MY DOG. Andrew Jackson.' But you will find me standing up to my rack, as the people's faithful representative, and the public's most obedient, very humble servant . . . ."

Not so fortunate in the elections of 1835, Crockett was again defeated and was soon on his way to Texas—to his Fate and to immortality. There had been a time, however, when he was on good terms with Andrew Jackson, for he had fought courageously in the Creek War under his command.

Sam Houston's story covers the period of a long, eventful and highly dramatic lifetime. Quite as picturesque as Crockett and, at times, even more erratic, he furnished material for many volumes of serious history, and also for romance by his deeds of high daring which have few parallels in American history.

There are many others whose stories are quite as remarkable, but who have frequently been less publicized. The names of many of them, in Tennessee and elsewhere, are to be found today only in the muster rolls and official reports of military organizations, or in the musty pages of records of the public affairs of their times. Any attempt to give adequate details concerning the thousands of Tennesseans who responded to the nation's call for men to serve in the Mexican War is futile; but their story is told by the men who led them and by the results of their labors and sacrifices.

The official papers of Aaron V. Brown, governor of Tennessee, testify to the valor of the citizens who responded en masse to the national government's call for volunteers. When Governor Brown received the War Department's call, dated May 16, 1846, he responded promptly by issuing a proclamation stating that the president was authorized to accept the services for the purpose of "prosecution of the existing war between the United States and the Republic of Mexico. . . ." Tennessee was asked to furnish one regiment of cavalry, two regiments of infantry, or riflemen . . . and included detailed instructions for recruiting men for these units— which totalled about twenty-eight hundred. The military officers, as well as Governor Brown, were overwhelmed when more than thirty thousand men—not approximately three thousand—responded. By the third of June there were twelve companies and William B. Campbell was elected colonel.[12]

Governor Brown, in an explanatory message to Colonel Campbell, ordered that his regiment, the First Regiment of Tennessee Volunteers, proceed, by means of steamboats chartered for that purpose, to New Orleans, where he was to report to Maj. Gen. Edmund Pendleton Gaines for further orders. He continued explaining to Colonel Campbell something of the difficulty of selecting, from the thousands who volunteered, the few actually required to fill the War Department's call.

"I could not take all," Governor Brown explained . . . and I therefore directed the four Major Generals of the State to select . . . the companies to be received from their respective divisions . . . they have selected you . . . as the fortunate ones on whom the glorious privilege of defending the rights and honors of the country has finally devolved. . . Others, no doubt, may feel some disappointment and mortification, that they, too, cannot share with you at this time in the toils and dangers, and honors of the present campaign . . . ."[13]

However, as the war progressed there was opportunity for other Tennessee volunteers to be put in the field, although there were always more volunteers than were requested in future calls for men. Among other Tennesseans who were soon in the field was William Trousdale, commissioned by President Polk as a colonel of infantry in the United States Army, and assigned to the Third Division of the army commanded by Maj. Gen. Gideon J. Pillow, also a Tennessean. Responding to another call in 1847, two other regiments and a battalion of six companies were soon enrolled, sent to New Orleans by river, and thence, by sea, to Vera Cruz, after which they were formed into a brigade and marched to Mexico City. By

324

November 10, 1847, the Fifth Tennessee Regiment, commanded by Col. W. R. McClellan, was mustered into service.

Other Tennesseans, some of whom had already migrated to the West, also swelled the total of the volunteers from their native state. Among them was Archibald Yell, who was born in Kentucky, but, at an early age, came with his family to Tennessee where he lived until early manhood. When he was only sixteen years old he volunteered for service under General Jackson in the Creek War. He then participated in the taking of Pensacola, and from there, marched with his brigade to New Orleans, where he distinguished himself for bravery in the battle of January Eighth.

In 1818 he volunteered again for service in the Seminole War and raised a company, of which he was chosen captain. Returning to Tennessee, he finished his education and, in 1827, was elected to the state legislature. Throughout these years he enjoyed the affection and confidence of General Jackson.

In 1832, he moved to Arkansas and was appointed receiver of public moneys. He resigned this position and was soon appointed judge on one of the district courts. When the Arkansas constitution was formed, he was elected to Congress, serving there until 1842, when he was elected governor of the state by a large majority. He resigned, however, in order to run for Congress, to which he was elected again in 1844. At the outbreak of the Mexican War, he resigned his seat in Congress and returned to Arkansas, and, at the head of her volunteers, was soon in active duty.

On the hard-fought field of Buena Vista, the Kentucky and Tennessee cavalry, under the command of Colonels Marshall and Yell, fought desperately to hold off a strong attack by the Mexicans. General Taylor had dispatched a party to their assistance, which saved the day, but shortly before they arrived, Colonel Yell received a lance wound in the mouth, which proved to be fatal.

William Trousdale, another of Tennessee's heroes in the Mexican War, was twice wounded at the battle of Chapultepec and, for conspicuous bravery on the field of battle, was made brigadier-general by Brevet of the United States Army. He had served with General Jackson at Pensacola and New Orleans and was a member of the Tennessee State Senate during the years of 1835-36. In 1849 he was elected governor of Tennessee, defeating the Whig candidate, Neill S. Brown, by a very small margin. When he ran for reelection, however, he was defeated, also by a small margin, by the Whig candidate, William B. Campbell. Trousdale was called "The War Horse of Sumner County," and Campbell was referred to during the political campaign as the commander of Tennessee's "Bloody First" regiment in the Mexican War. Following his defeat as governor, Trousdale was appointed United States Minister to Brazil.

Edmund Pendleton Gaines, whose services during the long period of his military career placed him among the greatest American generals, came to Tennessee from Virginia in 1790, when he was about twelve or thirteen years of age. His mother, a cultivated lady, looked well to his education and to that of her other children after they had moved to the western wilderness. During this period he was especially interested in studying mathematics and spent much of his time, as a young man, surveying lands. In 1799 he received his first commission, having been made an ensign of infantry. Soon he was appointed as a second lieutenant in the sixth infantry and from this period until 1806 was employed by the government as a surveyor and an army officer. Gaines became greatly involved during the great excitement over Aaron Burr's schemes for a supposed invasion of the lower country, for which he was accused and tried for treason. Under orders from the president Gaines arrested Burr, was appointed by Jefferson as United States marshal and, with a number of officers, attended Burr's trial. Although he was acting under orders from the president, Gaines and others came in for their share of criticism, but, with the acquittal of Colonel Burr, the excitement soon blew over.

He participated with great distinction in the War of 1812, his most brilliant action being his defense of Fort Erie on August 14, 1814. For his action in this important battle, he was awarded a gold medal by Congress and was presented swords by several states. From 1799, when he was first commissioned, through the War of 1812 and the Mexican War, he was famous for his outstanding service to his country. In 1812, he had been placed in command of the western military district and during this and subsequent periods, was active in the Seminole War, the Black Hawk War and lesser military engagements. His tie with Tennessee was strengthened by the fact that his second wife was Barbara Blount, daughter of the territorial governor, William Blount.

Gideon Pillow, one of the outstanding generals of the Mexican War, was born in Williamson County, Tennessee, June 10, 1806. Graduating at the University of Nashville in 1827, he read law under Judge Kennedy of Columbia, and was admitted to the Tennessee bar in 1829. He soon established an extensive practice and was noted for his eloquence and his forcefulness in prosecuting his cases. He was also inspector general of the state militia, having been appointed to that position by Governor Carroll. He was a son of Gideon Pillow, who emigrated from North Carolina about 1789, and participated in many of the Indian battles of that period. His sons, Gideon and William, soon followed in his footsteps. William, as a colonel, fought bravely under General Jackson during the Creek wars and was seriously wounded.

Gideon, in early manhood, had already won an important place in politics and, by 1844, had achieved such prominence that he was able to take an effective part in the successful effort of Tennessee Democrats to win for James K. Polk, not the nomination for the vice-presidency, but for the presidency itself. War would soon, however, become his major occupation. Shortly after news of General Taylor's campaign on the Rio Grande, he went promptly to the seat of war, tendering his services. He was assigned a large command of volunteers from Tennessee, Alabama and Georgia and, during the summer and fall of 1846, he conducted their discipline and military training with great success. By winter he, at the head of a Tennessee regiment of cavalry and two regiments of Illinois volunteers, with his own brigade of Tennessee troops, moved from Victoria, over the mountains, rivers and rugged plains, to Tampico, some four hundred and fifty miles distant. Crossing the Gulf at this place, he joined General Scott's army before Vera Cruz and was the second officer to debark his command.

He soon had two skirmishes with the enemy before the walls of Vera Cruz, in both of which he charged with great courage and force, and though the forces of the enemy greatly exceeded his own, he succeeded in driving them from the field. About the same time

327

he directed the erection of a naval battery which was of great importance in the taking of this stronghold. Meanwhile, he extended the American lines and prepared effectively for the impending siege. During the suspension of hostilities, he was chosen as one of the commissioners to negotiate the terms of surrender. On April 13, 1847, he was commissioned major-general.

This is but one of General Pillow's brilliant achievements during the Mexican War, but it was sufficient to win for him an appreciative notice of General Scott, who in an official order stated:

"It is due also to state, that in the part assigned to Brigadier (now Major) General Pillow and his brigade, the batteries attacked by them were much more formidable than that leader or the general-in-chief had supposed . . ." and, continuing, he praised General Pillow and his brigade in the highest terms, for their bravery.

Such recognition is typical of General Pillow's record in many of the most important battles of the war. He and his men were at Chapultepec and many other battles where superhuman courage and bravery were the accepted order of the day. Surviving many years after he had won these laurels, he took an important part in the War Between the States during the 1860s, as did many other Tennesseans who had fought in the Mexican War. Gen. Benjamin F. Cheatham was one of them and there were many, many others.

Another great soldier and statesman who served in the Mexican War was Jefferson Davis. Though not a Tennessean, he had, from the time when he visited the Jacksons at The Hermitage as a child, until the years when he served as President of the Confederate States of America, been closely associated with Tennesseans.

Among the other Tennesseans who participated in the tragic War Between the States were such outstanding men as Nathan Bedford Forrest, the matchless cavalry leader, tactician, and military genius; and David G. Farragut, one of the greatest admirals of the United States Navy.

Another Tennessean who played a great part in the winning and settling of the West was Thomas Hart Benton. He was born in Orange County, North Carolina, March 14, 1782. His father, Jesse Benton, was a lawyer and was associated with leading men west of the mountains at an early date, among them Richard Henderson

328

Thomas Hart Benton, prominent figure in the winning of the West. Photo courtesy of State of Tennessee Tourism Development Division.

Nathan Bedford Forrest, outstanding cavalry leader who participated in the War Between the States.

and others who were connected with the Transylvania Purchase of 1775. His mother, a member of a prominent Virginia family, brought her family to Williamson County, Tennessee after her husband's death.[14] At the time of his father's death, Thomas was attending the University of North Carolina, but he soon afterwards discontinued his studies there, moving with his family to Williamson County. He did not abandon his education, however, for he continued his studies and, by 1806, was admitted to the bar at Nashville, after which he began practice at Franklin, the county seat of Williamson County. Even at this early date, his brilliant mind and out-going personality won favorable attention and, in 1811, he was elected to the state legislature. Soon afterwards, he volunteered for military service and received the commission of lieutenant-colonel in the Thirty-ninth Infantry, which was commanded by Col. John Williams. He participated actively in the 1813 expedition to Natchez, Mississippi, after which, as one of Jackson's bright young men, he was closely associated with him and had the promise of going far as one of his favorite protegés, until the famous "brawl."

At the end of the war in 1815, Benton resigned his commission and emigrated to Missouri.

After he went to Missouri, Benton rose almost immediately to an amazing position of prominence and power, as did many other Tennesseans who moved into the new, unsettled territory of the West. John Spencer Bassett, in writing of Andrew Jackson, and others of this period of western expansion, attributes it to a kind of inborn sense of superiority. Of Jackson he said:

"He had the top man's feeling for the high places in society. Through his long life, there was never a disposition on the part of his associates to deny his pretension. He was accepted as a leader wherever he happened to be. Herein was the quality, given him by nature, which made him the man of distinction." [15]

Perhaps there was something more to it than Bassett indicated. While Tennesseans had their share of such a sense of superiority, so did most of the others who settled the West. Much of it was due, undoubtedly, to their pride of ownership of this vast new land, and not a little to the fact that from the time of their first settlements they had known the thrill of being freemen, capable of working out their own destinies and forming their governments according to their own liking.

Benton reached Missouri just as it was obtaining statehood and, in the process, had raised the hotly debated subject of the permission, or the prohibition, of slavery in new states. Being elected as a United States Senator for the new state, Benton began his long and illustrious career as a member of that body, and, from the very beginning, became one of the great national authorities in debates on this incendiary subject. He was not only an eye-witness to the proceedings of the Congress, the national government and the state of Missouri, in these stirring days, but he was an active participant in the debates on the floor of the Senate and was one of the adroit manipulators of the Missouri Compromise. His writings on this and other subjects of his times, in his *Thirty Years View,* are among the most detailed and revealing ever written on this important period in American History. Of this he wrote:

"Slavery agitation took its rise during this time (1819-20), in the form of attempted restriction on the state of Missouri—a prohibition to hold slaves to be placed upon her as a condition of her admission into the Union, and to be binding on her afterwards. This agitation came from the North, and under a federal lead, and soon swept both parties into a vortex. It was quieted, so far as that form of question was concerned, by admitting the state without restriction, and imposing it on the remainder of Louisiana territory north and west of the State, and above the parallel of 36 degrees and 30 minutes; which is the prolongation of the southern boundary line of Virginia and Kentucky. This was called a 'compromise,' and all was clear gain to the antislavery side of the question, and was done under the lead of the united slave state vote in the Senate, the majority of that vote in the House of Representatives, and the undivided sanction of a Southern administration . . . ."

Benton himself, though not a member of Missouri's constitutional convention, instigated this compromise and was responsible for its being put into the constitution. He was equally opposed to slavery agitation in the North and to slavery extension. The heated debates over the Missouri Compromise were but the forerunners of the great storm of controversy which would shake the nation to its very foundations and, for a time, tear it asunder.[16]

In 1823 Benton, arriving to take his seat in the Senate, found his chair adjoining that of the recently elected junior senator from Tennessee. He was Andrew Jackson! The two had not seen each other since their brawl in Nashville in 1813, but no sign of recognition passed between them. Other members, seeing the situation, offered to exchange seats with them, but both stubbornly refused.[17] In a few days they were named to a committee on military affairs, of which Jackson was chairman, upon which Jackson turned to the gentleman of Missouri, saying that they were on the same committee and that he would notify him when to attend a meeting. Benton replied politely, suggesting that the chairman call the meeting at a time suited to his own convenience, but nothing more was said between them. Again, in a few days, the two met in the drawing room of the White House. Benton bowed courteously and Jackson, smiling, stepped forward with an outstretched hand. The feud was ended and, for the rest of the older man's life, the two were once more fast friends. With almost his last breath, Andrew Jackson entrusted his friend William B. Lewis with messages for Sam Houston, Tom Benton, Frank Blair and Polk.

From his earliest days in the senate, Benton's career was steadily upward. Serving thirty years as a member of this important body, he became thoroughly familiar with both domestic and foreign affairs and, in his writings, left a rich heritage to future generations of Americans. His *Thirty Years View* and his important volumes, *Abridgement of the Debates of Congress,* have long been recognized for their formal recital of historic facts and also for the entertaining passages they contain.

Associated with Benton—and with Tennessee—was another important figure in winning the West, John Charles Fremont, the noted explorer, general, governor of California and of Arizona, and candidate for the presidency of the United States. Fremont was a brilliant, somewhat erratic, romantic, and more than ordinarily gifted character. He was born in Savannah, Georgia, on January 21, 1813. His father was a Frenchman, who made his living by teaching his native language, and his mother, Anne Beverly Whiting, was the daughter of a wealthy and prominent Virginia family. She, left

331

an orphan, was urged into a marriage when she was only seventeen, to a rich, gouty gentleman forty-five years her senior. She was granted a divorce from him by the Virginia legislature and was married to Fremont, who died in 1818, leaving her with three small children. She then moved from Savannah to Charleston, South Carolina, where her son Charles, only five years of age at the time of his father's death, was reared and educated. He became remarkable for his attainments in mathematics and for his interest in surveying and exploring.[18]

In 1837 he was employed to explore and survey the passes through the mountainous country of the Carolinas and Tennessee, for the purpose of locating a route for a proposed railroad between Charleston and Cincinnati. This work was ended abruptly by a severe financial depression in 1837 and, in the following fall, Fremont was engaged by the United States Army for a military reconnaisance of the mountainous Cherokee country in Georgia, North Carolina and Tennessee. Because Indian hostilities were anticipated, this survey was made hurriedly in the depth of winter. It was Fremont's first experience of exploring in mountain snows, but by no means his last, for in 1838-39, he accompanied M. Nicollet, a distinguished French scientist, in explorations between the Missouri and the British line.

While Fremont was in Washington reporting on these expeditions, he met Thomas Hart Benton's fifteen year old daughter, Jessie, and was soon engaged to her. Her parents objected to the marriage because of her youth, although they had a high personal regard for Fremont. Senator Benton, however, solved the problem by having the War Department issue an order transferring Fremont to an exploring expedition on the Des Moines River and the western frontiers. The romance did not end, however, for the next year, when Jessie had just reached a blossoming sweet sixteen, she and Fremont were secretly married on October 19, 1841. Soon Fremont suggested and promoted a geographical survey of the entire territory of the United States from the Missouri River to the Pacific Ocean, for the purpose of ascertaining the feasibility of overland communication between the two sides of the continent. Leaving Washington on May 2, 1842, he began his expedition on June 10, from a point on the Kansas River, a few miles beyond the Missouri border. Four months later, on October 10, 1842, he returned to his starting point by almost the same route he had traveled going out. Many hardships and dangers had been experienced, but Fremont had successfully carried out the purpose of his expedition. His report, made to Congress in the winter of 1842 and 1843, attracted both national and international attention.

Almost immediately, Fremont was off on another and even more hazardous expedition. He soon came into deep snow, which forced him to descend to a great basin, only to find himself in the depth of winter in a desert, his party in danger of death from cold and starvation. Through his astronomical observations, he found that he was in the latitude of the bay of San Francisco. However, a range of mountains, which Indians told him no man could pass, lay between him and the valleys of California. No inducement nor reward could persuade any of them to accompany him, so he boldly undertook the journey without the Indians as guides. Forty days later, he arrived at Sutter's Fort on the Sacramento River, he and his men thin and exhausted and of the sixty-seven horses with which he had started, only thirty-three had survived the trip. They were so weak and emaciated that they could hardly be led along. Continuing the trip, he skirted the western base of the Sierra Nevada, crossed that range through a gap, entered the great basin, and again visited the Salt Lake. He returned, through the South pass, reaching Kansas in July, 1844, after an absence of fourteen months. He was made captain in January, 1845, and in that year undertook his third expedition.

The object of the third expedition, which was probably the most exciting as well as the most productive of all, was the exploration of the great basin and maritime region of California. During the summer the headwaters of the streams which form the dividing line between the Mississippi valley and the Pacific Ocean, were examined and, by October, Fremont's party set up a camp on the shores of the Great Salt Lake. From this place he took a small party to explore the Sierra Nevada, and in the dead of winter, crossed it again with a few men, to secure supplies from California for his party. They met hostile Indians, but were successful in defending themselves and made their way to the San Joaquin valley, where he left his men to rest, while he went on to Monterey, then the capital

333

of California, to seek from the Mexican governor, General Castro, permission to continue his explorations in California. It was granted, but, almost immediately revoked. Fremont refused to abandon his explorations, however, and, at once, took a strong position on Hawk's peak, about thirty miles from Monterey. He cut down trees to build a fort, hoisted an American flag over it and, having plenty of ammunition, felt capable of defending his little party, which now numbered about sixty-two Americans. Writing to the American consul on March 10, 1846, he advised him:

"We have in no wise done wrong to the people or the authorities of this country, and if we are hemmed in and assaulted here, we will die, every man of us, under the flag of our country."

Threatened hourly by Mexican artillery, cavalry and infantry, Fremont waited for the attack. On the fourth day of the siege, becoming tired of inaction, he withdrew his party and marched toward the San Joaquin. A courier from General Castro, with a message proposing a cessation of hostilities, arrived at the deserted camp while the fires were still burning, so Fremont, unmolested, continued northward through the valley of the Sacramento into Oregon. On May 9, near Tlamath lake, he was found by a search party carrying dispatches from Washington which instructed him to watch over the interests of the United States in California, the government having reason to believe that Mexico would transfer this province to Great Britain. There was also the threat that General Castro would attempt to destroy the American settlements on the Sacramento, so he began his march back to California, finding that Castro was already moving toward these settlements.

The settlers rose and flocked to Fremont's standard and, under his leadership, successfully defended themselves. Telling this story, his father-in-law, in his *Thirty Years View,* said "All the northern part of California was freed from Mexican authority, independence was proclaimed, the flag of independence was raised, Castro flying to the south, the American settlers saved from destruction, and the British party in California counteracted and broken up in all their schemes."

On July 4, the American settlers celebrated by electing Fremont governor of California. On the tenth of that month, they learned that Commodore Sloate had taken possession of Monterey and Fremont proceeded to join the naval forces, marching to Monterey on the nineteenth with 160 mounted riflemen. On May 27, 1846, Fremont, having been promoted to the rank of lieutenant-colonel, organized a force of mounted men, known as the California Battalion. He was also appointed by Commodore Stockton as military commandant and civil governor of the territory.

The proposed independent government was abandoned when news was received of the outbreak of the war between the United States and Mexico. Soon General Stephen Watts Kearney, with a small force of dragoons, arrived in California and immediately a controversy arose between him and Commodore Stockton, as to who should be in command, since both had orders from Washington to conquer and organize a government in the country. Kearney, whose higher rank placed Fremont under his authority, ordered him to obey his commands, not those of Stockton, but Fremont decided to obey the naval officer. Orders from Washington instructed Stockton to yield the command to Kearney, which, of course, Fremont recognized and promptly acknowledged his authority. From the beginning Kearney showed marked animosity toward Fremont, eventually deciding to set out overland to the United States and ordering Fremont to accompany him. Reaching Fort Leavenworth on August 22, 1847, Kearney placed him under arrest and ordered him to Washington to report to the adjutant-general.

Passing through St. Louis, Fremont was greeted with great enthusiasm, presented publicly with a letter of appreciation and invited to the public dinner which citizens were planning in his honor. Because of the circumstances of his arrest, however, he felt it necessary to decline the dinner invitation and continued quietly on his way to Washington. Arriving there about the middle of September, Fremont asked for a speedy trial, but the court-martial, which began in November, 1847, lasted until January 31, 1848. As its result, he was found guilty of mutiny, disobedience to a superior officer, violation of good order and military discipline, and dismissed from the service. President Polk was requested by a majority of the members of the court to use clemency in carrying out the sentence. Polk refused to accept the verdict of mutiny, but let the others stand and

335

immediately remitted the penalty. Fremont, however, refused to admit any guilt whatever and did not accept the president's clemency. His reputation with the public, rather than being damaged by the court-martial, was not injured in any way—in fact he was regarded as more of a hero than ever.

Perhaps the most far-reaching of all Tennessee's contributions to the winning of the West was that made by James K. Polk while he was president of the United States. He, like Andrew Jackson, Sam Houston and many others, had long been a strong advocate of the annexation of the Republic of Texas, but it remained for him to be at the head of government when it was finally accomplished. Culminating many years of negotiation and discussion, it was finally agreed that the Republic of Texas become a part of the United States. Accordingly, on March 1, 1845, Congress passed a joint resolution providing that the "territory rightfully belonging to the Republic of Texas" should form a part of the American Union. John Tyler, whom Polk succeeded as president of the United States, signed the document on the same day it was passed, but it was several months before the annexation was actually consummated. Even then, however, the final chapters were not yet written, for Mexico did not willingly abide by the stipulations of her treaty. President Polk succeeded Tyler a few days after he had signed the congressional resolution and upon his shoulders fell the responsibility of bringing Texas into the Union as a full fledged state.[19]

In his inaugural address of March 4, 1845, the incoming president called attention to the fact that the people of Texas had expressed their desire to be annexed to the United States and pointed out that they were once a part of our country, had been ceded away to a foreign power and were now independent and possessed of the right to dispose of a part of their territory and to merge their sovereignty, as a separate, independent state, in ours. He then urged that by an immediate act of Congress, Texas be received into the Union on the same footing and with the same rights and privileges as the other states.

Continuing, he congratulated the late Congress which had approved the annexation and stated that it remained only for the two countries to agree upon the terms in order to consummate the deal.

"Perceiving no valid objection to the measure," he said, "and many reasons for its adoption, vitally affecting the peace, the safety, and the prosperity of both countries, I shall on this broad principle, and not in any narrow spirit of sectional policy, endeavor by all constitutional, honorable, and appropriate means, to consummate the expressed will of the people and the government of the United States, by the reannexation of Texas to our Union at the earliest practicable period." [20]

In his first annual message to Congress, December 2, 1845, President Polk reported that the terms of annexation offered by the United States had been accepted by Texas, both parties having pledged to the compact of their union. Urging Congress to act promptly upon this important subject, he pointed out that this accession of territory had been a bloodless achievement, that no arm of force had been raised to produce the result and that the sword had had no part in the victory.

"If we consider," he said, "the extent of territory involved in the annexation—its prospective influence on America—the means by which it has been accomplished, springing purely from the choice of the people themselves to share the blessings of our union—the history of the world may be challenged to furnish parallel."

Meanwhile, Mexico was showing an attitude of hostility against the United States by issuing proclamations and vowing the intention of making war on this country. The congress and the convention of the people of Texas invited the United States to send an army into their country to protect them from the threatened attack. President Polk, deeming it necessary as a precautionary measure, ordered a strong squadron to the coasts of Mexico and concentrated an efficient military force on the Texas frontier. They were ordered to commit no act of hostility, unless Mexico actually declared war, or made herself the aggressor by striking the first blow.

President Polk, continuing his first annual message, then gave a detailed report on the history and the present situation in regard to Oregon. He explained, in an able way, the negotiations on this subject between England and the United States in 1818, 1824, 1826,

337

1827 and 1828. Stating that when he came into office the situation was still unsettled, he discussed the subject at length, advising that by an earlier agreement a year's notice had to be given by either of the parties which wished to terminate the joint jurisdiction of this territory, he asked that such notice be authorized by Congress at once.

Polk's position on this subject was expressed as follows: "Though entertaining the settled conviction that the British pretensions of title could not be maintained to any portion of the Oregon territory, upon any principle of public law recognized by nations, yet, in deference to what had been done by my predecessors, and especially in consideration that the propositions of compromise had been thrice made by two preceding administrations, to adjust the question on the parallel of forty-nine degrees, and in two of them yielding to Great Britain the free navigation of the Columbia, and that the pending negotiation had been commenced on the basis of compromise, I deemed it my duty not abruptly to break off . . . ."

In regard to navigation of the Columbia River, he stated that he was unwilling to concede to any foreign power the right of free navigation of rivers which passed through the very heart of the country. Taking full responsibility, he directed that the offer of compromise be withdrawn and that the title of the United States to the whole Oregon territory be asserted. The mild looking, quiet Tennessean who now occupied the president's chair, thus, early in his administration, asserted with great force and determination, the rights of his country. Furthermore, his knowledge of law and his long legislative experience made him thoroughly capable of understanding and presenting to the Congress and the people of the United States full explanations of the complicated international problems with which they were now faced. As England was seeking full control of the Oregon country, she had also for many years, been looking with envious eyes upon Texas. As early as 1833, Sam Houston, in a letter to Andrew Jackson, informed him in detail on the situation in Texas and Mexico, telling him that Texas was facing an important crisis, since England was seeking to acquire it. But, he assured him, if the Texans made any transfer at all, its citizens would oppose anything but becoming a part of the United States.

The British efforts to acquire titles to both Texas and Oregon were to continue for several years, however, and were not settled until President Polk, with a surprising show of strength and courage, put an end to the long years of vacillating policies and settled the matter firmly and permanently.[21]

Concluding this lengthy and informative message on national affairs, President Polk called attention to the death of Andrew Jackson on June 8, 1845, and paid him this tribute:

"I trust it may not be deemed inappropriate on the occasion for me to dwell for a moment on the memory of the most eminent citizen of our country, who, during the summer that is gone by, has descended to the tomb. The enjoyment of contemplating, at the advanced age of near fourscore years, the happy condition of his country, cheered the last hours of Andrew Jackson, who departed this life in the hope of a blessed immortality . . . His great deeds had secured to him the affections of his fellow-citizens, and it was his happiness to witness the growth and glory of his country, which he loved so well. He departed amid the benedictions of millions of freemen.[22] The nation paid its tribute at his tomb. Coming generations will learn from his example the love of country and the rights of man. In his language on a similar occasion to the present, 'I now commend you, fellow citizens, to the guidance of Almighty God, with a full reliance on his merciful providence for the maintenance of our free institutions; and with an earnest supplication, that whatever errors it may be my lot to commit, in discharging the arduous duties which have devolved on me, will find a remedy in the harmony and wisdom of your counsels.' " [23]

Adding to the peace and satisfaction of his last days was the old hero's knowledge that in the hands of two of his most outstanding protegés, Sam Houston and James K. Polk, the nation was safe. Writing President Polk on May 26, 1845, a little less than two weeks before his death, he said:

"Texas comes into the Union with a united voice, and Genl. Houston, as I knew, puts his shoulder to the wheel to roll it in speedily. I knew British gold could not buy Sam Houston . . . My dear friend I have wrote thus far gasping for breath . . . What my affliction may end in God only knows. I am truly resigned to his will

339

whatever it may be. He does all things well, and I rejoice to see your administration succeeding so well. May a gracious providence preside over you in your administration and may you pass thro it and retire thro the plaudits of your country. . . ." [24]

Again, only two days before his death on June 8, he wrote another letter to Polk, still advising and still actively interested in his success. It was the last letter he ever wrote.

Meanwhile, the dying man had been advised that Sam Houston and his family were on the way to his bedside. Writing to his nephew, Major Andrew Jackson Donelson, then on important missions to Texas and Mexico, he said:

"I rejoice in the prudent course our mutual friend Genl. Houston has taken. It is what I calculated he would take and it is worthy of him, as a true patriot and friend of the rights of man and it will be profitable to him in any views hereafter in his own preferment. Be assured that Genl. Houston and his family will be received as he ought by the good citizens of Tennessee. My dear Major, I rejoice that you will nobly execute your mission and bring the lone star into our glorious Union . . . ."

The Houston party, though traveling with all possible speed, did not reach The Hermitage until a few hours after the old hero's death. The disappointment was great, for Sam Houston's ardent desire was to have Andrew Jackson lay his hands on his young son's head in blessing. Sadly leading the boy to the now prostrate form, the sorrowing father urged:

"Son, try to remember that you have looked upon the face of Andrew Jackson."

They, with other loyal followers—the great and the near-great—joined the family and neighbors as they carried Andrew Jackson's body to the tomb in the garden, where they placed it beside his beloved Rachel.

Soon after delivering his annual message, President Polk dispatched General Zachary Taylor, with an army, to hold the Texas country. War was officially declared by Congress on May 11, 1846 and, soon afterwards, Governor Aaron V. Brown, Tennessee's chief executive, issued a call for the 2,800 troops which had been requested of this state. Thirty thousand responded!

The late John Trotwood Moore, state historian, author and poet laureate of Tennessee, described this overwhelming response:

". . . Because of the large number of volunteers and their eagerness to serve, rules were laid down for the guidance of the four major-generals of the state in deciding what companies should be received from their respective divisions. . . By June third, companies had been organized into one regiment and formed the First Regiment of Tennessee Volunteers. They included the 'Harrison Guards' and the 'Nashville Blues,' two famous companies, as well as others under the command of able officers. The rendezvous for the troops in Middle Tennessee was Camp Taylor, about two miles down the Cumberland River from Nashville." [25]

Gen. William B. Campbell, of Smith County, was elected colonel; Gen. Samuel R. Anderson, of Sumner County, lieutenant-colonel. William Trousdale was commissioned colonel of infantry in the United States Army by President Polk in 1847, and many other leading Tennesseans took their place as officers of the Tennessee volunteers.

As the war went on other calls were made on Tennessee for troops and, in every case, her men volunteered in numbers far surpassing each call. Many Tennesseans, volunteers of the War of 1812, had served under Andrew Jackson, some serving as officers, and others, serving with conspicuous bravery in the ranks, also fought in the Mexican War. When the war ended and Texas was finally won, Tennessee had forever established her right to be called "The Volunteer State."

As for James K. Polk, he was not a warrior and he had not desired the war; but believing that it was a price which had to be paid in order to conclude the troublesome situation with Mexico, he prosecuted it ably and whole heartedly.

The objectives which Polk had set for his administration were, however of a different nature. His four goals were reduction of the tariff, an independent treasury, settlement of the Oregon question, and acquisition of California. He succeeded in reaching all four, but his greatest achievement was probably the permanent settlement of the Texas question.

In his fourth and final annual message, President Polk summed up the vast acquisitions of western territory which had taken place during the four years of his administration:

"Within less than four years the annexation of Texas to the Union has been consummated; all confusing title to the Oregon territory south of the forty-ninth degree of north latitude, being all that was insisted on by any of my predecessors, has been adjusted; and New Mexico and Upper California have been acquired by treaty. The area of these several territories, according to a report carefully prepared by the commissioner of the general land-office, from the most authentic information in his possession, and which is herewith transmitted, contains one million, one hundred and ninety-three thousand, and sixty-one square miles, or seven hundred and sixty-three millions, five hundred and fifty-nine thousand, and forty acres; while the area of the remaining twenty-nine states, and the territory not yet organized into states east of the Rocky Mountains, contains two million, fifty-nine thousand, five hundred and thirteen square miles. . . . These estimates show that the territories recently acquired, and over which our exclusive jurisdiction and dominion have been extended, constitute a country more than half as large as all that which was held by the United States before their acquisition." [26]

Continuing, he explained in minute detail the nature and the rich possibilities of the vast territory which had so recently become a part of the United States. In regard to Texas he pointed out the danger which would have attended its falling into the hands of a foreign power, as well as its fertility, the value of its rivers and harbors and its location. New Mexico, though inland and without a seaport, nevertheless, was already known for the richness of its minerals and its mines for precious metals, as well as fertility of soil which could support a large population.

Upper California, he said, ". . . irrespective of the vast mineral wealth recently developed there, holds at this day, in point of value and importance to the rest of the Union, the same relation that Louisiana did when that fine territory was acquired from France forty-five years ago. Extending nearly ten degrees of latitude along the Pacific, and embracing the only safe and commodious harbors on that coast, from many hundred miles, with a temperate climate, and an extensive interior of fertile lands, it is scarcely possible to estimate its wealth until it shall be brought under the government of our laws, and its resources fully developed. . . ."

In spite of his great accomplishments, President Polk did not seek re-election for a second term. He was never robust and the burden of government had rested heavily upon his shoulders. Preparing for his retirement he purchased the handsome residence of Felix Grundy in Nashville, and it was to this home—later known as "Polk Place"—that he came after his eventful administration had closed. He was arranging his library and preparing to establish himself for a long, pleasant retirement, when he fell victim to the cholera during the epidemic of 1849, and died after living in his new home some three months. He was fifty-four years of age.

Mrs. Polk survived her husband for many years, maintaining her household at "Polk Place," but remaining in semi-retirement. In her drawing room she received distinguished guests, not only from Tennessee, but from all parts of the nation. Yet her heart was never far away from the white-columned tomb in her garden. Her death occurred in August, 1891 and, eventually, "Polk Place" was sold, but the tomb in the garden was removed to the grounds of the nearby capitol of Tennessee.

Eighty years had passed since the log cabin home of the first white family had been built on the Watauga at Boone's Creek, but in this brief time a continent had been crossed and a new generation of pioneers, many of whom were sons or grandsons of the Wataugans and members of other early Tennessee settlements, were pouring across the plains to build their homes and establish their independent governments by free men on the shores of the Pacific Ocean. The "dangerous example" of the Wataugans had, indeed, traveled a long way!

A great nation, in which Tennesseans were privileged to play an important part, was being built, but with this privilege they and others who marched in the vanguard with them had great responsibility. Andrew Jackson spoke earnestly of this in his farewell address, delivered March 3, 1837, at the end of his second term as President of the United States.

THE DANGEROUS EXAMPLE

"Knowing that the path of freedom is continually beset by enemies, who often assume the disguise of friends," he warned, "I have
devoted the last hours of my public life to warn you of the dangers.
The progress of the United States, under our free and happy institutions, has surpassed the most sanguine hopes of the founders of
the republic. Our growth has been rapid beyond all former example,
in numbers, in wealth, in knowledge, and all the useful arts which
contribute to the comforts and convenience of man; and from the
earliest ages of history to the present day, there never have been
thirteen millions of people associated together in one political body
who enjoyed so much freedom and happiness as the people of these
United States. You have no longer any cause to fear danger from
abroad; your strength and power are well known throughout the
civilized world, as well as the high and gallant bearing of your sons.
It is from within, among yourselves, from cupidity, from corruption,
from disappointed ambition, and inordinate thirst for power, that
factions will be formed and liberty endangered. It is against such
designs, whatever disguise the actors may assume, that you have
especially to guard yourselves. You have the highest of human trusts
committed to your care. Providence has showered on this favored
land blessings without number, and has chosen you as the guardians
of freedom, to preserve it for the benefit of the human race . . .

"My own race is nearly run; advanced age and failing health
warn me that before long I must pass beyond the reach of human
events, and cease to feel the vicissitudes of human affairs. I thank
God that my life has been spent in a land of liberty, and that he has
given me a heart to love my country with the affection of a son.
And filled with gratitude for your constant and unwavering kindness, I bid you a last and affectionate farewell.

Then, placing his hands, in spirit, upon the heads of the American people, he pronounced this benediction:

"May He, who holds in his hands the destinies of nations, make
you worthy of the favors he has bestowed and enable you, with
pure hearts, and pure hands, and sleepless vigilance, to guard and
defend, to the end of time, the great charge he has committed to
your keeping."

344

Selected
Bibliography

Adair, James. *The History of the American Indians*. Particularly Those Nations Adjoining the Mississippi, East and West Florida, Georgia, South and North Carolina, and Virginia. London: 1775. Also Judge Samuel Cole Williams' annotated reprint, 1930.

American State Papers. Vols. I and II. Washington: Gales and Seaton, 1834. Documents Legislative and Executive, Personal Reports and Letters.

The American's Own Book. Containing the Declaration of Independence, with the lives of the signers; the Constitution of the United States; the inaugural addresses, portraits of presidents of the United States; biographical sketches, etc. New York: Leavitt & Allen, 1855.

American Archives, 5th Series. Vol. III. Donelson (Donaldson), Earl (Earle) references, etc.

Ashe, Thomas. Travels in America (Performed in 1806). Tennessee exports: "fine waggon and saddle horses, beef, cattle, ginseng, deerskin, and furs, cotton, hemp, flax; also timber, pork and flour. . . ." Published 1808.

Bancroft, Aaron, D.D. *The Life of George Washington, First President of the United States*. 2 vols. Boston: T. Ballington, 1826.

Bancroft, George. *History of the United States*. 10 vols. Boston: Little, Brown & Co., 1834-1874.

Bassett, John Spencer. *Correspondence of Andrew Jackson*. 6 vols. Washington: Carnegie Institution, 1926.

Benton, Thomas Hart. *Thirty Years' View*. 2 vols. New York: D. Appleton & Co., 1854.

Benton, Thomas Hart. *An Abridgment of the Debates of Congress,* from 1789 to 1856. 16 vols. New York and London: D. Appleton & Co., 1857-1861.

Bisset, Robert. *History of the Reign of George III, to the Termination of the Late War*. 4 vols. Philadelphia: Lewis and Weaver, 1811.

Boggs, Mae Helene Bacon. *My Playhouse was a Concord Coach*. An Anthology of Newspaper Clippings and Documents Relating to Those who made California History During the Years of 1822-1888. Dedicated to the author's uncle, the late William Lyncoya Smith, who was named by Andrew Jackson. n.p., n.d.

Brackenridge, Hugh Henry. *Law Miscellanies.* Notes on Blackstone's Commentaries, Showing the Variations of the Law of Pennsylvania from the Law of England, and What Acts of Assembly Might Require to be Repealed or Modified. Philadelphia: P. Byrne, 1814.

Byrd, Col. William. *A History of the Dividing Line.* The Westover Manuscript Containing the History of the Dividing Line Between Virginia and North Carolina; A Journey to the Land of Eden and a Progress to the Mines. Petersburg: n.p., 1841.

Caldwell, Joshua W. *Sketches of Bench and Bar in Tennessee.* Knoxville: Ogden Brothers & Co., 1898.

Caldwell, Mary French. *Andrew Jackson's Hermitage,* 1933; *General Jackson's Lady,* 1936; *The Duck's Back,* 1952; *Tennessee: The Volunteer State,* 1968.

Carroll, Bartholomew Rivers. *Historical Collections of South Carolina.* 2 vols. n.p., 1836.

Caruthers, Dr. William A. *The Knights of the Golden Horseshoe.* n.p., 1844. See also Davis, Curtis Carroll. *Chronicler of the Cavaliers.* Also essay by John Easten Cooke, *Appleton's Journal,* II, 175-6, September 1869.

Claiborne, Nathaniel Herbert. *Notes on the War in the South.* Contains biographical sketches of Montgomery, Sevier, Jackson, Governor Claiborne and others. n.p., n.d.

Claiborne, W. C. C. *Official Letterbooks of W. C. C. Claiborne 1801-1816.* Edited by Dunbar Rowland. Jackson: Mississippi Department of Archives and History, 1917.

Clayton, W. W. *History of Davidson County, Tennessee.* Philadelphia: Lewis & Company, 1880.

Clement, Maude Carter. *History of Pittsylvania County.* Lynchburg: n.p., 1929.

A Concise History of the United States from the Discovery until 1813. 4th ed. Philadelphia: 1813.

Confidential State Papers. Vol. 10. (American State Papers). Contains much valuable correspondence in relation to Tennessee, the far South, the Mississippi River, Governor William Blount and the so-called conspiracies of the times. Also letters from Spanish Chargés des Affaires, Joseph Ignatius de Viar and Joseph de Jaudenes to Thomas Jefferson, Secretary of State, Philadelphia. May 25, 1792 and many others.

Crane, Verner W. "The Tennessee River as the Road to Carolina: the Beginnings of Exploration and Trade." *Mississippi Valley Historical Review,* III, 3-18.

Creekmore, Betsy Beeler. *Knoxville.* Knoxville: University of Tennessee Press, 1958.

Crew, H. W. *History of Nashville, Tennessee.* Nashville: Barbee & Smith, 1890.

Dana, Charles A. and Ripley, George, eds. *The New American Cyclopedia.* New York and London: D. Appleton & Co., 1859. Important for biographers of leading personages of the period.

Dinwiddie, Robert. *Official Records of Robert Dinwiddie of Virginia.* Dinwiddie Records. Vol. I. Correspondence of Governor Dinwiddie and Governor Glen of South Carolina and other important correspondence. 1751-1758.

Dorris, Mary C. *Preservation of the Hermitage.* Nashville: n.p., 1915.

Draper, Lyman C. *History of the Battle of King's Mountain, October 7th, 1780, and the Events Which Led to It.* Cincinnati: Peter G. Thompson, 1881.

Du Pratz, M. Le Page. *The History of Louisiana* or of the Western Parts of Virginia and the Carolinas. With Some Notes and Observations Relating to our Colonies. 2 vols. Printed for T. Becket and P. A. De Hondt in the Strand, 1763.

Dusenbery, B. M., compiler. *Monument to the Memory of General Andrew Jackson,* containing twenty-five Eulogies and Sermons Delivered on the Occasion of His Death. Troy: Samuel Hanna, 1846.

Eaton, John. *The Life of Andrew Jackson,* to which is added a brief History of the Seminole War and Cession and Government of Florida. Philadelphia: n.p., 1828.

The Federalist on the New Constitution. Written in 1788 by Mr. Hamilton, Mr. Madison, and Mr. Jay, with an Appendix Containing the Letters of Pacificus and Helvidius, etc. A new edition written by Mr. Madison and corrected by himself. Hallowell: Glazier, Masters and Smith, 1842.

Filson, John. *Kentucke and the Adventures of Colonel Daniel Boone.* Wilmington: James Adams, 1784. Reprint with Introduction by Willard Rouse Jillson. Louisville: John P. Morton & Co., 1934.

French, B. F. *Historical Collections of Louisiana.* Embracing Many Rare and Valuable Documents Relating to the Natural, Civil and Political History of the State. Compiled with Historical and Biographical Notes and Introduction by B. F. French. New York: n.p., 1846. Part I. Tonty's Memoirs, 1691. Published in Paris, 1697.

Frost, John. *Pictorial Life of George Washington.* Philadelphia: n.p., 1858.

Frost, John. *The American Generals from the Founding of the Republic to the Present Time.* Philadelphia: J. W. Bradley, 1848.

Frost, John. *Pictorial History of the Mexican War.* Philadelphia: Thomas, Cowperthwait & Co., 1849.

Goodpasture, A. V. "Indian Wars and Warriors." *Tennessee Historical Quarterly.* Vol. IV. Nos. 1, 2, 3, 4. Nashville: 1918.

Haywood, Judge John. *The Civil and Political History of the State of Tennessee from the Earliest Settlement up to the Year of 1796, Including the Boundaries of the State.* Knoxville: Heiskell & Brown, 1823.

Haywood, Judge John. *Natural and Aboriginal History of Tennessee Up to the First Settlements Therein by the White People in the Year 1768.* Nashville: George Wilson, 1823.

Haywood, Judge John. *A Revisal of All the Public Acts of the State of North Carolina and the State of Tennessee Now in Force in the State of Tennessee.* Revised in the Winter of 1809 by John Haywood Esq., Attorney at Law, and formerly a Judge of the Superior Courts of North Carolina. Nashville: Thomas O. Bradford, 1809.

Headley, J. T. *The Second War with England.* 2 vols. New York: Charles Scribner, 1853.

Heiskell, Judge Samuel G. *Andrew Jackson & Early Tennessee History.* 3 vols. Nashville: n.p., 1918.

Hickey, W. *The Constitution of the United States of America.* With an alphabetical analysis; the Declaration of Independence; the Articles of Confederation; the prominent political acts of George Washington; electoral votes for all of the Presidents and Vice-Presidents; the high authorities and civil officers of government, from March 4, 1789, to March 4, 1847. Philadelphia: 1854.

Howe, Henry. *Historical Collections of the Great West.* 2 vols. Greeneville, Tenn.: James A. Roberts, 1854.

Hume, David. *History of England.* 6 vols. Philadelphia: n.p., 1795.

Irving, Washington. *Life of George Washington.* 5 vols. n.p., n.d.

James, Marquis. *The Raven.* Indianapolis: Bobbs-Merrill Co., 1929.

James, Marquis. *The Life of Andrew Jackson.* Part One: The Border Captain; Part Two: Portrait of a President. Indianapolis: Bobbs-Merrill Co., 1938.

Jefferson, Thomas. *The Writings of Thomas Jefferson.* Memoir, Correspondence, and Miscellanies from the Papers of Thomas Jefferson. Edited by Thomas Jefferson Randolph. Charlottesville: F. Carr & Co., 1829.

Jones, Hugh. *The Present State of Virginia.* London: 1724. Reprinted for the Virginia Historical Society. Chapel Hill: 1956.

Journals of the Commons House of Assembly of South Carolina. Two sessions, 1697. Records of appearance of Frenchmen from the Mississippi in South Carolina.

Journal of the Virginia House of Burgesses. Vol. 1. Passages on such subjects as the French Broad River; Alexander Spotswood's messages to the House of Burgesses; Fortifications; Death of King William III—notes on succession; Indian Trade; Sir Francis Nicholson, Governor of Virginia; Five Nations (Indians); Spotswood's treaty with the Five Nations—1716; advisability of extending frontiers to the mountains; Spotswood's removal, etc.

LaTour, Maj. A. Lacarriere. *Historical Memoir of The War in West Florida and Louisiana, 1814 and 1815.* Translated from the French by H. P. Nugent. Philadelphia: n.p., 1816.

Lawson, John. (Original Title Page) "The History of Carolina; Containing the Natural History of that Country; Together with the Present State Thereof; and a Journal of a Thousand Miles Travel'd thro' Several Nations of Indians, Giving a Particular Account of Their Customs, Manners, etc." London: 1714. Printed for W. Taylor.

Lee, Henry. *Memoir of the War in the Southern Department.* Written in 1809. One early critic said: "It is written with candor and impartiality, and possesses the charm peculiar to writers who have witnessed with their own eyes the scenes which they describe." Later edition published in New York in 1870. Edited by the author's sons Henry and Robert Edward Lee.

Legislative Journal of Colonial Virginia, III, 1588-9.

Lempriere's Biographical Dictionary, or *Sketches of Celebrated Characters of Every Age and Nation.* Hartford: D. F. Robinson & Co., 1827.

Liancourt, La Rochefoucauld. *Voyages dans les Etats-Unis D'Amerique fait, en 1795, 1796 et 1797.* n.p., n.d.

Life Magazine (July 3, 1950) pp. 36-58.

Logan, John H. *History of The Upper Country of South Carolina.* Charleston: n.p., 1859.

Longacre, James B. and Herring, James. *National Portrait Gallery of Distinguishd Americans.* 4 vols. New York: Monson Bancroft, n.d.

Lorain, John. *Hints to Emigrants, or a comparative Estimate of the Advantages of Pennsylvania, and the Western Territory, etc.* Philadelphia: Littell & Henry, 1819.

Lossing, Benson J. *The Pictorial Field-Book of the Revolution,* or, Illustrations by Pen and Pencil of the History, Biography, Scenery, Relics, and Traditions of the War for Independence. 2 vols. New York: Harper & Brothers, 1852.

Madison, James. *Madison Papers.* Edited by Henry D. Gilpin. Mobile: Allston Mygatt, 1842.

Marbois, Barbé Marquis de. *History of Louisiana.* Philadelphia: n.p., 1830.

Maas, Jacob. *The Jackson Wreath.* Philadelphia: n.p., 1829.

Moore, H. N. *The Life and Times of General Francis Marion.* Philadelphia: John Perry, 1845.

Moore, John Trotwood and Foster, Austin P. *Tennessee, the Volunteer State.* 4 vols. Chicago and Nashville: 1923.

Monette, John W. *History of the Discovery and Settlement of the Valley of the Mississippi.* New York: Harper Brothers, 1846.

Moultrie, Gen. William. *Memoirs of the American Revolution.* 2 vols. New York: 1802.

Nelson, Anson. *Memorial to Sarah Childress Polk.* New York: n.p., 1892.

Nolte, Vincent. *Fifty Years in Both Hemispheres;* or Reminiscences of the Life of a Former Merchant, Late of New Orleans. Translated from the German. (Highly interesting and amusing, but totally unreliable.) New York: 1854.

North Carolina State Records. Vol. 24, Chapter XLVI, pp. 765-6. An Act to Empower the Free Holders of Washington, Sullivan, and Green to Return Their Representatives Otherwise Than Is Heretofore Directed.
"Whereas, it is represented to the General Assembly that many of the inhabitants of Washington, Green and Sullivan counties have withdrawn their allegiance from this State, etc., etc. . . . Pardon and total oblivion offered." (State of Franklin)

Nye, S. & Co. *The Spirit of '76.* A weekly newspaper which advocated the Whig cause. Nashville: March 14, 1840. (First issue)

Parton, James. *Life of Andrew Jackson.* 3 vols. New York: 1860.

Polk, James Knox. *Addresses and Messages.* Compiled by Edwin Williams. Vol. III. New York: n.p., 1840.

Polk, James Knox. *The Diary of a President.* Edited by Allan Nevins. New York: n.p., 1929.

Polk, James Knox. *A Political Biography,* by Eugene Irving McCormac. Berkeley: University of California Press, 1922.

Polk, James Knox. *Diary of James K. Polk.* Manuscripts owned by the Chicago Historical Society. Chicago: n.p., 1910.

Polk, James Knox. *The Correspondence of James K. Polk.* Edited by Herbert Weaver and Paul H. Bergeron. Nashville: Vanderbilt University Press, 1972.

Putnam, A. W. *History of Middle Tennessee, or Life and Times of James Robertson.* Nashville: 1859.

Ramsay, David. *History of the American Revolution.* 2 vols. Boston: 1858.

Ramsey, J. G. M. *The Annals of Tennessee to the End of the Eighteenth Century.* Charleston: 1853.

Roosevelt, Theodore. *The Winning of the West.*

Scott, Joseph. *Scott's U.S. Gazeteer.* Important for information and maps of the Southwest Territory and the entire United States, 1795.

Scott, Nancy N. *A Memoir of Hugh Lawson White.* Philadelphia: 1856.

Sealafield, Charles. *The Americans as They Are:* Described in a Tour Through the Valley of the Missisippi. London: 1828.

Silver, James W. *Edmund Pendleton Gaines, Frontier General.* Baton Rouge: Louisiana State University Press, 1949.

Sparks, Jared. *The Writings of George Washington.* 12 vols. Boston: 1858.

Spencer, J. A. *History of the United States from the Earliest Period to the Administration of James Buchanan.* New York: 1858.

Spotswood, Alexander. *The Official Letters of Alexander Spotswood, Lieut. Governor of the Colony of Virginia, 1710-1722.* From the manuscripts in the collection of the Virginia Historical Society, with introduction and notes by R. A. Brock.

The Territorial Papers of the United States. Vol. 4. "The Territory South of the River Ohio, 1790-1796." Washington: U. S. Government Printing Office, 1936.

Travels West of the Alleghenies. Includes the travels of Richaux and others. Cleveland: Arthur H. Clark Co., 1904.

The Tennessee Farmer. Tennessee's first agricultural journal. Jonesboro: 1834.

Truth's Advoate. Anti-Jackson paper. Cincinnati: 1828.

United States Laws. Vols. 1, 3, 4. Important for treaties with the Cherokees, the opening of post roads and general progress of the west.

Virginia Calendar of State Papers.

Walker, Alexander. *Jackson at New Orleans.* New York: n.p., 1856.

de Warville, J. P. Brissot. *New Travels in the United States of America,
Performed in 1788.* Translated from the French. Boston: n.p., 1797.

Weems, M. L. (Parson). *The Life of Washington.* 9th ed. Philadelphia: n.p., 1809. Printed for Matthew Carey. (Contains "cherry tree"
story.) Weems was rector of the Mount Vernon parish.

Whitaker, Arthur P. *The Spanish American Frontier.* Boston: n.p.,
1927.

White, Dr. Robert H. *Tennessee, Its Growth and Progress.* Nashville:
n.p., 1936.

White, Dr. Robert H. *Tennessee, Old and New,* 1946.

White, Dr. Robert H. *Messages of the Governors.* Vol. I, 1952.

Wilkinson, Gen. James. *Memoirs of My Own Times.* Philadelphia:
n.p., 1816.

Williams, Judge Samuel Cole.

William Tatum, Wataugan, 1923.

History of the Courts of Chancery of Tennessee, 1923.

History of the Lost State of Franklin, 1924.

Memoirs of Lieutenant Henry Timberlake, 1927.

Early Travels in the Tennessee Country, 1928.

Adair's History of the American Indians, 1929.

The Beginnings of West, Tennessee, 1930.

History of Codification in Tennessee, 1932.

Dawn of Tennessee Valley and Tennessee History, 1937.

General Nathaniel Taylor, 1940.

The Lincolns and Tennessee, 1942.

Phases of the History of the Supreme Court of Tennessee, 1944.

Tennessee During the Revolutionary War, 1944.

Williamson, ————. *History of North Carolina.* Philadelphia, 1812.

Wilson, Alexander. *Ornithology of the Natural History of the Birds of
the United States.* Philadelphia: 1828. This work is important for
Wilson's study of birds, but is almost equally so for his excellent notes
on his travels through Tennessee and the South.

Wirt, William. *Sketches of the Life and Character of Patrick Henry.*
15th ed. Hartford, 1854.

APPENDIX A

Southern Indians and the Cherokee Country—1761

English colonial authorities, from the earliest days, were fully aware of the threat offered by the activities of the French and the Spanish to the south and the west of them. Particularly, they were concerned about the possibility of Indian wars which might be incited by either or both of these powers. For more than a half-century after the Treaty of Ryswick (1697) the governors of the British provinces kept themselves well informed on affairs in the Indian country. One of the many interesting documents on this subject is the statement of Gov. Arthur Dobbs of North Carolina in 1761, entitled: "The Colony, Its Climate, Soil, Population, Government, Resources, etc."

Governor Dobbs, describing the Indian country, said:

"The Cherokee Indians are situated among and beyond the Mountains to the Westward of our present Settlements, their upper towns beyond the Mountains are within the parallels of this Province, the middle and lower Towns West of the South Carolina Frontier, they were lately esteemed to be a powerful Tribe, and to consist of about 3,000 fighting men, they are now upon account of the War, Sickness and Famine supposed to be reduced to about 2,000.

"The Shawnees upon the Ohio to the Westward of the Virginia frontier is the next most considerable Nation to the Northward of this Province, and the Chickasaws near the Mississippi to the Southward of the Tenassee or Cherokee river who consist of about 400 fighting men are the most warlike Tribe and always firm friends to the English. To the Southward of these are the upper and lower Creeks about 3000 fighting men on the Western frontier of South Carolina and Georgia and beyond them the Choctaws.

"There have been no Treaties made between this Province and any Nation of Indians except a late Treaty made between the Virginians and the Cherokees in 1755 by Mr. Randolph and Col. Byrd who were joined by a Commission from this Province Col. Waddell. . . . There has been a small Trade carried on by a few Indian Traders from this Province with the Catawbas and Cherokees for furs and peltry, but no Regulations by law ever made in this Province.

"There are no French or Spanish Settlements near this Province the nearest at present is a Stockaded fort called l'Assumption lately erected upon the Tenasse or Cherokee river which falls into the Ohio above its

Entrance into the Mississippi, which is a great check to ye Chickasaws our most valuable Indian Allies, and has had a great Influence upon the Cherokees in spiriting them up and supplying them with Ammunition to make war upon this and the neighbouring Colonies. The French have another upon the Oubach called by them the River St. Jerome which falls into the North side of the Ohio before it enters into the Mississippi, by which they had a Communication with Le Detroit between the Lakes Huron and Erie from Louisiana; but as I apprehend it belonged to the Government of Canada it has or ought to have been given up by the Capitulation and Evacuation of Canada. I believe the French had not above 100 men in either of these forts. The other Forts which affect the Southern Provinces belonging to the French are the Alabama fort situated upon a branch of the Mobile, and another called fort Tombeebee higher up on the Mobile River to confine and distress the Chickasaws our allies and to awe the Choctaws and influence the Creek Indians; these are also stockaded forts and have above 100 men in each fort.

"The only Spanish Fort which affects our Colony of Georgia is St. Augustine and Garrison of which is about 300 men which I apprehend is maintained by the Pope; these are at constant war with the adjoining Indians and do not extend their plantations and in time of peace an advantageous trade is carried on through them with the Havana, their Forts of Sta Rosa and Pensacola on the Florida Coast in the Bay of Mexico are no Detriment to our Colonies but a Confinement to the French at Mobile.

"The grand Settlement of the French upon the Mississippi and Mobile are the only places dangerous to our Colonies as they will always spirit up the Creeks Choctaws and Cherokees to molest our Southern Colonies and embroil us with the Indians. . . ."

This, in general, was the picture of conditions surrounding the Tennessee country about the time when the white men were beginning to make serious and continued efforts to penetrate its interior.

APPENDIX B

Treaty of Lochaber

Miscellaneous notes on the Journal of the Virginia House of Burgesses, Volume 12, 1768, 1770, 1772 and 1775.

xiv—"Replying, a month later, to Stuart's communication of July 12th, Governor Botetourt authorized him to draw upon the Mess. Norton & Son of London for £2900 sterling, the amount set by him for the purchase of the Cherokee lands.

Williamsburg, Aug. 9th, 1770

Sir

I have inclosed to you an authority to draw upon Messrs. Norton & Son for £2900 Sterling by which you will perceive that the 384,17.6 which you have desired, together with £15. in order to enable you to purchase gold by bills for 300 are both added to the estimate of £2500 with which you originally engaged to procure for this dominion from the Indians those lands, to the purchase of which His Majesty has been graciously pleased to consent. I have likewise appointed Col. Donelson a member of the House of Burgesses to meet you at Lochaber upon Friday the 5th of October that he may be able to report from view, to our General Assembly, the whole of that transaction, may fix with you a proper time for running the line and may be instructed in the knowledge of every thing which will be wanted for that material purpose.

I am extremely pleased with the assurance you have given me that the strictest economy shall be observed; and as it has ever been the first object of my life to be remarkable for good faith and punctuality, I shall depend upon you in the present instance for that credit with the Indians which my actions shall deserve.

I will be answerable that Messrs. Norton and Son shall pay due honour to your Bills for £2900 sterling.

Extremely your obedient
BOTETOURT.

Hon. John Stuart, Esq.

On the 18th day of October following, a congress of leading Chiefs of the Cherokee Nation was held at Lochaber in the province of South Carolina, and the treaty negotiated between the Cherokee Nation and Great Britain. A copy of the deed of cession, resulting from this convention, was delivered to Colonel Donelson, representative appointed by

Lord Botetourt to be present upon that occasion, and forwarded by him to Governor Nelson at Williamsburg. Application for a grant—charter, etc. made "in behalf of the company by Thomas Walpole, a London banker, Benjamin Franklin, John Sargeant, and Samuel Wharton, but was opposed by Lord Hillsborough in a report that gave Franklin an opportunity to make such a crushing reply as to lead to Hillsborough's resignation from the cabinet . . .

"The grant of these lands to the Ohio Company created much concern in Virginia, since a great many grants to soldiers for services in Indian wars had been made in that section. Washington writing to Lord Botetourt, from Mt. Vernon, on October 5th called attention to this attempt upon the part of the Ohio Company to acquire lands in the section recently ceded by the Indians to Virginia, and urged that some action be taken to protect the interest of the soldiers, many of whom had already settled upon the disputed lands."

Washington's letter continues "and though the exigency of our affairs rendered it impractical for us to settle this country for some years after the date of the proclamation, and the policy of government forbid it for a few years longer, yet the causes not being removed and the land given to some as a recompense for their losses, and fought after by others for private emolument, have we not a title to be regarded among the first? We fain would hope so. We flatter ourselves that in this point of view Your Excellency will also consider us, and by your kind interposition and favourable representation of our case His Majesty will be graciously pleased to confirm the 200,000 acres of land to us, agreeable to the terms of the Proclamation. Or if it should be judged necessary to be more particular in the location of it, and your Lordship will be pleased to cause the same to be signified to me, I will point out immediately thereupon, the particular spots on which we would beg to have our surveys made; as part of the land prayed for in our petition of the 15th of December last, to wit, that on Sandy creek, will not be comprehended within the line running from Holston's river to the mouth of the Great Kanhawa. . . ."

Another interesting excerpt is taken from the Journal of the Virginia House of Burgesses, Vol. 12, p. xxvii. It is dated June 22, 1770.

"The Association entered into last Friday, the 22nd Instant, by the Gentlemen of the House of Burgesses, and the Body of Merchants Assembled in this city. . . ."

1—Committee of five chosen for each county. Authorized to publicize violators.

2—By example, etc., "We the subscribers" to encourage industry and frugality and discourage luxury and extravagence,

3—Agree not to import for sale or personal use—spirits, cider, perry, beer, ale, porter, malt, beef, fish, butter, cheese, tallow, candies, fruit, pickles, confectionary, chairs, tables, looking glasses, carriages, joiners work riband, India goods, boots, saddles, fine cloth, etc. etc.

4—Not to import slaves.

Among the signers Peyton Randolph, Moderator, Andrew Sprowle, chairman, . . . Edmund Pendleton, Archibald Cary, Richard Lee, Benjamin Harrison, John Donelson, Henry Lee, Thomas Jefferson, George Washington.

The State Papers, official records and personal correspondence of men in public life in Maryland, Pennsylvania, Virginia, the Carolinas and Georgia, offer a rich field for extensive original research to students and writers of the present, as well as future generations.

APPENDIX C

Who Owns the Land?

Indian titles to land which now lies within the boundaries of the state of Tennessee and her sister states were slowly extinguished. Little by little the white man advanced beyond his old settlements along the eastern seaboard and the Indian, retreating before him, gradually surrendered the mountains, the rivers and the fertile valleys which had been his heritage. It is a glorious chapter in the annals of human progress, but a tragic one in the history of the American Indian, when the view is taken that the Indians inhabiting the land at the time of the white man's discoveries were the true and rightful owners of the lands. The fact is that long before these Indians existed other human beings had lived, used the land and left the record of their being in the land itself. Their bones and artifacts bear testimony that the Indians whom the white men found here were not, by any means, the first to inhabit the North American continent. Who, then, was the rightful owner? By what right could they claim its total possession? These are questions which have long been debated by lawyers, philosophers, and historians, and, for that matter, they are still subjects of controversy. What problems will arise as exploration of outer space progresses?

Long before the first white settlements were formed west of the Appalachian Mountains, European powers had declared their sovereignty over the vast territory between the Atlantic and Pacific oceans. The boundaries to these claims were described vaguely and, often, incorrectly, with the result that England, France and Spain asserted conflicting and frequently changing claims to the interior of the continent. Generally speaking, ownership of land has been based upon three rights: the right of discovery, the right of a conqueror to lands his troops had marched over, and the right of purchase, which was the major basis of the acquisition of Indian lands by the white settlers. Who then has the right to occupy and improve a land?

An interesting discussion of this long debated subject appears in *Law Miscellanies,* by Hugh Henry Brackenridge, published in 1814, and often called the "Pennsylvania Blackstone," since it deals with the variations of the laws of Pennsylvania and other American states from the law of England, upon which they were largely based.

"This leads to the question," Judge Brackenridge comments, "as to the right of men themselves, with regard to portions of the earth . . . The right of Great Britain to the soil of North America, founded on the first

359

discovery of the coast, however just in its nature, yet was limited in its extent, by the right of the natives, and the right of other nations. The right of the natives has been generally supposed not to limit but exclude all others. For the law of nature vests the soil in the first occupant, and these from the earliest times had possessed the country. But shall a few tribes thinly scattered over the immense continent retain possession of it, while other parts of the globe are overcharged with inhabitants?"

After a long argument, based partly on Biblical quotations, Judge Brackenridge pointed out that the Creator had commanded the first couple to ". . . store the earth with inhabitants . . ." and that obedience, naturally, called for the cultivation of land for their sustenance. He comes to this conclusion:

"The aborigines of this continent can therefore have but small pretence to a soil which they have never cultivated. The most they can with justice claim, is a right to those spots of ground where their wigwams have been planted, and to so much of the soil around them as may be necessary to produce grain to support them, their families, in town upon the coast, or in the inland country, where they have inhabited. Perhaps they may have some priority right to occupy a different country, should it be their choice to change the situation where former circumstances may have placed them. . ."

However, Judge Brackenridge considered it advisable for lands to be purchased from the Indians, rather than by ancient rights of discovery or conquest.

It was by formally negotiated treaties and purchase that most of the lands were acquired by the American colonies and, later, by the government of the United States. Titles were thus extinguished to most of the Indian lands. These treaties followed each other in long and complicated succession and vast sums were paid to the Indians in both goods, which they usually preferred, and money for their ceded lands. Under the government of the United States a kind of paternal protection was extended over the Indian tribes and they were taught the arts—as well as too many of the vices—of civilization. Many tribes, notably the Cherokees, made remarkable advancement.

However, the period which intervened between the establishment of the Watauga settlements in 1769 and the final extinguishment of Indian titles to lands within the present boundaries of Tennessee was characterized by continuous conflict between the white settlers and the red men. Neither side was without blame, but it can be said for the Tennessee pioneers that they attempted to extinguish Indian claims to the land by just and fair purchase, and that long after the red men had violated their treaties, they restrained themselves from offensive warfare as long as it was humanly possible to do so. Under George Washington's administration, only defensive warfare was permitted by the federal government, which, in its effort to placate the Indians, often deliberately sacrificed the settlers along the western frontiers. It was not until after Sevier and Robertson conducted their final punitive campaigns in 1793 and 1794 that the settlers knew any degree of safety.

Not until 1818, when Andrew Jackson and Isaac Shelby, "late governor of Kentucky," completed their treaty with the Chickasaws were Indian claims to the rich territory now known as West Tennessee extinguished.

William Blount, after his appointment as territorial governor, was important in adjusting the difficulties which faced the western settlers. He pled their cause, guarded their lives and property as well as he could with the limited military forces at his disposal—made treaties with the Indians and paved the way for future expansion and development.

APPENDIX D

The Dangerous Example

The letter written at Williamsburg, May 10, 1774, by the Earl of Dunmore, the last colonial governor of Virginia, to the Earl of Dartmouth, then the British Secretary of State, urged that George III yield to the demands of his American colonies for titles to land beyond the Appalachian Mountains, and warned His Majesty that:

"Whatever may be the law with respect to title, there are, I think, divers reasons which should induce his majesty to comply with the petition, so far at least, as to admit the petitioners and their acquisitions, if not into this government, into some other. For if the title should be thought defective, it would still, at such a distance from the seat of any authority, be utterly impractical to void it, or prevent the occupying of the lands, which being known to be of an extraordinary degree of fertility, experience shows nothing (so fond as the Americans are of migration) can stop the concourse of people that actually begin to draw toward them; and should the petition be rejected, your lordship may assure yourself, it is no chimerical conjecture that, so far from interrupting the progress of their settlement, it would have a direct contrary tendency, by forcing the people to adopt a form of government of their own, which it would be easy to frame in such a manner as to prove an additional encouragement to all dissatisfied of every other government, to flock to that. In effect, we have an example of the very case, there being actually a set of people in the back part of this colony, bordering on the Cherokee country, who finding they could not obtain the land they fancied, under any of the neighboring governments, have settled upon it without, and, contented themselves with becoming in a manner tributary to the Indians, and have appointed magistrates, and framed laws for their present occasions, and to all intents and purposes, erected themselves into, though an inconsiderable, yet a separate State; the consequence of which may prove hereafter detrimental to the peace and security of the other colonies; IT AT LEAST SETS A DANGEROUS EXAMPLE TO THE PEOPLE OF AMERICA, OF FORMING GOVERNMENTS DISTINCT FROM AND INDEPENDENT OF HIS MAJESTY'S AUTHORITY . . . ."

APPENDIX E

1776 Petition of the Inhabitants of Washington District

"To the Hon. the Provincial Council of North Carolina:

"The humble petition of the inhabitants of Washington District, including the River Wataugah, Nonachukie, etc., in committee assembled, Humbly Sheweth, that about six years ago, Col. Donelson, (in behalf of the Colony of Virginia,) held a treaty with the Cherokee Indians, in order to purchase the lands of the Western Frontiers; in consequence of which Treaty, many of our petitioners settled on the lands of the Wataugah, etc., expecting to be within the Virginia line, and consequently hold their lands by their improvements as first settlers; but to their great disappointment, when the lines was run they were (contrary to their expectation) left out; finding themselves thus disappointed, and being too inconveniently situated to remove back, and feeling an unwillingness to loose the labour bestowed on their plantations, they applied to the Cherokee Indians, and leased the land for the term of ten years, before the expiration of which term, it appeared that many persons of distinction were actually making purchases forever; thus yielding a precedent, (supposing many of them who were gentlemen of the law, to be better judges of the constitution than we were,) and considering the bad consequences it must be attended with, should the reversion be purchased out of our hands, we next proceeded to make a purchase of the lands, reserving those in our possession in sufficient tracts for our own use, and resolving to dispose of the remainder for the good of the community. This purchase was made and the lands acknowledged to us and our heirs forever, in an open treaty, in Wataugah Old Fields, a deed being obtained from the chiefs of the said Cherokee nation, for themselves and their whole nation, conveying a fee simple right to the said lands, to us and our heirs forever, which deed was for and in consideration of the sum of two thousand pounds sterling, (paid to them in goods,) for which consideration they acknowledged themselves fully satisfied, contented and paid; and agreed, for themselves, their whole nation, their heirs, etc., forever to resign, warrant and defend said lands to us, and our heirs, etc., against themselves, their heirs, etc.

"The purchase was no sooner made, than we were alarmed by the reports of the present unhappy differences between Great Britain and America, on which report, (taking the now united colonies for our guide,) we proceeded to choose a committee, which was done unanimously by consent of the people. This committee (willing to become a party in the present unhappy contest) resolved, (which is now on our records,) to adhere strictly to the rules and orders of the Continental Congress, and in open committee acknowledged themselves indebted to the united colonies their full proportion of the Continental expense.

"Finding ourselves on the Frontiers, and being apprehensive that, for the want of a proper legislature, we might become a shelter for such as endeavoured to defraud their creditors; considering also the necessity of recording Deeds, Wills, and doing other public business; we, by consent of the people, formed a court for the purposes above mentioned, taking (by desire of our constituents) the Virginia laws for our guide, so near as the situation of affairs could admit; this was intended for ourselves, and was done by the consent of every individual; but, wherever we had to deal with people out of our district, we have ruled them to bail, to abide by our determinations, (which was, in fact, leaving the matter to reference), otherways we dismissed their suit, lest we should in any way intrude on the legislature of the colonies. In short, we have endeavoured so strictly to do justice, that we have admitted common proof against ourselves, on accounts, etc., from the colonies, without pretending a right to require the Colony Seal.

"We therefore trust we shall be considered as we deserve, and not as we have (no doubt) been many times represented, as a lawless mob. It is for this very reason we can assure you that we petition: we now again repeat it, that it is want of proper authority to try and punish felons, we can only mention to you murderers, horse-thieves and robbers, and are sorry to say that some of them have escaped us for want of authority. We trust, however, this will not long be the case; and we again repeat it, that its for this reason we petition to this Honourable Assembly.

"Above we have given you an abstract of our proceedings, since our settling on Wataugah, Nonachuckie, etc., in regard to our civil affairs. We have shown you the causes of our first settling and the disappointments we have met with, the reason of our lease and of our purchase, the manner in which we purchased, and how we hold of the Indians in fee simple; the causes of our forming a committee, and the legality of its election; the same of our Court proceedings, and our reasons for petitioning in regard to our legislature.

"We now proceed to give you some account of our military establishments, which were chosen agreeable to the rules established by convention, and officers appointed by the committee. This being done, we thought it proper to raise a company on the District service, as our proportion, to act in the common cause on the seashore. A company of fine riflemen were accordingly enlisted, and put under Capt. James Robertson, and were actually embodied, when we received sundry letters and depositions, (copies of which we now enclose you,) you will readily judge there was occasion for them in another place, where we daily expected an attack. We therefore thought proper to station them on our Frontiers, in defense of the common cause, at the expense and risque of our own private fortunes, till further public orders, which we flatter ourselves will give no offence. We have enclosed you sundry proceedings at the station where our men now remain.

"We shall now submit the whole to your candid and impartial judgment. We pray your mature and deliberate consideration in our behalf, that you may annex us to your Province, (whether as county, district, or other division,) *in such manner as may enable us to share in the glorious cause of Liberty;* enforce our laws under authority, and in every respect become the best members of society; and for ourselves and constituents we hope, we may venture to assure you, that we shall adhere strictly to your determinations, and that nothing will be lacking or any thing neglected, that may add weight (in the civil or military establishments) to the glorious cause in which we are now struggling, or contribute to the welfare of our own or ages yet to come.

"That you may strictly examine every part of this our Petition, and delay no time in annexing us to your Province, in such manner as your wisdom shall direct, is the hearty prayer of those who, for themselves and their constituents, as in duty bound, shall ever pray."

Signers—Members of the Committee: John Carter, chn., Charles Robertson, James Robertson, Zach. Isbell, John Sevier, Jas. Smith. Jacob Brown, Wm. Bean, John Jones, George Rusel, Jacob Womack, and Robert Lucas.

Members: Jacob Womack, Joseph Dunham, Rice Durron, Edward Hopson, Lew. Bowyer, D. Atty., Joseph Buller, Andw. Greer, Joab (his mark) Mitchell, Gideon Morris, Shadrack Morris, William Crockett, Thos. Dedmon, David Hickey, Mark Mitchell, Hugh Blair, Elias Pebeer, Jos. Brown, John Neave, John Robinson, Christopher Cunningham, Jas. Easeley, Ambrose Hodge, Dan'l Morris, Wm. Cox, James Easley, John Haile, Elijah Robertson, William Clark, John (his mark) Dunham, Wm. Overall, Mat Hawkins, John Brown, Jos. Brown, Job Bumper, Isaac Wilson, Richard Norton, George Hutson, Thomas Simpson, Valentine Sevier, Jonathan Tipton, Robert Sevier, Drury Goodan, Richard Fletcher, Ellexander Grear, Andrew Grear, Jun., Teeler Nave, Lewis

367

Jones, John I. Cox, John Cox jr., Abraham Cox, Emanuel Shote, Tho. Houghton, Jos. Luske, Wm. Reeves, David Hughes, Landon Carter, John McCormick, David Crockett, Edw'd Cox. Tho's Hughes, William Robertson, Henry Siler, Frederick Calvit, William Newberry, Adam Sherrell, Samuel Sherrell, junr., Ossa Rose, Henry Bates, junr., Jos. Grimes, Christopher Cunningham, sen., Joshua Barton, sen., Henry Gates, jun., Will'm Dod, Govers Morris, Wm. Bates, Ge. Hartt, Isaac Wilson, Jno. Waddell, Jarrett Williams, Oldham Hightower, Abednego Hix, Charles McCartney, Frederick Vaughn, Jos. McCartney, Mark Robertson, Joseph Calvit, Joshua Houghton, John Chukinbeard, James Cooper, William Brokees, Julius Robertson, John King, Michael Hider, John Davis and John Barley.

The document itself is without date, but it was received and officially acknowledged on August 22, 1776.

"It had been probably drawn up in the early part of that year," Ramsey says. "Nothing has been found after the most careful examination, to show what action was taken by the Provincial Council in reference to the petition. It is probable, however, that in the exercise of its now omnipotent and unrestricted authority, the Council advised the settlers to send forward their representatives to the Provincial Congress at Halifax, as it is known they did as delegates from 'Washington District, Watauga Settlement . . . .' "

Notes To Chapter I

[1] James Adair, *History of the American Indians*, p. 243.

[2] Robert Dinwiddie, *Records*, Vol. I, p. 62.

[3] Moore and Foster, *Tennessee, the Volunteer State*, p. 85.

[4, 5, 6] George Bancroft, *History of the United States*. Vol. VI, p. 47n. Also p. 30 and 130.

The Duke de Choiseul was called "the greatest minister of France since Richelieu." He was one of the best informed men in Europe on American affairs at that time. His intimate friend, Monsieur le Comte du Chatelet, was also well informed on America and was aware of the increasing momentum of the American controversy. In 1768, Choiseul, aware of this situation, appointed du Chatelet as ambassador to England, in order that he might correspond with him concerning the impending break between Great Britain and her American colonies. Le Comte du Chatelet, incidentally, was the son of the much talked about woman with whom Voltaire had been intimately connected. (Bancroft, *op. cit.* p. 130.)

Barre, member of the British Parliament, was an impassioned advocate of the Americans. He was associated with Pitt, Conway, and others in the repeal of the hated Townshend acts early in 1769.

[7] Bancroft, *op. cit.* Vol. VI, pp. 253-255.

[8] *Ibid.* Vol. VI, pp. 222-223.

[9] Judge John Haywood, *Civil and Political History of Tennessee*, p. 51.

[10] Washington Irving, *Life of George Washington*, Vol. I, p. 369.

[11] Haywood, *op. cit.*, p. 55.

[12] Ramsey, *Annals*, pp. 111-112.

[13] Haywood, *op. cit.*, p. 55.

[14] Ramsey, *Annals*, p. 106.

[15] Bancroft, *op. cit.*, Vol. VI, p. 401.

[16] *Ibid.*, Vol. IX, pp. 166-68.

[17] Ramsey, *Annals*, pp. 114-115.

[18] B. J. Lossing, Vol. II, pp. 489, 618.

[19] Ramsey, *Annals*, p. 117.

[20] Archibald Henderson, *Conquest of the Old Southwest*, pp. 221-226.

[21] Ramsey, *Annals*, pp. 128-129.

[22] B. J. Lossing, *op. cit.*, Vol. II, pp. 122-123.

[23] Ramsey, p. 143; Williams, *Tennessee During the Revolutionary War*, p. 24; Moore and Foster, *op. cit.*, p. 164.

[24] Samuel Cole Williams, *op. cit.*, p. 25. Also *North Carolina Colonial Records*, Vol. X, p. 793.

[25] *Ibid.*, p. 17 *et seq.*

[26] Ramsey, *Annals*, pp. 134-140.

Notes To Chapter II

[1] Ramsey, *Annals,* p. 139.

[2] Moore and Foster, *Tennessee the Volunteer State,* p. 165.

[3] Judge Samuel G. Heiskell, *Andrew Jackson and Early Tennessee History,*
Vol. I, p. 23.

[4] Ramsey, *Annals,* pp. 147-48. Also Williams, *Tennessee During the Revolutionary War,* pp. 25-26.

Judge Williams' footnote on the attempt to clear British agents of responsibility for the savage wars waged against the transmontane settlements. This
footnote reads:

"Stuart to Lord Germain, May 20, 1776. N.C. Col. Recs. X, 607. An
effort has been made by a recent historian to acquit Stuart of complicity in
bringing the Cherokees to war against the white settlers; indeed, to show that
Stuart tried to restrain them. This is contrary to the firm conviction of the
revolutionary leaders of the South at that time. Stedman, a Briton who wrote
a history of the American Revolution, had been a British officer under
Clinton, and he says (Vol. I, p. 248); "British agents were again employed
in engaging the Indians to make a diversion and to enter the Southern Colonies on their back and defenseless parts."

Stuart and Clinton were solicitous to avoid making a record so as to
escape the odium incident to being parties to such an attack by savages; and
Stuart's letters and reports should be read in that light. But secret messages
such as the one intercepted by the Americans in the hands of the South
Carolina Tory, Moses Kirkland, disclosed the true attitude. Ramsay, *History
of the American Revolution,* II, 140. The recent historian referred to, Hamer,
did not reckon on the finesse and suppression on the part of Stuart and his
brother Henry, but he seems ready to believe the Wataugans resorted to
worse.

Author's note: The Henry Stuart letter, said by some writers to have been
a forgery, was only a small part of the British-Indian conspiracy, so whether
it was forged or was genuine has little weight in the over-all picture of the
British-Indian conspiracy which was designed to launch attacks along the
entire western frontier, from Detroit to the Gulf of Mexico. See the following testimony given by irrefutable sources in the affair of Governor Hamilton. Neither can it be denied that the Revolution west of the mountains
was quite as important, if not more so, than that fought by the thirteen
"original states." Hundreds of documents which support this statement may
be found easily in published works, as well as still unpublished manuscripts
and state papers.

(From *Jefferson's Writings*—Vol. I—Randolph edition—Report of council in Virginia taking evidence against GoverNer Hamilton and British-Indian
war in west. Based on some of Hamilton's own proclamations).

pp. 455-456—"The board proceeded to the consideration of the letters of
Colonel (George Rogers) Clarke, and other papers relating to Henry
Hamilton, Esq. who has acted for some years past, as Lieutenant Governor
of the settlement at and about Detroit, and commandant of the British
garrison there. . . .

"They find that Governor Hamilton has executed the task of inciting the

Indians to perpetrate their accustomed cruelties on the citizens of the United States, without distinction of age, sex, or condition, with an eagerness and avidity which evince, that the general nature of his charge harmonized with his particular disposition . . . etc . . . etc.

"That Governor Hamilton gave standing rewards for scalps, but offered none for prisoners, which induced the Indians, after making their captives carry their baggage into the neighborhood of the fort, there put them to death, and carried in their scalps to the Governor, who welcomed their return and success by a discharge of cannon. That when a prisoner, brought alive, and destined to death by the Indians, the fire already kindled, and himself bound to the stake, was dextrously withdrawn and secreted from them by the humanity of a fellow prisoner, a large reward was offered for the discovery of the victim, which having tempted a servant to betray his concealment . . . he was again restored into the hands of the savages. . . ."

More details pp. 456-57-58.

[5] Williams, *Tennessee During the Revolutionary War*, p. 32. Also Ramsey, *Annals*, pp. 133-34.

[6] *American Historical Magazine*, Vol. VII, p. 360 *et seq.*

[7] *Life Magazine*, July 3, 1950.

[8] *General William Moultrie's Memoirs*, p. 90 *et seq.*

[9] *Tennessee Historical Magazine*, pp. 132-40. Article by Judge Samuel Cole Williams.

[10] This quotation is taken from p. 215 of a small leather bound book, titled *History of the United States*. Except for the gold lettering of the title on the spine of the book, there is nothing to identify it—for, unfortunately, the title page is missing. From its contents it appears to have been published shortly after 1826. It was a part of the Judge John Overton library, or, perhaps of his nephew, John Claybrooke. It is now in the library of the author.

[11] A. V. Goodpasture, "Indian Wars and Warriors," *Tennessee Historical Society Magazine*, 1918. Vol. IV, Numbers 1, 2, 3, 4.

[12] *Knoxville Gazette*, April 3, 1793.

[13] Ramsey, *Annals*, p. 154.

[14] Theodore Roosevelt, *Winning of the West*, Vol. I, p. 289.

[15] Williams, *Tennessee During the Revolutionary War*, p. 45.

[16] *Ibid.*, p. 48.

[17] Ramsey, *Annals*, p. 168.

[18] Williams, *Tennessee During the Revolutionary War*, p. 57.

[19] *North Carolina Colonial Records*, Vol. X, p. 892.

[20] Ramsey, *Annals*, p. 169.

[21] B. J. Lossing, *op. cit.*, Vol. II, p. 287.

[22] Filson, *Adventures of Daniel Boone*.

[23] Lossing, *op. cit.*, p. 288.

[24] *Ibid.*, 288n.

[25] Ramsey, *Annals*, p. 184.

[26] Williams, *op. cit.*, p. 94.

[27] *Ibid.*, p. 94.

[28] Thomas Jefferson Randolph, *Writings of Thomas Jefferson*, Vol. I, p. 454 (Appendix).

[29] Ramsey, *Annals,* p. 188.

[30] Randolph, *op. cit.,* Vol. I, p. 163.

[31] Williams, *Tennessee During the Revolutionary War,* pp. 98-99. Death of John Stuart and capture of Hamilton.

[32] L. C. Draper, *King's Mountain and Its Heroes,* p. 19.

[33] Ramsey, *Annals,* pp. 211-212.

[34] *Ibid.,* p. 223.

[35] Lee, *Memoirs,* pp. 199-200.

[36] L. C. Draper, *King's Mountain and Its Heroes,* p. 49.

[37] Ramsey, *Annals,* p. 226.

[38] Williams, *Tennessee During the Revolutionary War,* p. 144n.

[39] Samuel G. Heiskell, *Andrew Jackson and Early Tennessee History,* p. 241.

[40] *Ibid.,* p. 252.

[41] Williams, *op. cit.,* p. 152.

[42] Lee, *Memoirs,* p. 199-200.

[43] L. C. Draper, *King's Mountain and Its Heroes,* p. 196.

[44] Ramsey, *Annals,* p. 235.

[45] *Ibid.,* p. 241.

[46] Williams, *Tennessee During the Revolutionary War,* p. 155n.

[47] Heiskell, *Andrew Jackson and Early Tennessee History,* Vol. I, pp. 398-399. Also *New York Times,* 1855.

[48] Ramsey, *Annals,* p. 246.

[49] Draper, *op. cit.,* p. 284.

[50] Randolph, *Jefferson's Writings,* Vol. I, pp. 455-456. (Appendix).

[51] *Ibid.,* Vol. I, p. 295.

[52] Bassett, *Correspondence of Andrew Jackson,* Vol. I, pp. 2-4.

[53] *Ibid., Vol.* VI, pp. 253-54.

[54] Isaac Shelby. Autobiography quoted by Williams, *Tennessee During the Revolutionary War,* p. 219.

Notes To Chapter III

[1] Ramsey, *Annals,* p. 194.

[2] *Southwestern Monthly,* William Hall Narrative, 1852.

[3] A. W. Putnam, *History of Middle Tennessee,* Preface, p. xi.

[4] Col. John Donelson. Excerpts from his diary of the voyage of the flotilla from Fort Patrick Henry to the Great Salt Lick. (Published in full by Putnam, Ramsey and others.)

[5] Putnam, *History of Middle Tennessee,* p. 76. "Mrs. Peyton, whose infant was killed in the confusion of unloading the boat of Jonathan Jennings, during the attack upon it by the Indians, was the daughter of Jonathan Jennings and the mother of the Hon. Bailey Peyton. Her husband, Ephraim Peyton, had accompanied Capt. Robertson with stock by land."

[6] Putnam, *op. cit.,* p. 80.

[7] *Ibid.*, pp. 85-86.

[8] General Francis Nash, hero of the American Revolution. Slain at the Battle of Germantown, 1777.

[9] Putnam, *op. cit.*, p. 81.

[10] *Ibid.*, p. 107.

[11] Mary French Caldwell, *General Jackson's Lady*, pp. 77-78.

[12] Moore & Foster, *Tennessee, the Volunteer State*, p. 173.

[13] Putnam, *op. cit.*, p. 133.

[14] *Ibid.*, pp. 127-28.

[15] Moore & Foster, *Tennessee, the Volunteer State.* p. 171: "As early as June 1778, Governor Jefferson had instructed Colonel George Rogers Clark to establish a military post near the mouth of the Ohio. Just at that time, however, he was engaged in his marvelous campaign in the Northwest which resulted in the capture of Governor Hamilton, at Vincennes, February 25, 1779. In March, Colonel Clark reached the conclusion that the only method of maintaining American authority in Illinois was to evacuate the present posts, and center their whole force at, or near, the mouth of the Ohio; which would still be ineffective unless a considerable number of families could be settled around the fort, for the purpose of drawing reinforcements and victualing the garrison. (Calendar of Virginia State Papers, Vol. I, pp. 338-39.) Soon afterward he took two hundred men from the Falls of the Ohio, and proceeding down the river, built Fort Jefferson, and established a settlement at the Iron Banks, about five miles below the mouth of the Ohio, and within the hunting grounds of the Chickasaw Indians. (Collins, *History of Kentucky*, p. 39.) As soon as the Chickasaws learned that this fort had been erected, and a number of families settled about it, without consent, they took up arms to defend their hunting ground. (Va. Calendar State Papers, Vol. 3, p. 284.) They not only laid siege to Fort Jefferson, but they invaded the frontiers of Kentucky, and even presented as far as the settlements on the Cumberland."

[16] Ramsey, *Annals*, pp. 271-73.

[17] Samuel Cole Williams, *Tennessee During the Revolutionary War*, p. 239.

Notes To Chapter IV

[1] Williams, *Dawn of History in the Tennessee Country*, pp. 121-22.

[2] *Ibid.*, p. 25.

[3] Samuel G. Heiskell, *Andrew Jackson and Early Tennessee History*, pp. 40-41.

[4] Nancy N. Scott, *Memoirs of Hugh Lawson White*, p. 235 *et seq.*

[5] Ramsey, *Annals*, p. 290.

[6] *Ibid.*, p. 292.

[7] Williams, *The Lost State of Franklin*, pp. 43-44.

[8] *Ibid.*, p. 38.

[9] *Ibid.*, pp. 54-55.

[10] Judge John Allison, *Dropped Stitches*, p. 28.

[11] Williams, *Lost State of Franklin*, p. 55.

[12] Ramsey, *Annals*, p. 293.

[13] *Ibid.*, p. 307.

[14] Williams, *Lost State of Franklin*, pp. 61-62.

[15] *Ibid.*, p. 65 et seq.

[16] Williams, *Lost State of Franklin*, p. 76; also *North Carolina State Records*, XXII, p. 649 et seq.

[17] Ramsey, *Annals*, p. 319.

[18] *Ibid.*, p. 318.

[19] *Ibid.*, p. 320.

[20] Williams, *Lost State of Franklin*, p. 93.

[21] Ramsey, *Annals*, p. 338.

[22] *Ibid.*, p. 342.

[23] Williams, *Lost State of Franklin*, p. 100.

[24] Thomas Jefferson Randolph, *The Writings of Thomas Jefferson*, Vol. I, p. 309.

[25] Ramsey, *Annals*, pp. 348-50.

[26] Washington Irving, *Life of Washington*, Vol. IV, p. 496.

[27] Ramsey, *Annals*, p. 406.

[28] Judge John Haywood, *The Civil and Political History of Tennessee*.

[29] Ramsey, *Annals*, p. 471.

[30] *Ibid.*, p. 418.

[31] *Ibid.*, pp. 428-29.

Notes To Chapter V

[1] Clarence Edwin Carter, *Territorial Papers of the United States*, Vol. IV. The Territory South of the River Ohio. U.S. Government Printing Office, 1936.

[2] *Ibid.*, pp. 24, 33, Footnote p. 46.

[3] *Ibid.*, p. 37.

[4] *Ibid.*, pp. 26-27.

[5] *Ibid.*, p. 33n.

[6] Ramsey, *Annals*, pp. 645-46.

[7] American State Papers—Indian Affairs—Vol. I (See Blount and Secretary of War Correspondence—1792-93.)

[8] American State Papers, Indian Affairs, Vol. I.

[9] Mary French Caldwell, *Andrew Jackson's Hermitage*, pp. 13-14.

[10] Territorial Papers, p. 407. Nov. 28, 1795.

[11] Samuel G. Heiskell, *Andrew Jackson and Early Tennessee History*, Vol. II, p. 530.

[12] Moore & Foster, *Tennessee, the Volunteer State*, p. 156.

[13] Ramsey, *Annals*, p. 652.

[14] Robert H. White, *Tennessee: Its Growth and Progress*, pp. 66-67.

Notes To Chapter VI

[1] Robert H. White, *Messages of the Governors of Tennessee*, Vol. I, p. 3.
[2] Thomas Hart Benton, *Abridgment of the Debates of Congress*, Vol. I, p. 531.
[3] *Ibid.*, pp. 601-602.
[4] *Ibid.*, p. 758.
[5] *Ibid.*, p. 754.
[6] *Ibid.*, p. 602.
[7] *Ibid.*, p. 603.
[8] Robert H. White, *op. cit.*, Vol. I, p. 9.
[9] *Ibid.*, pp. 5-6.
[10] *Ibid.*, p. 35.
[11] Judge Samuel G. Heiskell, *Andrew Jackson and Early Tennessee History*, Vol. I.
[12] Confidential State Papers, Vol. 10, p. 171.
[13] American State Papers and Public Documents, Vol. II, pp. 36-37.
[14] Confidential State Papers, Vol. 10, p. 176.

Notes To Chapter VII

[1] Robert H. White, *Messages of the Governors of Tennessee*, Vol. I, p. 161-179.
[2] *Ibid.*, Vol. I, p. 151.
[3] *Ibid.*, Vol. I, p. 256.
[4] Tennessee Senate Journal, 1809, pp. 28, 29.
[5] Judge Samuel G. Heiskell, *Andrew Jackson and Early Tennessee History*, Vol. I, p. 171.
[6] The building in which this session of the Legislature met was located at the corner of Broad Street and Eighth Avenue (formerly Spruce Street), Nashville. The present Hume-Fogg High School building is at present located on this site.
[7] White, *op. cit.*, Vol. I, p. 372 *et seq.*
[8] White, *op. cit.*, Vol. I, pp. 379-383.
[9] John Spencer Bassett, *Correspondence of Andrew Jackson*, Vol. I, pp. 220-23.
[10] White, *op. cit.*, Vol. I, p. 382.
[11] Bassett, *op. cit.*, Vol. I, pp. 238-242.
[12] *Ibid.*, Vol. I, p. 240.
[13] *Ibid.*, Vol. I, p. 243.
[14] *Ibid.*, Vol. I, p. 256.
[15] *Ibid.*, p. 258 ff.
[16] Bassett, *op. cit.*, Vol. I, p. 274.
[17] *Ibid.*, Vol. I, pp. 306-07.
[18] *Ibid.*, Vol. I, p. 307.

[19] James Parton, *Life of Andrew Jackson*, Vol. I, pp. 387-89.

[20] *Ibid.*, Vol. I, pp. 411-21.

[21] Bassett, *Correspondence of Andrew Jackson*, Vol. I, pp. 319-20.

[22] Reid and Eaton, *History of the Life of Andrew Jackson*, pp. 34-37.

[23] Marquis James, *The Life of Andrew Jackson*, p. 166.

[24] John Spencer Bassett, Vol. I, p. 357.

[25] Reid and Eaton, *op. cit.*, p. 46.

[26] Bassett, *op. cit.*, Vol. I, p. 365.

[27] *Ibid.*, Vol. I, p. 444 *et seq.*

[28] Bassett, *op. cit.*, Vol. I, pp. 444-47.

[29] Moore and Foster, *Tennessee, the Volunteer State*, pp. 354-56.

[30] James Parton, *op. cit.*, Vol. I, pp. 428-29.

[31] Bassett, *op. cit.*, Vol. I, p. 494.

[32] *Ibid.*, Vol. I, p. 499.

[33] *Ibid.*, Vol. II, pp. 15-16.

[34] *Ibid.*, Vol. II, pp. 68-70. To Governor Blount.

[35] *Ibid.*, Vol. II, p. 106. "The enemy may attempt a landing at Pascagoula, and from thence to penetrate the country in that direction, and by that means cut off our supplies from New Orleans." Letter to James Winchester, Nov. 22, 1814, when Jackson left the command at Mobile to Winchester and struck out, on November 22, accompanied only by his small staff for the arduous journey on horseback, for New Orleans, in order that he might personally examine the nature of the country.

[36] Bassett, *op. cit.*, Vol. II, p. 102.

[37] Mary French Caldwell, *General Jackson's Lady*, p. 313.

[38] James Parton, *op. cit.*, Vol. II, pp. 29-30.

[39] *Ibid.*, Vol. II, pp. 30-31.

[40] Bassett, *op. cit.*, Vol. II, pp. 127-128.

[41] Reid and Eaton, *op. cit.*, pp. 231-232.

[42] Bassett, *op. cit.*, Vol. II, p. 150.

[43] Mary C. Dorris, *Preservation of the Hermitage.*

[44] Bassett, *op. cit.*, Vol. I, pp. 461-62.

[45] Marquis James, *Andrew Jackson, the Border Captain*, pp. 191-92.

[46] Mary French Caldwell, *General Jackson's Lady*, pp. 319-21.

[47] *Ibid.*, p. 337.

[48] Mary French Caldwell, *Andrew Jackson's Hermitage*, pp. 56-57.

Notes To Chapter VIII

[1] John Spencer Bassett, *Correspondence of Andrew Jackson*, Vol. II, 277 *et seq.*

[2] Edwin Williams, *Statesman's Manual*, Vol. II, p. 952.

[3] Bassett, *op. cit.*, Vol. V, p. 345.

[4] John Frost, *American Generals*, pp. 835-36.

[5] John Frost, *The Mexican War* (1849), p. 166.
[6] *Ibid.*, p. 169.
[7] Bassett, *op. cit.*, Vol. V, pp. 411-12.
[8] *Ibid.*, Vol. V, p. 425.
[9] *Ibid.*, Vol. V, p. 438.
[10] Moore and Foster, *op. cit.*, p. 411.
[11] Robert H. White, *Messages*, Vol. III, pp. 460-61.
[12] *Ibid.*, Vol. III, pp. 458-59.

Notes To Chapter IX

[1] J. A. Spencer, *History of the United States*, Vol. III, p. 47 *et seq.*
[2] *Ibid.*, Vol. III, pp. 44-45.
[3] Henry Howe, *The Great West*, p. 221n.
[4] J. A. Spencer, *op. cit.*, p. 49.
[5] Alexander Wilson, *Ornithology, or the Natural History of the Birds of the United States.*
[6] John Frost, *American Generals . . . and Other Distinguished Officers*, p. 594.
[7] *Ibid.*, p. 597.
[8] *Papers of Mirabeau Bonaparte Lamar*, Vol. I, p. 34. Texas State Library. Other references to Long story in Yoakum's *History of Texas.*
[9] John Spencer Bassett, *Correspondence of Andrew Jackson*, Vol. V, pp. 309-10.
[10] John Frost, *op. cit.*, pp. 905-06.
[11] "gee-wo-haw." Terms used usually by plowmen in telling mules the direction to right or left, or stop.
[12] Robert H. White, *Messages of the Governors of Tennessee*, Vol. IV, p. 120 *et seq.*
[13] *Ibid.*, p. 125.
[14] Judge Joshua W. Caldwell, *Bench and Bar*, p. 29.
[15] Bassett, *op. cit.*, Vol. I, p. vii.
[16] Thomas Hart Benton, *Thirty Years' View*, p. 9.
[17] Marquis James, *The Life of Andrew Jackson*, p. 382.
[18] *Appleton's New American Cyclopedia.* 1859. Fremont, pp. 743-47.
[19] John Frost, *The Mexican War*, 1849.
[20] Edwin Williams, *Statesman's Manual*, Vol. III, p. 1446.
[21] Marquis James, *The Raven*, p. 190.
[22] *Stateman's Manual*, Vol. III, pp. 1473-74.
[23] *Ibid.*, Vol. II, p. 714.
[24] John Bassett, *op. cit.*, Vol. VI, p. 412.
[25] Moore and Foster, *Tennessee, the Volunteer State*, p. 437.
[26] *Statesman's Manual*, Vol. III, p. 1760.

Index